CREATIVE
HOMEOWNER®

NEW
MOST-POPULAR
1-STORY
HOME PLANS

CREATIVE HOMEOWNER®, Upper Saddle River, New Jersey

VP/Editorial Director: Timothy O. Bakke
Production Manager: Kimberly H. Vivas

Home Plans Editor: Kenneth D. Stuts, CPBD
Home Plans Designer Liaison: Timothy Mulligan

Design and Layout: Arrowhead Direct (David Kroha,
    Cindy DiPierdomenico, Judith Kroha); Maureen Mulligan

Cover Design: David Geer

Current Printing (last digit)
10 9 8

New Most Popular 1-Story Home Plans
Library of Congress Control Number: 2007921261
ISBN-10: 1-58011-355-9
ISBN-13: 978-1-58011-355-7

CREATIVE HOMEOWNER®
A Division of Federal Marketing Corp.
24 Park Way
Upper Saddle River, NJ 07458
www.creativehomeowner.com

Note: The homes as shown in the photographs and renderings in this book may differ from the actual blueprints. When studying the house of your choice, please check the floor plans carefully.

Front cover: *main plan* 481028, page 223; *left to right plan* 161093, page 311; *plan* 441014, page 292; *plan* 481028, page 223; *plan* 561005, page 290 **page 1:** *plan* 151529, page 194 **page 3:** *top to bottom plan* 151536, page 304; *plan* 161093, page 311; *plan* 161102, page 322 **page 4:** *plan* 121116, page 377 **page 5:** *plan* 121117, page 374 **page 6:** *top to bottom plan* 481137, page 380; *plan* 391049, page 385 **page 7:** *plan* 481132, page 387 **page 68:** *top* courtesy of Thomasville; *bottom both* courtesy of Rubbermaid **page 69:** courtesy of IKEA **page 70:** courtesy of ClosetMaid **page 71:** courtesy of ClosetMaid; *bottom* courtesy of Rubbermaid **pages 72–73:** *all* courtesy of Rubbermaid **pages 74–75:** *all* courtesy of Diamond Cabinets **pages 138–145:** *all* illustrations by Warren Cutler, Tony Davis (site plans), Elizabeth Eaton, Biruta Hansen, Paul Mirocha, Gordon Morrison, Michael Rothman, Michael Wanke **page 206:** Jessie Walker **page 207:** *top* Mark Lohman; *bottom both* www.davidduncanlivingston.com **page 208:** *top* Mark Samu/CH, design: Mari Gardner Design; *bottom* Jessie Walker **page 210:** courtesy of Thibaut **page 211:** Mark Lohman **page 212:** Mark Lohman, design: Janet Lohman Interior Design **page 213:** Jessie Walker **page 272:** courtesy of Kraftmaid Cabinetry **page 273:** *top* courtesy of Merillat; *bottom* courtesy of Kraftmaid Cabinetry **pages 274–275:** *top right & center* courtesy of Kraftmaid Cabinetry; *bottom right* courtesy of American Olean **pages 276–277:** *top right* courtesy of Kraftmaid Cabinetry; *bottom right* courtesy of Diamond Cabinets; *top left* courtesy of Wellborn Cabinets **page 278:** *top* courtesy of Wellborn Cabinets; *bottom* courtesy of Diamond Cabinets **page 279:** *top right* courtesy of Rev-A-Shelf; *bottom right* courtesy of Merillat; *top left* courtesy of Iron-A-Way **page 280:** courtesy of Wellborn Cabinets **page 281:** *top* courtesy of Merillat; *bottom* courtesy of Moen **page 282:** *top right* courtesy of Canac Cabinetry; *bottom right* courtesy of Wellborn Cabinets; *top left* courtesy of Thibaut **page 283:** courtesy of American Olean **page 421:** *plan* 391059, page 401 **page 425:** *top to bottom plan* 271078, page 403; *plan* 271059, page 406; *plan* 351018, page 408 **page 432:** *top to bottom plan* 271061, page 409; *plan* 121009, page 412; *plan* 131045, page 416 **back cover:** *top plan* 271002, page 341; *middle plan* 161095, page 318; *left to right plan* 481028, page 223; *plan* 16095, page 318; *plan* 441014, page 292.

Contents

Getting Started

Maybe you can't wait to bang the first nail. Or you may be just as happy leaving town until the windows are cleaned. The extent of your involvement with the construction phase is up to you. Your time, interests, and abilities can help you decide how to get the project from lines on paper to reality. But building a house requires more than putting pieces together. Whoever is in charge of the process must competently manage people as well as supplies, materials, and construction. He or she will have to

- Make a project schedule to plan the orderly progress of the work. This can be a bar chart that shows the time period of activity by each trade.
- Establish a budget for each category of work, such as foundation, framing, and finish carpentry.
- Arrange for a source of construction financing.
- Get a building permit and post it conspicuously at the construction site.
- Line up supply sources and order materials.
- Find subcontractors and negotiate their contracts.
- Coordinate the work so that it progresses smoothly with the fewest conflicts.
- Notify inspectors at the appropriate milestones.
- Make payments to suppliers and subcontractors.

You as the Builder

You'll have to take care of every logistical detail yourself if you decide to act as your own builder or general contractor. But along with the responsibilities of managing the project, you gain the flexibility to do as much of your own work as you want and subcontract out the rest. Before taking this path, however, be sure you have the time and capabilities. Do you also have the

time and ability to schedule the work, hire and coordinate subs, order materials, and keep ahead of the accounting required to manage the project successfully? If you do, you stand to save the amount that a general contractor would charge to take on these responsibilities, normally 15 to 30 percent of the construction cost. If you take this responsibility on but mismanage the project, the potential savings will erode and may even cost you more than if you had hired a builder in the first place. A subcontractor might charge extra for hav-

Acting as the builder, above, requires the ability to hire and manage subcontractors.

Building a home, opposite, includes the need to schedule building inspections at the appropriate milestones.

ing to return to the site to complete work that was originally scheduled for an earlier date. Or perhaps because you didn't order the windows at the beginning, you now have to pay for a recent cost increase. (If you had hired a builder in the first place he or she would absorb the increase.)

Hiring a Builder to Handle Construction

A builder or general contractor will manage every aspect of the construction process. Your role after signing the construction contract will be to make regular progress payments and ensure that the work for which you are paying has been completed. You will also consult with the builder and agree to any changes that may have to be made along the way.

Leads for finding builders might come from friends or neighbors who have had contractors build, remodel, or add to their homes. Real-estate agents and bankers may have some names handy but are more likely familiar with the builder's ability to complete projects on time and budget than the quality of the work itself.

The next step is to narrow your list of candidates to three or four who you think can do a quality job and work harmoniously with you. Phone each builder to see whether he or she is interested in being considered for your project. If so, invite the

builder to an interview at your home. The meeting will serve two purposes. You'll be able to ask the candidate about his or her experience, and you'll be able to see whether or not your personalities are compatible. Go over the plans with the builder to make certain that he or she understands the scope of the project. Ask if they have constructed similar houses. Get references, and check the builder's standing with the Better Business Bureau. Develop a short list of builders, say three, and ask them to submit bids for the project.

Contracts

Lump-Sum Contracts

A lump-sum, or fixed-fee, contract lets you know from the beginning just what the project will cost, barring any changes made because of your requests or unforeseen conditions. This form works well for projects that promise few surprises and are well defined from the outset by a complete set of contract documents. You can enter into a fixed-price contract by negotiating with a single builder on your short list or by obtaining bids from three or four builders. If you go the latter route, give each bidder a set of documents and allow at least two weeks for them to submit their bids. When you get the bids, decide who you want and call the others to thank them for their efforts. You don't have to accept the lowest bid, but it probably makes sense to do so since you have already honed the list to builders you trust. Inform this builder of your intentions to finalize a contract.

Cost-Plus-Fee Contracts

Under a cost-plus-fee contract, you agree to pay the builder for the costs of labor and materials, as verified by receipts, plus a fee that represents the builder's overhead and profit. This arrangement is sometimes referred to as "time and materials." The fee can range between 15 and 30 percent of the incurred costs. Because you ultimately pick up the tab—whatever the costs—the contractor is never at risk, as he is with a lump-sum contract. You won't know the final total cost of a cost-plus-fee contract until the project is built and paid for. If you can live with that uncertainty, there are offsetting advantages. First, this form allows you to accommodate unknown conditions much more easily than does a lump-sum contract. And rather than being tied down by the project documents, you will be free to make changes at any point along the way. This can be a trap, though. Watching the project take shape will spark the desire to add something or do something differently. Each change costs more, and the accumulation can easily exceed your budget. Because of the uncertainty of the final tab and the built-in advantage to the contractor, you should think twice before entering into this form of contract.

Contract Content

The conditions of your agreement should be spelled out thoroughly in writing and signed by both parties, whatever contractual arrangement you make with your builder. Your contract should include provisions for the following:

- The names and addresses of the owner and builder.
- A description of the work to be included ("As described in the plans and specifications dated . . .").
- The date that the work will be completed if time is of the essence.
- The contract price for lump-sum contracts and the builder's allowed profit and overhead costs for changes.
- The builder's fee for cost-plus-fee contracts and the method of accounting and requesting payment.
- The criteria for progress payments (monthly, by project milestones) and the conditions of final payment.
- A list of each drawing and specification section that is to be included as part of the contract.
- Requirements for guarantees. (One year is the standard period for which contractors guarantee the entire project, but you may require specific guarantees on

When submitting bids, all of the builders should base their estimates on the same specifications. Once the work begins, communicate with your builder to keep the work proceeding smoothly.

Inspect your newly built home, if possible, before the builder closes it up and finishes it.

certain parts of the project, such as a 20-year guarantee on the roofing.)

- Provisions for insurance.
- A description of how changes in the work orders will be handled.

The builder may have a standard contract that you can tailor to the specifics of your project. These contain complete specific conditions with blanks that you can fill in to fit your project and a set of "general conditions" that cover a host of issues from insurance to termination provisions. It's always a good idea to have an attorney review the draft of your completed contract before signing it.

Working with Your Builder

The construction phase officially begins when you have a signed copy of the contract and copies of any insurance required from the builder. It's not unheard of for a builder to request an initial payment of 10 to 20 percent of the total cost to cover mobilization costs, those costs associated with obtaining permits and getting set up to begin the actual construction. If you agree to this, keep a careful eye on the progress of the work to ensure that the total paid out at any one time doesn't get too far out of sync with the actual work completed.

What about changes? From here on, it's up to you and your builder to proceed in good faith and to keep the channels of communication open. Even so, changes of one sort or another beset every project, and they usually add to its cost.

Light at the End of the Tunnel.

The builder's request for a final inspection marks the end of the construction phase—almost. At the final inspection meeting, you and the builder will inspect the work, noting any defects or incomplete items on a "punch list." When the builder tidies up the punch list items, you should reinspect. Sometimes, builders go on to another job and take forever to clean up the last few details, so only after all items on the list have been completed satisfactorily should you release the final payment, which often accounts for the builder's profit.

Some Final Words

Having a positive attitude is important when undertaking a project as large as building a home. A positive attitude can help you ride out the rigors and stress of the construction process.

Stay Flexible. Expect problems, because they certainly will occur. Weather can upset the schedule you have established for subcontractors. A supplier may get behind on deliveries, which also affects the schedule. An unexpected pipe may surprise you during excavation. Just as certain, every problem that comes along has a solution if you are open to it.

Be Patient. The extra days it may take to resolve a construction problem will be forgotten once the project is completed.

Express Yourself. If what you see isn't exactly what you thought you were getting, don't be afraid to look into changing it. Or you may spot an unforeseen opportunity for an improvement. Changes usually cost more money, though, so don't make frivolous decisions.

Finally, watching your home go up is exciting, so stay upbeat. Get away from your project from time to time. Dine out. Take time to relax. A positive attitude will make for smoother relations with your builder. An optimistic outlook will yield better-quality work if you are doing your own construction. And though the project might seem endless while it is under way, keep in mind that all the planning and construction will fade to a faint memory at some time in the future, and you will be getting a lifetime of pleasure from a home that is just right for you.

Plan #111004

Dimensions: 76' W x 85' D
Levels: 1
Square Footage: 2,968
Bedrooms: 4
Full Bathrooms: 3½
Foundation: Crawl space or slab
Materials List Available: No
Price Category: G

Images provided by designer/architect. Living Room

If you've been looking for a home that includes a special master suite, this one could be the answer to your dreams.

Features:

- **Living Room:** Make a sitting area around the fireplace here so that the whole family can enjoy the warmth on chilly days and winter evenings. A door from this room leads to the rear covered porch, making this room the heart of your home.

- **Kitchen:** An island with a cooktop makes cooking a pleasure in this well-designed kitchen, and the breakfast bar invites visitors at all times of day.

- **Utility Room:** A sink and a built-in ironing board make this room totally practical.

- **Master Suite:** A private fireplace in the corner sets a romantic tone for this bedroom, and the door to the covered porch allows you to sit outside on warm summer nights. The bath has two vanities, a divided walk-in closet, a standing shower, and a deluxe corner bathtub.

CAD FILE AVAILABLE

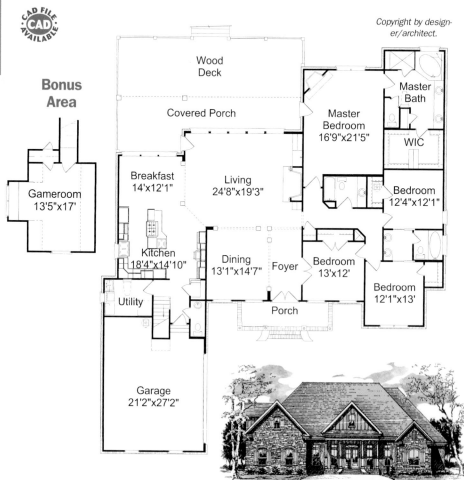

Copyright by designer/architect.

Kitchen

Dining Room

Master Bath

Master Bath

How to Quit Smoking — Lighting Your Fireplace

Before attempting to light a wood fire, make certain that the damper is open all the way. This allows a good draft (flow of air up the chimney) to prevent smoke from blowing back into the room. To ensure a good draft—particularly if your home is well insulated —open a window a bit when lighting a fire.

The opposite of draft is downdraft, which occurs when cold air flows down the chimney and into the room. If the fireplace is properly designed and maintained, the smoke shelf will prevent backpuffing from downdraft most of the time by redirecting cold air currents back up the chimney. The open damper also helps prevent backpuffing.

Also, build a fire slowly to let the chimney liner heat up, which will create a good draft and minimize the chances of downdraft.

Don't wait until fall to inspect the chimney. Do this job, or call a chimney sweep, when the weather is mild. Because some repairs take a while to make, it's best to have them done when the fireplace is not normally in use. If you do the inspection yourself, wear old clothes, eye goggles, and a mask.

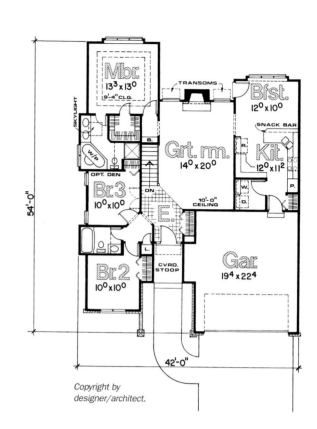

Plan #121002

Dimensions: 42' W x 54' D

Levels: 1

Square Footage: 1,347

Bedrooms: 3

Bathrooms: 2

Foundation: Basement

Materials List Available: Yes

Price Category: B

Images provided by designer/architect.

This home, as shown in the photograph, may differ from the actual blueprints. For more detailed information, please check the floor plans carefully.

Copyright by designer/architect.

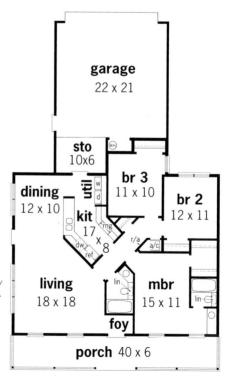

Plan #211018

Dimensions: 40' W x 64' D

Levels: 1

Square Footage: 1,266

Bedrooms: 3

Bathrooms: 2

Foundation: Crawl space

Materials List Available: Yes

Price Category: B

Images provided by designer/architect.

Copyright by designer/architect.

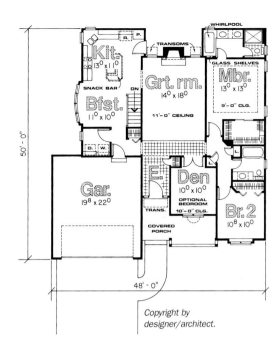

Optional Third Bedroom Floor Plan

Plan #121056

Dimensions: 48' W x 50' D

Levels: 1

Square Footage: 1,479

Bedrooms: 2

Bathrooms: 2

Foundation: Basement

Materials List Available: Yes

Price Category: B

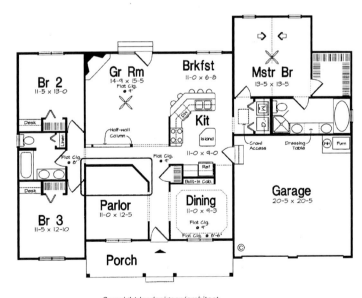

Optional Basement Stairs

Plan #391038

Dimensions: 59' W x 44' D

Levels: 1

Square Footage: 1,642

Bedrooms: 3

Bathrooms: 2

Foundation: Crawl space, slab, or basement

Materials List Available: Yes

Price Category: C

Plan #131005

Dimensions: 70' W x 37'4" D
Levels: 1
Square Footage: 1,595
Bedrooms: 3
Bathrooms: 2
Foundation: Crawl space, slab, or basement
Materials List Available: Yes
Price Category: D

SMARTtip

Create a Courtyard

Create a private walled-garden retreat with fences covered by climbing vines. Add height with trellises, and divide spaces with clipped boxwood hedges. Include an (almost) instant patio by digging away an area of sod and then covering it with a layer of sand and landscaping mesh to discourage weeds. Then cover it with pea gravel, and add a garden bench, statuary, and perhaps an antique or two. The result? European ambiance for even the most nondescript suburban yard.

Images provided by designer/architect.

With the finest features of an open design in the main living areas, this home gives privacy where you need it. Best of all, it's wheelchair accessible.

Features:

• Foyer: A high ceiling gives this area real presence and serves to blend it seamlessly with the great room and the dining room.

• Great Room: The open design allows you to use this room as an extension of the dining room or, if you wish, furnish it to create a private reading nook or visually separate media center.

• Breakfast Room: Both this room and the adjacent well-appointed kitchen flow into the rest of the living area. However, access to the rear porch, where you can sit out and enjoy the weather while you eat, distinguishes this room.

• Master Suite: Located in the same wing as the other bedrooms, this suite has a separate entrance and features a vaulted ceiling, three closets, and a compartmental bath.

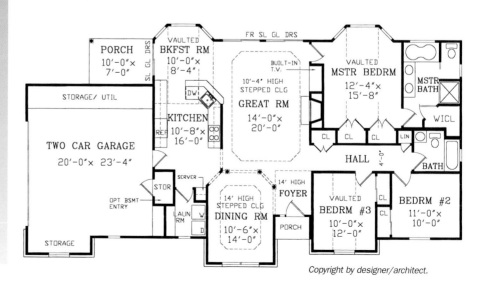

Copyright by designer/architect.

Foyer

Dining Room

Great Room

Living Room

SMARTtip

Natural Trellis

Create a natural rustic trellis that might even, if growing conditions are right, produce its own pretty blooms. Cut and place saplings in the ground as uprights. Then weave old grapevines with smaller saplings for the lattice.

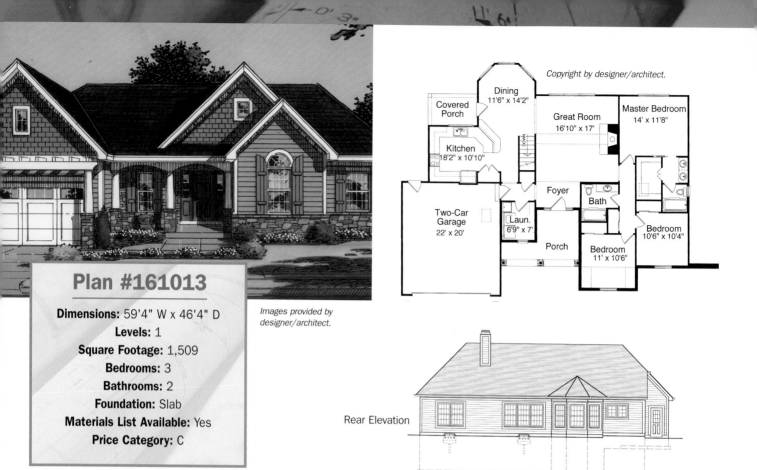

Plan #161013

Dimensions: 59'4" W x 46'4" D

Levels: 1

Square Footage: 1,509

Bedrooms: 3

Bathrooms: 2

Foundation: Slab

Materials List Available: Yes

Price Category: C

Images provided by designer/architect.

Rear Elevation

Plan #161014

Dimensions: 51'8" W x 49'8" D

Levels: 1

Square Footage: 1,698

Bedrooms: 3

Bathrooms: 2

Foundation: Slab

Materials List Available: Yes

Price Category: C

Images provided by designer/architect.

CAD FILE AVAILABLE

Rear Elevation

Copyright by designer/architect.

Plan #321010

Dimensions: 59' W x 37'8" D
Levels: 1
Square Footage: 1,787
Bedrooms: 3
Bathrooms: 2
Foundation: Basement
Materials List Available: Yes
Price Category: C

Images provided by designer/architect.

CAD FILE AVAILABLE

SMARTtip
Country Décor in Your Bathroom

Collections are often part of a country decor, even in the bathroom. All you need is three or more of anything that have size, shape, or color in common. You can mass them on walls, on shelves, on the windowsills, or even along the edge of the tub.

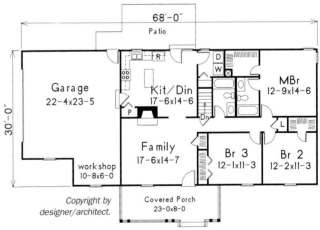

Copyright by designer/architect.

Plan #321013

Dimensions: 68' W x 30' D
Levels: 1
Square Footage: 1,360
Bedrooms: 3
Bathrooms: 2
Foundation: Crawl space, slab, or basement
Materials List Available: Yes
Price Category: B

Images provided by designer/architect.

CAD FILE AVAILABLE

SMARTtip
Glass Doors and Fire Safety

Professionals recommend keeping glass doors open while a fire is burning. When the doors are left completely open, the burning flame has a more realistic appearance and the glass doesn't become soiled by swirling ashes. When the doors are closed, heat from a large hot fire can break the glass.

Plan #131014

Dimensions: 48' W x 43'4" D
Levels: 1
Square Footage: 1,380
Bedrooms: 3
Bathrooms: 2
Foundation: Crawl space, slab, or basement
Materials List Available: Yes
Price Category: C

Images provided by designer/architect.

The exterior of this home looks formal, thanks to its twin dormers, gables, and the bay windows that flank the columned porch, but the inside is contemporary in both design and features.

Features:

- **Great Room:** Centrally located, this great room has a 10-ft. ceiling. A fireplace, built-in cabinets, and windows that overlook the rear covered porch make it as practical as it is attractive.

- **Dining Room:** A bay window adds to the charm of this versatile room.

- **Kitchen:** This U-shaped room is designed to make cooking and cleaning jobs efficient.

- **Master Suite:** With a bay window, a walk-in closet, and a private bath with an oval tub, the master suite may be your favorite area.

- **Additional Bedrooms:** Located on the opposite side of the house from the master suite, these rooms share a full bath in the hall.

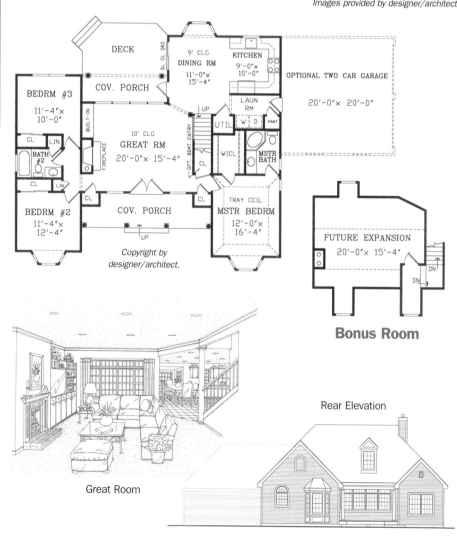

DECK

9' CLG
DINING RM
11'-0" x
15'-4"

KITCHEN
9'-0" x
10'-0"

COV. PORCH

BEDRM #3
11'-4" x
10'-0"

LAUN RM

OPTIONAL TWO CAR GARAGE
20'-0" x 20'-0"

10' CLG
GREAT RM
20'-0" x 15'-4"

BATH #2

UTIL

WICL

MSTR BATH

BEDRM #2
11'-4" x
12'-4"

COV. PORCH

MSTR BEDRM
12'-0" x
16'-4"
TRAY CEIL

Copyright by designer/architect.

FUTURE EXPANSION
20'-0" x 15'-4"

Bonus Room

Great Room

Rear Elevation

Plan #101002

Dimensions: 46' W x 42' D
Levels: 1
Square Footage: 1,296
Bedrooms: 3
Bathrooms: 2
Foundation: Crawl space, slab, basement
Materials List Available: No
Price Category: C

This affordable compact home is also strikingly attractive.

Features:

- Ceiling Height: 8 ft.

- Foyer: Beveled glass front provides a luxurious entry.

- Family Room: This spacious 16-ft. x 20-ft. room has a vaulted ceiling.

- Laundry Room: There is ample space to fold clothes.

- Master Bedroom Suite: Split from other bedrooms, this suite has many his and her features.

- Kitchen: This galley kitchen offers open traffic patterns with ample counter space.

- Breakfast Eating Area: A growing family will find additional seating space that leads to a covered porch providing a pleasant retreat.

Images provided by designer/architect.

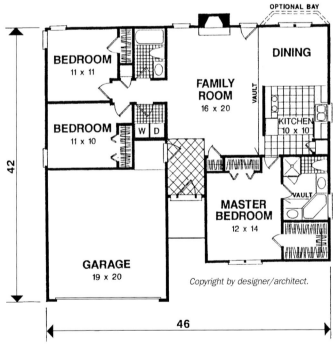

Copyright by designer/architect.

SMARTtip

Preparing Walls for Paint

Poor surface preparation is the number-one cause of paint failure. Preparing surfaces properly—including removing loose paint and thoroughly sanding—may be tedious, but it's important for a good-looking and long-lasting finish.

Plan #221015

Dimensions: 69'8" W x 46' D

Levels: 1

Square Footage: 1,926

Bedrooms: 3

Bathrooms: 2½

Foundation: Basement; walkout basement for fee

Materials List Available: No

Price Category: D

You'll love the open plan in this lovely ranch and admire its many features, which are usually reserved for much larger homes.

Features:

- Ceiling Height: 8 ft.

- Great Room: A vaulted ceiling and tall windows surrounding the centrally located fireplace give distinction to this handsome room.

- Dining Room: Positioned just off the entry, this formal room makes a lovely spot for quiet dinner parties.

- Dining Nook: This nook sits between the kitchen and the great room. Central doors in the bayed area open to the backyard.

- Kitchen: An island will invite visitors while you cook in this well-planned kitchen, with its corner pantry and ample counter space.

- Master Suite: A tray ceiling, bay window, walk-in closet, and bath with whirlpool tub, dual-sink vanity, and standing shower pamper you here.

Images provided by designer/architect.

Rear Elevation

Copyright by designer/architect.

Images provided by designer/architect.

Plan #301002

Dimensions: 57'2" W x 54'10" D
Levels: 1
Square Footage: 1,845
Bedrooms: 3
Bathrooms: 2½
Foundation: Slab or crawl space
Materials List Available: Yes
Price Category: D

Although compact, this home is filled with surprisingly luxurious features.

Features:

- Ceiling Height: 8 ft. unless otherwise noted.

- Front Porch: Guests will be sheltered from the rain by this lovely little porch.

- Foyer: This elegant foyer features a 10-ft. ceiling and is open to the dining room and the rear great room.

- Dining Room: The 10-ft. ceiling from the foyer continues into this spacious dining room.

- Family Room: This family room features a vaulted ceiling and a fireplace with built-in bookcases.

- Kitchen: This kitchen boasts a pantry and plenty of storage and counter space.

- Master Bedroom: This master bedroom includes a cathedral ceiling and two walk-in closets. The master bath has two vanities, a corner spa, and a walk-in closet.

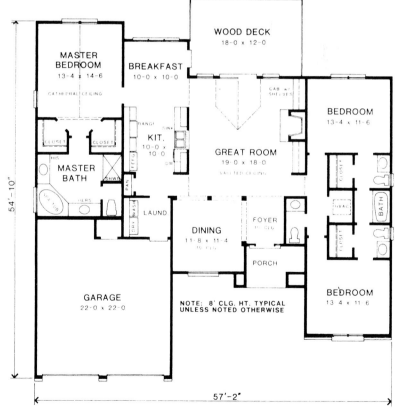

Copyright by designer/architect.

Plan #161002

Dimensions: 64'2" W x 44'2" D
Levels: 1
Square Footage: 1,860
Bedrooms: 3
Bathrooms: 2
Foundation: Basement
Materials List Available: Yes
Price Category: D

Images provided by designer/architect.

The brick, stone, and cedar shake facade provides color and texture to the exterior, while the unique nooks and angles inside this delightful one-level home give it character.

Features:

- Great Room/Dining Room: This spacious great room is furnished with a wood-burning fireplace, a high ceiling, and French doors. Wide entrances to the breakfast room and dining room expand its space to comfortably hold large gatherings.

- Kitchen: The breakfast bar offers additional seating. The covered porch lets you enjoy a view of the landscape and is conveniently located for outdoor meals off this kitchen and breakfast area.

- Master Suite: The master suite is a private retreat. An alcove creates a comfortable sitting area, and an angled entry leads to the bath with whirlpool and a double-bowl vanity.

Left Side Elevation

Rear Elevation

Right Side Elevation

Copyright by designer/architect.

Dining Room

Living Room / Dining Room

Great Room/Breakfast Area

Great Room

SMARTtip

Installing Rods and Poles

The way to install a rod or pole depends on the type it is, the brackets that will hold it, the weight of the window treatment, and the surface to which it is being fastened. Given below are some general guidelines, but for specific installation procedures, refer to the instructions that accompany the rod or pole.

- Use a stepladder to reach high places.

- Use the proper tools.

- Take accurate measurements.

- Work with a helper.

- If attaching a bracket to wood, first drill small pilot holes to avoid splitting the wood.

- Consider using wall anchors, particularly for the heavier window treatments.

- Use a level as needed to help you position the brackets for the pole or rod.

- Take care not to drill or hammer into any pipes or electrical wiring.

Because they're designed to stand out, decorative poles and their finials require more room for installation than conventional drapery rods. Finials add inches to the ends of a window treatment, so make sure you have enough wall room to display your hardware to its full advantage. And because decorative rods are often heavy, be certain your window frames and walls can support the weight.

Plan #161012

Dimensions: 69' W x 50'10" D

Levels: 1

Square Footage: 1,648

Bedrooms: 3

Bathrooms: 2

Foundation: Basement

Materials List Available: Yes

Price Category: C

Images provided by designer/architect.

This delightful brick home, with multiple gables and an inviting front porch, offers an exciting interior with varied ceiling heights and an open floor plan.

Features:

- **Great Room:** This great room showcases an 11-ft. ceiling and a gas fireplace. Enjoy a beverage seated at the convenient bar, and move freely through a generous opening to the relaxed dining area.

- **Kitchen:** This galley kitchen is expanded by easy access to the garage and laundry room.

- **Master Suite:** You will appreciate the openness of this large master bedroom, which features an 11-ft. ceiling. You can also retreat to the privacy of an adjoining covered porch.

- **Library:** Thoughtful design allows you to exercise the option of converting the bedroom off the foyer into a library.

Right Side Elevation

Left Side Elevation

Rear Elevation

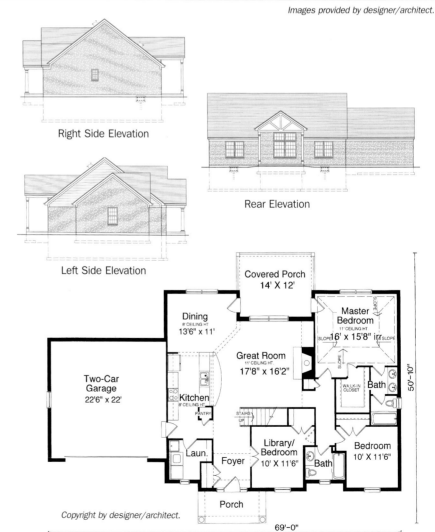

Copyright by designer/architect.

Plan #391019

Dimensions: 56' W x 32' D
Levels: 1
Square Footage: 1,792
Bedrooms: 3
Bathrooms: 2
Foundation: Basement
Materials List Available: Yes
Price Category: C

Images provided by designer/architect.

This southern-style cottage with sociable porch fits in almost anywhere, from a leafy lane to hillside or curbside and renders a lot of living space and hospitality.

Features:

- Family Room: This room features a central stone fireplace, plus two walls of windows to usher in the light. Sloping ceilings and decorative beams boost its rustic charm. An enormously generous space, it opens wide to the corner kitchen.

- Dining Room: This room has its own level of sophistication, including entry outside to the deck.

- Utility Areas: The family-sized pantry and laundry area are set off by themselves to avoid interference with everyday living.

- Master Suite: A leisurely hall leads to the master bedroom and private full bath,

wide walk-in closets, and a trio of windows.

- Bedrooms: Across the hall the two secondary bedrooms share a roomy bath and a view of the front porch.

Side/Rear View

Copyright by designer/ architect.

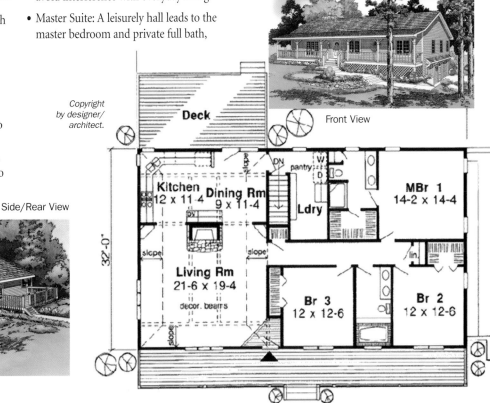

Front View

Plan #271081

Dimensions: 86' W x 54' D

Levels: 1

Square Footage: 2,539

Bedrooms: 3

Bathrooms: 2

Foundation: Slab

Materials List Available: No

Price Category: E

This traditional home is sure to impress your guests and even your neighbors.

Features:

- Living Room: This quiet space off the foyer is perfect for pleasant conversation.

- Family Room: A perfect gathering spot, this room is nicely enhanced by a fireplace.

- Kitchen: This room easily serves the bayed morning room and the formal dining room.

- Master Suite: The master bedroom overlooks a side patio, and boasts a private bath with a skylight and a whirlpool tub.

- Library: This cozy room is perfect for curling up with a good novel. It would also make a great extra bedroom.

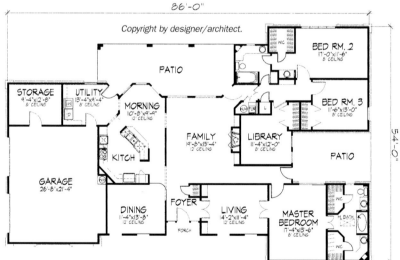

SMARTtip

Determining Curtain Length

Follow length guidelines for foolproof results, but remember that they're not rules. Go ahead and play with curtain and drapery lengths. Instead of shortening long panels at the hem, for instance, take up excess material by blousing them over tiebacks for a pleasing effect.

Plan #101012

Dimensions: 69'4" W x 62'9" D

Levels: 1

Square Footage: 2,288

Bedrooms: 3

Bathrooms: 2½

Foundation: Crawl space, slab, basement, or walkout

Materials List Available: No

Price Category: E

This classic brick ranch boasts traditional styling and an exciting up-to-date floor plan.

Features:

• Ceiling Height: 9 ft. unless otherwise noted.

• Front Porch: Guests will be welcome by this inviting front porch, which features a 12-ft. ceiling.

Images provided by designer/architect.

• Family Room: This warm and inviting room measures 16 ft. x 19 ft. It features a 14-ft. ceiling and a rear wall of windows. French doors lead to an enormous deck.

• Kitchen: This unique angled kitchen is open to the hearth room and eating areas, all of which enjoy vaulted ceilings and are surrounded by windows. The hearth room has a TV niche.

• Master Suite: This 16-ft. x 15-ft. master suite is truly sumptuous, with its

12-ft. ceiling, sitting area, two walk-in closets, and full-featured bath.

• Bonus Room: Here is plenty of storage or room for future expansion. Just beyond the entry are stairs leading to a bonus room measuring approximately 12 ft. x 21 ft.

Copyright by designer/architect.

Living Room

Plan #321001

Dimensions: 83' W x 42' D

Levels: 1

Square Footage: 1,721

Bedrooms: 3

Bathrooms: 2

Foundation: Crawl space, slab, or basement

Materials List Available: Yes

Price Category: C

This home, as shown in the photograph, may differ from the actual blueprints. For more detailed information, please check the floor plans carefully.

Images provided by designer/architect

CAD FILE AVAILABLE

Rear View

Copyright by designer/architect.

You'll love the atrium which creates a warm, naturally lit space inside this gracious home, as well as the roof dormers that give the house wonderful curb appeal from the outside.

Features:

- Great Room: Bathed in light from the atrium window wall, this room, with its vaulted ceiling, will be the hub of your family life.

- Dining Room: This room also has a vaulted ceiling and is lit by the atrium, but you can draw drapes at night to create a cozy, warm feeling.

- Kitchen: Designed for functionality, this step-saving kitchen is easy to organize and makes cooking a pleasure.

- Breakfast Room: For convenience, this room is located between the kitchen and the rear covered porch.

- Master Suite: Retire with pleasure to this lovely retreat, with its luxurious bath.

Plan #101011

Dimensions: 71'2" W x 58'1" D
Levels: 1
Square Footage: 2,184
Bedrooms: 3
Bathrooms: 3
Foundation: Crawl space, slab, basement, or walkout
Materials List Available: Yes
Price Category: E

Images provided by designer/architect.

A classic design and spacious interior add up to a flexible design suitable to any modern lifestyle.

CAD FILE AVAILABLE

Features:

• Ceiling Height: 9 ft. unless otherwise noted.

• Formal Dining Room: A decorative square column and a tray ceiling adorn this elegant dining room.

• Screened Porch: Enjoy summer breezes in style by stepping out of the French doors into this vaulted screened porch.

• Kitchen: Does everyone want to hang out in the kitchen while you are cooking? No problem. True to the home's country style, this huge 14-ft.-3-in. x 22-ft.-6-in. has plenty of room for helpers.

• Patio or Deck: This pleasant outdoor area is accessible from both the screened porch and the master bedroom.

• Master Suite: This luxurious suite includes a double tray ceiling, a sitting area, two walk-in closets, and an exquisite bath.

Kitchen

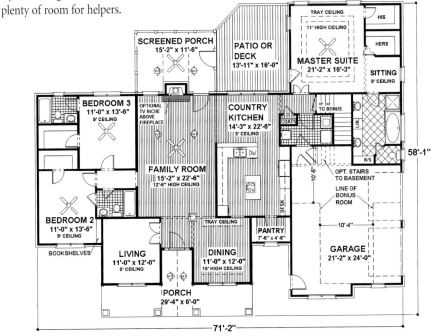

Copyright by designer/architect.

Plan #131007

Dimensions: 59'10" W x 47'8" D
Levels: 1
Square Footage: 1,595
Bedrooms: 3
Bathrooms: 2
Foundation: Crawl space, slab, basement, or walkout
Materials List Available: Yes
Price Category: D

Imagine living in this home, with its traditional country comfort and individual brand of charm.

Features:

- Exterior elements: The mixture of a front porch with a cameo front door, decorative posts, bay windows, and dormers will delight you.

- Great Room: A tray ceiling gives distinction to this large room, and a wet bar eases entertaining.

- Screened Porch: At dusk and dawn, this porch is sure to be your favorite outdoor spot.

- Kitchen: Eat any meal in this large kitchen for a touch of homey charm.

- Dining Room: Perfect for hosting a formal dinner, this bayed dining room can increase your enjoyment of simple family meals.

- Master Bedroom: For the sake of privacy, this room is somewhat secluded. Decorate to emphasize the elegant tray ceiling.

Images provided by designer/architect.

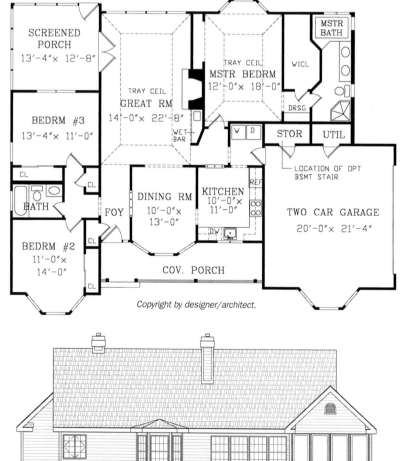

Copyright by designer/architect.

Rear Elevation

Alternate Front View

Foyer / Dining Room

Great Room

Add the Extras

Simple or plain, it's the little conveniences and miscellaneous touches that push the dining experience to perfection. Here are some extra things to think about.

- You can never have too many serving trays when you entertain outside. For carrying food or drinks from the kitchen or the grill, trays are indispensable.

- A serving cart on wheels makes a perfect movable outdoor bar and provides an additional serving surface. Look for one at yard sales or buy one new.

- Chances are you won't have a sideboard, but a few small tables to hold excess items are great substitutes for one. They're also easier to position in the different places where you need them.

- For cooler weather or even a summer's evening with a bit of nip in the air, nothing beats an outdoor fireplace for comfort. You could build one into the house, but various types of stand-alone units are sold in home centers. To add a Southwest ambiance, consider a chiminea, a clay fireplace. Try burning some piñon pine, and you'll feel as if you're in Santa Fe. Be sure to follow manufacturers' instructions when using these fireplaces. You might also have to store them during the winter.

- Pots of fragrant plants—lavender, scented geraniums, flowering tobacco, or jasmine—provide a sensual aroma. Flowers such as roses climbing up an arbor or trellis are beautiful, evoke a romantic feeling, and lend a delicate scent to the atmosphere as well.

Nothing adds romance and intrigue to an evening soiree as candlelight does. Include just a few candles for an intimate dinner. Use more for a larger gathering, placing one or more on each table. Scatter luminaries around the yard. As the beautiful evening dusk begins, light candles, a few at a time, so your eyes can adjust to the dimming light. Not only do the candles illuminate the night in a magical way but they can also keep bugs at bay.

Plan #311002

Dimensions: 56'6" W x 82' D
Levels: 1
Square Footage: 2,402
Bedrooms: 4
Bathrooms: 2½
Foundation: Crawl space, slab
Materials List Available: Yes
Price Category: E

This lovely home has an open floor plan in the main living area but privacy in the bedrooms.

Features:

- Foyer: With an 11-ft. ceiling, this foyer opens to both the great room and the dining room.

- Great Room: A 10-ft. ceiling and handsome fireplace highlight this spacious room, which is open to both the kitchen and breakfast room.

- Dining Room: A butler's pantry and built-in china closet spell convenience in this lovely room.

- Breakfast Room: Bask in the sunshine flowing through the bay windows in this room, which opens to the rear porch.

- Kitchen: Designed for efficiency, this kitchen will charm all the cooks in the family.

- Master Suite: It's easy to feel pampered by the huge closet and bath with corner tub and two vanities.

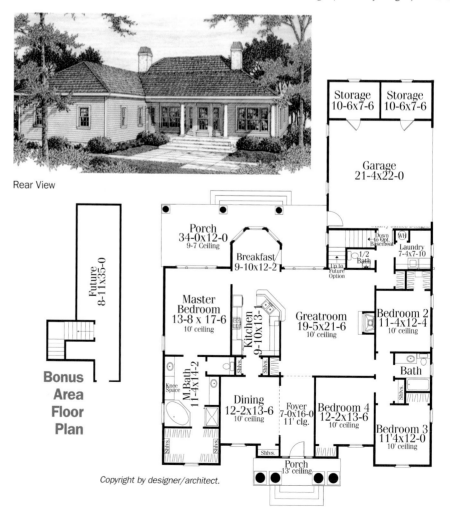

Rear View

Copyright by designer/architect.

Plan #151037

Dimensions: 50' W x 56' D

Levels: 1

Square Footage: 1,538

Bedrooms: 3

Bathrooms: 2

Foundation: Crawl space, slab, or basement

CompleteCost List Available: Yes

Price Category: C

Images provided by designer/architect.

You'll love this traditional-looking home, with its covered porch and interesting front windows.

Features:

- Ceiling Height: 8 ft.

- Great Room: This large room has a boxed window that emphasizes its dimensions and a fireplace where everyone will gather on chilly evenings. A door opens to the backyard.

- Dining Room: A bay window overlooking the front porch makes this room easy to decorate.

- Kitchen: This well-planned kitchen features ample counter space, a full pantry, and an eating bar that it shares with the dining room.

- Master Suite: A pan ceiling in this lovely room gives an elegant touch. The huge private bath includes two walk-in closets, a whirlpool tub, a dual-sink vanity, and a skylight in the ceiling.

- Additional Bedrooms: On the opposite side of the house, these bedrooms share a large bath, and both feature excellent closet space.

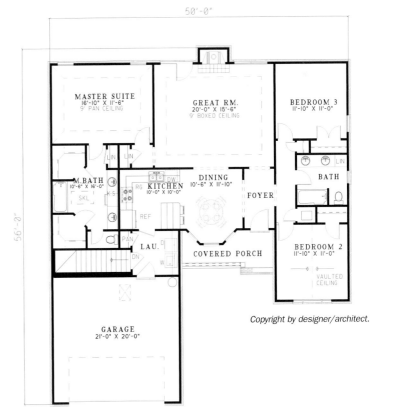

Copyright by designer/architect.

Plan #161003

Dimensions: 60' W x 47' D
Levels: 1
Square Footage: 1,508
Bedrooms: 3
Bathrooms: 2
Foundation: Basement
Materials List Available: Yes
Price Category: C

Multiple gables and a cozy front porch invite you to this enchanting one-story home.

Features:

- Great Room: This bright and cheery room features a sloped ceiling and fireplace. The great room is designed for convenience, with easy access to the foyer and dining area, creating the look and feel of a home much larger than its actual size.

- Dining Area: Adjacent to the great room, this dining area has multiple windows and angles that add light and dimension.

- Kitchen: This spacious kitchen is designed for easy work patterns with an abundance of counter and cabinet space. It also features a snack bar.

- Master Bedroom: Designed for step-saving convenience, this master bedroom includes a compartmented bath, double-bowl vanity, and large walk-in closet.

Images provided by designer/architect.

Copyright by designer/architect.

Rear Elevation

Plan #151034

Dimensions: 58'6" W x 64'6" D

Levels: 1

Square Footage: 2,133

Bedrooms: 3

Bathrooms: 2

Foundation: Crawl space, slab, or basement

CompleteCost List Available: Yes

Price Category: D

You'll love the high ceilings, open floor plan, and contemporary design features in this home.

Features:

- Great Room: A pass-through tiled fireplace between this lovely large room and the adjacent hearth room allows you to notice the mirror effect created by the 10-ft. boxed ceilings in both rooms.

- Dining Room: An 11-ft. ceiling and 8-in. boxed column give formality to this lovely room, where you're certain to entertain.

- Kitchen: If you're a cook, this room may become your favorite spot in the house, thanks to its great design, which includes plenty of work and storage space, and a very practical layout.

- Master Suite: A 10-ft. boxed ceiling gives elegance to this room. A pocket door opens to the private bath, with its huge walk-in closet, glass-blocked whirlpool tub, separate glass shower, and private toilet room.

CAD FILE AVAILABLE

This home, as shown in the photograph, may differ from the actual blueprints. For more detailed information, please check the floor plans carefully.

Images provided by designer/architect.

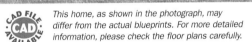

Copyright by designer/architect.

Rendering reflects floor plan

Plan #291002

Dimensions: 62'8" W x 38'4" D
Levels: 1
Square Footage: 1,550
Bedrooms: 3
Bathrooms: 2
Foundation: Basement
Materials List Available: No
Price Category: C

This comfortable Southwestern-style ranch house will fit perfectly into any setting.

Features:

- Ceiling Height: 8 ft. unless otherwise noted.

- Front Porch: This scalloped front porch offers plenty of room for enjoying a cool summer breeze.

- Foyer: Upon entering this impressive foyer you'll be greeted by a soaring space encompassing the living room and dining room.

- Living/Dining Area: This combined living room and dining room has a handsome fireplace as its focal point. When dinner is served, guests will flow casually into the dining area.

- Kitchen: Take your cooking up a notch in this terrific kitchen. It features a 42-in.-high counter that will do double-duty as a snack bar for family meals and a wet bar for entertaining.

- Master Suite: This master retreat is separated from the other bedrooms and features an elegant vaulted ceiling. The dressing area has a compartmentalized bath and a walk-in closet.

Images provided by designer/architect.

Rear View

Copyright by designer/architect.

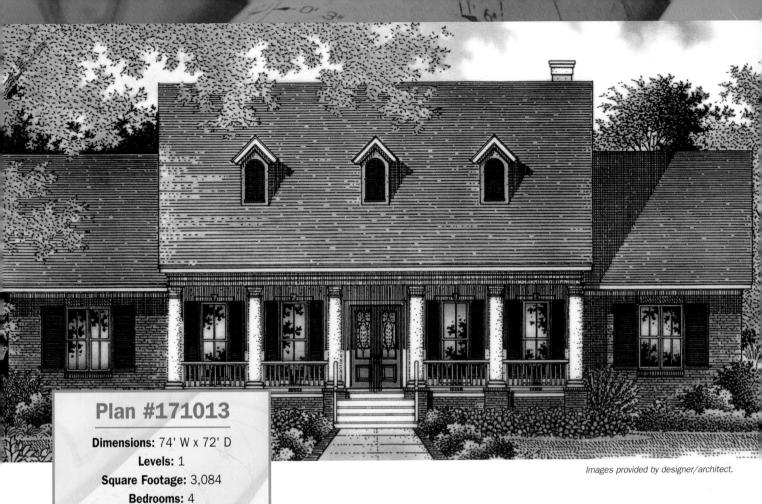

Images provided by designer/architect.

Plan #171013

Dimensions: 74' W x 72' D

Levels: 1

Square Footage: 3,084

Bedrooms: 4

Bathrooms: 3½

Foundation: Crawl space or slab

Materials List Available: Yes

Price Category: G

Impressive porch columns add to the country charm of this amenity-filled family home.

Features:

- Ceiling Height: 10 ft.

- Foyer: The sense of style continues from the front porch into this foyer, which opens to the formal dining room and the living room.

- Dining Room: Two handsome support columns accentuate the elegance of this dining room.

- Living Room: This living room features a cozy corner fireplace and plenty of room for the entire family to gather and relax.

- Kitchen: You'll be inspired to new culinary heights in this kitchen, which offers plenty of counter space, a snack bar, a built-in pantry, and a china closet.

- Master Suite: The bedroom of this master suite has a fireplace and overlooks a rear courtyard. The bath has two vanities a large walk-in closet, a deluxe tub, a walk-in shower, and a skylight.

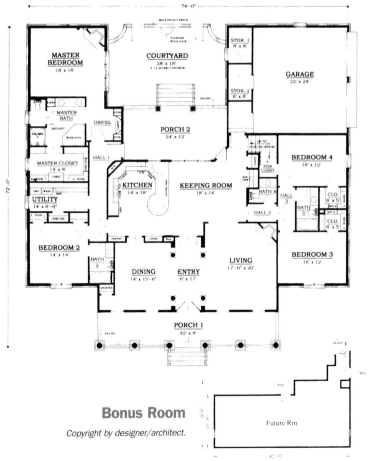

Bonus Room

Copyright by designer/architect.

Plan #211003

Dimensions: 62' W x 64' D
Levels: 1
Square Footage: 1,856
Bedrooms: 3
Bathrooms: 2
Foundation: Crawl space or slab
Materials List Available: Yes
Price Category: D

SMARTtip

Fire Extinguishers

The word PASS is an easy way to remember the proper way to use a fire extinguisher.

Pull the pin at the top of the extinguisher that keeps the handle from being accidentally pressed.

Aim the nozzle of the extinguisher toward the base of the fire.

Squeeze the handle to discharge the extinguisher. Stand approximately 8 feet away from the fire.

Sweep the nozzle back and forth at the base of the fire. After the fire appears to be out, watch it carefully because it may reignite!

The traditional style of this home is blended with all the amenities required for today's lifestyle.

Features:

• Ceiling Height: 8 ft. unless otherwise noted.

• Front Porch: Guests will feel welcome arriving at the front door under this sheltering front porch.

• Dining Room: This large room will accommodate dinner parties of all sizes, from large formal gatherings to more intimate family get-togethers.

• Living Room: Guests and family alike will feel right at home in this inviting room. Sunlight streaming through the skylights in the 12-ft. ceiling, combined with the handsome fireplace, makes the space both airy and warm.

• Back Patio: When warm weather comes around, step out the sliding glass doors in the living room to enjoy entertaining or just relaxing on this patio.

• Kitchen: A cathedral ceiling soars over this efficient modern kitchen. It includes an eating area that is perfect for informal family meals.

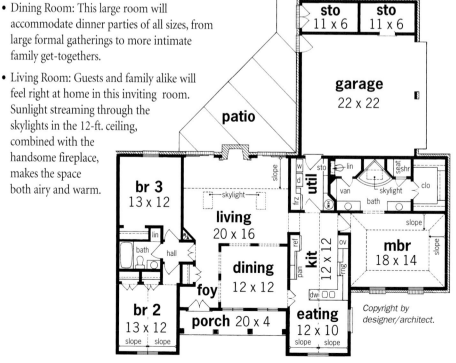

Copyright by designer/architect.

Plan #321008

Dimensions: 57' W x 52'2" D
Levels: 1
Square Footage: 1,761
Bedrooms: 4
Bathrooms: 2
Foundation: Basement
Materials List Available: Yes
Price Category: C

One look at the roof dormers and planter boxes that grace the outside of this ranch, and you'll know that the interior is planned for comfortable family living.

Features:

- **Great Room:** A vaulted ceiling in this room points up its generous dimensions. Put a grouping of chairs near the fireplace to take advantage of the cozy spot it creates in chilly weather.

- **Kitchen:** Open to the great room, this kitchen has been planned for convenience. It features a pass-through to the dining area for easy serving when you've got a crowd to feed.

- **Master Bedroom:** A vaulted ceiling here makes you feel especially pampered, and the walk-in closet and amenity-filled bath add to that feeling.

- **Additional Bedrooms:** Great closet space characterizes all the rooms in this home, making it easy for children of any age to keep it organized and tidy.

Images provided by designer/architect.

Copyright by designer/architect.

MBr 14-6x13-0 vaulted clg

Br 2 11-0x10-0

Br 3 11-0x10-0

Br 4 12-0x10-0 vaulted clg

Great Rm 16-0x17-10 vaulted clg

Dining 12-4x10-0

Covered Porch

Patio

Brkfst 11-8x10-8

Kit 11-5x 12-9

Garage 20-4x20-10

Dn

L

P

R

W
D

52'-2"

57'-0"

SMARTtip

Hanging Wallpaper

Use liner paper to smooth out a damaged wall and to provide uniform support for expensive paper.

Plan #151060

Dimensions: 80'11" W x 95'8" D

Levels: 1

Square Footage: 3,554

Bedrooms: 3

Bathrooms: 3

Foundation: Crawl space, slab basement, or walkout

CompleteCost List Available: Yes

Price Category: F

This large home has everything and was designed for abundant living.

Features:

• Great Room: This large entertaining area features a 12-ft.-high ceiling.

• Dining Room: This formal area has 8-in. round columns framing the entry to the foyer and the great room.

• Master Suite: You'll reach this private retreat, located on the opposite side of the home from the secondary bedrooms, through an arched opening off the foyer.

• Garage: This large three-car garage has a storage nook.

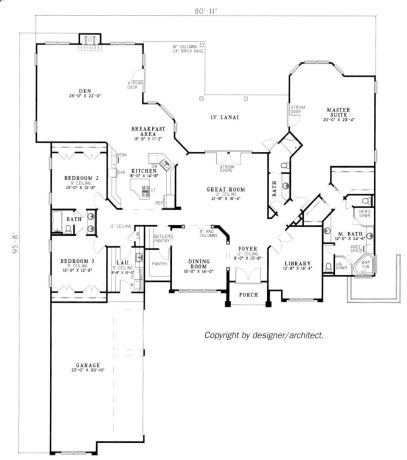

Plan #121001

Dimensions: 56' W x 58' D
Levels: 1
Square Footage: 1,911
Bedrooms: 3
Bathrooms: 2
Foundation: Basement
Materials List Available: Yes
Price Category: D

Detailed, soaring ceilings and top-notch amenities set this distinctive home apart.

Features:

• Ceiling Height: 8 ft. except as noted.

• Great Room: A soaring ceiling and six tall transom-topped windows make this a light and airy spot for entertaining.

• Formal Dining Room: The entry enjoys a pleasing view of this dining room's detailed 12-ft. ceiling and picture window.

• Great Room: At the back of the home, a see-through fireplace in this great room is joined by a built-in entertainment center.

• Hearth Room: This bayed room shares the see-through fireplace with the great room.

• Master Suite: Enjoy the stars and the sun in the private bath's whirlpool and separate shower. The bath features the same decorative ceiling as the dining room.

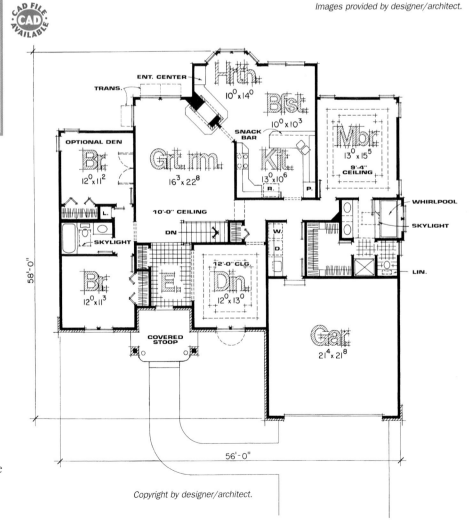

Copyright by designer/architect.

Plan #221020

Dimensions: 69'8" W x 43' D
Levels: 1
Square Footage: 1,859
Bedrooms: 3
Bathrooms: 2½
Foundation: Basement
Materials List Available: No
Price Category: D

Images provided by designer/architect.

You'll love this design if you're looking for a compact home with amenities usually found in much larger designs.

Features:

- Ceiling Height: 8 ft.

- Living Room: A vaulted ceiling gives an elegant feeling, and a bank of windows lets natural light pour in during the daytime.

- Dining Room: Located just off the entry for the convenience of your guests, this room is ideal for intimate family meals or formal dinner parties.

- Kitchen: Just across from the dining room, this kitchen is distinguished by its ample counter space. The adjacent nook is large enough to use as a casual dining area, and it features access to the backyard.

- Master Suite: The large bay window lends interest to this room, and you'll love the walk-in closet and private bath, with its whirlpool tub, standing shower, and dual-sink vanity.

Rear Elevation

Copyright by designer/architect.

Plan #131009

Dimensions: 64'10" W x 57'8" D
Levels: 1
Square Footage: 2,018
Bedrooms: 3
Bathrooms: 2
Foundation: Crawl space, slab, or basement
Materials List Available: Yes
Price Category: E

Images provided by designer/architect.

The pavilion-styled great room at the heart of this H-shaped ranch gives it an unusual elegance that you're sure to enjoy.

Features:

- **Great Room:** The tray ceiling sets off this room, and a fireplace warms it on chilly nights and cool days. Two sets of sliding glass doors leading to the backyard terrace let in natural light and create an efficient traffic flow.

- **Kitchen:** Designed for a gourmet cook, this kitchen features a snack bar that everyone will enjoy and easy access to the breakfast room.

- **Breakfast Room:** Open to the columned rear porch, this breakfast room is an ideal spot for company or family brunches.

- **Master Suite:** A sitting area and access to the porch make the bedroom luxurious, while the private bath featuring a whirlpool tub creates a spa atmosphere.

VAULTED
BEDRM #2
14'-8" x 11'-0"
CL CL

BEDRM #3
11'-0" x 13'-0"

BATH #2
STOR UTIL
LOCATION OF
OPT. BSMT STAIR

TWO CAR GARAGE
20'-0" x 21'-0"

ALT. FRONT ENTRY GARAGE

TERRACE
BUILT-IN

11'-6" HIGH STEPPED CLG
GREAT RM
21'-0" x 16'-0"
TV
CL

COV. PORCH
24'-8" x 10'-2"

9'-6" HIGH CEILING
BKFST RM
13'-0" x 20'-2"
DW
KITCHEN
REF
PANT

SITTING
CL. OR BUILT-IN
11'-6" HIGH STEPPED CLG
MSTR BEDRM
13'-0" x 18'-0"

HIGH CEIL
GALLERY

COV. PORCH

9'-6" HIGH STEPPED CLG
DINING RM
12'-0" x 14'-0"

DRSG
WICL
WICL
LIN

9'-6" HIGH STEPPED CLG
MSTR BATH
STEAM SHOWER
SEAT

Copyright by designer/architect.

Great Room

Plan #191032

Dimensions: 80'4" W x 52' D
Levels: 1
Square Footage: 2,091
Bedrooms: 3
Bathrooms: 2
Foundation: Slab
Materials List Available: No
Price Category: D

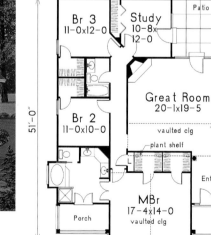

CAD FILE AVAILABLE

Plan #321030

Dimensions: 61' W x 51' D
Levels: 1
Square Footage: 2,029
Bedrooms: 4
Bathrooms: 2
Foundation: Crawl space, slab, basement, or walkout
Materials List Available: Yes
Price Category: D

SMARTtip

Measuring Angles

A sure-fire way to accurately measure the wall-frame acute angle is to cut a piece of scrap lumber to emulate the angle, and then measure it.

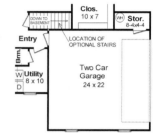

Plan #351006

Dimensions: 72'10" W x 41' D

Levels: 1

Square Footage: 1,638

Bedrooms: 3

Bathrooms: 2

Foundation: Crawl space, slab, or basement

Materials List Available: Yes

Price Category: D

Images provided by designer/architect.

CAD FILE AVAILABLE

Stair Location for Basement Option

Copyright by designer/architect.

Images provided by designer/architect.

Copyright by designer/architect.

Plan #121034

Dimensions: 92'8" W x 59'4" D

Levels: 1

Square Footage: 2,223

Bedrooms: 1

Bathrooms: 2½

Foundation: Basement; crawl space for fee

Materials List Available: Yes

Price Category: E

CAD FILE AVAILABLE

Optional Basement Level Floor Plan

Plan #131006

Dimensions: 61' W x 53'6" D
Levels: 1
Square Footage: 2,193
Bedrooms: 3
Bathrooms: 2
Foundation: Crawl space, slab, or basement
Materials List Available: Yes
Price Category: E

This compact home is perfect for a small lot, but even so, has all the features of a much larger home, thanks to its space-saving interior design that lets one area flow into the next.

Features:

- Great Room: This wonderful room is sure to be the heart of your home. Visually, it flows from the foyer and dining room to the rear of the house, giving you enough space to create a private nook or two in it or treat it as a single, large room.

- Dining Room: Emphasize the formality of this room by decorating with subdued colors and sumptuous fabrics.

- Kitchen: Designed for efficiency, this kitchen features ample counter space and cabinets in a layout guaranteed to please you.

- Master Suite: You'll love the amenities in this private master suite, with its lovely bedroom and a bath filled with contemporary fixtures.

Kitchen

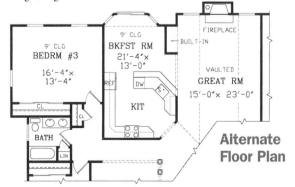

Alternate Floor Plan

Plan #131020

Dimensions: 67'2" W x 48'10" D

Levels: 1

Square Footage: 1,735

Bedrooms: 3

Bathrooms: 2

Foundation: Crawl space, slab, or basement

Materials List Available: Yes

Price Category: D

This gorgeous ranch is designed for entertaining but is also comfortable for family living.

Features:

- **Living Room:** A 9-ft. stepped ceiling highlights the spaciousness of this room, which gives a view of one of the two covered porches.

- **Dining Room:** Also with a 9-ft. stepped ceiling and a view of the porch, this room features a bay window.

- **Family Room:** An 11-ft. vaulted ceiling and gliding French doors to the porch define this central gathering area.

- **Kitchen:** Enjoy the skylight, a fireplace that's shared with the family room, a central island cooktop, and a snack bar in this room.

- **Master Suite:** The tray ceiling is 9 ft. 9 in. high, and this area includes a sitting area and a bath with a whirlpool tub and dual-sink vanity.

Images provided by designer/architect.

Copyright by designer/architect.

Photos provided by designer/architect.

Kitchen

Foyer/Dining Room

Plan #321002

Dimensions: 72' W x 28' D

Levels: 1

Square Footage: 1,400

Bedrooms: 3

Bathrooms: 2

Foundation: Crawl space, basement

Materials List Available: Yes

Price Category: B

If you're looking for a well-designed compact home with contemporary amenities, this could be the home of your dreams.

Features:

- Porch: Just the right size for some rockers and a swing, this porch could become your outdoor living area when the weather is fine.

- Living Room: A vaulted ceiling adds to the spacious feeling in this room, where friends and family are sure to gather.

- Kitchen: This space-saving design, in combination with the ample counter and cabinet space, makes cooking a pleasure.

- Utility Room: This large room is fitted with cabinets for extra storage space. You'll find storage space in the large garage, too.

- Master Bedroom: This room is somewhat secluded for privacy, making it an ideal place for some quiet time at the end of the day.

Images provided by designer/architect.

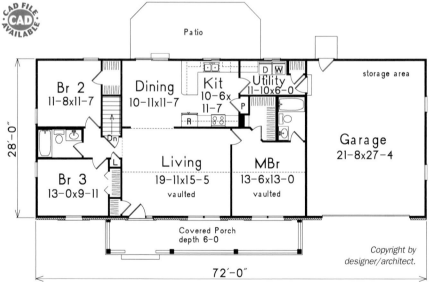

Copyright by designer/architect.

SMARTtip

Fabric Draping Ability

Test a fabric's draping ability by looking at a large piece in a fabric store. Gather at least two to three yards of material, holding one end in your hand. Check how it drapes. Does it fall into folds easily? Also look at the pattern when it is gathered. Does the design become lost in the folds? Ask a salesclerk or a friend to hold the fabric, and look at it from a few feet away.

Plan #151009

Dimensions: 44' W x 86'2" D
Levels: 1
Square Footage: 1,601
Bedrooms: 3
Bathrooms: 2
Foundation: Crawl space, slab
CompleteCost List Available: Yes
Price Category: C

This can be the perfect home for a site with views you can enjoy in all seasons and at all times.

Features:

- Porches: Enjoy the front porch with its 10-ft. ceiling and the more private back porch where you can set up a grill or just get away from it all.

- Foyer: With a 10-ft. ceiling, this foyer opens to the great room for a warm welcome.

- Great Room: Your family will love the media center and the easy access to the rear porch.

- Kitchen: This well-designed kitchen is open to the dining room and the breakfast nook, which also opens to the rear porch.

- Master Suite: The bedroom has a 10-ft. boxed ceiling and a door to the rear. The bath includes a corner whirlpool tub with glass block windows.

- Bedrooms: Bedroom 2 has a vaulted ceiling, while bedroom 3 features a built-in desk.

Copyright by designer/architect.

Images provided by designer/architect.

SMARTtip

Fertilizing Your Grass

Fertilizers contain nutrients balanced for different kinds of growth. The ratio of nutrients is indicated on the package by three numbers (for example, 10-10-10). The first specifies nitrogen content; the second, phosphorus; and the third, potash.

Nitrogen helps grass blades to grow and improves the quality and thickness of the turf. Fertilizers contain up to 30 percent nitrogen.

Phosphorus helps grass to develop a healthy root system. It also speeds up the maturation process of the plant.

Potash helps grass stay healthy by providing amino acids and proteins to the plants.

Plan #161026

Dimensions: 67'6" W x 63'6" D
Levels: 1
Square Footage: 2,041
Bedrooms: 3
Bathrooms: 2
Foundation: Basement
Materials List Available: No
Price Category: D

You'll love the special features of this home, which has been designed for efficiency and comfort.

CAD FILE AVAILABLE

Features:

- **Foyer:** This raised foyer offers a view through the great room and beyond it to the covered deck.

- **Great Room:** Elegant windows allow versatility — decorate casually or more formally.

- **Kitchen:** You'll find ample counter space and cabinets in this spacious room, which adjoins the dining room and opens onto the rear yard.

- **Library:** Curl up on the window seat that wraps around the tower in this quiet spot.

- **Laundry Room:** A tub makes this large room practical for crafts as well as laundry.

- **Master Suite:** A vaulted ceiling gives grace to the sitting area, and the garden bath with a walk-in closet and whirlpool tub adds luxury.

Rear Elevation

Main Level Floor Plan

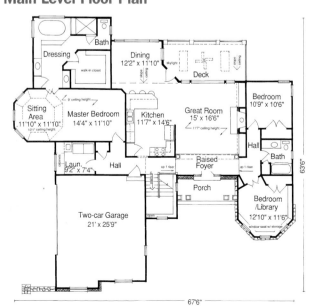

Bath
Dressing
walk-in closet
Dining 12'2" x 11'10"
skylight
Deck
Bedroom 10'9" x 10'6"
Sitting Area 11'10" x 11'10"
Master Bedroom 14'4" x 11'10"
Kitchen 11'7" x 14'6"
Great Room 15' x 16'6"
Hall
Laun. 9'2" x 7'4"
Hall
Raised Foyer
Bath
up 1 riser
up 1 riser
Porch
Two-car Garage 21' x 25'9"
Bedroom /Library 12'10" x 11'6"
window seat w/ storage

67'6"

63'6"

Basement Level Floor Plan

Patio
Rec. Room
Kitchen
Bath
Saurla
Basement Storage
Bedroom 11'11" x 13'
Bath
Exercise Room 11'11" x 15'2"

Left Side Elevation

Right Side Elevation

Front View

Living Room

Plan #311001

Dimensions: 65'11" W x 67'9" D
Levels: 1
Square Footage: 2,085
Bedrooms: 3
Bathrooms: 2½
Foundation: Crawl space, slab, or basement
Materials List Available: No
Price Category: D

Images provided by designer/architect.

Rear View

Copyright by designer/architect.

Optional Bonus Area

Plan #311004

Dimensions: 68'2" W x 57'4" D
Levels: 1
Square Footage: 2,046
Bedrooms: 3
Bathrooms: 2½
Foundation: Crawl space, slab, or basement
Materials List Available: Yes
Price Category: D

Images provided by designer/architect.

Copyright by designer/architect.

Rear View

Copyright by designer/architect.

Plan #271060

Dimensions: 72' W x 64'8" D

Levels: 1

Square Footage: 1,726

Bedrooms: 2

Bathrooms: 2½

Foundation: Walkout basement

Materials List Available: No

Price Category: C

Images provided by designer/architect.

CAD FILE AVAILABLE

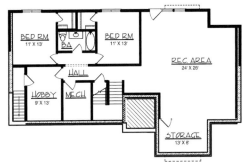

Optional Basement Level Floor Plan

Plan #351082

Dimensions: 65' W x 56'8" D

Levels: 1

Square Footage: 1,800

Bedrooms: 3

Bathrooms: 2½

Foundation: Crawl space, slab or basement

Material List Available: Yes

Price Category: E

Images provided by designer/architect.

CAD FILE AVAILABLE

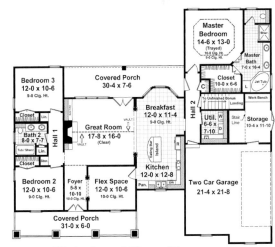

Main Level Floor Plan

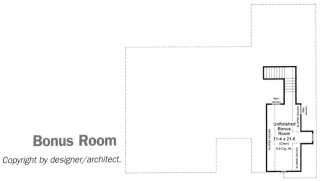

Bonus Room

Copyright by designer/architect.

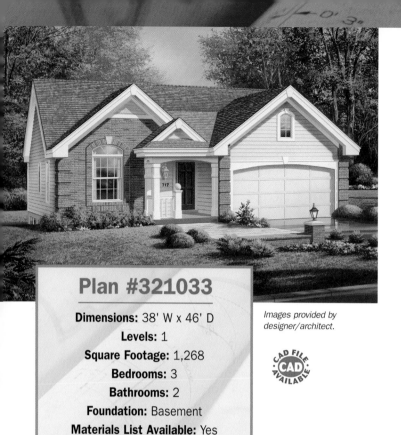

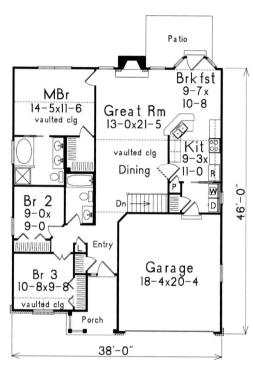

Images provided by designer/architect.

Copyright by designer/architect.

Plan #321033

Dimensions: 38' W x 46' D

Levels: 1

Square Footage: 1,268

Bedrooms: 3

Bathrooms: 2

Foundation: Basement

Materials List Available: Yes

Price Category: B

CAD FILE AVAILABLE

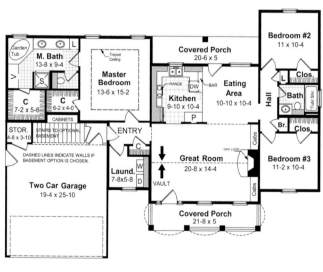

Images provided by designer/architect.

Copyright by designer/architect.

Plan #351005

Dimensions: 61' W x 47'4" D

Levels: 1

Square Footage: 1,501

Bedrooms: 3

Bathrooms: 2

Foundation: Crawl space, slab, or basement

Materials List Available: Yes

Price Category: D

CAD FILE AVAILABLE

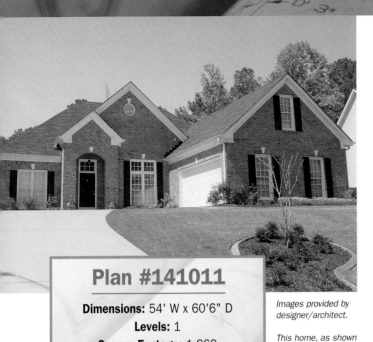

Plan #141011

Dimensions: 54' W x 60'6" D

Levels: 1

Square Footage: 1,869

Bedrooms: 3

Bathrooms: 2

Foundation: Crawl space, slab, or basement

Materials List Available: Yes

Price Category: D

Images provided by designer/architect.

This home, as shown in the photograph, may differ from the actual blueprints. For more detailed information, please check the floor plans carefully.

Bonus Area Floor Plan →

Copyright by designer/architect.

Floor plan labels: Patio / Deck; Bdrm.3 10⁸ x 11⁶; Living 15⁶ x 22⁶ 12' High Ceil.; Brkfst. 11⁸ x 9⁸; Master Bdrm. 13⁶ x 17⁴; Bth.2; Kit. 11⁸ x 12⁰; M.Bath Vaulted; Bdrm.2 10⁸ x 11⁶ Plant Shelf Above; Foyer 6⁰ x 10⁶ 12' Ceil.; Dining 11⁰ x 12⁰ 12' High Ceil.; Laund.; Plant Shelf Above; Opt. Location For Bsmt. Stairs; Bonus 13⁴ x 23⁸; Double Garage 21⁸ x 21⁸; 54-0; 60-6

Plan #341035

Dimensions: 60' W x 28' D

Levels: 1

Square Footage: 1,680

Bedrooms: 4

Bathrooms: 2

Foundation: Crawl space, slab; basement option for fee

Materials List Available: Yes

Price Category: C

Images provided by designer/architect.

Floor plan labels: DECK 12'-0" X 10'-0"; GARDEN TUB; BATH 1; CLOSET; KITCHEN 13'-1" X 13'-5" ISLAND; BEDROOM 2 10'-6" X 13'-5"; BATH 2; BEDROOM 3 10'-6" X 10'-11"; CLOSET; SHWR; BEDROOM 1 13'-11" X 13'-5"; DINING ROOM 12'-4" X 13'-5"; PREFAB VENTLESS GAS LOG FIREPLACE; LIVING ROOM 18'-10" X 13'-5"; BEDROOM 4 10'-6" X 10'-11"; PANTRY; SHELVES; PORCH; 28'-0"; 60'-0"

Copyright by designer/architect.

Plan #131044

Dimensions: 57'6" W x 42'4" D
Levels: 1
Square Footage: 1,994
Bedrooms: 3
Bathrooms: 2
Foundation: Crawl space, slab, or basement
Materials List Available: Yes
Price Category: E

Images provided by designer/architect.

Under a covered porch, Victorian-detailed bay windows grace each side of the brick-faced facade at the center of this ranch-style home, giving it a formal air.

Features:

- Ceiling Height: 10-ft. ceilings grace the central living area and the master bedroom of this home.

- Foyer: Round top windows make this area and the flanking rooms bright and cheery.

- Great Room: A fireplace and built-ins that are visible from anywhere in this large room make it a natural gathering place for friends and family.

- Optional Office: Use the room just off the central hall as a home office, fourth bedroom, or study.

- Master Suite: You'll love the bay window, tray ceiling, two walk-in closets, and private bath.

- Bonus Space: Finish this large area in the attic for extra living space, or use it for storage.

Rear Elevation

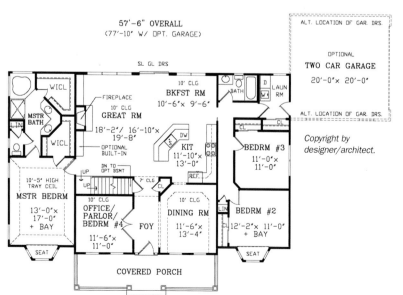

Copyright by designer/architect.

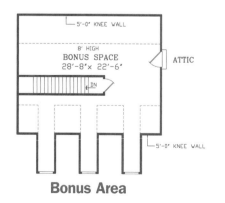

Bonus Area

Plan #151050

Dimensions: 69'2" W x 74'10" D

Levels: 1

Square Footage: 2,096

Bedrooms: 3

Bathrooms: 2½

Foundation: Crawl space, slab, or basement

CompleteCost List Available: Yes

Price Category: D

Images provided by designer/architect.

You'll love this spacious home for both its elegance and its convenient design.

Features:

- Ceiling Height: 8 ft.

- Great Room: A 9-ft. boxed ceiling complements this large room, which sits just beyond the front gallery. A fireplace and door to the rear porch make it a natural gathering spot.

- Kitchen: This well-designed kitchen includes a central work island and shares an angled eating bar with the adjacent breakfast room.

- Breakfast Room: This room's bay window is gorgeous, and the door to the garage is practical.

- Master Suite: You'll love the 9-ft. boxed ceiling in the bedroom and the vaulted ceiling in the bath, which also includes two walk-in closets, a corner whirlpool tub, split vanities, a shower, and a separate toilet room.

- Workshop: A huge workshop with half-bath is ideal for anyone who loves to build or repair.

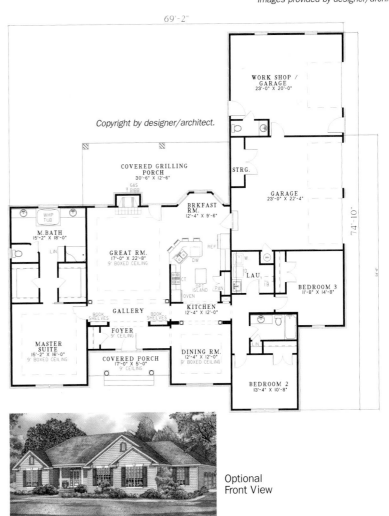

Copyright by designer/architect.

Optional
Front View

Plan #391034

Dimensions: 72'4" W x 43' D

Levels: 1

Square Footage: 1,737

Bedrooms: 3

Bathrooms: 2

Foundation: Crawl space, slab, or basement

Material List Available: Yes

Price Category: C

Images provided by designer/architect.

This home, as shown in the photograph, may differ from the actual blueprints. For more detailed information, please check the floor plans carefully.

Copyright by designer/architect.

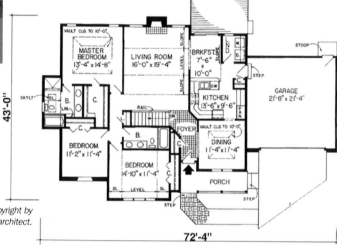

Plan #151243

Dimensions: 35' W x 80'6" D

Levels: 1

Square Footage: 1,923

Bedrooms: 3

Bathrooms: 2

Foundation: Crawl space or slab

CompleteCost List Available: Yes

Price Category: D

Images provided by designer/architect.

Copyright by designer/architect.

Plan #321011

Dimensions: 83' W x 50'4" D
Levels: 1
Square Footage: 2,874
Bedrooms: 4
Bathrooms: 2½
Foundation: Basement
Materials List Available: Yes
Price Category: F

Images provided by designer/architect.

CAD FILE AVAILABLE

SMARTtip

Drilling for Kitchen Plumbing

Drill holes for plumbing and waste lines before installing the cabinets. It is easier to work when the cabinets are out in the middle of the floor, and there is no danger of knocking them out of alignment when creating the holes if they are not screwed to the wall studs or one another yet.

Plan #151196

Dimensions: 89' W x 49'4" D
Levels: 1
Square Footage: 1,800
Bedrooms: 3
Bathrooms: 2
Foundation: Crawl space, slab
CompleteCost List Available: Yes
Price Category: D

Images provided by designer/architect.

CAD FILE AVAILABLE

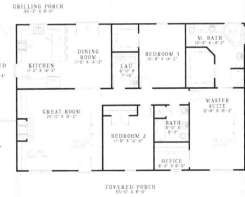

Plan #151005

Dimensions: 58' W x 54'10" D

Levels: 1

Square Footage: 1,940

Bedrooms: 4

Bathrooms: 2

Foundation: Crawl space, slab, or basement

CompleteCost List Available: Yes

Price Category: D

Images provided by designer/architect.

Copyright by designer/architect.

Plan #361004

Dimensions: 77' W x 81' D

Levels: 1

Square Footage: 2,191

Bedrooms: 3

Bathrooms: 2

Foundation: Basement, crawl space

Materials List Available: No

Price Category: D

Images provided by designer/architect.

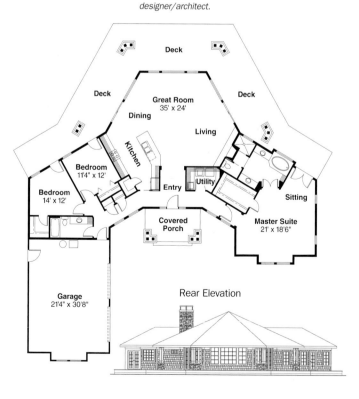

Copyright by designer/architect.

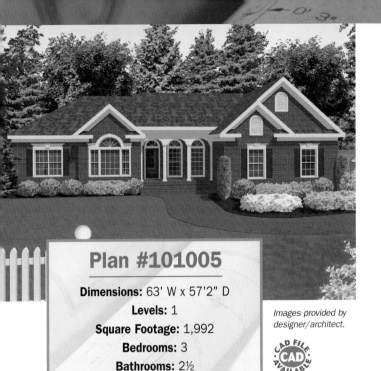

Copyright by designer/architect.

Plan #101005

Dimensions: 63' W x 57'2" D

Levels: 1

Square Footage: 1,992

Bedrooms: 3

Bathrooms: 2½

Foundation: Crawl space, slab, or basement

Materials List Available: Yes

Price Category: D

Images provided by designer/architect.

CAD FILE AVAILABLE

Rear View

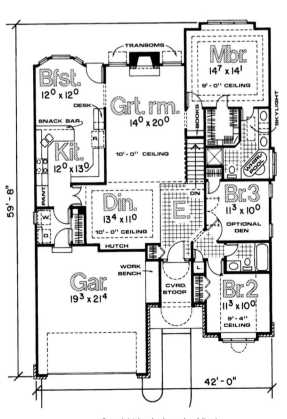

Plan #121118

Dimensions: 42' W x 59'8" D

Levels: 1

Square Footage: 1,636

Bedrooms: 3

Bathrooms: 2

Foundation: Basement; crawl space for fee

Material List Available: Yes

Price Category: C

Images provided by designer/architect.

Copyright by designer/architect.

Copyright by designer/architect.

Images provided by designer/architect.

Plan #481031

Dimensions: 98' W x 72' D

Levels: 1

Square Footage: 4,707

Main Level Sq. Ft.: 2,518

Basement Level Sq. Ft.: 2,189

Bedrooms: 4

Bathrooms: 3½

Foundation: Walkout basement

Material List Available: No

Price Category: I

Basement Level Floor Plan

Plan #151104

Dimensions: 43' W x 55' D

Levels: 1

Square Footage: 1,860

Bedrooms: 3

Bathrooms: 2

Foundation: Crawl space or slab; basement for fee

CompleteCost List Available: Yes

Price Category: D

Images provided by designer/architect.

Main Level Floor Plan

Bonus Area

Copyright by designer/architect.

Images provided by designer/architect.

Master Bdrm. 15⁰ x 14⁸

M.Bath

Covered Patio

Bdrm.3 10⁶ x 10⁰

Bath 2

Kit./Brkfst. 10⁸ x 12⁶

Computer Station

Bdrm.2 10⁶ x 10⁰

Lin.

W. D. Clts.

Dining 14¹⁰ x 10⁰

Wh Furn.

Disp. Stairs

Vaults to 14' High

Double Garage 19⁰ x 20⁸

Living Area 17⁰ x 15⁶

Vaults to 9'-10" High

Ref. P

Dw

Plant Shelf Above

Optional Screen porch

Optional Sun porch

Copyright by designer/architect.

Plan #141004

Dimensions: 37' W x 61' D

Levels: 1

Square Footage: 1,514

Bedrooms: 3

Bathrooms: 2

Foundation: Slab, basement

Materials List Available: Yes

Price Category: C

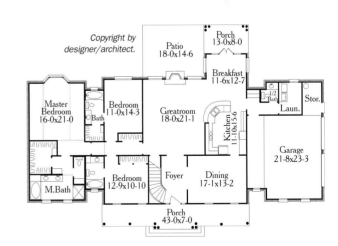

Copyright by designer/architect.

Images provided by designer/architect.

Master Bedroom 16-0x21-0

Bedroom 11-0x14-3

Greatroom 18-0x21-1

Kitchen 11-10x15-6

Breakfast 11-6x12-7

Patio 18-0x14-6

Porch 13-0x8-0

Bath

1/2 Bath

Laun.

Stor.

M.Bath

Bedroom 12-9x10-10

Foyer

Dining 17-1x13-2

Garage 21-8x23-3

Porch 43-0x7-0

Plan #311005

Dimensions: 87' W x 57'3" D

Levels: 1

Square Footage: 2,497

Bedrooms: 3

Bathrooms: 2½

Foundation: Crawl space, slab, or basement

Materials List Available: Yes

Price Category: E

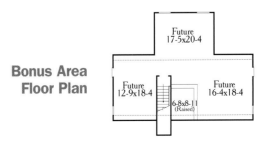

Future 17-5x20-4

Bonus Area Floor Plan

Future 12-9x18-4

Future 16-4x18-4

6-8x8-11 (Raised)

Plan #221004

Dimensions: 67'8" W x 43' D

Levels: 1

Square Footage: 1,763

Bedrooms: 3

Bathrooms: 2

Foundation: Basement

Materials List Available: No

Price Category: C

Images provided by designer/architect.

You'll love the spacious feeling provided by the open design of this traditional ranch.

Features:

- Ceiling Height: 8 ft.

- Dining Room: This formal room is perfect for entertaining groups both large and small, and the open design makes it easy to serve.

- Living Room: The vaulted ceiling here and in the dining room adds to the elegance of these rooms. Use window treatments that emphasize these ceilings for a truly sumptuous look.

- Kitchen: Designed for practicality and efficiency, this kitchen will thrill all the cooks in the family. An attached dining nook makes a natural gathering place for friends and family.

- Master Suite: The private bath in this suite features a double vanity and whirlpool tub. You'll find a walk-in closet in the bedroom.

- Garage: You'll love the extra storage space in this two-car garage.

Rear Elevation

Copyright by designer/architect.

Plan #101004

Dimensions: 55'8" W x 56'6" D
Levels: 1
Square Footage: 1,787
Bedrooms: 3
Bathrooms: 2
Foundation: Crawl space, slab, or basement
Materials List Available: Yes
Price Category: D

Images provided by designer/architect.

This carefully designed ranch provides the feel and features of a much larger home.

Features:

- Ceiling Height: 9 ft. unless otherwise noted.

- Entry: Guests will step up onto the inviting front porch and into this entry, with its impressive 11-ft. ceiling.

- Dining Room: Open to the entry and to its left is this elegant dining room, perfect for entertaining or informal family gatherings.

- Family Room: This family gathering place features an 11-ft. ceiling to enhance its sense of spaciousness.

- Kitchen: This intelligently designed kitchen has an open plan. A breakfast bar and a serving bar are features that add to its convenience.

- Master Suite: This suite is loaded with amenities, including a double-step tray ceiling, direct access to the screened porch, a sitting room, deluxe bath, and his and her walk-in closets.

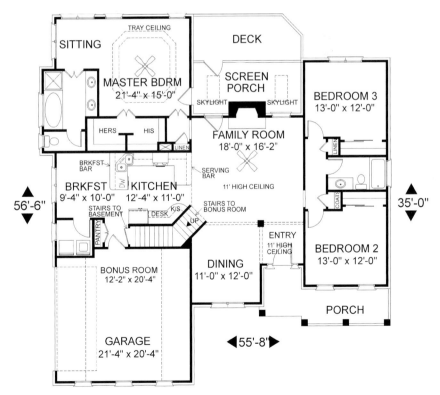

Copyright by designer/architect.

Plan #271073

Dimensions: 69' W x 56' D
Levels: 1
Square Footage: 1,920
Bedrooms: 3
Bathrooms: 2½
Foundation: Walkout basement
Materials List Available: No
Price Category: D

Images provided by designer/architect.

A great floor plan and plenty of space make this home perfect for people who welcome family members back home to visit.

Features:

- Great Room: This vaulted space shares a see-through fireplace with a cozy hearth room.

- Kitchen: An angled island and a step-in pantry are the highlights of this room.

- Study: Double doors introduce this versatile space, which shows off a nice bay window.

- Master Suite: Double doors lead to the bedroom. The private bath hosts a whirlpool tub and a separate shower.

- Basement: This level contains more bedrooms and family spaces for visiting relatives.

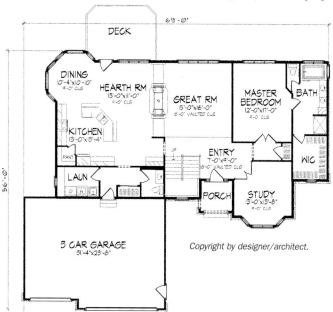

Copyright by designer/architect.

Basement Level Floor Plan

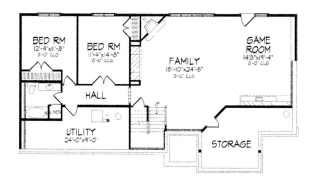

Plan #321003

Dimensions: 67'4" W x 48' D

Levels: 1

Square Footage: 1,791

Bedrooms: 4

Bathrooms: 2

Foundation: Basement

Materials List Available: Yes

Price Category: C

The traditional good looks of the exterior of this home are complemented by the stunning contemporary design of the interior.

Features:

• Great Room: With a vaulted ceiling to highlight its spacious dimensions, this room is certain to be the central gathering spot for friends and family.

• Dining Room: Also with a vaulted ceiling, this room has an octagonal shape for added interest. Windows here and in the great room look out to the covered patio.

• Kitchen: A center island gives a convenient work space in this well-designed kitchen, which features a pass-through to the dining room for easy serving, and large, walk-in pantry for storage.

• Breakfast Room: A bay window lets sunshine pour in to start your morning with a smile.

• Master Bedroom: A vaulted ceiling and a sitting area make you feel truly pampered in this room.

Images provided by designer/architect.

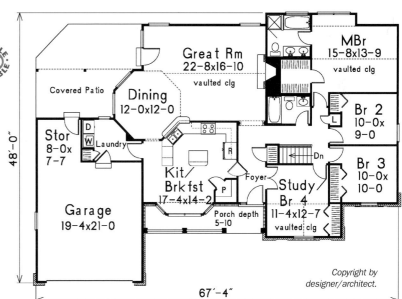

Copyright by designer/architect.

SMARTtip

Bay & Bow Windows

Occasionally too little room exists between the window frame (if there is one) and the ceiling. In this situation you might be able to use ceiling-mounted hardware. Alternatively, a cornice across the top and a rod mounted inside the cornice will give you the dual benefit of visually lowering the top of the window and concealing the hardware.

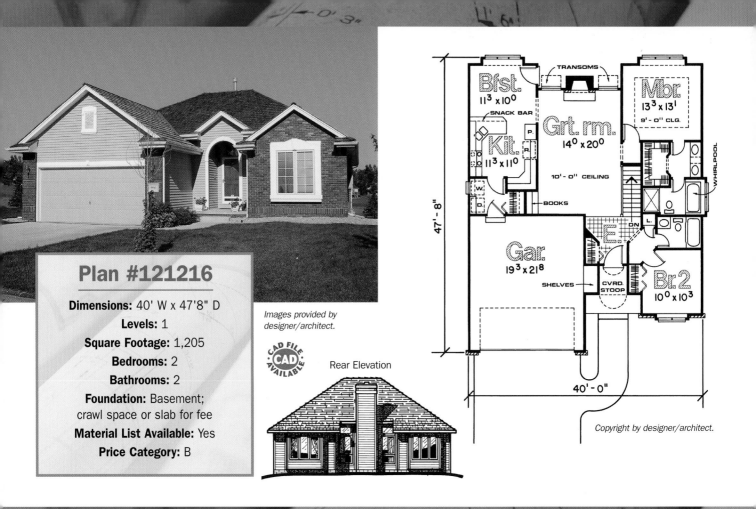

Plan #121216

Dimensions: 40' W x 47'8" D

Levels: 1

Square Footage: 1,205

Bedrooms: 2

Bathrooms: 2

Foundation: Basement; crawl space or slab for fee

Material List Available: Yes

Price Category: B

Images provided by designer/architect.

Rear Elevation

Copyright by designer/architect.

Plan #271082

Dimensions: 71' W x 62' D

Levels: 1

Square Footage: 2,074

Bedrooms: 4

Bathrooms: 2

Foundation: Crawl space or slab

Materials List Available: No

Price Category: D

Images provided by designer/architect.

Copyright by designer/architect.

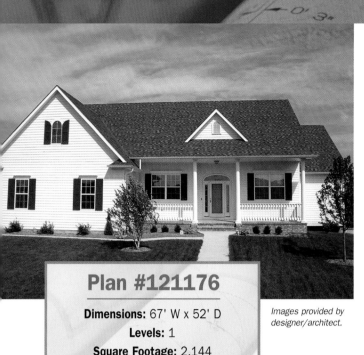

Plan #121176

Dimensions: 67' W x 52' D

Levels: 1

Square Footage: 2,144

Bedrooms: 4

Bathrooms: 2

Foundation: Slab; basement for fee

Material List Available: Yes

Price Category: D

Images provided by designer/architect.

BEDROOM 3
10'6" X 11'6"
9' CLG

BEDROOM 2
10'10" X 11'6"
9' CLG

NOOK
10'6" X 11'6"

PORCH

SITTING

KITCHEN
14'4" X 12'
PANTRY

VAULTED

MASTER SUITE
13'4" X 15'6"
10' CLG

EATING BAR

LIVING ROOM
16' X 19'4"
14' CLG

BEDROOM 4
10'6" X 11'6"
9' CLG

VAULTED

BARREL ARCH

AC

OPTIONAL DOOR

DN

DINING ROOM
10'8" X 11'8"
11' CLG

STUDY
10'4" X 11'8"
11' CLG

OPTIONAL BASEMENT STAIRS

ARCH

ARCH

GARAGE
20'4" X 23'8"

PORCH
11' CLG

67'

52'

Copyright by designer/architect.

Plan #221001

Dimensions: 87' W x 60' D

Levels: 1

Square Footage: 2,600

Bedrooms: 3

Bathrooms: 2½

Foundation: Basement

Materials List Available: No

Price Category: F

Images provided by designer/architect.

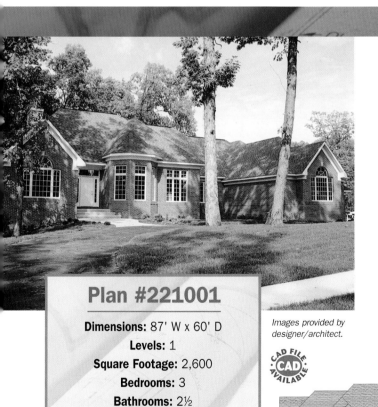

BR. #2
11'4" X 12'

GRT. RM.
18'6" X 21'

NK.
11'8" X 12'8"

KIT.
16'10" X 12'6"

SIT. AREA
14' X 20'8"

MBR.

DEN/BR.
CATHEDRAL CEILING
12'4" X 14'

E.

DIN.
11'8" X 14'6"

3 CAR GAR.
29'6" X 36'8"

CATHEDRAL CEILING

60'-0"

87'-0"

Copyright by designer/architect.

CAD CAD FILE AVAILABLE

Rear Elevation

Kitchen

Clutter-Cutting Tips for Your Home

O ne of the great things about moving into a new home is all that new, uncluttered closet space you gain. But if you are like most homeowners, storage of all types will quickly become scarce, especially in a smaller cottage home. Here are some tips for expanding and organizing storage space.

Shelving Types

Shelving is an easy and economical way to add extra storage space in almost any part of your home—along walls, inside closets, and even in the basement or garage. Building shelves doesn't usually require a lot of skill or specialized tools, so this is one project just about any do-it-yourselfer can handle. And unless you decide to use hardwood—which looks great but costs a bundle—it won't cost a lot to install them either.

Solid wood shelving is the way to go when you want to show off the wood or your work.

Plywood and particleboard offer a couple of advantages when it comes to shelving, though. They cost less than solid wood, and can be bought faced with decorative surfaces. They also come in sheets, which makes them ideal for a really wide

Home offices require a mix of storage options: open shelving, drawers, and file cabinets.

shelf. Inexpensive, manufactured storage units ready for assembly often are made from melamine-coated particleboard.

Wood trim will help match your new shelves to the rest of the room or add some interesting detail. Trim is also a handy way to hide seams, gaps, exposed edges of plywood, and other blemishes. You can get trim in either hardwood or softwood. If you plan on finishing a project with stain or sealer, make sure the trim

matches the wood you used for the rest of the project.

Bracket Options

There are two basic types of ready-to-hang shelving supports: stationary shelf brackets and shelving standards. Stationary brackets come in many sizes and styles, and range from utilitarian to decorative. Shelving standards are slotted metal strips that support various types of shelf brackets.

Mounting Brackets

For maximum strength, anchor shelf supports to wall studs. If your shelf will carry a light load, you can anchor its supports between studs with mollies or toggle bolts. Attaching supports directly to the studs is always better, though, because sooner or later something heavy will wind up on the shelf. Use masonry anchors to attach shelf supports to brick or concrete. You can also attach shelf supports to a ledger attached to wall studs with 3-inch drywall screws.

Ready-made shelving, above, offers a quick alternative to building your own shelves.

Mud rooms and areas near the entrance the family uses most should have storage for coats, hats, and boots.

Shelf Standards. Metal shelf standards can be mounted directly to walls or, for a more decorative look, you can insert the standards in grooves routed into the wood itself or into hardwood strips.

Cut the standards to fit with a hacksaw, and attach them to wall studs with 3-inch drywall screws. Use a carpenter's level to make sure that both standards are plumb and that the corresponding mounting slots are level. Mount standards 6 inches from the ends of shelving to prevent sagging. For long wall shelves, install standards every 48 inches.

Many kitchen and closet storage systems use wire grids that attach to walls with molded plastic brackets. If you anticipate light loads, you can mount these brackets to drywall using the screws and expansion anchors usually included with such systems. But for heavier loads, use drywall screws to fasten the brackets directly to the wall studs.

Customized Storage

Built-in storage units are an excellent way to make the most of existing storage space in your home. Ready-made or custom-made built-in shelving units, entertainment centers, kitchen cabinets, medicine cabinets, window seats, and under-bed drawers are not only inexpensive and easy to assemble, they allow you to add a unique, personalized touch to your living spaces.

Built-in Shelving

A built-in shelving unit can create valuable storage capacity from an overlooked wall space, such as the area between windows or between a door and its adjacent corner. To construct the shelving, you'll need 1x10 or 1x12 lumber for side panels, top and base panels, and shelves; four 2x2 strips for spreaders; trim molding to conceal gaps along the top and bottom of the unit; 12d

common nails and 6d finishing nails. If the unit will be bearing heavy loads, use hardwood boards, and make sure that the shelves span no more than 36 inches. To make installation easier, cut the side pieces an inch shorter than the ceiling height. (This way, you'll be able to tilt the unit into position without scraping the ceiling.) Paint or stain the wood pieces before assembling the unit. Hang the shelves from pegs or end clips inserted into holes drilled in the side pieces.

Adding Closet Space

What homeowner, even a new homeowner, hasn't complained about having too little closet space? Fortunately, there are almost always ways to find a bit more closet space or to make the closet space you have more efficient. Often, it isn't the space that is lacking but how the space is organized that is the problem. The trick is to find ways to help you organize the space.

Ventilated closet systems help keep your belongings neat and within easy reach.

Organizing Systems. The easiest and most obvious solution is one of the many commercial closet organizing systems now on the market. There are a number of configurations available, and you can customize most systems to meet your needs. Constructing your own version of a commercial closet organizer is another option. With a combination of shelves and plywood partitions, you can divide a closet into storage zones, with a single clothes pole on one side for full-length garments; double clothes poles on the other side for half-length garments like jackets, skirts, or slacks; a column of narrow shelves between the two for folded items or shoes; and one or more closet-wide shelves on top.

Before designing a closet system, above, inventory all of the items you want to store in the closet.

Metal shelf standards can provide a quick solution for creating shelving in areas where it is needed.

Cedar Closets

Both solid cedar boards and composite cedar panels have only moderate resistance to insects, and are used more for their pleasant aroma and appearance. The sheets of pressed red and tan particles are no less aromatic than solid wood, but the panels are 40 to 50 percent less expensive, and are easier to install. Solid boards require more carpentry work, and are likely to produce a fair amount of waste unless you piece the courses and create more joints. To gain the maximum effect, every inside surface should be covered, including the ceiling and the back of the door. The simplest option is to use ¼-inch-thick panels, which are easy to cut into big sections that cover walls in one or two pieces. Try to keep cedar seams in boards or panels from falling over drywall seams. No stain, sealer, or clear finish is needed; just leave the wood raw. The cedar aroma will fade over the years as natural oils crystallize on the surface. But you can easily regenerate the

For garages and basements, you'll find a combination of shelving and hanging hooks keeps tools and equipment organized, left.

Storage for basements, garages, and workshops, opposite below, should include a cabinet that locks for storage of dangerous chemicals.

Specialized storage accessories, such as the sports storage system shown at right, not only keeps items organized but they also keep them in ready-to-play condition.

scent from the panels by scuffing the surface with fine sandpaper.

Ideas for Basements, Garages, and Workshops

Workshops and other utility areas such as garages, attics, and basements can benefit from storage upgrades as much as any other room in the home—perhaps even more so, as utility areas are prone to clutter. Convenience, flexibility, and safety are the things to keep in mind when reorganizing your work space. Try to provide storage space for tools and hardware as near as possible to where they'll be used. In addition to a sturdy workbench, utility shelving

is a mainstay in any workshop. You can buy ready-to-assemble units or make your own using ¾-inch particleboard or plywood shelves and ¾x1½-inch (1x2) hardwood stock for cleats (nailed to the wall), ribs (nailed to the front underside of the shelves), and vertical shelf supports.

DIY Utility Storage. Don't forget about pegboard. To make a pegboard tool rack, attach washers to the back of the pegboard with hot glue, spacing the washers to coincide with wall studs. Position the pegboard so that the rear washers are located over studs. Drive drywall screws through finish washers and the pegboard into studs. (Use masonry anchors for concrete walls.)

Finally, try to take advantage of any oth-

erwise wasted space. The area in your garage above your parked car is the ideal spot for a U-shaped lumber storage rack, made of 1x4 stock and connecting plates. The space in front of the car could be used for a storage cabinet or even a workbench.

Instant Storage. To utilize the overhead space in your garage, build deep storage platforms supported by ledgers screwed to wall studs and threaded rods hooked to ceiling joists or rafters. You can also hang tools from the walls by mounting pegboard. You can buy sets with a variety of hooks and brackets for tools. For small items, such as jars of nails, make shallow shelves by nailing 1x4 boards between the exposed studs.

Suit storage to your needs. The narrow pullout pantry above is located between the refrigerator and a food-preparation area. Notice how you can access the shelves from both sides of the pantry when it is extended.

Kitchen Storage

The type of storage in a kitchen is almost as important as the amount. Some people like at least a few open shelves for displaying attractive china or glassware; others want absolutely everything tucked away behind doors.

What are your storage needs? The answer depends partly on your food shopping habits and partly on how many pots, pans, and other pieces of kitchen equipment you have or would like to have. A family that goes food shopping several times a week and prepares mostly fresh foods needs more refrigerator space, less freezer capacity, and fewer cabinets than a family that prefers packaged or prepared foods and makes only infrequent forays to the local supermarket.

Planning

To help clarify your needs, mentally walk yourself through a typical meal and list the utensils used to prepare food, where you got them, and your progress throughout the work area. And don't limit yourself to full-scale meals. Much kitchen work is devoted to preparing snacks, reheating leftovers, and making lunches for the kids to take to school.

Food Preparation. During food preparation, the sink and stove come into use. Some families rely heavily on the microwave for reheating. Using water means repeated trips to the sink, so that area might be the best place to keep a steamer, salad spinner, and coffee and tea canisters, as well as glassware and cups. Near the stove you may want storage for odd-shaped items such as a fish poacher or wok. You can hang frequently used pans and utensils from a convenient rack; stow other items in cabinets so that they do not collect grease.

During the Meal. When the food is ready, you must take it to the table. If the eating space is nearby, a work counter might turn into a serving counter. If the dining space is in another room, a pass-through facilitates serving.

Storage accessories, such as the pullout pot holder above, come as options from some cabinet manufacturers, or you can install them later yourself. Notice how the side rails hold the pot lids in place. The cabinet below features space for small baskets.

After the Meal. When the meal ends, dishes must go from the table to the sink or dishwasher, and leftovers to storage containers and the refrigerator. Now the stove and counters need to be wiped down and the sink scoured. When the dishwasher finishes its cycle, everything must be put away.

Open versus Closed Storage. Shelves, pegboards, pot racks, cup hooks, magnetic knife racks, and the like put your utensils on view, which is a good way to personalize your kitchen.

But open storage has drawbacks. Items left out in the open can look messy unless they are kept neatly arranged. Another option is to install glass doors on wall cabinets. This handily solves the dust problem but often costs more than solid doors.

Plan #161056

Dimensions: 86'2" W x 63'8" D
Levels: 1
Square Footage: 5,068
Main Level Sq. Ft.: 3,171
Basement Level Sq. Ft.: 1,897
Bedrooms: 4
Bathrooms: 3½
Foundation: Basement or walkout
Material List Available: Yes
Price Category: J

This home is dedicated to comfort and high lifestyle and sets the standard for excellence.

Features:

- Open Plan: A wraparound island with seating is adorned with pillars and arched openings, and it separates the kitchen from the great room and breakfast room. This design element allows the rooms to remain visually open and, paired with a 9-ft. ceiling height, creates a spacious area.

- Great Room: A gas fireplace warms this gathering area, and the wall of windows across the rear brings the outdoors in. The built-in entertainment center will be a hit with the entire family.

- Master Suite: Delighting you with its size and luxury, this retreat enjoys a stepped ceiling in the sleeping area. The master bath features a garden bathtub and an oversized walk-in closet.

- Lower Level: Open stairs introduce this lower level, which mimics the size of the first floor, and, with a 9-ft. ceiling height, offers the same elegant feel of the first floor. Additional bedrooms, a game room, an exercise area, and storage are available options.

Images provided by designer/architect.

Rear Elevation

Great Room

Rear View

Dining Room

Outdoor Grill Area

Kitchen

Living Room

Copyright by designer/architect.

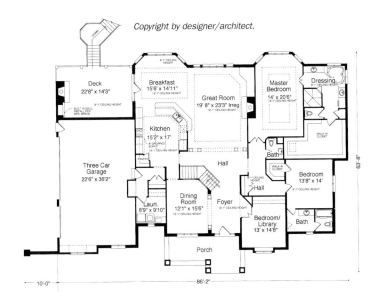

Optional Basement Level Floor Plan

Master Bath

Master Bedroom

Plan #121006

Dimensions: 46' W x 58' D

Levels: 1

Square Footage: 1,762

Bedrooms: 3

Bathrooms: 2

Foundation: Slab

Materials List Available: Yes

Price Category: C

The entry has a trio of arched openings that leads you to other areas of this amenity-packed home.

Features:

- Ceiling Height: 8 ft. except as noted.

- Eating Bar: Conveniently located between the kitchen and family room, this is sure to be a favorite spot for informal entertaining and family gatherings.

- Family room: A wall of windows, a fireplace, and a vaulted ceiling stretching to 11 ft. work together to make this a bright and warm room.

- Kitchen: There's no shortage of counter space in this well-planned kitchen that features a center island in addition to the eating bar.

- Master Suite: Luxuriate at the end of the day in this large bedroom with its decorative tray ceiling and walk-in closet. Enjoy the pampering bath with its sunlit corner whirlpool flanked by vanities.

- Garage: Two bays provide room for cars and plenty of storage as well.

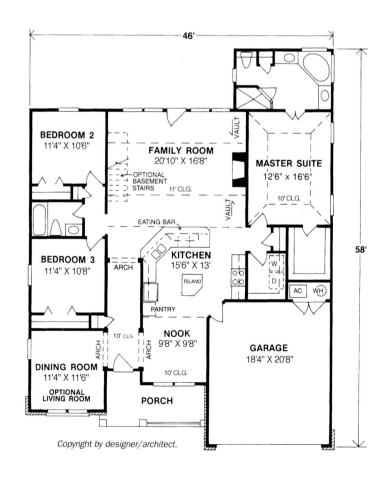

Plan #151089

Dimensions: 84' W x 55'6" D
Levels: 1
Square Footage: 1,921
Bedrooms: 3
Bathrooms: 3
Foundation: Crawl space, slab, or basement
CompleteCost List Available: Yes
Price Category: D

If your family loves to combine indoor and out-door living, this home's fabulous porches and deck space make it perfect.

Features:

- **Porches:** A huge wraparound front porch, sizable rear porch, and deck that joins them give you space for entertaining or simply lounging.

- **Living Room:** A fireplace and built-in media center could be the focal points in this large room.

- **Hearth Room:** Open to both the living room and kitchen, this hearth room also features a fireplace.

- **Kitchen:** This step-saving kitchen includes ample storage and work space, as well as an angled bar it shares with the hearth room. Atrium doors lead to the rear porch.

- **Bonus Upper Level:** A large game room and a full bath make this area a favorite with the children.

Images provided by designer/architect.

Copyright by designer/architect.

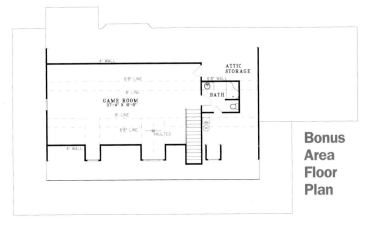

Bonus Area Floor Plan

Plan #301005

Dimensions: 71' W x 42' D
Levels: 1
Square Footage: 1,930
Bedrooms: 3
Bathrooms: 2
Foundation: Crawl space, slab
Materials List Available: Yes
Price Category: D

This home features an old-fashioned rocking-chair porch that enhances the streetscape.

Features:

- Ceiling Height: 8 ft.

- Dining Room: When the weather is warm, guests can step through French doors from this elegant dining room and enjoy a breeze on the rear screened porch.

- Family Room: This family room is a warm and inviting place to gather, with its handsome fireplace and built-in bookcases.

- Kitchen: This kitchen offers plenty of counter space for preparing your favorite recipes. Its U-shape creates a convenient open traffic pattern.

- Master Suite: You'll look forward to retiring at the end of the day in this truly luxurious master suite. The bedroom has a fireplace and opens through French doors to a private rear deck. The bath features a corner spa tub, a walk-in shower, double vanities, and a linen closet.

Images provided by designer/architect.

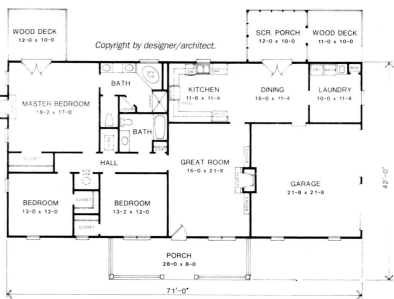

Copyright by designer/architect.

SMARTtip

Light With Shutters

For the maximum the amount of light coming through shutters, use the largest panel possible on the window. Make sure the shutters have the same number of louvers per panel so that all of the windows in the room look unified. However, don't choose a panel that is over 48 inches high, because the shutter becomes unwieldy. Also, any window that is wider than 96 inches requires extra framing to support the shutters.

Plan #351004

Dimensions: 78' W x 49'6" D
Levels: 1
Square Footage: 1,852
Bedrooms: 3
Bathrooms: 2½
Foundation: Crawl space, slab, or basement
Materials List Available: Yes
Price Category: D

Images provided by designer/architect.

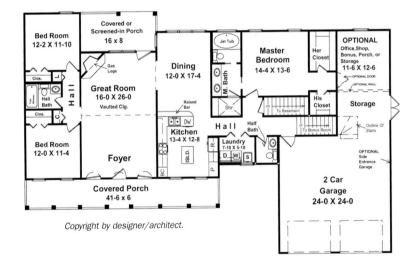

Copyright by designer/architect.

You'll love this design if you've been looking for a one-story home large enough for both a busy family life and lots of entertaining.

Features:

- Great Room: A vaulted ceiling, substantial corner fireplace, and door to the rear porch give character to this sizable, airy room.

- Dining Room: This well-positioned room, lit by a wall of windows, can comfortably hold a crowd.

- Kitchen: The center island and deep pantry add efficiency to this well-planned kitchen, which also features a raised snack bar.

- Master Suite: Two walk-in closets and a bath with jet tub and separate shower complement the spacious bedroom here.

- Garage Storage: Barn doors make it easy to store yard equipment and tools here. Finish the optional area at the rear of the garage or overhead for a home office or media room.

Rear
Elevation

Bonus Room

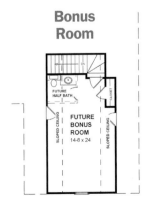

Plan #131001

Dimensions: 72'4" W x 32'4" D

Levels: 1

Square Footage: 1,615

Bedrooms: 3

Bathrooms: 2

Foundation: Crawl space, slab, basement, or walkout

Materials List Available: Yes

Price Category: D

Images provided by designer/architect.

Copyright by designer/architect.

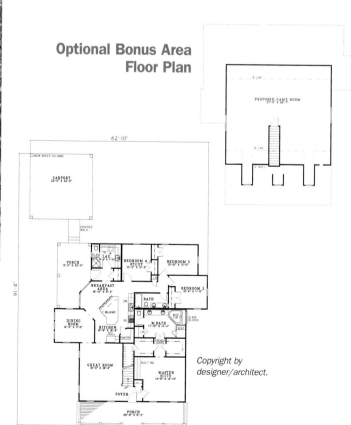

Optional Bonus Area Floor Plan

Plan #151113

Dimensions: 62'10" W x 91'4" D

Levels: 1

Square Footage: 2,186

Bedrooms: 4

Bathrooms: 3

Foundation: Crawl space, slab, or basement

CompleteCost List Available: Yes

Price Category: D

Images provided by designer/architect.

Copyright by designer/architect.

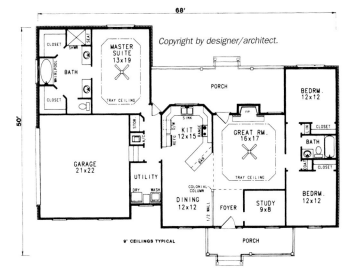

Copyright by designer/architect.

Images provided by designer/architect.

Plan #171009

Dimensions: 68' W x 50' D

Levels: 1

Square Footage: 1,771

Bedrooms: 3

Bathrooms: 2

Foundation: Crawl space, slab

Materials List Available: Yes

Price Category: C

Plan #131004

Dimensions: 59'4" W x 35'8" D

Levels: 1

Square Footage: 1,097

Bedrooms: 3

Bathrooms: 2

Foundation: Crawl space, slab, or basement

Materials List Available: Yes

Price Category: C

Images provided by designer/architect.

This home, as shown in the photograph, may differ from the actual blueprints. For more detailed information, please check the floor plans carefully.

Alternate Basement Floor Plan

Copyright by designer/architect.

Plan #151015

Dimensions: 72'4" W x 48'4" D
Levels: 2
Square Footage: 2,789
Main Level Sq. Ft.: 1,977
Upper Level Sq. Ft.: 812
Bedrooms: 4
Bathrooms: 3
Foundation: Crawl space, slab, or basement
CompleteCost List Available: Yes
Price Category: F

Images provided by designer/architect.

The spacious kitchen that opens to the breakfast room and the hearth room make this family home ideal for entertaining.

Features:

- **Great Room:** The fireplace will make a cozy winter focal point in this versatile space.
- **Hearth Room:** Enjoy the built-in entertainment center, built-in shelving, and fireplace here.
- **Dining Room:** A swing door leading to the kitchen is as attractive as it is practical.
- **Study:** A private bath and walk-in closet make this room an ideal spot for guests when needed.
- **Kitchen:** An island work area, a computer desk, and an eat-in bar add convenience and utility.
- **Master Suite:** Two vanities, two walk-in closets, a shower with a seat, and a whirlpool tub highlight this private space.

Main Level Floor Plan

Upper Level Floor Plan

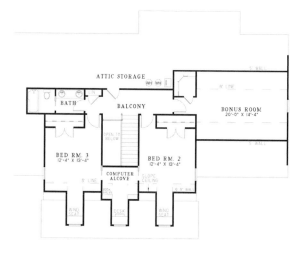

Plan #241007

Dimensions: 58'10" W x 59'1" D

Levels: 1

Square Footage: 2,036

Bedrooms: 3

Bathrooms: 2

Foundation: Crawl space, slab

Materials List Available: No

Price Category: D

Enjoy summer breezes while relaxing on the large front porch of this charming country cottage.

Features:

- Great Room: Whether you enter from the front door or from the kitchen, you will feel welcome in this comfortable great room, which features a corner fireplace.

- Kitchen: This well-designed kitchen with extensive counter space offers a delightful eating bar, perfect for quick or informal meals.

- Master Suite: This luxurious master suite, located on the first floor for privacy, features his and her walk-in closets, separate vanities, a deluxe corner tub, a linen closet, and a walk-in shower.

- Additional Bedrooms: Two secondary bedrooms and an optional, large game room —well suited for a growing family—are located on the second floor.

Images provided by designer/architect.

Copyright by designer/architect.

Bonus Area Floor Plan

FUTURE BATH

DN

FUTURE GAMEROOM
15'-0" X 20'-0"

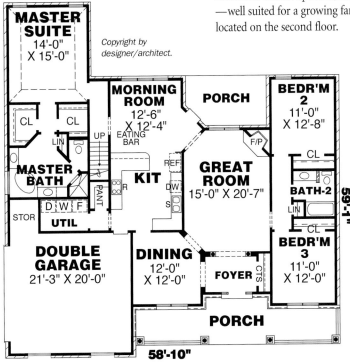

MASTER SUITE
14'-0" X 15'-0"

CL   CL

LIN

MASTER BATH

D W F

STOR   UTIL

DOUBLE GARAGE
21'-3" X 20'-0"

MORNING ROOM
12'-6" X 12'-4"

UP

EATING BAR

KIT

PANT

REF

DW

PORCH

GREAT ROOM
15'-0" X 20'-7"

BEDR'M 2
11'-0" X 12'-8"

F/P

CL

BATH-2

LIN

59'-1"

DINING
12'-0" X 12'-0"

FOYER

CTS

BEDR'M 3
11'-0" X 12'-0"

CL

PORCH

58'-10"

Plan #251001

Dimensions: 61'3" W x 40'6" D
Levels: 1
Square Footage: 1,253
Bedrooms: 3
Bathrooms: 2
Foundation: Crawl space, slab
Materials List Available: No
Price Category: B

Images provided by designer/architect.

• Master Bedroom: This master bedroom features a large walk-in closet. It has its own master bath with a single vanity, a tub, and a walk-in shower.

• Garage: This attached garage provides plenty of extra storage space, as well as parking for two cars.

This charming country home has a classic full front porch for enjoying summertime breezes.

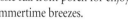

Features:

• Ceiling Height: 8 ft.

• Foyer: Guests will walk through the front porch into this foyer, which opens to the family room.

• Screened Porch: A second porch is screened and is located at the rear of the home off the dining room, so your guests can step out for a bit of fresh air after dinner.

• Family Room: Family and friends will be drawn to this large open space, with its handsome fireplace and sloped ceiling.

• Kitchen: This open and airy kitchen is a pleasure in which to work. It has ample counter space and a pantry.

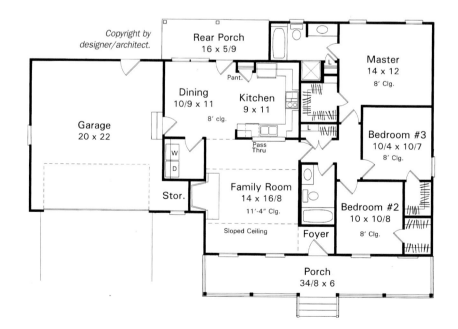

Plan #131002

Dimensions: 70'1" W x 60'7" D
Levels: 1
Square Footage: 1,709
Bedrooms: 3
Bathrooms: 2½
Foundation: Slab or basement
Materials List Available: Yes
Price Category: D

Images provided by designer/architect.

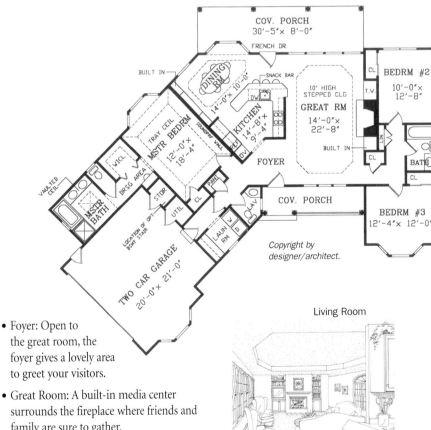

COV. PORCH
30'-5" x 8'-0"

FRENCH DR

BUILT IN

DINING RM
14'-0" x 10'-0"

SNACK BAR

KITCHEN
14'-8" x 9'-4"

10' HIGH
STEPPED CLG
GREAT RM
14'-0" x 22'-8"

BUILT IN

CL

BEDRM #2
10'-0" x 12'-8"

T.V.

TRAY CEIL

MSTR BEDRM
12'-0" x 18'-4"

FOYER

BATH

CL

VAULTED CEIL

WIC

DRSG AREA

MSTR BATH

STDR

UTIL

CL

PANT

LAV

COV. PORCH

BEDRM #3
12'-4" x 12'-0"

LAUN RM

LOCATION OF OPT BSMT STAIR

Copyright by designer/architect.

TWO CAR GARAGE
20'-0" x 21'-0"

Rear View

You'll love the way this angled ranch brings out the best in a corner lot or on a slope.

Features:

- Ceiling Height: 8 ft.

- Front Porch: Hang baskets of plants from the roof of this porch, which is just the right size for a couple of rockers and a side table.

- Dining Room: Well-placed windows flood this room with sunlight during the day and a built-in cabinet gives ample storage space for all your china, linens, and collectables.

- Foyer: Open to the great room, the foyer gives a lovely area to greet your visitors.

- Great Room: A built-in media center surrounds the fireplace where friends and family are sure to gather.

- Master Suite: You'll love the privacy of this somewhat isolated but easily accessed room. Decorate to show off the large bay window and tray ceiling, and enjoy the luxury of a separate toilet room.

Living Room

Plan #561006

Dimensions: 61'4" W x 72'8" D
Levels: 1
Square Footage: 2,408
Bedrooms: 3
Bathrooms: 2½
Foundation: Basement
Material List Available: Yes
Price Category: E

This magnificent farmhouse design, with its traditional front porch and rear screened-in porch, is more than just a home.

Features:

- **Great Room:** Gather by the glowing fire on cold nights, or expand your entertaining space any other time. This great room is at the center of everything and has plenty of space for friends, family, and anyone else you can think to invite.

- **Kitchen:** A built-in pantry and ample counter space make a great work area for the family cook and the aspiring chef alike. An open transition to the breakfast area simplifies morning chaos, while a defined separation formalizes the dining room.

- **Master Suite:** This area is a welcome retreat where you can shut out the frenzied world and simply relax. The attached master bath includes dual walk-in closets, his and her

sinks, a standing shower, and a separate tub — perfect for busy mornings and romantic evenings.

- **Secondary Bedrooms:** These bedrooms boast ample closet space and equal distance to a full bathroom. They're also off the beaten path, creating a calmer space for study and sleep.

Images provided by designer/architect.

Rear Elevation

Copyright by designer/architect.

Plan #351089

Dimensions: 79'4" W x 53'6" D
Levels: 1
Square Footage: 2,505
Bedrooms: 3
Bathrooms: 3
Foundation: Crawl space or slab
Material List Available: Yes
Price Category: F

Images provided by designer/architect.

Rear View

This colonial farmhouse has beautiful architectural features and a unique interior design, a combination that you'll love to come home to.

Features:

- Porches: Columns and arched windows add a graceful touch to the front porch, which opens into a large, inviting foyer. The breakfast area opens on either side to porches, one covered and one you can choose to be covered or screened. Either way, you'll be able to relax over breakfast on the porch.

- Great Room: Vaulted ceilings, windows opening to the covered porch, and a gas

fireplace provide a warm welcome for guests and make this a great space for gatherings.

- Kitchen: Working from the concept of the kitchen as the heart of the home, this design centralizes it between the breakfast room/sunroom, dining room, and great room for easy transitions between preparing and serving. It features plenty of workspace, a raised bar, and a desk area for organizing mail, grocery lists, and the family calendar.

- Master Suite: This suite has a unique design, with his and her bathrooms and closets. "Her bath" features a vanity and jetted tub, while "his" has a stall shower with seat and sink. But there's no harm in sharing.

- Garage: This attached garage has enough space for two cars, as well as room for his "toys" and a workshop.

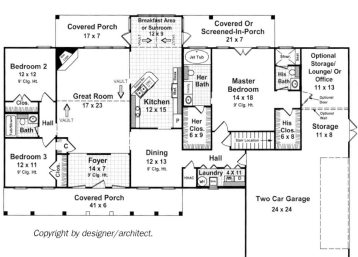

Copyright by designer/architect.

Bonus Area Floor Plan

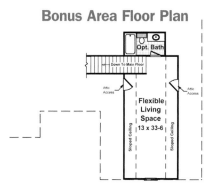

Plan #121010

Dimensions: 50' W x 62' D
Levels: 1
Square Footage: 1,902
Bedrooms: 2
Bathrooms: 2
Foundation: Basement
Materials List Available: Yes
Price Category: D

Images provided by designer/architect.

This home is replete with architectural details that provide a convenient and gracious lifestyle.

Features:

• Ceiling Height: 8 ft.

• Great Room: The entry enjoys a long view into this room. Family and friends will be drawn to the warmth of its handsome fireplace flanked by windows.

• Breakfast Area: You'll pass through cased openings from the great room into the cozy breakfast area that

will lure the whole family to linger over informal meals.

• Kitchen: Another cased opening leads from the breakfast area into the well-designed kitchen with its convenient island.

• Master Bedroom: To the right of the great room special ceiling details highlight the master bedroom where a cased opening and columns lead to a private sitting area.

• Den/Library: Whether you are listening to music or relaxing with a book, this special room will always enhance your lifestyle.

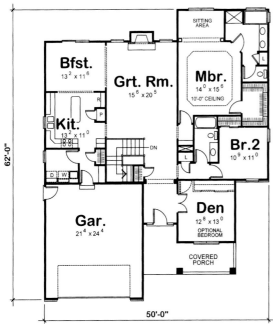

Copyright by designer/architect.

SMARTtip

Accentuating Your Fireplace with Faux Effects

Experiment with faux effects to add an aged look or a specific style to a fireplace mantel and surround. Craft stores sell inexpensive kits with directions for adding the appearance of antiqued or paneled wood or plaster, rusticated stone, marble, terra cotta, and other effects that make any style achievable.

Plan #351020

Dimensions: 54' W x 48' D

Levels: 1

Square Footage: 1,488

Bedrooms: 3

Bathrooms: 2

Foundation: Crawl space, slab, or basement

Materials List Available: Yes

Price Category: C

Images provided by designer/architect.

This is a lot of house for its size and is an excellent example of the popular split bedroom layout.

Features:

- **Great Room:** This large room is open to the dining room.

- **Kitchen:** This fully equipped kitchen has a peninsula counter and is open into the dining room.

- **Master Suite:** This private area, located on the other side of the home from the secondary bedrooms, features large walk-in closets and bath areas.

- **Bedrooms:** The two secondary bedrooms have large closets and share a hall bathroom.

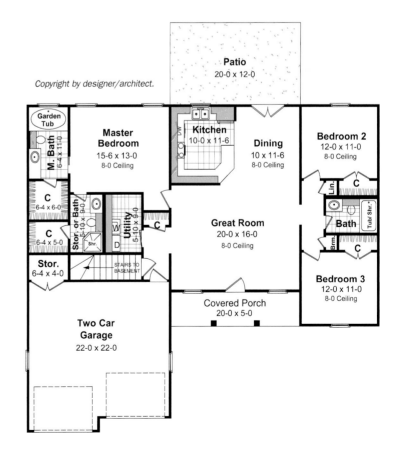

Copyright by designer/architect.

Plan #201084

Dimensions: 66'10" W x 54'5" D
Levels: 1
Square Footage: 2,056
Bedrooms: 3
Bathrooms: 2
Foundation: Crawl space, slab
Materials List Available: Yes
Price Category: G

This classic family home features beautiful country styling with lots of curb appeal.

Features:

- Ceiling Height: 8 ft.

- Open Plan: When guests arrive, they'll enter a foyer that is open to the dining room and den. This open area makes the home seem especially spacious and offers the flexibility for all kinds of entertaining and family activities.

- Kitchen: You'll love preparing meals in this large, well-designed kitchen. There's plenty of counter space, and the breakfast bar is perfect impromptu family meals.

- Master Suite: This spacious and elegant master suite is separated from the other bedroom for maximum privacy.

- Bonus Room: This unfinished bonus room awaits the time to add another bedroom or a home office.

- Garage: This attached garage offers parking for two cars, plus plenty of storage space.

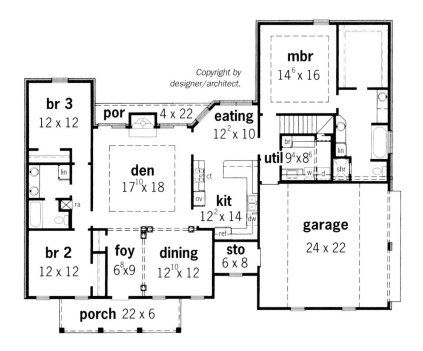

Copyright by designer/architect.

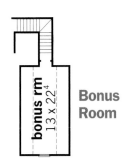

Bonus Room

Plan #131013

Dimensions: 50' W x 41'8" D
Levels: 1
Square Footage: 1,489
Bedrooms: 3
Bathrooms: 2
Foundation: Crawl space, slab or basement
Materials List Available: Yes
Price Category: C

You'll love the Victorian details on the exterior of this charming ranch-style home.

Features:

- Front Porch: This porch is large enough so that you can sit out on warm summer nights to catch a breeze or create a garden of potted ornamentals.

- Great Room: Running from the front of the house to the rear, this great room is bathed in natural light from both directions. The volume ceiling adds a luxurious feeling to it, and the fireplace creates a cozy place on chilly afternoons.

- Kitchen: Cooking will be a pleasure in this kitchen, thanks to the thoughtful layout and well-designed work areas.

- Master Suite: Enjoy the quiet in this room, where it will be easy to relax and unwind, no matter what the time of day. The walk-in closet gives you plenty of storage space, and you're sure to appreciate both the privacy and large size of the master bath.

Images provided by designer/architect.

WICL

TRAY CEIL
MSTR BEDRM
12'-4" x 15'-2"

MSTR BATH

LIN

BATH

BKFST RM
8'-2"/ 10'-4" x 15'-8"

10'-0" CLG STEPPED CLG
GREAT RM
15'-4" x 20'-6"

DW KIT

LAUN RM

REF

STEPPED CLG
DINING RM
10'-0" x 11'-0"

CL

OPTIONAL
TWO CAR GARAGE
20'-4" x 19'-6"

CL

CL CL

COV. PORCH

VAULTED
BEDRM #2
11'-2" x 10'-0"

VAULTED
BEDRM #3
10'-4" x 12'-0"

SEAT

Copyright by designer/architect.

Rear Elevation

Plan #101006

Dimensions: 63' W x 58' D
Levels: 1
Square Footage: 1,982
Bedrooms: 3
Bathrooms: 2½
Foundation: Crawl space, slab basement, or walkout
Materials List Available: Yes
Price Category: D

Radius-top windows and siding accented with wood shingles give this home a distinctive look.

Features:

- **Ceiling Height:** 9 ft. unless otherwise noted.
- **Family Room:** This room is perfect for all kinds of informal family activities. A vaulted ceiling adds to its sense of spaciousness.
- **Dining Room:** This room, with its tray ceiling, is designed for elegant dining.
- **Porch:** When the weather gets warm, you'll enjoy stepping out onto this large screened porch to catch a breeze.
- **Master Suite:** You'll love ending your day and getting up in the morning to this exquisite master suite, with its vaulted ceiling, sitting area, and large walk-in closet.
- **Bonus Room:** Just off the kitchen are stairs leading to this enormous bonus room, offering more than 330 sq. ft. of future expansion space.

Images provided by designer/architect.

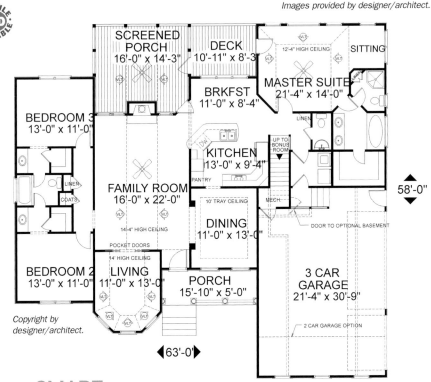

Copyright by designer/architect.

SMARTtip

Art in Pools

The tiled walls and floor of a pool make great canvases for art, so incorporate a serious or whimsical design. Also, make the stairs wide and shallow to form a wading area for kids.

Plan #101008

Dimensions: 68' W x 53' D

Levels: 1

Square Footage: 2,088

Bedrooms: 3

Bathrooms: 2½

Foundation: Crawl space, slab, or basement

Materials List Available: Yes

Price Category: E

This ranch sports an attractive brick-and-stucco exterior accented with quoins and layered trim.

Features:

- Ceiling Height: 11 ft. unless otherwise noted.

- Kitchen: You'll love cooking in this bright, airy kitchen, which is lit by an abundance of windows.

- Breakfast room: Off the kitchen is this breakfast room, the perfect spot for informal family meals.

- Master Suite: You'll look forward to retiring at the end of the day to this truly exceptional master suite, with its grand bath, spacious walk-in closet, and direct access to the porch.

- Morning Porch: Greet the day with your first cup of coffee on this porch, which is accessible from the master suite.

- Secondary Bedrooms: These bedrooms measure a generous 11 ft. x 14 ft. They share a compartmented bath.

Images provided by designer/architect.

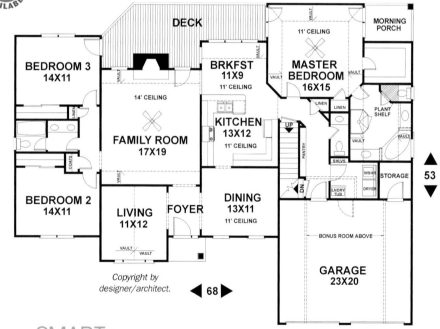

Copyright by designer/architect.

SMARTtip

Accentuating Your Bathroom with Details

No matter how big or small the room, details will pull the style together. Some of the best details that you can include are the smallest—drawer pulls from an antique store or shells in a glass jar or just left on the countertop. Add period flavor with crown molding, or dress up contemporary fixtures with polished stone fittings.

Images provided by designer/architect.

Plan #141002

Dimensions: 37' W x 53' D
Levels: 1
Square Footage: 1,365
Bedrooms: 3
Bathrooms: 2
Foundation: Slab or basement
Materials List Available: No
Price Category: B

This warm country cottage-style house is perfect for the growing family.

Features:

• Ceiling Height: 8 ft. unless otherwise noted.

• Foyer: Guests will be greeted by a full vaulted ceiling that soars to a height of 11 ft. 8 in.

• Dining Area: This dining area flows from the foyer but is defined by a plant shelf over a column.

• Kitchen: This kitchen is open and spacious, with large windows facing the front of the house so that the cook can keep an eye on the kids playing in the front yard. It includes a pass-through over the sink.

• Master Bedroom: This bedroom is separated from the others to create more privacy. Its distinctive look comes from a ceiling that slopes to flat at 9 ft. 6 in.

• Laundry: For maximum efficiency, the washer and dryer are closeted in the hall of the secondary bedrooms.

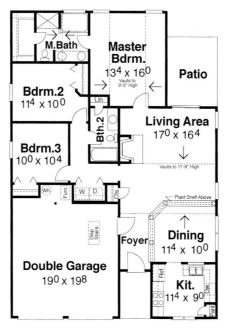

Copyright by designer/architect.

Plan #151822

Dimensions: 108'10" W x 73'10" D

Levels: 1

Square Footage: 3,602

Bedrooms: 4

Bathrooms: 3½

Foundation: Crawl space or slab; basement or walkout for fee

CompleteCost List Available: Yes

Price Category: H

Images provided by designer/architect.

- **Master Suite:** Who cares about the spacious bedroom when such a master bath exists? It features an enormous walk-in closet, his and her vanities, an extra-large glass shower, and a whirlpool tub, which is illuminated through glass blocks.

- **Secondary Bedrooms:** All three bedrooms feature their own walk-in closet and access to a private full bathroom. Bedroom 4 is a small version of a master suite, with its own full bathroom with whirlpool tub and separate stall shower.

Perfect for the modern family, this home is both spacious and efficiently designed.

Features:

- **Outdoor Space:** This large porch is great for welcoming guests in or sitting outside for a chat with the neighbors. The rear grilling porch, with entrances from the great room and bedroom 4, adds to the entertaining area available to you.

- **Great Room:** Flanked by windows, a fireplace, and built-in storage, this great room is waiting for occupants and guests to enjoy it.

- **Kitchen:** This kitchen features ample work and storage space, a large island, a walk-in closet, and a long snack bar, which provides a transition into both the breakfast room and the great room. An adjacent butler's pantry leads into the formal dining room, providing easy transitions between meal preparation and serving.

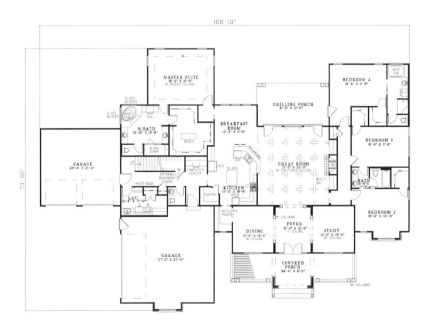

Copyright by designer/architect.

Plan #161115

Dimensions: 79'8" W x 44'2" D
Levels: 1
Square Footage: 2,253
Bedrooms: 4
Bathrooms: 3
Foundation: Walkout basement
Material List Available: Yes
Price Category: E

Images provided by designer/architect.

This one-level home offers a beautiful exterior of brick and stone with shake siding.

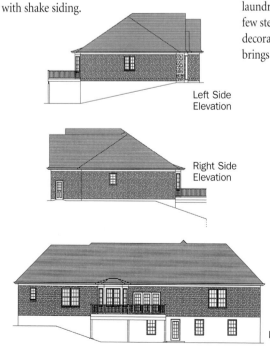

Left Side Elevation

Right Side Elevation

Rear Elevation

Features:

- Great Room: This open gathering area features an 11-foot-high ceiling and access to the rear yard. Turn on the corner gas fireplace, and fill the room with warmth and charm.

- Kitchen: This peninsula kitchen with built-in pantry and counter seating offers easy access to both formal and informal dining. The laundry facilities and the garage are just a few steps away. A magnificent bay window decorates the breakfast room and brings natural light into the area.

- Master Suite: This retreat offers a furniture alcove in the sleeping area and a walk-in closet. The private bath features a double-bowl vanity and a whirlpool tub.

- Guest Suite: This private bedroom suite is located behind the three-car garage and offers a welcoming environment for your overnight guests.

- Basement: This full walkout basement expands the living space of the delightful home.

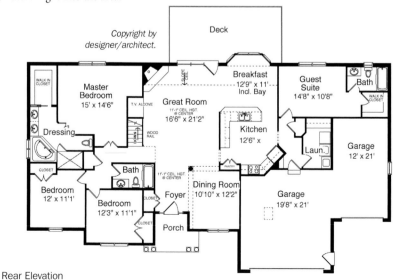

Copyright by designer/architect.

Plan #191001

Dimensions: 62' W x 72' D

Levels: 1

Square Footage: 2,156

Bedrooms: 4

Bathrooms: 3

Foundation: Crawl space, slab, or basement

Materials List Available: No

Price Category: D

Images provided by designer/architect.

This lovely home has the best of old and new — a traditional appearance combined with fabulous comforts and conveniences.

Features:

- Great Room: A tray ceiling gives stature to this expansive room, and its many windows let natural light stream into it.

- Kitchen: When you're standing at the sink in this gorgeous kitchen, you'll have a good view of the patio. But if you turn around, you'll see the island cooktop, wall oven, walk-in pantry, and snack bar, all of which make this kitchen such a pleasure.

- Master Suite: Somewhat isolated for privacy, this area is ideal for an evening or weekend retreat. Relax in the gracious bedroom or luxuriate in the spa-style bath, with its corner whirlpool tub, large shower, two sinks, and access to the walk-in closet, which measures a full 8 ft. x 10 ft.

- Mudroom: No matter whether you live where mud season is as reliable as spring thaws or where rain is a seasonal event, you'll love having a spot to confine the muddy mess.

Front View

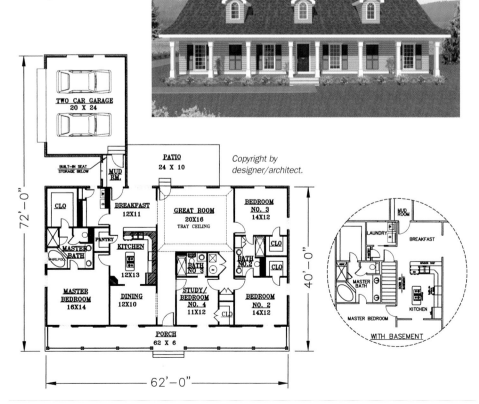

Copyright by designer/architect.

Plan #431001

Dimensions: 58'8" W x 62' D
Levels: 1
Square Footage: 1,792
Bedrooms: 3
Bathrooms: 2½
Foundation: Crawl space or basement
Material List Available: Yes
Price Category: C

Your neighbors will envy this Southern-style home.

Features:

- **Great Room:** The entry overlooks this room, where a fireplace warms gatherings on chilly evenings. A large window and French doors allow a view of the yard.

- **Kitchen:** The primary workstation in this kitchen is a peninsula, which faces the fireplace in the great room. The peninsula is equipped with a sink and snack counter.

- **Master Suite:** This private space is located on the other side of the home from the other bedrooms. It contains expansive his and her walk-in closets, a spa tub, and a double vanity area in the salon.

- **Bedrooms:** Two additional bedrooms are separated from the master suite. Both bedrooms have large closets and share a hall bathroom.

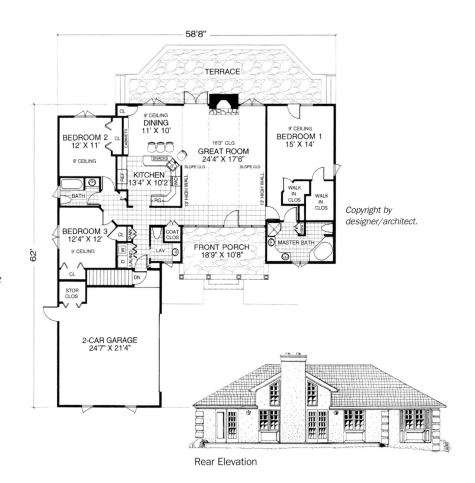

Rear Elevation

Plan #361444

Dimensions: 53' W x 58'8"D
Levels: 1
Square Footage: 1,605
Bedrooms: 3
Bathrooms: 2
Foundation: Crawl space or basement
Material List Available: No
Price Category: D

Stucco detailing accents this single-level home. The interior features large gathering spaces.

Features:

- Entry: Two bold columns frame this entry, creating a small welcoming porch.

- Living Room: At the center of everything, this living room will be the heart of the home. Its unhampered transition into the dining areas and kitchen creates a feeling of openness that will welcome guests.

- Dining Room: This room will impress your dinner guests. The double window gives a front-yard view while allowing natural light into the space.

- Master Suite: Everyone knows how important the master bath is to the success of the master suite design, and this bath does not disappoint. His and her sinks, a large tub with a view, and a separate standing shower combine to create both a retreat and a remedy for hectic mornings.

- Secondary Bedrooms: These bedrooms boast ample closet space and equal distance to a full bathroom. They're also off the beaten path, creating a calmer space for study and sleep.

Plan #141022

Dimensions: 90' W x 93' D

Levels: 1

Square Footage: 2,911

Bedrooms: 3

Bathrooms: 2½

Foundation: Basement

Materials List Available: No

Price Category: F

Second-floor dormers accent this charming country ranch, which features a gracious porch that spans its entire front. A detached garage, connected by a covered extension, creates an impressive, expansive effect.

Features:

- Living Room: As you enter the foyer, you are immediately drawn to this dramatic, bayed living room.

- Study: Flanking the foyer, this cozy study features built-in shelving and a direct-vent fireplace.

- Kitchen: From a massive, partially covered deck, a wall of glass floods this spacious kitchen, breakfast bay, and keeping room with light.

- Master Suite: Enjoy the complete privacy provided by this strategically located master suite.

- Guest Quarters: You can convert the bonus room, above the garage, into a guest apartment.

Images provided by designer/architect.

Rear View

Copyright by designer/architect.

Plan #311061

Dimensions: 73' W x 71' D

Levels: 1

Square Footage: 2,570

Bedrooms: 3

Bathrooms: 2½

Foundation: Crawl space, slab, or basement

Material List Available: Yes

Price Category: E

Images provided by designer/architect.

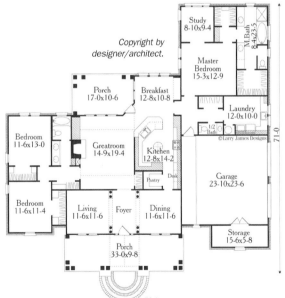

Copyright by designer/architect.

©Larry James Designs

Basement Stair Location

This Southern-style house is a dream. With its beautiful bay windows and inviting entryway, you're sure to love owning this home.

Features:

- Great room: A vaulted ceiling highlights the spaciousness of this room. Large windows light up the room and accent the beautiful porch on the rear side of the home. The fireplace is a beautiful and useful feature, especially in chilly winter months.

- Master Suite: This space features dual walk-in closets, a dressing area, private toilet, a separate shower, and garden tub. A study is strategically located at the back end of the home, making the area an exceptional space to work from home, even when it is busy with activity.

- Garage: This two-car garage has an attached storage area. The garage connects to the laundry room, which contains a small bathroom.

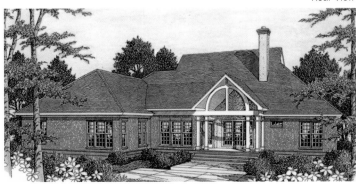

Rear View

Plan #191021

Dimensions: 70' W x 80' D

Levels: 1

Square Footage: 3,029

Bedrooms: 4

Bathrooms: 3

Foundation: Slab

Material List Available: No

Price Category: G

Images provided by designer/architect.

This southern-style ranch home is the perfect place to raise your family.

Features:

- Great Room: This large gathering area features a tray ceiling and a grand fireplace. The open floor plan allows flow between the breakfast room and the dining room, enabling all three areas to act as one.

- Kitchen: This peninsula kitchen boasts a built-in pantry and is open to the breakfast area. The laundry facilities and garage are just a few steps away.

- Master Suite: The bath provides you with respite from the outside world. This spacious inviting area, which includes a walk-in closet, has everything you need to comfortably unwind.

- Garage: A spacious two-car garage is attached to the rear of the home, providing necessary space in an economical design.

Copyright by designer/architect.

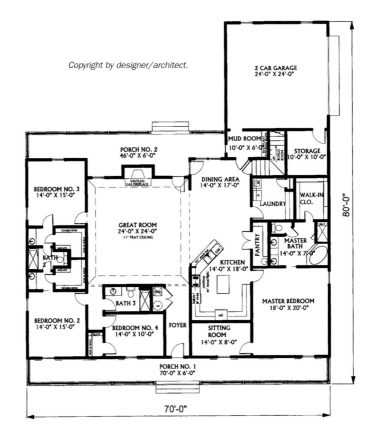

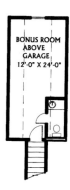

Bonus Area Floor Plan

Plan #101009

Dimensions: 70'2" W x 59' D
Levels: 1
Square Footage: 2,097
Bedrooms: 3
Bathrooms: 3
Foundation: Crawl space, slab, or basement
Materials List Available: Yes
Price Category: E

Round columns enhance this country porch design, which will nestle into any neighborhood.

Features:

- Ceiling Height: 9 ft. unless otherwise noted.

- Family Room: This large family room seems even more spacious, thanks to the vaulted ceiling. It's the perfect spot for all kinds of family activities.

- Dining Room: This elegant dining room is adorned with a decorative round column and a tray ceiling.

- Kitchen: You'll love the convenience of this enormous 14-ft.-3-in. x 22-ft.-6-in. country kitchen, which is open to the family room.

- Screened Porch: A French door leads to this breezy porch, with its vaulted ceiling.

- Master Suite: This sumptuous suite includes a double tray ceiling, a sitting area, a large walk-in closet, and a luxurious bath.

- Patio or Deck: This area is accessible from both the screened porch and master suite.

Images provided by designer/architect.

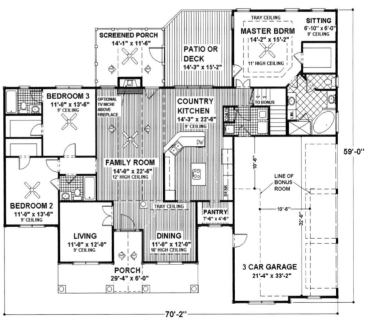

Copyright by designer/architect.

SMARTtip

Single-Level Decks

A single-level deck can use a strong vertical element, such as a pergola or a gazebo, to make it interesting. A simple and less-expensive option is a potted conical shrub or a clematis growing on a trellis.

Plan #151168

Dimensions: 66' W x 65'2" D
Levels: 1
Square Footage: 2,261
Bedrooms: 4
Bathrooms: 2½
Foundation: Crawl space, slab, basement, or daylight basement
CompleteCost List Available: Yes
Price Category: E

Images provided by designer/architect.

The well-planned layout of this home will delight your family if you want plenty of space for group activities, as well as private times.

Features:

- **Great Room:** Natural light flows into this room, with its door to the covered porch and fireplace.

- **Outdoor Areas:** Relax and enjoy the rear covered porch, the patio, and the front covered porch.

- **Dining Room:** An 11-ft. boxed ceiling and entry columns let you decorate for formality here.

- **Kitchen:** The central island has space for working as well as a snack bar, and you'll love the pantry.

- **Breakfast Room:** Set the table in the deep bay to enjoy the morning light.

- **Master Suite:** A 9-ft. boxed ceiling and door to the rear porch make the bedroom luxurious, and the bath has two walk-in closets and a whirlpool tub, separate shower, and dual vanity.

Copyright by designer/architect.

Bonus Area

Plan #251004

Dimensions: 50'9" W x 42'1" D
Levels: 1
Square Footage: 1,550
Bedrooms: 3
Bathrooms: 2
Foundation: Crawl space, slab
Materials List Available: Yes
Price Category: C

Images provided by designer/architect.

Combine the old-fashioned appeal of a country farmhouse with all the comforts of modern living.

Features:

- Ceiling Height: 9 ft.
- Foyer: When guests enter this inviting foyer, they will be greeted by a view of the lovely family room.
- Family Room: Usher family and friends into this welcoming family room, where they can warm up in front of the fireplace. The room's 12-ft. ceiling enhances its sense of spaciousness.

- Kitchen: Gather around and keep the cook company at the snack bar in this roomy kitchen. There's still plenty of counter space for food preparation, thanks to the kitchen island.
- Master Bedroom: This elegant master bedroom features a large walk-in closet and a 9-ft. recessed ceiling.
- Master Bath. This master bath includes a double vanity, a tub, and a walk-in shower.
- Garage: This attached garage provides plenty of extra storage space, as well as parking for two cars.

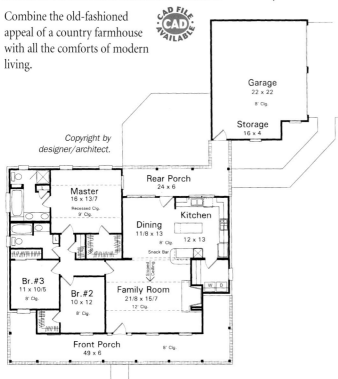

Copyright by designer/architect.

SMARTtip

Shaker Style in Your Bathroom

This warm, likable style fits in perfectly with a country home because of its old-fashioned values. But it blends in well with contemporary interiors, too, because of its clean lines and plain geometric shapes. In fact, adding a few Shaker elements can warm up the sometimes cold look of a thoroughly modern room.

Plan #311060

Dimensions: 66'1" W x 77'7" D

Levels: 1

Square Footage: 2,585

Bedrooms: 4

Bathrooms: 2½

Foundation: Crawl space, slab, or basement

Material List Available: Yes

Price Category: E

Images provided by designer/architect.

This Southern-style house was designed for both efficiency and beauty.

Features:

- Great Room: The appeal of this room is its access to other areas of the home, including a private porch that contains skylights.

- Kitchen: A snack-bar island and large pantry closet are features of this kitchen, as well as a breakfast nook. A desk area is a bonus for multi-tasking moms and dads; cook dinner while helping the kids with homework.

- Master Suite: Enjoy the grandiose features of this master suite, with its dual vanities, two walk-in closets, private toilet, and garden tub. You're sure to find a retreat from daily stress here.

- Additional Bedrooms: Three additional bedrooms, an ample laundry room, and half bathroom are only a few more of the exciting features offered by the design.

Storage
21-6x11-0

Garage
21-6x25-6

Porch
19-2x12-0

Master Bedroom/ Sitting Room
12-9x23-8

M.Bath
104x13-6

77-7

Laun.
9-0x8-7

1/2 Bath

Greatroom
19-1x17-5

Bedroom
12-0x13-6

Kitchen
18-0x11-6

Bath

Breakfast
14-0x9-0

Dining
11-6x13-6

Foyer

Bedroom
11-6x13-6

Bedroom
12-0x11-7

Porch

66-1

Basement Stair Location

Copyright by designer/architect.

Basement Stair Location

1/2 Bath

Greatroom

Kitchen

Dining

Rear View

Plan #351013

Dimensions: 30' W x 36' D
Levels: 1
Square Footage: 800
Bedrooms: 2
Bathrooms: 1
Foundation: Crawl space or basement
Materials List Available: Yes
Price Category: B

Images provided by designer/architect.

The design and layout of this home bring back the memories of days gone by and places in which we feel comfortable.

Features:

- **Living Room:** When you enter this room from the front porch, you can feel the warmth from its fireplace.

- **Kitchen:** This kitchen features a raised bar and is open to the living room.

- **Bedrooms:** Two equally sized bedrooms share a common bathroom located in the hall.

- **Screened Porch:** Located in the rear of the home and accessible from bedroom 1 and the kitchen, this area is for relaxing.

Copyright by designer/architect.

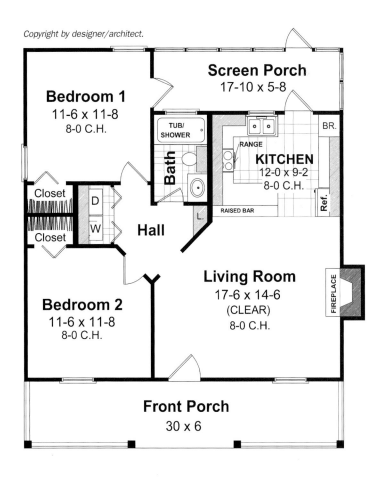

This home, as shown in the photograph, may differ from the actual blueprints. For more detailed information, please check the floor plans carefully.

Images provided by designer/architect.

Copyright by designer/architect.

Rendering reflects floor plan

Plan #121012

Dimensions: 40' W x 48'8" D
Levels: 1
Square Footage: 1,195
Bedrooms: 3
Bathrooms: 2
Foundation: Basement
Materials List Available: Yes
Price Category: B

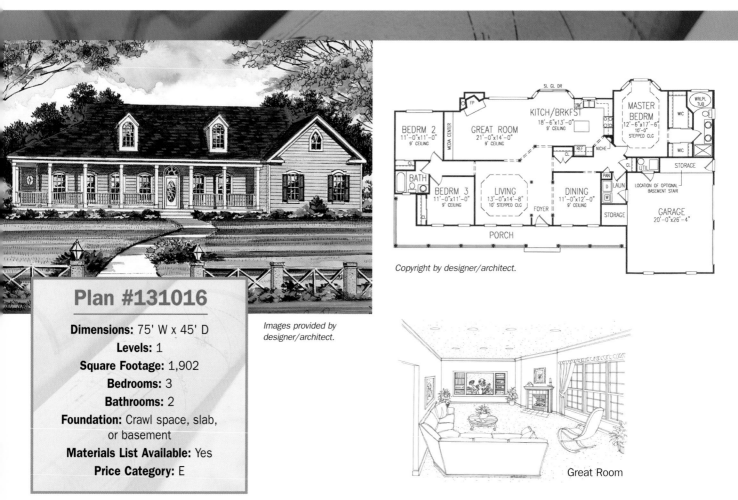

Copyright by designer/architect.

Images provided by designer/architect.

Great Room

Plan #131016

Dimensions: 75' W x 45' D
Levels: 1
Square Footage: 1,902
Bedrooms: 3
Bathrooms: 2
Foundation: Crawl space, slab, or basement
Materials List Available: Yes
Price Category: E

Plan #171011

Dimensions: 70' W x 58' D

Levels: 1

Square Footage: 2,069

Bedrooms: 3

Bathrooms: 2½

Foundation: Crawl space, slab

Materials List Available: Yes

Price Category: D

Images provided by designer/architect.

Copyright by designer/architect.

Plan #191016

Dimensions: 113' W x 56' D

Levels: 1

Square Footage: 2,421

Bedrooms: 3

Bathrooms: 2

Foundation: Crawl space or slab

Material List Available: No

Price Category: E

Images provided by designer/architect.

Copyright by designer/architect.

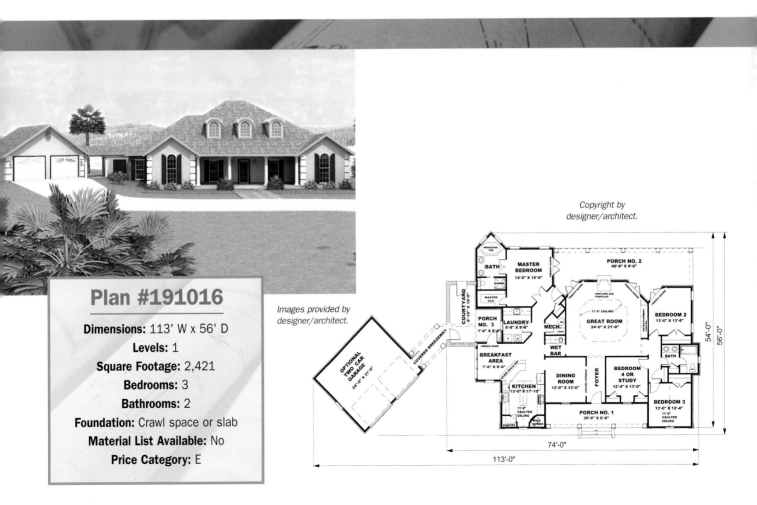

Plan #441002

Dimensions: 70' W x 51' D

Levels: 1

Square Footage: 1,873

Bedrooms: 3

Bathrooms: 2

Foundation: Crawl space

Materials List Available: Yes

Price Category: D

Images provided by designer/architect.

Rear Elevation

Plan #351055

Dimensions: 73'8" W x 58'4" D

Levels: 1

Square Footage: 2,251

Bedrooms: 3

Bathrooms: 2½

Foundation: Crawl space, slab or basement

Material List Available: Yes

Price Category: F

Images provided by designer/architect.

Rear Elevation

Bonus Room

Images provided by designer/architect.

Copyright by designer/architect.

Plan #151101

Dimensions: 87'10" W x 54'6" D

Levels: 1

Square Footage: 2,804

Bedrooms: 4

Bathrooms: 2½

Foundation: Slab

CompleteCost List Available: Yes

Price Category: F

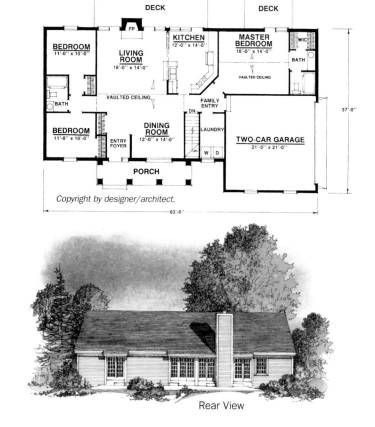

Images provided by designer/architect.

Copyright by designer/architect.

Rear View

Plan #291001

Dimensions: 63' W x 37' D

Levels: 1

Square Footage: 1,550

Bedrooms: 3

Bathrooms: 2

Foundation: Basement

Materials List Available: No

Price Category: C

Plan #131017

Dimensions: 69'8" W x 39'4" D
Levels: 1
Square Footage: 1,480
Bedrooms: 3
Bathrooms: 2
Foundation: Crawl space, slab, or basement
Materials List Available: Yes
Price Category: C

Images provided by designer/architect.

This fully accessible home is designed for wheelchair access to every area, giving everyone true enjoyment and freedom of movement.

Features:

- Great Room: Facing towards the rear, this great room features a volume ceiling that adds to the spacious feeling of the room.

- Kitchen: Designed for total convenience and easy work patterns, this kitchen also offers a view out to the covered front porch.

- Master Bedroom: Enjoy the quiet in this room which is sure to become your favorite place to relax at the end of the day.

- Additional Bedrooms: Both rooms have easy access to a full bath and feature nicely sized closet spaces.

- Garage: Use the extra space in this attached garage for storage.

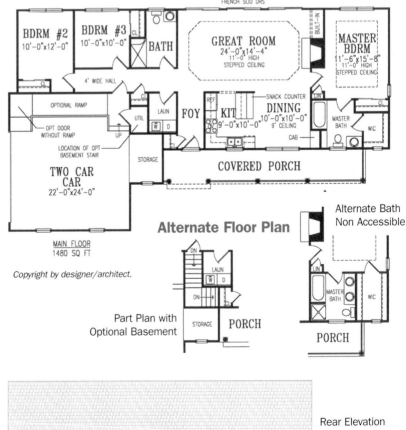

Copyright by designer/architect.

Plan #271074

Dimensions: 68' W x 86' D
Levels: 1
Square Footage: 2,400
Bedrooms: 4
Bathrooms: 3
Foundation: Crawl space or slab
Materials List Available: No
Price Category: E

Perfect for families with aging relatives or boomerang children, this home includes a completely separate suite at the rear.

Features:

• **Living Room:** A corner fireplace casts a friendly glow over this gathering space.

• **Kitchen:** This efficient space offers a serving bar that extends toward the eating nook and the formal dining room.

• **Master Suite:** A cathedral ceiling presides over this deluxe suite, which boasts a whirlpool tub, dual-sink vanity, and walk-in closet.

• **In-law Suite:** This separate wing has its own vaulted living room, plus a kitchen, a dining room, and a bedroom suite.

Copyright by designer/architect.

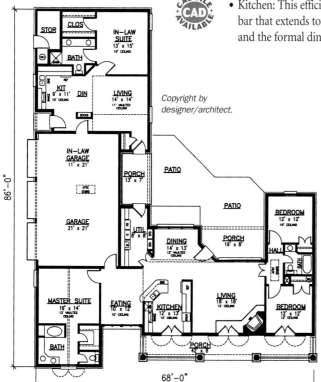

SMARTtip

Adding Professional Flair to Window Treatments

You can give your window treatment designs a professional look by using decorator tricks to customize readymades or dress your own home-sewn designs. These could include contrast linings, tassels, cording, ribbons, or couture trimmings such as buttons, coins, or bows applied to edges. Another trick is to sew a fine wire into the hem of curtains or valances to create a pliable edge that you can shape yourself. Small weights that you can sew into the hem of drapery panels or jabots will make them hang better. For more inspiration look at fashion magazines and visit showrooms.

Images provided by designer/architect.

Plan #251003

Dimensions: 42' W x 42' D

Levels: 1

Square Footage: 1,393

Bedrooms: 3

Bathrooms: 2

Foundation: Crawl space or slab

Materials List Available: Yes

Price Category: B

Come home to this three-bedroom home with front porch and unattached garage.

Features:

- **Family Room:** This room feels large and warm, with its high ceiling and cozy fireplace.

- **Kitchen:** This island kitchen with dining area has plenty of cabinet space.

- **Master Bedroom:** This large master bedroom features a walk-in closet and a view of the backyard.

- **Master Bath:** Located in the rear of the home, this master bath features a soaking tub and a separate shower.

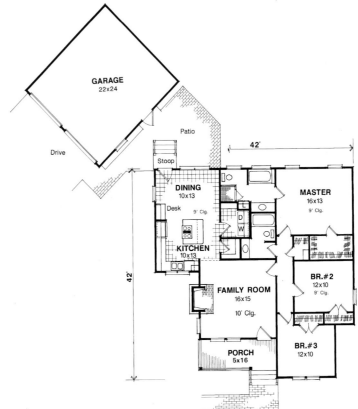

Copyright by designer/architect.

Plan #101026

Dimensions: 50' W x 57'4" D
Levels: 1
Square Footage: 1,420
Bedrooms: 3
Bathrooms: 2
Foundation: Crawl space
Materials List Available: No
Price Category: B

CAD FILE AVAILABLE

Excellent looks and a great personality make this home a perfect match for your family.

Features:

- Family Room: Large windows look onto the front yard in this large all-purpose area, which is open to the dining area.

- Kitchen: This U-shaped kitchen has a raised bar and is open into the dining and family rooms.

- Master Suite: This area features large bay windows looking onto the backyard. The luxurious private bath has a double vanity and a walk-in closet.

- Bedrooms: The two secondary bedrooms have large closets and share a hall bathroom.

- Laundry Area: Conveniently located near the bedrooms, this room has bifold doors to keep utility area out of view.

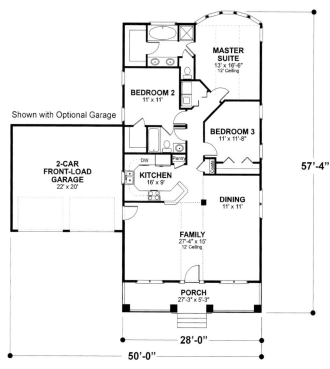

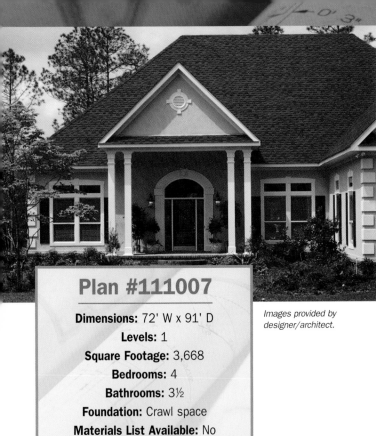

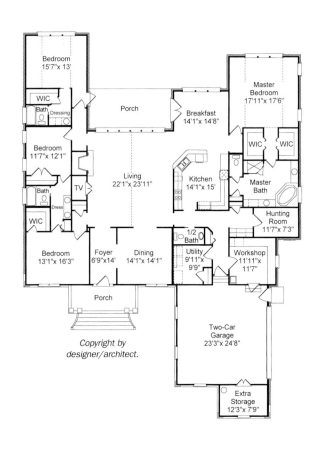

Plan #111007

Dimensions: 72' W x 91' D

Levels: 1

Square Footage: 3,668

Bedrooms: 4

Bathrooms: 3½

Foundation: Crawl space

Materials List Available: No

Price Category: I

Images provided by designer/architect.

Copyright by designer/architect.

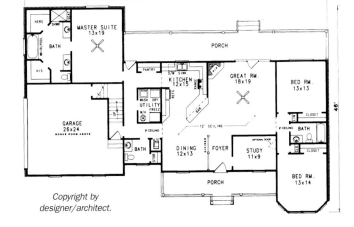

Plan #171015

Dimensions: 79' W x 52' D

Levels: 1

Square Footage: 2,089

Bedrooms: 3

Bathrooms: 2½

Foundation: Crawl space, slab

Materials List Available: Yes

Price Category: D

Images provided by designer/architect.

Copyright by designer/architect.

Bonus Area

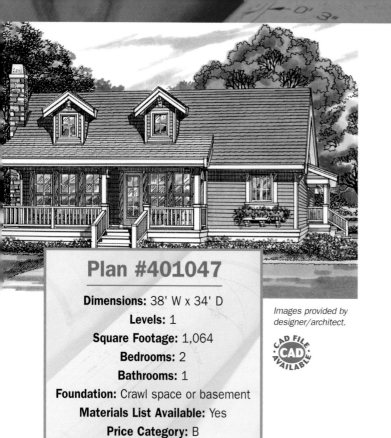

Plan #401047

Dimensions: 38' W x 34' D

Levels: 1

Square Footage: 1,064

Bedrooms: 2

Bathrooms: 1

Foundation: Crawl space or basement

Materials List Available: Yes

Price Category: B

Images provided by designer/architect.

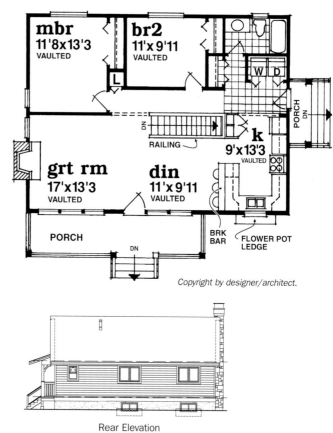

mbr
11'8x13'3
VAULTED

br2
11'x9'11
VAULTED

W D

DN

RAILING

k
9'x13'3
VAULTED

PORCH
DN

grt rm
17'x13'3
VAULTED

din
11'x9'11
VAULTED

PORCH

DN

BRK BAR

FLOWER POT LEDGE

Copyright by designer/architect.

Rear Elevation

Plan #421008

Dimensions: 74'6" W x 43' D

Levels: 1

Square Footage: 1,954

Bedrooms: 3

Bathrooms: 2½

Foundation: Crawl space, slab, or basement

Material List Available: Yes

Price Category: D

Images provided by designer/architect.

PATIO
42'-6"x12'-0"

STORAGE
HW
LNDRY/MUD ROOM
16'-11"x8'-5"
MECH
F

BREAKFAST
11'-7"x11'-2"

MASTER BATH
JACC.

PLANTS

GARAGE
20'-8"x20'-8"

KITCHEN
11'-7"x11'-0"

GREAT ROOM
13'-0"x29'-5"
(VAULTED)

MASTER BEDROOM
15'-0"x13'-1"
(VAULTED)

W.I.C.

SHWR.

BATH

FRIG

LINEN

FORMAL DINING
11'-7"x12'-1"

OPTIONAL HALF-WALL

BEDROOM #2
11'-0"x12'-0"

W.I.C.

BEDROOM #3
11'-7"x10'-6"

W.I.C.

COVERED PORCH
32'-6"x10'-0"

Copyright by designer/architect.

**Optional Basement
Level Floor Plan**

STORAGE

LNDRY/
1/2 BATH

MUDROOM
14'-4"x8'-11"

DN

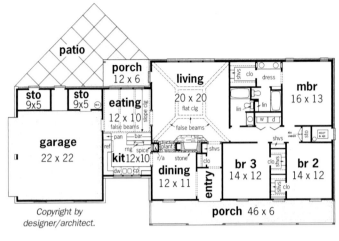

patio

porch
12 x 6

living
20 x 20
flat clg

sto
9x5

sto
9x5

eating
12 x 10
false beams

mbr
16 x 13

garage
22 x 22

kit 12x10

dining
12 x 11

entry

br 3
14 x 12

br 2
14 x 12

porch 46 x 6

Copyright by designer/architect.

Plan #211036

Dimensions: 80' W x 40' D
Levels: 1
Square Footage: 1,800
Bedrooms: 3
Bathrooms: 2
Foundation: Slab
Materials List Available: Yes
Price Category: D

Images provided by designer/architect.

SMARTtip

Dimmer Switches

You can dim lights just slightly to extend lamp life and save energy, and there will be very little perceptible change in light level. For instance, dimming the light to 50 percent will be perceived as though the light were only dimmed to 70 percent. Therefore, there is no dramatic dilation or constriction of the eye due to light level change.

Plan #211005

Dimensions: 68' W x 64' D
Levels: 1
Square Footage: 2,000
Bedrooms: 3
Bathrooms: 2
Foundation: Crawl space or slab
Materials List Available: Yes
Price Category: D

Images provided by designer/architect.

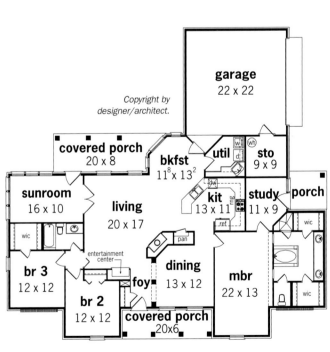

Copyright by designer/architect.

garage
22 x 22

covered porch
20 x 8

bkfst
11⁸ x 13²

util

sto
9 x 9

sunroom
16 x 10

living
20 x 17

kit
13 x 11

study
11 x 9

porch

wic

entertainment center

pan

br 3
12 x 12

foy

dining
13 x 12

mbr
22 x 13

br 2
12 x 12

covered porch
20x6

wic

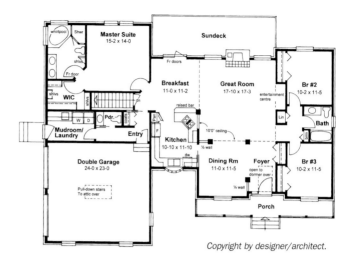

Copyright by designer/architect.

Plan #281020

Dimensions: 60' W x 48' D

Levels: 1

Square Footage: 1,912

Bedrooms: 3

Bathrooms: 2½

Foundation: Basement

Materials List Available: Yes

Price Category: D

Images provided by designer/architect.

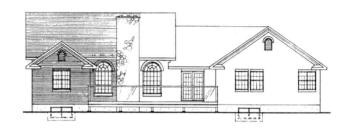

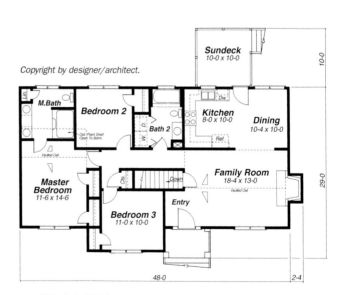

Copyright by designer/architect.

Plan #141001

Dimensions: 48' W x 29' D

Levels: 1

Square Footage: 1,208

Bedrooms: 3

Bathrooms: 2

Foundation: Basement

Materials List Available: Yes

Price Category: B

Images provided by designer/architect.

SMARTtip

Hydro-seeding

An alternative to traditional seeding is hydro-seeding. In this process, a slurry of grass seed, wood fibers, and fertilizer is spray-applied in one step. Hydro-seeding is relatively inexpensive. Compared with seeding by hand, hydro-seeding is also very fast.

Plan #211030

Dimensions: 75' W x 37' D
Levels: 1
Square Footage: 1,600
Bedrooms: 3
Bathrooms: 2
Foundation: Slab
Materials List Available: Yes
Price Category: C

You'll love the way your family can make use of the well-designed living space in this home.

Images provided by designer/architect.

Features:

- **Living Room:** The exposed beams in the 16-ft. tall vaulted ceiling, stone hearth for the fireplace, and 6-in. sunken floor add up to pure luxury.

- **Dining Room:** A divider sets off this room, but even so, it feels open to the other areas.

- **Kitchen:** A built-in snack bar separates this room from the dining room. A large pantry closet and amply counter area make it a cook's delight.

- **Sewing Room:** Set between the kitchen and the laundry room, this area is ideal for the sewer.

- **Master Suite:** A sunken floor and sitting room are luxurious amenities to add to the walk-in closet and bath with separate tub and shower.

- **Storage Room:** Just off the garage, this large room has open space and built-in shelves.

Copyright by designer/architect.

Plan #271003

Dimensions: 64'8" W x 40'4" D

Levels: 1

Square footage: 1,452

Bedrooms: 3

Bathrooms: 2

Foundation: Full basement

Materials List Available: Yes

Price Category: B

Images provided by designer/architect.

This traditional home boasts a striking facade that introduces an extraordinary split-level floor plan.

Features:

- Living Room: This expansive space boasts fabulous windows, a lovely fireplace, and a soaring vaulted ceiling.

- Dining Room: The vaulted ceiling extends over this eating space, too, which is just steps from the kitchen.

- Kitchen: The U-shaped meal-prep area boasts its own vaulted ceiling, a nearby breakfast nook, and a built-in menu desk.

- Master Suite: A walk-in closet and private access to a full bath headline the amenities here.

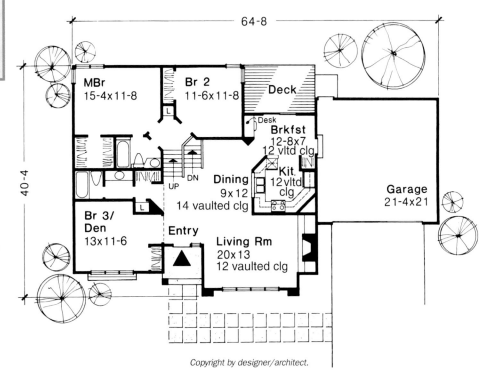

Copyright by designer/architect.

Plan #101022

Dimensions: 66'2" W x 62' D

Levels: 1

Square Footage: 1,992

Bedrooms: 3

Bathrooms: 3

Foundation: Crawl space, slab, or basement

Materials List Available: Yes

Price Category: D

The exterior of this lovely home is traditional, but the unusually shaped rooms and amenities are contemporary.

Features:

- Foyer: This two-story foyer is open to the family room, but columns divide it from the dining room.

- Family Room: A gas fireplace and TV niche, flanked by doors to the covered porch, sit at the rear of this seven-sided, spacious room.

- Breakfast Room: Set off from the family room by columns, this area shares a snack bar with the kitchen and has windows looking over the porch.

- Bedroom 3: Use this room as a living room if you wish, and transform the guest room to a media room or a family bedroom.

- Master Suite: The bedroom features a tray ceiling, has his and her dressing areas, and opens to the porch. The bath has a large corner tub, separate shower, linen closet, and two vanities.

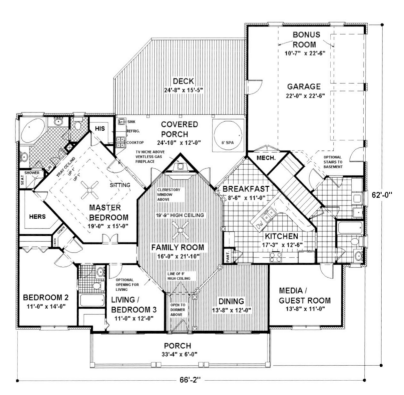

Plan #161098

Dimensions: 72' W x 55'10" D
Levels: 1
Square Footage: 2,283
Bedrooms: 3
Bathrooms: 2
Foundation: Basement
Material List Available: No
Price Category: E

This home, as shown in the photograph, may differ from the actual blueprints. For more detailed information, please check the floor plans carefully.

Images provided by designer/architect.

This spacious single-level home with 9-ft.-high ceiling heights is designed with formal and informal spaces.

Features:

- Dining Room: This open room and the great room are defined by columns and dropped ceilings.

- Great Room: This gathering area features a fireplace and a triple sliding glass door to the rear yard.

- Kitchen: This spacious kitchen with large pantry and angled counter serves the informal dining area and solarium, creating a comfortably relaxed gathering place.

- Master Suite: Designed for luxury, this suite, with its high-style tray ceiling, offers a whirlpool tub, double-bowl vanity, and large walk-in closet.

Rear Elevation

Copyright by designer/architect.

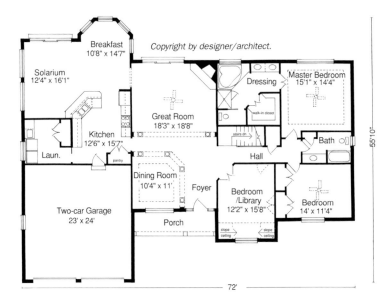

Kitchen

Plan #441009

Dimensions: 94' W x 53' D

Levels: 1

Square Footage: 2,650

Bedrooms: 4

Bathrooms: 2½

Foundation: Crawl space; slab or basement available for fee

Materials List Available: No

Price Category: F

Images provided by designer/architect.

You'll love to call this plan home. It's large enough for the whole family and has a façade that will make you the envy of the neighborhood.

CAD FILE CAD AVAILABLE

Features:

- **Foyer:** The covered porch protects the entry, which has a transom and sidelights to brighten this space.

- **Great Room:** To the left of the foyer, beyond decorative columns, lies this vaulted room, with its fireplace and media center. Additional columns separate the room from the vaulted formal dining room.

- **Kitchen:** A casual nook and this island work center are just around the corner from the great room. The second covered porch can be reached via a door in the nook.

- **Master Suite:** This luxurious space boasts a vaulted salon, a private niche that could be a small study, and a view of the front yard. The master bath features a spa tub, separate shower, compartmented toilet, huge walk-in closet, and access to the laundry room.

- **Bedrooms:** The two additional bedrooms are located at the back of the plan and share the Jack-and-Jill bathroom.

Copyright by designer/architect.

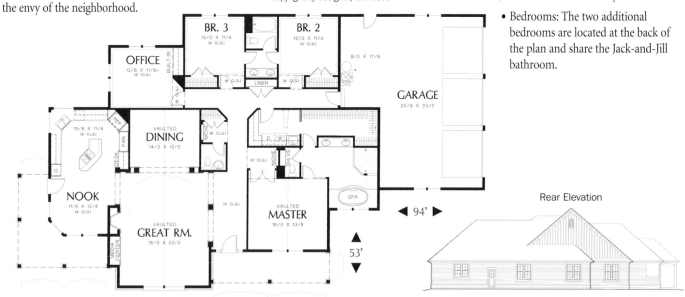

Rear Elevation

Plan #361223

Dimensions: 143'1" W x 96' D

Levels: 1

Square Footage: 2,966

Bedrooms: 3

Bathrooms: 2½

Foundation: Basement, crawl space

Material List Available: No

Price Category: F

CAD FILE AVAILABLE • CAD

Cottage-like architectural details and an abundance of windows add warmth and personality to this generously designed home.

Features:

• Great Room: You'll love the view of your private patio through the wall of windows in this room.

• Kitchen: This open work area contains ample counter space, an island cooktop, and a large pantry. An octagon-shaped breakfast nook completes the kitchen area.

• Master Suite: The double doors provide an air of seclusion for this suite. The bedroom features a French door to the front porch. The adjoining bath is equipped with a whirlpool tub, a shower, a double-sink vanity, and two walk-in closets.

• Secondary Bedrooms: The two additional bedrooms, each with access to the hall bathroom, occupy the right wing of this home.

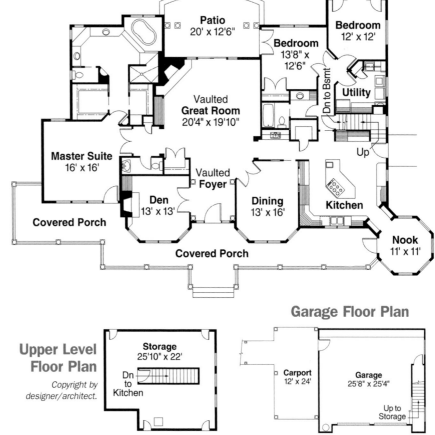

Patio
20' x 12'6"

Bedroom
13'8" x 12'6"

Bedroom
12' x 12'

Vaulted Great Room
20'4" x 19'10"

Dn to Bsmt

Utility

Master Suite
16' x 16'

Vaulted Foyer

Up

Den
13' x 13'

Dining
13' x 16'

Kitchen

Covered Porch

Covered Porch

Nook
11' x 11'

Upper Level Floor Plan

Copyright by designer/architect.

Storage
25'10" x 22'

Dn to Kitchen

Garage Floor Plan

Carport
12' x 24'

Garage
25'8" x 25'4"

Up to Storage

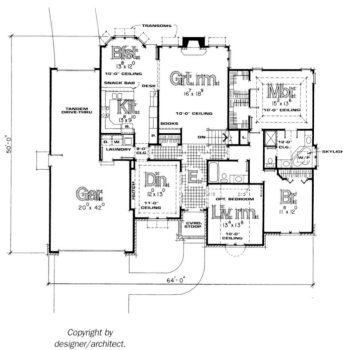

Plan #121050

Dimensions: 64' W x 50' D

Levels: 1

Square Footage: 1,996

Bedrooms: 2

Bathrooms: 2

Foundation: Basement

Materials List Available: Yes

Price Category: D

Images provided by designer/architect.

Copyright by designer/architect.

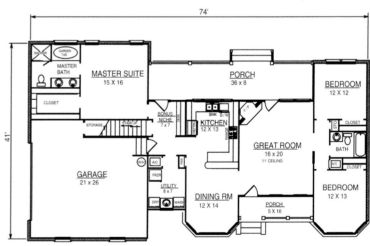

Plan #171023

Dimensions: 74' W x 41' D

Levels: 1

Square Footage: 1,684

Bedrooms: 3

Bathrooms: 2

Foundation: Crawl space or slab

Material List Available: Yes

Price Category: C

Images provided by designer/architect.

Copyright by designer/architect.

Plan #131035

Dimensions: 65'4" W x 45'10" D

Levels: 1

Square Footage: 1,892

Bedrooms: 3

Bathrooms: 2½

Foundation: Crawl space, slab, or basement

Materials List Available: Yes

Price Category: E

Images provided by designer/architect.

Rear Elevation

Bonus Area

Copyright by designer/architect.

Plan #241041

Dimensions: 65' W x 45' D

Levels: 1

Square Footage: 1,612

Bedrooms: 3

Bathrooms: 2

Foundation: Slab

Material List Available: No

Price Category: C

Images provided by designer/architect.

Copyright by designer/architect.

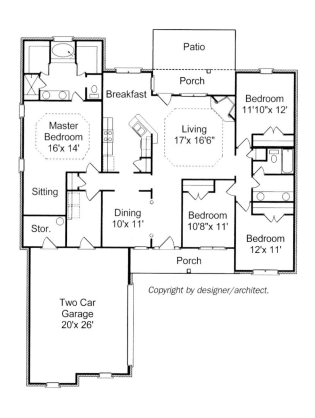

Images provided by designer/architect.

Copyright by designer/architect.

Plan #111015

Dimensions: 64' W x 58' D

Levels: 1

Square Footage: 2,208

Bedrooms: 4

Bathrooms: 2

Foundation: Slab

Materials List Available: No

Price Category: F

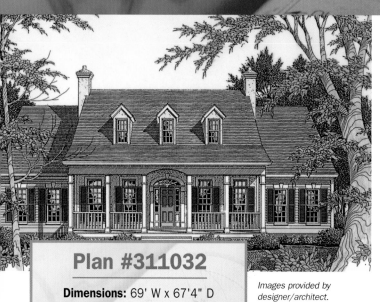

Images provided by designer/architect.

Plan #311032

Dimensions: 69' W x 67'4" D

Levels: 1

Square Footage: 2,127

Bedrooms: 3

Bathrooms: 2½

Foundation: Crawl space, slab or basement

Material List Available: No

Price Category: D

Bonus Area Floor Plan

Copyright by designer/architect.

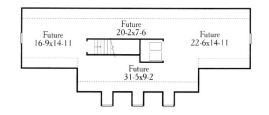

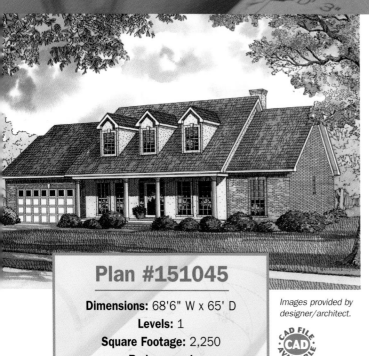

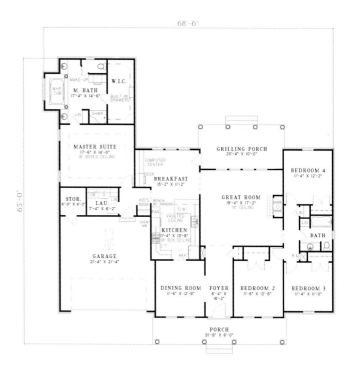

68'-6"

Images provided by
designer/architect.

CAD FILE AVAILABLE — CAD

Plan #151045

Dimensions: 68'6" W x 65' D

Levels: 1

Square Footage: 2,250

Bedrooms: 4

Bathrooms: 2

Foundation: Crawl space, slab;
basement for fee

CompleteCost List Available: Yes

Price Category: E

Copyright by designer/architect.

Images provided by
designer/architect.

Plan #211067

Dimensions: 96' W x 90' D

Levels: 1

Square Footage: 4,038

Bedrooms: 4

Bathrooms: 4½

Foundation: Crawl space

Materials List Available: Yes

Price Category: I

Copyright by
designer/architect.

Plan #211048

Dimensions: 66' W x 60' D
Levels: 1
Square Footage: 2,002
Bedrooms: 3
Bathrooms: 2
Foundation: Crawl space, slab
Materials List Available: Yes
Price Category: D

This southern-style home is filled with inviting spaces and will fit into any neighborhood.

Features:

- Ceiling Height: 8 ft.

- Front Porch: Enjoy summer breezes on this porch, which features accented shutters that are both functional and stylish.

- Living Room: From the porch, French doors lead into the side-lit entry and this gracious living room.

- Sundeck: You can bask in the summer sun on this private rear deck, or if you prefer, enjoy a cool breeze under the shade of the rear porch. Each is accessible through its own set of French doors.

- Master Suite: This suite is secluded from the rest of the house for privacy, making it the perfect retreat at the end of a busy day. From the bedroom, open double doors to gain access to the luxurious bath, with a dual-sink vanity and his and her walk-in closets.

Images provided by designer/architect.

Copyright by designer/architect.

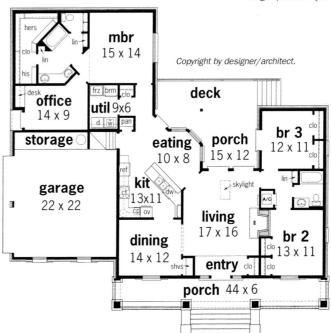

SMARTtip

Eye Appeal

Not everything in a landscaping plan needs to be in the ground. You might want to consider hanging flowering plants on a front porch or placing hardy potted plants on outdoor steps and decks or strategically along a paved walkway. Even a window box, viewed from outside, becomes a part of the landscaping.

Plan #211002

Dimensions: 68' W x 62' D
Levels: 1
Square Footage: 1,792
Bedrooms: 3
Bathrooms: 2
Foundation: Crawl space
Materials List Available: Yes
Price Category: C

Images provided by designer/architect.

Arched windows on the front of this home give it a European style that you're sure to love.

SMARTtip

Water Features

Water features create the ambiance of a soothing oasis on a deck. A water-filled urn becomes a mirror that reflects the sky— making a small deck look larger. Fish flashing in an ornamental pool add color and act as a focal point for a deck with no view.

A water fountain introduces a pleasant rhythmical sound that helps drown out the background noises of traffic and nearby neighbors.

Features:

• Living Room: The 12-ft. ceiling in this large, open room enhances its spacious feeling. A fireplace adds warmth on chilly days and cool evenings.

• Dining Room: Decorate to accentuate the 12-ft. ceiling and formal feeling of this room.

• Kitchen: Designed for comfort and efficiency, this room also has a 12-ft. ceiling. The cozy breakfast bar is a natural gathering spot for friends and family.

• Master Suite: A split design guarantees privacy here. A sloped cathedral ceiling adds elegance, and a walk-in closet makes it practical. The bath has two vanities, a tub, and a walk-in shower.

• Garage: Park two cars here, and use the balance of this 520 sq. ft. area as a handy storage area.

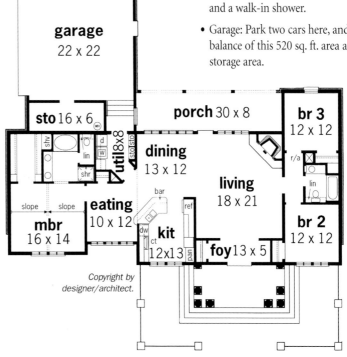

Copyright by designer/architect.

Plan #351021

Dimensions: 61' W x 47'4" D
Levels: 1
Square Footage: 1,500
Bedrooms: 3
Bathrooms: 2
Foundation: Crawl space, slab, or basement
Materials List Available: Yes
Price Category: *D*

Images provided by designer/architect.

This lovely home provides a functional split-floor-plan layout with many of the features that your family desires.

Features:

- **Great Room:** This large gathering area, with a vaulted ceiling, has a gas log fireplace.

- **Kitchen:** This open kitchen layout has plenty of counter space for that growing family.

- **Master Suite:** This expansive master bedroom and bath has plenty of storage space in its separate walk-in closets.

- **Garage:** This two-car garage has a storage area.

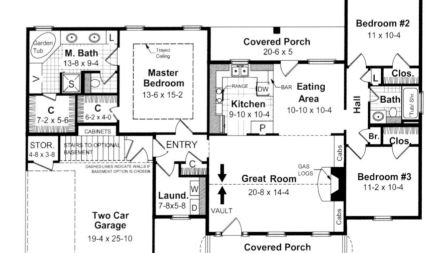

Copyright by designer/architect.

Plan #101013

Dimensions: 72' W x 66' D

Levels: 1

Square Footage: 2,564

Bedrooms: 3

Bathrooms: 2½

Foundation: Basement; crawl space or slab for fee

Materials List Available: Yes

Price Category: F

Images provided by designer/architect.

This exciting design combines a striking classic exterior with a highly functional floor plan.

Features:

- Ceiling Height: 9 ft. unless otherwise noted.

- Family Room: This warm and inviting room measures 18 ft. x 22 ft. It features a 14-ft. ceiling and a rear wall of windows. French doors lead to an enormous deck.

- Kitchen: This unique angled kitchen is open to the hearth room and eating areas, all of which enjoy vaulted ceilings and are surrounded by windows. The hearth room has a TV niche.

- Master Suite: This 19-ft. x 18-ft. master suite is truly sumptuous, with its 12-ft. ceiling, sitting area, two walk-in closets, and full-featured bath.

- Secondary Bedrooms: Each of the secondary bedrooms measures 11 ft. x 14 ft. and has direct access to a shared bath.

- Bonus Room: Just beyond the entry are stairs leading to this bonus room, which measures approximately 12 ft. x 21 ft.—plenty of room for storage or future expansion.

Master Bedroom

Copyright by designer/architect.

Plan #271007

Dimensions: 51'5" W x 40'9" D
Levels: 1
Square Footage: 1,283
Bedrooms: 3
Bathrooms: 2
Foundation: Basement
Materials List Available: Yes
Price Category: B

This charming traditional home has an appealing exterior and is full of exceptional interior features.

Features:

• Great Room: This room is just off the front foyer and boasts a dramatic vaulted ceiling and inviting fireplace.

• Dining room: Open to the great room, this area overlooks the delightful rear deck.

• Kitchen: This area is efficiently designed with a pantry and a sunny vaulted breakfast nook, which leads to the deck, making breakfast alfresco a daily option.

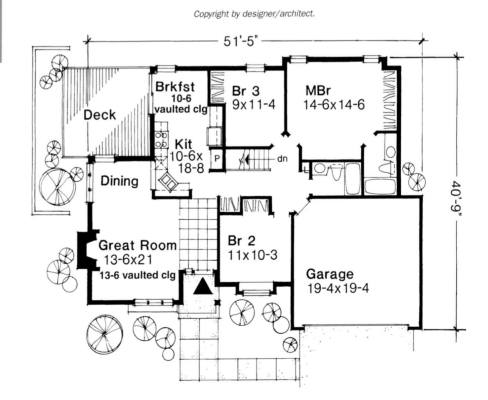

Plan #211011

Dimensions: 84' W x 54' D
Levels: 1
Square Footage: 2,791
Bedrooms: 3 or 4
Bathrooms: 2
Foundation: Slab or crawl space
Materials List Available: Yes
Price Category: F

SMARTtip

Types of Decks

Ground-level decks resemble a low platform and are best for flat locations. They can be the most economical type to build because they don't require stairs.

Raised decks can rise just a few steps up or meet the second story of a house. Lifted high on post supports, they adapt well to uneven or sloped locations.

Multilevel decks feature two or more stories and are connected by stairways or ramps. They can follow the contours of a sloped lot, unifying the deck with the outdoors.

Images provided by designer/architect.

Plenty of room plus an open, flexible floor plan make this a home that will adapt to your needs.

Features:

- Ceiling Height: 8 ft. unless otherwise noted.
- Living Room: This distinctive room features a 12-ft. ceiling and is designed so that it can also serve as a master suite with a sitting room.
- Family Room: The whole family will want to gather in this large, inviting family room.
- Morning Room: The family room blends

into this sunny spot, which is perfect for informal family meals.

- Kitchen: This spacious kitchen offers a smart layout. It is also contiguous to the family room.
- Master Suite: You'll look forward to the end of the day when you can enjoy this master suite. It includes a huge, luxurious master bath with two large walk-in closets and two vanity sinks.
- Optional Bedroom: This optional fourth bedroom is located so that it can easily serve as a library, den, office, or music room.

Copyright by designer/architect.

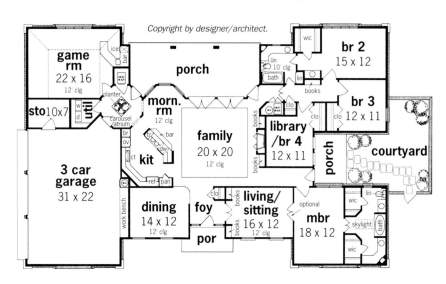

Planning Your Landscape

Landscapes change over the years. As plants grow, the overall look evolves from sparse to lush. Trees cast cool shade where the sun used to shine. Shrubs and hedges grow tall and dense enough to provide privacy. Perennials and ground covers spread to form colorful patches of foliage and flowers. Meanwhile, paths, arbors, fences, and other structures gain the patina of age.

Constant change over the years—sometimes rapid and dramatic, sometimes slow and subtle—is one of the joys of landscaping. It is also one of the challenges. Anticipating how fast plants will grow and how big they will eventually get is difficult, even for professional designers.

To illustrate the kinds of changes to expect in a planting, these pages show a landscape design at three different "ages." Even though a new planting may look sparse at first, it will soon fill in. And because of careful spacing, the planting will look as good in 10 to 15 years as it does after 3 to 5. It will, of course, look different, but that's part of the fun.

At Planting

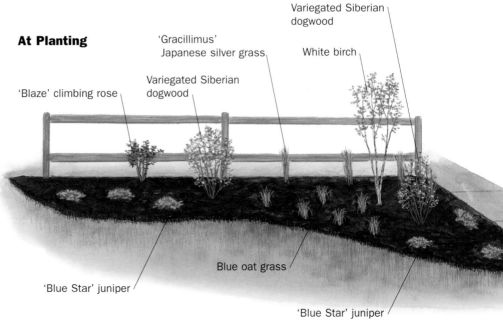

- Variegated Siberian dogwood
- 'Gracillimus' Japanese silver grass
- White birch
- 'Blaze' climbing rose
- Variegated Siberian dogwood
- Blue oat grass
- 'Blue Star' juniper
- 'Blue Star' juniper

Three to Five Years

At Planting—Here's how the corner might appear in early summer immediately after planting. The white birch tree is only 5 to 6 ft. tall, with trunks no thicker than broomsticks. The variegated Siberian dogwoods each have a few main stems about 3 to 4 ft. tall. The 'Blaze' rose has just short stubs where the nursery cut back the old stems, but it will grow fast and may bloom the first year. The 'Blue Star' junipers are low mounds about 6 to 10 in. wide. The blue oat grass forms small, thin clumps of sparse foliage. The 'Gracillimus' Japanese silver grass may still be dormant, or it may have a short tuft of new foliage. Both grasses will grow vigorously the first year.

Three to Five Years—The birch tree has grown 1 to 2 ft. taller every year but is still quite slender. Near the base, it's starting to show the white bark typical of maturity. The variegated Siberian dogwoods are well established now. If you cut them to the ground every year or two in spring, they grow back 4 to 6 ft. tall by midsummer, with strong, straight stems. The 'Blaze' rose covers the fence, and you need to prune out a few of its older stems every spring. The slow-growing 'Blue Star' junipers make a series of low mounds; you still see them as individuals, not a continuous patch. The grasses have reached maturity and form lush, robust clumps. It would be a good idea to divide and replant them now, to keep them vigorous.

Ten to Fifteen Years—The birch tree is becoming a fine specimen, 20 to 30 ft. tall, with gleaming white bark on its trunks. Prune away the lower limbs up to 6 to 8 ft. above ground to expose its trunks and to keep it from crowding and shading the other plants. The variegated dogwoods and 'Blaze' rose continue to thrive and respond well to regular pruning. The 'Blue Star' junipers have finally merged into a continuous mass of glossy foliage. The blue oat grass and Japanese silver grass will still look good if they have been divided and replanted over the years. If you get tired of the grasses, you could replace them with cinnamon fern and astilbe, as shown here, or other perennials or shrubs.

Ten to Fifteen Years

Cinnamon fern

Astilbe

A Step Up
Plant a Foundation Garden

'Techny' American **C** arborvitae

Germander **H**

'Blue Star' juniper **D**

'Sarah Bernhardt' **F** peony

Rare is the home without foundation plantings. These simple skirtings of greenery hide unattractive concrete block underpinnings and help overcome the impression that the house is hovering a few feet above the ground. Useful as these plantings are, they are too often just monochromatic expanses of clipped yews, dull as dishwater. But, as this design shows, a durable, low-maintenance foundation planting can be more varied, more colorful, and more fun.

Broad-leaved and coniferous evergreen shrubs anchor this planting and provide four-season cover for the foundation. But they also offer contrasting shapes and textures and a range of colors from icy blue through a variety of greens to maroon.

What makes this design special is the smaller plants fronting the foundation shrubs. Including perenni-

als, grasses, and low shrubs in the mix expands the foundation planting into a small front-yard garden. From spring until frost, flowers in white, pink, magenta, and mauve stand out against the blue-and-green backdrop. When the last flower fades in autumn, the evergreen foliage takes center stage, serving through the winter as a welcome reminder that the world will green up again.

Plants and Projects

Eye-catching as the flowers in this planting are, the foliage is the key to its success in every season. The evergreens are attractive year-round. And each of the perennials has been chosen as much for its foliage as for its flowers. A thorough cleanup and maintenance pruning spring and fall will keep the planting looking its best.

A 'Wichita Blue' juniper *Juniperus scopulorum* (use 1 plant) This slow-growing, upright evergreen shrub has a neat pyramidal form and lovely silver-blue foliage and blue berries to add year-round color at the corner of the house.

B 'PJM' rhododendron

Rhododendron (use 5) An informal row of these hardy evergreen shrubs beautifully conceals the foundation. Vivid magenta flowers in early spring, small dark green leaves that turn maroon in winter, all on a compact plant.

C 'Techny' American arborvitae *Thuja occidentalis* (use 1) This cone-shaped, slow-growing evergreen fills the corner near the front steps with fragrant, rich green, fine-textured foliage.

D 'Blue Star' juniper *Juniperus squamata* (use 3) The sparkly blue foliage and irregular mounded form of this low-growing evergreen shrub look great next to the peony and germander.

E 'Sea Urchin' blue fescue grass *Festuca ovina* var. *glauca* (use 3) The very fine blue leaves of this perennial grass contrast handsomely with the dark green rhododendrons behind. Flower spikes rise above the neat, soft-looking mounds in early summer.

F 'Sarah Bernhardt' peony *Paeonia* (use 3) A sentimental favorite, this perennial offers fragrant pink double flowers in early summer. Forms a multistemmed clump with attractive foliage that will look nice next to the steps through the summer.

G White astilbe *Astilbe* (use 3) The lacy dark green foliage and fluffy white flower plumes of

this tough perennial stand out against the blue foliage of its neighbors. Flowers in June or July.

H Germander *Teucrium chamaedrys* (use 1) This rugged little shrub forms a tidy mound of small, dark, shiny evergreen leaves next to the walk. Mauve flowers bloom in late summer.

I 'Sheffield' chrysanthemum *Dendranthema* x *grandiflorum* (use 1) A longtime regional favorite, this hardy perennial forms a broad mound of fragrant graygreen foliage. Small, clear pink, daisylike blossoms cover the plant from September until frost.

I 'Sheffield' chrysanthemum

E 'Sea Urchin' blue fescue grass

B 'PJM' rhododendron

G White astilbe

A 'Wichita Blue' juniper

Note: All plants are appropriate for USDA Hardiness Zones 4, 5, and 6.

Site: Sunny

Season: Fall

Concept: A mixture of easy-care perennials and shrubs provides a colorful setting for a home's public face.

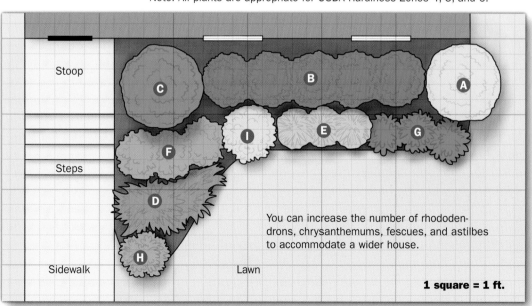

Stoop

Steps

Sidewalk

Lawn

You can increase the number of rhododendrons, chrysanthemums, fescues, and astilbes to accommodate a wider house.

1 square = 1 ft.

Angle of Repose

Make a Back-Door Garden for a Sheltered Niche

Many homes offer the opportunity to tuck a garden into a protected corner. In the front yard, such spots are ideal for an entry garden or a landscaping display that showcases your house when viewed from the sidewalk or the street. If the planting is in the backyard, like the site shown here, it can be more intimate, part of a comfortable outdoor room you can enjoy from a nearby patio or window.

The curved bed wraps around the small patio, increasingly shaded by the neighboring crab apple as the years pass. The planting has been designed with spring especially in mind, so we're showing that season here. Dozens of bulbs light up the corner in April and May, assisted by several early-blooming trees and shrubs. Flowers in white, pink, yellow, purple, and blue carpet the ground

or twinkle on bare branches above. Several impart a delicious scent to the fresh spring air.

Early flowers aren't the only pleasures of spring in the garden. Watch buds fatten and burst into leaf on the deciduous trees and shrubs, and mark the progress of the season as new, succulent shoots of summer perennials emerge.

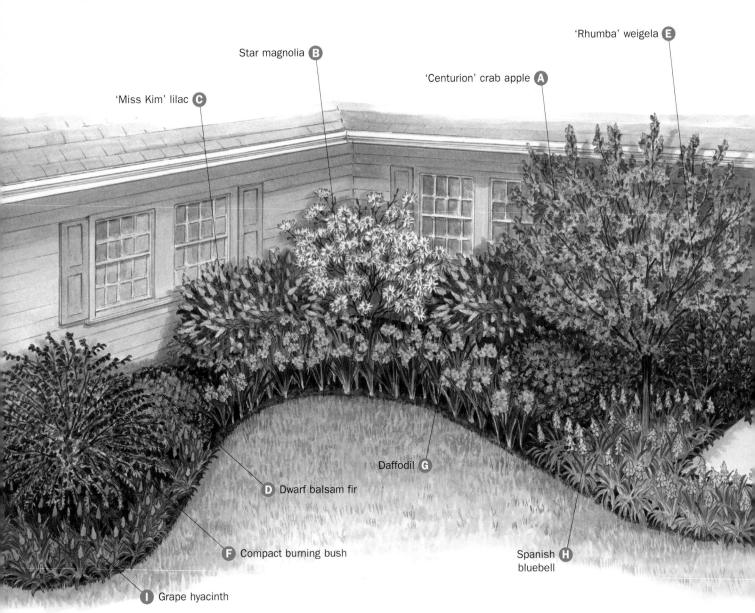

'Rhumba' weigela **E**

Star magnolia **B**

'Centurion' crab apple **A**

'Miss Kim' lilac **C**

Daffodil **G**

D Dwarf balsam fir

F Compact burning bush

Spanish **H** bluebell

I Grape hyacinth

Note: All plants are appropriate for USDA Hardiness Zones 4, 5, and 6.

Plants and Projects

Once established, these plants require little maintenance. The shrubs won't overgrow nearby windows, and the trees will need little pruning. Every few years you will have to divide the bulbs.

A **'Centurion' crab apple** *Malus* (use 1 plant)
A small deciduous tree with cheerful rosy pink flowers in May, attractive summer foliage, and glossy little fruits that last into winter. Will broaden to shade the terrace as it ages.

B **Star magnolia** *Magnolia stellata* (use 1)
This small, rounded, multi-trunked deciduous tree won't outgrow the corner. Delightful white flowers bloom in early spring, before leaves appear.

C **'Miss Kim' lilac** *Syringa patula* (use 2)
This well-behaved, compact deciduous shrub has clusters of purple flowers in May. Open nearby windows to enjoy their wonderful scent.

D **Dwarf balsam fir** *Abies balsamea* 'Nana' (use 1)
Lustrous dark green needles and a compact rounded form make this low-growing evergreen shrub an ideal companion for the taller deciduous shrubs and a good backdrop for spring bulbs.

E **'Rhumba' weigela** *Weigela florida* (use 1)
With dark red flowers in summer and dark green-and-purple leaves, this compact deciduous shrub is eye-catching throughout the growing season.

F **Compact burning bush** *Euonymus alatus* 'Compacta' (use 1)
This deciduous shrub lights up the end of the planting with its dependable fall color: the dark green leaves turn pale copper and then bright crimson red.

G **Daffodil** *Narcissus* (use 35)
One of the cheeriest spring sights is the butter yellow trumpets of this prince of flowering bulbs. To keep the flowers coming each year, you must let the foliage die down naturally, but the daylilies will hide it as they grow.

H **Spanish bluebell** *Endymion hispanica* (use 24)
Dangling above attractive grassy foliage, the pretty blue bell-like flowers of this spring bulb dapple the ground beneath the crab apple. When its foliage gets ragged, you can pull or trim it.

I **Grape hyacinth** *Muscari armeniacum* (use 35 or more)
These little bulbs will spread happily beneath the burning bush, making a carpet of grassy foliage topped with fragrant dark blue-purple flowers arranged in grapelike clusters.

J **Planter**
Extend springtime color onto the patio with Darwin tulips and pansies in the large planter next to the door. Plant tulip bulbs in fall; replace them every few years. Add a few dozen pansy plants in early spring.

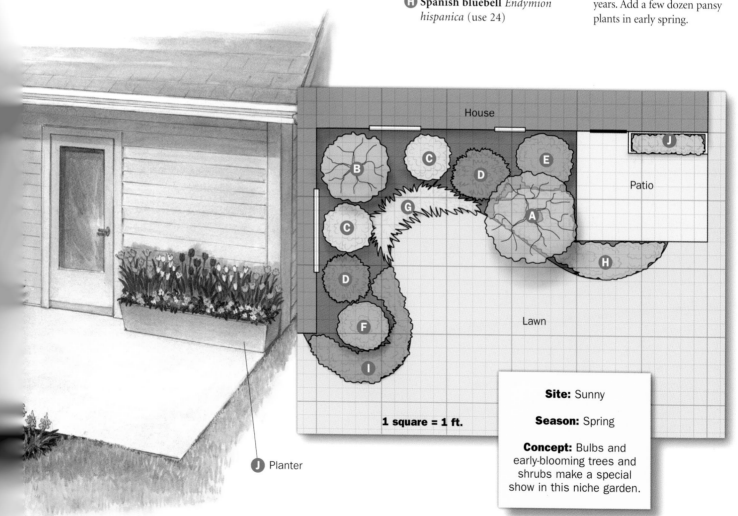

J Planter

House

Patio

Lawn

1 square = 1 ft.

Site: Sunny

Season: Spring

Concept: Bulbs and early-blooming trees and shrubs make a special show in this niche garden.

A Neighborly Corner

Beautify a Boundary with Easy-Care Plants

The corner where your property meets your neighbor's and the sidewalk can be a kind of grassy no-man's-land. This design defines the boundary with a planting that can be enjoyed by the property owners as well as by people passing by.

Because of its exposed location, remote from the house and close to the street, this is a less personal planting than those in other more private parts of your property.

It is meant to be appreciated from a distance. Anchored by a multitrunked birch tree, attractive grasses and shrubs are arrayed in large masses at several heights. An existing split-rail fence on the property line now serves as a scaffold for a rose trained around its rails. While not intended as a barrier, the planting also provides a modest physical and psychological screen from activity on the street.

> **Site:** Sunny
>
> **Season:** Summer
>
> **Concept:** Enhance the property line with a low-care, neighbor-friendly planting of trees and shrubs.

Variegated **C** Siberian dogwood

'Blaze' **B** climbing rose

'Blue Star' juniper **D**

1 square = 1 ft.

Fence

Lawn

Sidewalk

Note: All plants are appropriate for USDA Hardiness Zones 4, 5, and 6.

Plants and Projects

These plants all have a four-season presence, including the grasses, whose foliage stands up as well as many shrubs to the rigors of winter. Good gardens make good neighbors, so we've used well-behaved plants that won't make extra work for the person next door—or for you. The rose will need training throughout the summer, there will be some birch leaves to rake in fall, and the grasses must be trimmed back in late winter or early spring.

A **White birch** Betula platyphylla 'White Spire' (use 1 plant)

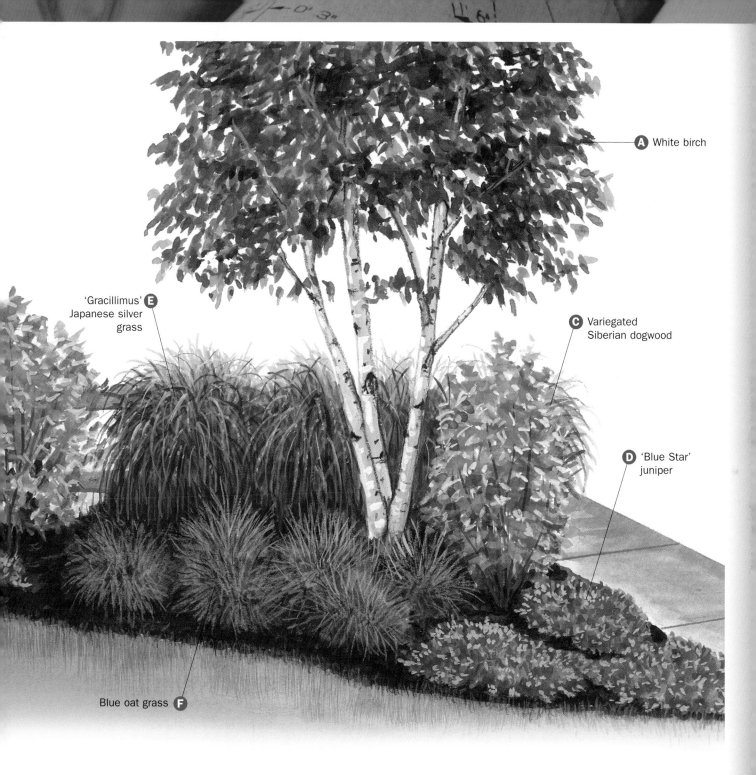

A White birch

'Gracillimus' **E** Japanese silver grass

C Variegated Siberian dogwood

D 'Blue Star' juniper

Blue oat grass **F**

A deciduous tree grown for its graceful upright form and striking white bark. Green leaves dance in the summer breezes and turn a pretty yellow in fall. Buy a multi-trunked specimen, and keep the lower limbs pruned so it won't cast too much shade on the shrubs and grasses underneath.

B **'Blaze' climbing rose** *Rosa* (use 1)
This vigorous climbing rose has long flexible canes that can be trained horizontally. Tied to or wrapped around the rails, they'll cover the fence quickly. Bears lots of red semidouble flowers in June; blooms off and on until frost. The flowers are only mildly fragrant.

C **Variegated Siberian dogwood** *Cornus alba* 'Elegantissima' (use 2)
A deciduous shrub with eye-catching features year-round: white flowers in spring, white-and-green leaves in summer, and pale blue berries in fall. In winter, dark red stems provide a lovely contrast to the blue foliage of the juniper.

D **'Blue Star' juniper** *Juniperus squamata* (use 6)
This evergreen shrub forms an irregular sparkling blue mass. It grows slowly and never needs pruning. An excellent ground cover, it is a nice counterpoint to the flowing grasses.

E **'Gracillimus' Japanese silver grass** *Miscanthus* (use 4)
This perennial grass is always beautiful, but never more so than in fall and winter, when silvery plumes of tiny seeds wave above an arching clump of tan foliage. Earlier, the narrow leaves are green striped with white.

F **Blue oat grass** *Helictotrichon sempervirens* (use 6)
Less than half as tall as the silver grass, this perennial is just as lovely. Dense compact mounds bristle with wiry blue leaves, which often live through the winter. Thin stalks carry slender seed heads that turn tan in winter.

Plan #321035

Dimensions: 55'8" W x 46' D
Levels: 1
Square Footage: 1,384
Bedrooms: 2
Bathrooms: 2
Foundation: Walkout
Materials List Available: Yes
Price Category: B

Images provided by designer/architect.

You'll love the way the two-story atrium windows meld this home with your sloped site.

Features:

- Great Room: A masonry fireplace, vaulted ceiling, huge bayed area, and stairs to the atrium below make this room a natural gathering spot.

- Dining Area: You'll love sitting here and admiring the view by sunlight or starlight.

- Kitchen: An angled bar is both a snack bar and work space in this well-designed kitchen with an attached laundry room.

- Master Suite: Double doors open into the spacious bedroom with a huge walk-in closet. The bath has a garden tub, separate shower, and double vanity.

- Optional Basement Plan: Take advantage of this space to build a family room, media room, or home studio that's lit by the huge atrium windows and opens to the patio.

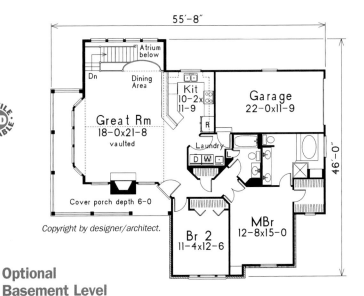

Copyright by designer/architect.

Optional Basement Level Floor Plan

Rear View

Plan #391042

Dimensions: 50' W x 40' D
Levels: 1
Square Footage: 1,307
Bedrooms: 3
Bathrooms: 2
Foundation: Crawl space, slab, or basement
Materials List Available: Yes
Price Category: B

This comfortable home has an air of cozy seclusion in an economical design.

Features:

- Living Room: Open ceiling beams lend height and space to this roomy living room. It is an area that's ideal for gathering and entertainment.

- Kitchen: This efficiently designed L-shape kitchen opens directly into the dining room, making transitions simple. The laundry room is just a few footsteps away, the perfect distance for cleaning up table linens and other kitchen messes.

- Master Suite: Imagine a relaxing breakfast in bed in a room with a vaulted ceiling, a large closet. and a full master bath. Close enough to the other bedrooms without sacrificing privacy, you can be near your loved ones.

- Bedrooms: Both secondary bedrooms have easy access to the nearby full bathroom. If a third bedroom is unnecessary, the space could be used equally well as a den.

This home, as shown in the photograph, may differ from the actual blueprints. For more detailed information, please check the floor plans carefully.

Images provided by designer/architect.

Copyright by designer/architect.

Rear View

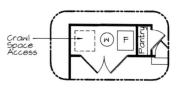

Slab/Crawl Space Option Floor Plan

Plan #401033

Dimensions: 62' W x 29' D

Levels: 1

Square Footage: 1,405

Bedrooms: 3

Bathrooms: 2

Foundation: Basement

Materials List Available: Yes

Price Category: B

This three-bedroom leisure home is perfect for the family that spends casual time out of doors. An expansive wall of glass gives a spectacular view from the great room and accentuates the high vaulted ceilings throughout the design.

Features:

- Great Room: This room is warmed by a hearth and is open to the dining room and L-shaped kitchen.

- Kitchen: A triangular snack bar graces this kitchen and provides space for casual meals.

- Bedrooms: The bedrooms are split, with the master bedroom on the right side of the plan and family bedrooms on the left.

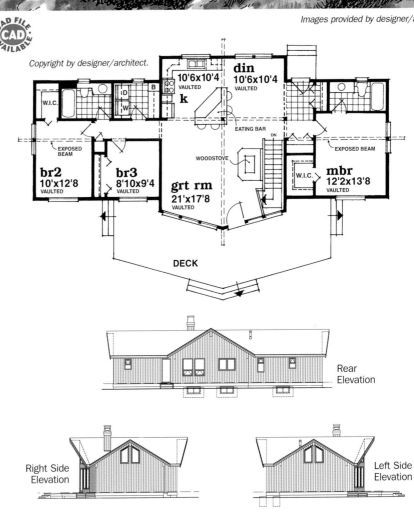

Rear Elevation

Right Side Elevation

Left Side Elevation

Plan #121013

Dimensions: 40' W x 55'8" D
Levels: 1
Square Footage: 1,375
Bedrooms: 1
Bathrooms: 2
Foundation: Basement
Materials List Available: Yes
Price Category: B

Images provided by designer/architect.

This convenient open plan is well-suited to retirement or as a starter home.

Features:

- Ceiling Height: 8 ft., unless otherwise noted.

- Den: To the left of the entry, French doors lead to a den that can convert to a second bedroom.

- Kitchen: A center island doubles as a snack bar while the breakfast area includes a pantry and a desk for compiling shopping lists and menus.

- Open Plan: The sense of spaciousness is enhanced by the large open area that includes the family room, kitchen, and breakfast area.

- Family Room: A handsome fireplace invites family and friends to gather in this area.

- Porch: Step through the breakfast area to enjoy the fresh air on this secluded porch.

- Master Bedroom: This distinctive bedroom features a boxed ceiling. It's served by a private bath with a walk-in closet.

CAD FILE AVAILABLE

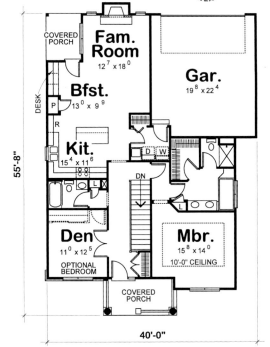

Copyright by designer/architect.

SMARTtip

Paint Color Choices for Your Home

Earth tones are easy to decorate with because they are neutral colors. Use neutral or muted tones, such as light grays, browns, or greens with either lighter or darker shades for accenting.

Use bright colors sparingly, to catch the eye. Painting the front door a bright color creates a cheerful entryway.

Investigate home shows, magazines, and houses in your area for color ideas. Paint suppliers can also give you valuable tips on appropriate color schemes.

Colors that look just right on a color card may need to be toned down for painting large areas. If in doubt, buy a quart of paint and test it.

Images provided by designer/architect.

Copyright by designer/architect.

Rear Elevation

Plan #221008

Dimensions: 60'4" W x 46' D

Levels: 1

Square Footage: 1,540

Bedrooms: 3

Bathrooms: 2

Foundation: Basement

Materials List Available: No

Price Category: C

Images provided by designer/architect.

Copyright by designer/architect.

CAD FILE AVAILABLE

Plan #321025

Dimensions: 28' W x 28' D

Levels: 1

Square Footage: 914

Bedrooms: 2

Bathrooms: 1

Foundation: Walkout

Materials List Available: Yes

Price Category: A

Optional Basement Level Floor Plan

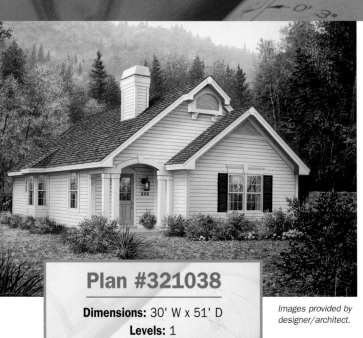

Plan #321038

Dimensions: 30' W x 51' D
Levels: 1
Square Footage: 1,452
Bedrooms: 4
Bathrooms: 2
Foundation: Basement
Materials List Available: Yes
Price Category: B

Images provided by designer/architect.

CAD FILE AVAILABLE

Copyright by designer/architect.

Plan #391069

Dimensions: 56' W x 48' D
Levels: 1
Square Footage: 1,492
Bedrooms: 3
Bathrooms: 2
Foundation: Crawl space, slab, or basement
Materials List Available: Yes
Price Category: B

Images provided by designer/architect.

Copyright by designer/architect.

Optional Floor Plan

Plan #321040

Dimensions: 35' W x 40'8" D

Levels: 1

Square Footage: 1,084

Bedrooms: 2

Bathrooms: 2

Foundation: Basement

Materials List Available: Yes

Price Category: B

Images provided by designer/architect.

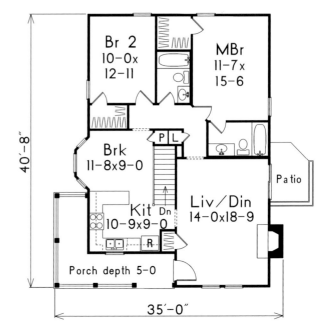

Copyright by designer/architect.

Plan #151749

Dimensions: 76' W x 50' D

Levels: 1

Square Footage: 1,616

Bedrooms: 3

Bathrooms: 2

Foundation: Crawl space

CompleteCost List Available: Yes

Price Category: C

Images provided by designer/architect.

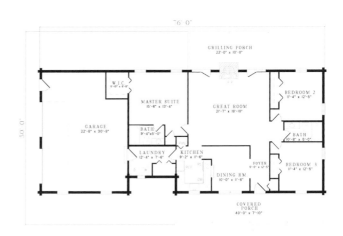

Copyright by designer/architect.

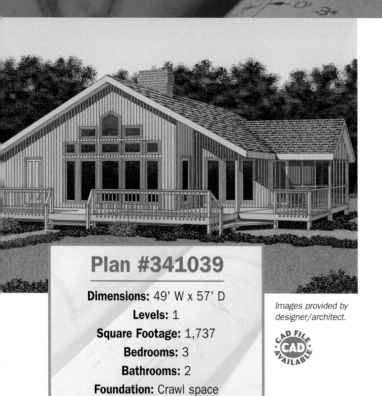

Plan #341039

Dimensions: 49' W x 57' D

Levels: 1

Square Footage: 1,737

Bedrooms: 3

Bathrooms: 2

Foundation: Crawl space

Material List Available: Yes

Price Category: C

Images provided by designer/architect.

CAD FILE AVAILABLE

BEDROOM 2
15'-0" X 11'-5"

BATH 1

BEDROOM 1
13'-9" X 15'-0"

CLOSET

CLOS.

BEDROOM 3
11'-5" X 10'-9"

BATH 2

KITCHEN
15'-5" X 15'-9"

ISLAND

SCREENED PORCH

PANTRY

CLOSET

DINING AREA

GREAT ROOM
29'-2" X 14'-9"

COVERED DECK

DECK

VAULTED CEILING

57'-0"

DECK

49'-0"

Copyright by designer/architect.

Plan #271023

Dimensions: 60' W x 48'4" D

Levels: 1

Square Footage: 1,993

Bedrooms: 3

Bathrooms: 2

Foundation: Basement

Materials List Available: Yes

Price Category: D

Images provided by designer/architect.

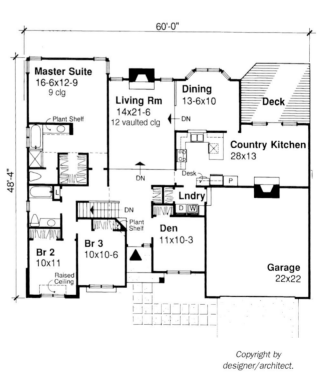

60'-0"

Master Suite
16-6x12-9
9 clg

Plant Shelf

Living Rm
14x21-6
12 vaulted clg

Dining
13-6x10

Deck

Country Kitchen
28x13

Desk

48'-4"

Lndry

Plant Shelf

Br 2
10x11

Br 3
10x10-6

Den
11x10-3

Garage
22x22

Raised Ceiling

Copyright by designer/architect.

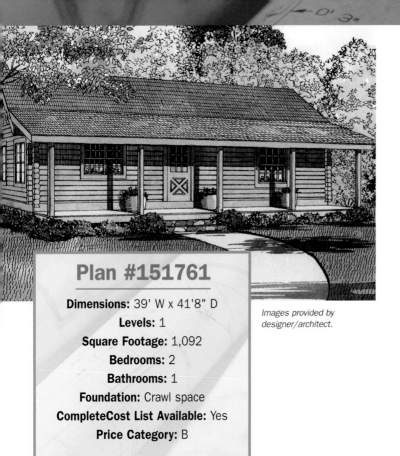

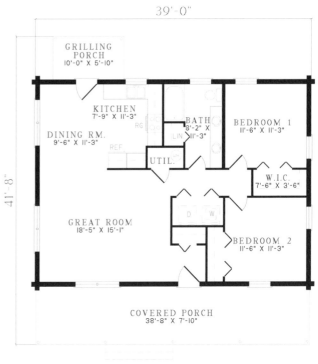

GRILLING PORCH
10'-0" X 5'-10"

KITCHEN
7'-9" X 11'-3"

DINING RM.
9'-6" X 11'-3"

BATH
8'-2" X
11'-3"

BEDROOM 1
11'-6" X 11'-3"

UTIL.

W.I.C.
7'-6" X 3'-6"

GREAT ROOM
18'-5" X 15'-1"

BEDROOM 2
11'-6" X 11'-3"

COVERED PORCH
38'-8" X 7'-10"

39'-0"

41'-8"

Images provided by designer/architect.

Copyright by designer/architect.

Plan #151761

Dimensions: 39' W x 41'8" D

Levels: 1

Square Footage: 1,092

Bedrooms: 2

Bathrooms: 1

Foundation: Crawl space

CompleteCost List Available: Yes

Price Category: B

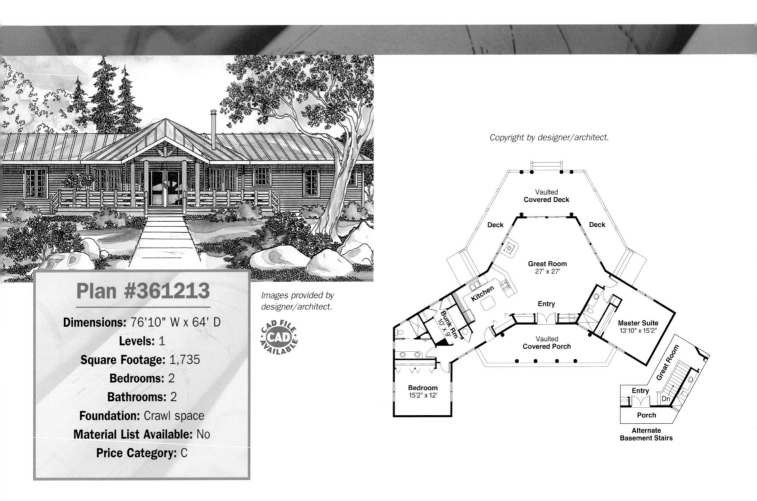

Copyright by designer/architect.

Images provided by designer/architect.

CAD FILE AVAILABLE

Vaulted Covered Deck

Deck

Deck

Great Room
27' x 27'

Kitchen

Bunk Rm
10' x 9'

Entry

Master Suite
13'10" x 15'2"

Vaulted Covered Porch

Great Room

Bedroom
15'2" x 12'

Entry

Dn

Porch

Alternate Basement Stairs

Plan #361213

Dimensions: 76'10" W x 64' D

Levels: 1

Square Footage: 1,735

Bedrooms: 2

Bathrooms: 2

Foundation: Crawl space

Material List Available: No

Price Category: C

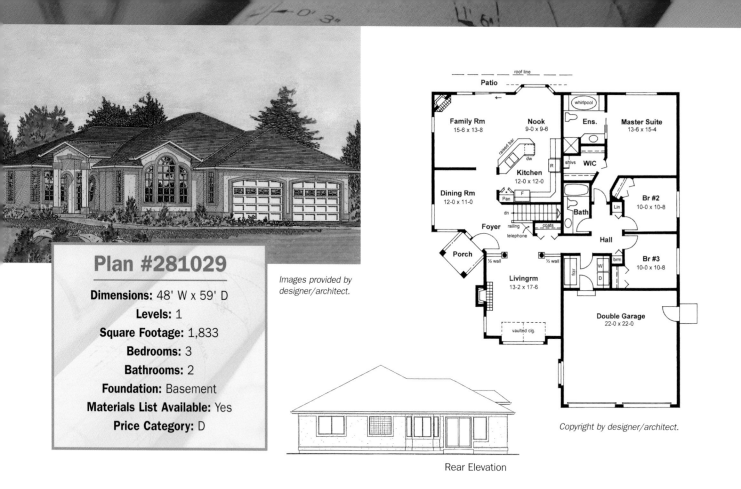

Plan #281029

Dimensions: 48' W x 59' D

Levels: 1

Square Footage: 1,833

Bedrooms: 3

Bathrooms: 2

Foundation: Basement

Materials List Available: Yes

Price Category: D

Images provided by designer/architect.

Copyright by designer/architect.

Rear Elevation

Plan #181013

Dimensions: 44' W x 30' D

Levels: 1

Square Footage: 1,147

Bedrooms: 3

Bathrooms: 1

Foundation: Basement

Material List Available: Yes

Price Category: B

Images provided by designer/architect.

CAD FILE AVAILABLE

Copyright by designer/architect.

Plan #401020

Dimensions: 55'6" W x 30' D

Levels: 1

Square Footage: 1,230

Bedrooms: 3

Bathrooms: 2

Foundation: Basement, crawl space

Materials List Available: Yes

Price Category: B

This is a grand vacation or retirement home, designed for views and the outdoor lifestyle. The full-width deck complements the abundant windows in the rooms that face it.

Features:

- **Living Room:** This area, with a vaulted ceiling, a fireplace, and full-height windows overlooking the deck, is made for gathering.

- **Dining Room:** This room is open to the living room; it has sliding glass doors that lead to the outdoors.

- **Kitchen:** This room has a pass-through counter to the dining room and is U-shaped in design.

- **Bedrooms:** Two family bedrooms in the middle of the plan share a full bath.

- **Master Suite:** This area has a private bath and deck views.

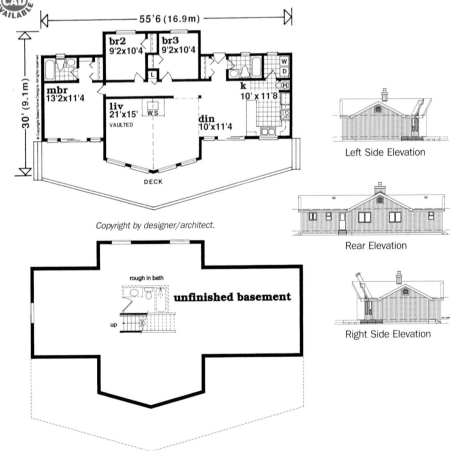

Copyright by designer/architect.

Optional Basement Level Floor Plan

Left Side Elevation

Rear Elevation

Right Side Elevation

Plan #151528

Dimensions: 41'4" W x 84'2" D
Levels: 1
Square Footage: 1,747
Bedrooms: 2
Bathrooms: 2
Foundation: Crawl space or slab
CompleteCost List Available: Yes
Price Category: C

This Craftsman-inspired design combines a rustic exterior with an elegant interior. The 10-ft.-high ceilings and abundance of windows enhance the family areas with plenty of natural lighting.

CAD FILE AVAILABLE

Features:

• Great Room: Featuring a fireplace and built-in computer center, this central gathering area is open to the breakfast room and has access to the rear covered porch.

• Kitchen: This combination kitchen and break fast room enjoys a bar counter for additional seating. Note the large laundry room with pantry, which is located between the kitchen and the garage.

• Master Suite: You'll spend many luxurious hours in this beautiful suite, with its 10-ft.-high boxed ceiling, his and her walk-in closets, and large bath with glass shower, whirlpool tub, and double vanity.

• Bedrooms: On the same side of the home as the master suite are these two other bedrooms, which have large closets and an adjoining bath room between them.

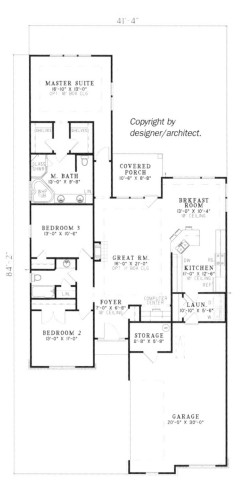

Front View

Plan #321009

Dimensions: 55'8" W x 46'4" D
Levels: 1
Square Footage: 1,684
Opt. Finished Basement Sq. Ft.: 611
Bedrooms: 3
Bathrooms: 2
Foundation: Walkout
Materials List Available: Yes
Price Category: C

Features:

- **Porch:** This wraparound porch is an ideal spot to watch the sun come up or go down. Add potted plants to create a lush atmosphere or grow some culinary herbs.

- **Great Room:** You couldn't ask for more luxury than this room provides, with its vaulted ceiling, large bay window, fireplace, dining balcony, and atrium window wall.

- **Kitchen:** No matter whether you're an avid cook or not, you'll relish the thoughtful design of this room.

- **Master Suite:** This suite is truly a retreat you'll treasure. It has two large walk-in closets for good storage space, and sliding doors that open to an exterior balcony where you can sit out to enjoy the stars. The amenity-filled bath adds to your enjoyment of this suite.

If you've got a site with great views, you'll love this home, which is designed to make the most of them.

CAD FILE AVAILABLE

Rear View

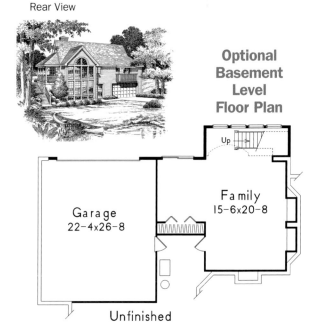

Optional Basement Level Floor Plan

55'-8"

46'-4"

Balcony

MBr 18-4x13-0

Kit 10-2x 11-9

Dining

Dn

Great Rm 16-0x21-4 vaulted

Entry

Br 2 12-8x14-0

Br 3 11-4x12-6

Porch depth 6-0

Copyright by designer/architect.

Up

Garage 22-4x26-8

Family 15-6x20-8

Unfinished

Images provided by designer/architect.

Plan #521017

Dimensions: 94'11" W x 94'10" D
Levels: 1
Square Footage: 2,359
Bedrooms: 3
Bathrooms: 3
Foundation: Slab
Material List Available: No
Price Category: E

This country-style ranch home is ideal for a growing family. The covered front porch houses a window-lined exterior, illustrating to guests how open and welcoming the home is.

Features:

- Living Room: This large space features a fireplace and built-in storage, and it opens onto the large deck, which is perfect for barbecues and soaking up the sun.

- Kitchen: An efficient and convenient design, this L-shaped kitchen includes an island with sinks and a raised bar. It opens into the breakfast room and open dining area and onto the screened porch. The space is ideal for warm indoor meals or fun, insect-free meals outside.

- Master Suite: Lined with windows, this already-spacious area opens up in sunlit comfort. Amenities include a walk-in closet and full master bath, which includes dual sinks, a large standing shower, and an over-sized tub set beneath bay windows.

- Secondary Bedrooms: Both bedrooms include a large closet, access to a full bathroom, and enough space to accommodate any design you can create.

- Garage: This two-car garage includes extra space for storage or hobbies and is far enough from the house for all the hammer strokes and buzzing saws of a busy workshop without disturbing the household.

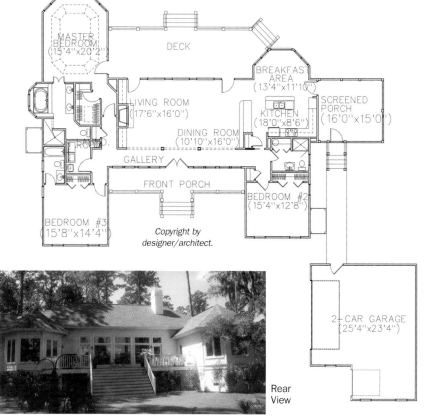

Copyright by designer/architect.

Rear View

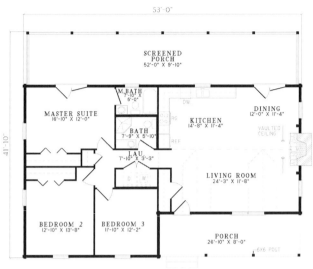

Plan #151797

Dimensions: 53' W x 41'10" D

Levels: 1

Square Footage: 1,480

Bedrooms: 3

Bathrooms: 2

Foundation: Crawl space

CompleteCost List Available: Yes

Price Category: B

Images provided by designer/architect.

Copyright by designer/architect.

Plan #451316

Dimensions: 89'6" W x 61'1" D

Levels: 1

Square Footage: 6,824

Main Level Sq. Ft.: 3,412

Lower Level Sq. Ft.: 3,412

Bedrooms: 3

Bathrooms: 5

Foundation: Walkout

Material List Available: No

Price Category: K

Images provided by designer/architect.

CAD FILE AVAILABLE

Basement Level Floor Plan

Copyright by designer/architect.

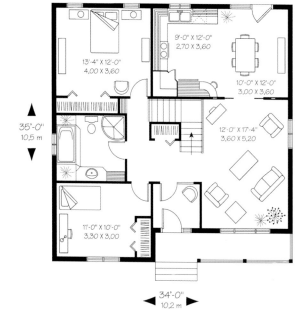

Plan #181012

Dimensions: 34' W x 35' D

Levels: 1

Square Footage: 1,113

Bedrooms: 2

Bathrooms: 1

Foundation: Basement

Materials List Available: Yes

Price Category: B

CAD FILE AVAILABLE

13'-4" X 12'-0"
4,00 X 3,60

9'-0" X 12'-0"
2,70 X 3,60

10'-0" X 12'-0"
3,00 X 3,60

12'-0" X 17'-4"
3,60 X 5,20

11'-0" X 10'-0"
3,30 X 3,00

35'-0"
10,5 m

34'-0"
10,2 m

Plan #611033

Dimensions: 132'3" W x 98'5" D

Levels: 1

Square Footage: 5,449

Bedrooms: 4

Bathrooms: 6½

Foundation: Slab

CompleteCost List Available: Yes

Price Category: I

CAD FILE AVAILABLE

132'-3"

98'-5"

Plan #271285

Dimensions: 54' W x 58' D
Levels: 1
Square Footage: 1,972
Bedrooms: 3
Bathrooms: 2½
Foundation: Crawl space or basement
Material List Available: No
Price Category: D

Images provided by designer/architect.

The Spanish-style exterior has Old-World appeal with its detailed ironwork, overhanging eaves, and textured walls.

Features:

- **Entry:** This dramatic entryway leads to the sunken living room, which adjoins the formal dining room. A gorgeous fireplace warms up the entire space.

- **Kitchen:** This area features a snack bar where stools or high backed chairs will make the space perfect for informal dining.

- **Passive Sunroom:** At the center of this gorgeous, efficiently designed home, is this sun-drenched area that you can use as a year-round garden, greenhouse, or finished sunroom. Built-in thermal storage collects heat that is later released into the main living areas.

- **Master Suite:** This private area contains a well-designed bath and his and her closets.

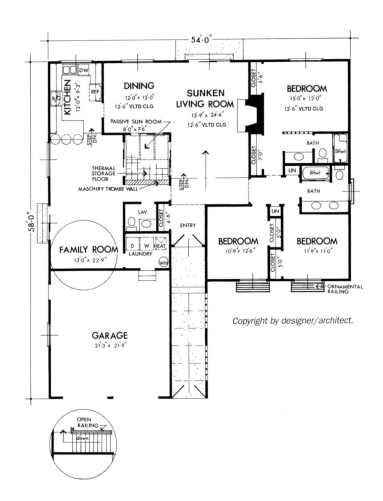

Copyright by designer/architect.

Plan #281018

Dimensions: 50' W x 52'6" D
Levels: 1
Square Footage: 1,565
Bedrooms: 3
Bathrooms: 2
Foundation: Basement
Materials List Available: Yes
Price Category: C

Images provided by designer/architect.

You'll love the arched window that announces the grace of this home to the rest of the world.

Features:

- **Living Room:** Scissor trusses on the ceiling and a superb window design make this room elegant.

- **Dining Room:** Open to the living room, this dining room features an expansive window area and contains a convenient, inset china closet.

- **Family Room:** A gas fireplace in the corner and a doorway to the patio make this room the heart of the house.

- **Breakfast Room:** The bay window here makes it a lovely spot at any time of day.

- **Kitchen:** A raised snack bar shared with both the family and breakfast rooms adds a nice touch to this well-planned, attractive kitchen.

- **Master Suite:** A bay window, walk-in closet, and private bath add up to luxurious comfort in this suite.

Rear Elevation

Left Side Elevation

Right Side Elevation

Copyright by designer/architect.

Plan #151495

Dimensions: 67'2" W x 64'8" D

Levels: 1

Square Footage: 2,121

Bedrooms: 3

Bathrooms: 2

Foundation: Slab

CompleteCost List Available: Yes

Price Category: D

Images provided by designer/architect.

Copyright by designer/architect.

Plan #311058

Dimensions: 55' W x 76'4" D

Levels: 1

Square Footage: 1,702

Bedrooms: 3

Bathrooms: 2

Foundation: Crawl space, slab, or basement

Material List Available: Yes

Price Category: C

Images provided by designer/architect.

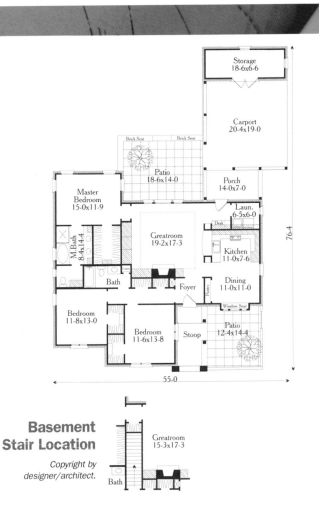

Basement Stair Location

Copyright by designer/architect.

Plan #361030

Dimensions: 92' W x 66' D

Levels: 1

Square Footage: 2,619

Bedrooms: 2

Bathrooms: 2½

Foundation: Crawl space

Material List Available: No

Price Category: F

Images provided by designer/architect.

CAD FILE AVAILABLE

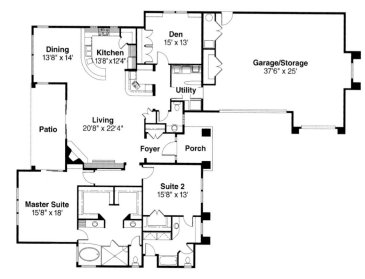

Dining 13'8" x 14'
Kitchen 13'8" x12'4"
Den 15' x 13'
Garage/Storage 37'6" x 25'
Utility
Patio
Living 20'8" x 22'4"
Foyer
Porch
Master Suite 15'8" x 18'
Suite 2 15'8" x 13'

Copyright by designer/architect.

Plan #271079

Dimensions: 104' W x 55' D

Levels: 1

Square Footage: 2,228

Bedrooms: 1-3

Bathrooms: 1½

Foundation: Daylight basement

Materials List Available: No

Price Category: E

Images provided by designer/architect.

CAD FILE AVAILABLE

Copyright by designer/architect.

BAR 11' X 11'
BED RM 10' X 16'
FAMILY RM 21' X 16'
BILLARDS 22' X 18'
STORAGE 8' X 24'
BED RM 13' X 14'
BATH
EXERCISE 13' X 11'
MECH 11' X 11'

Optional Basement Level Floor Plan

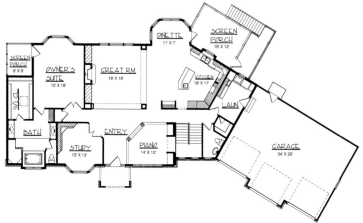

SCREEN PORCH 8' X 9'
OWNER'S SUITE 15' X 19'
GREAT RM 18' X 18'
DINETTE 11' X 7'
SCREEN PORCH 18' X 12'
KITCHEN 19' X 17'
LAUN
BATH
STUDY 13' X 13'
ENTRY
PIANO 14' X 12'
GARAGE 34' X 26'

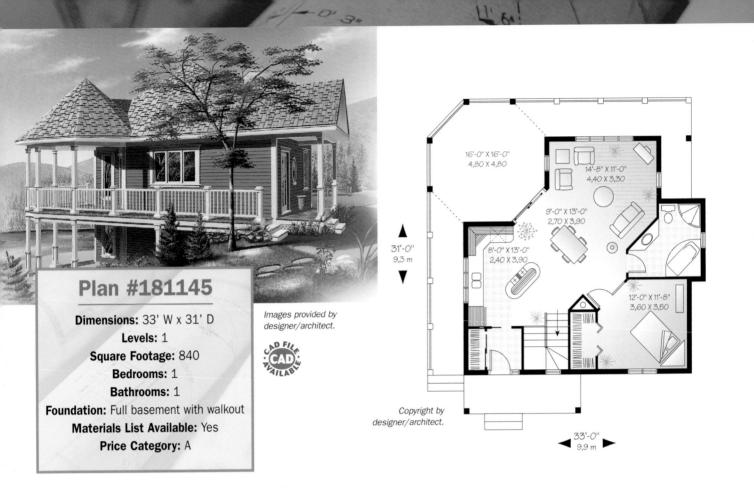

Plan #181145

Dimensions: 33' W x 31' D

Levels: 1

Square Footage: 840

Bedrooms: 1

Bathrooms: 1

Foundation: Full basement with walkout

Materials List Available: Yes

Price Category: A

Images provided by designer/architect.

CAD FILE AVAILABLE

16'-0" X 16'-0"
4,80 X 4,80

14'-8" X 11'-0"
4,40 X 3,30

9'-0" X 13'-0"
2,70 X 3,90

8'-0" X 13'-0"
2,40 X 3,90

12'-0" X 11'-8"
3,60 X 3,50

31'-0"
9,3 m

33'-0"
9,9 m

Copyright by designer/architect.

Plan #361469

Dimensions: 74'6" W x 78'6" D

Levels: 1

Square Footage: 2,261

Bedrooms: 3

Bathrooms: 2½

Foundation: Crawl space

Material List Available: No

Price Category: E

Images provided by designer/architect.

CAD FILE AVAILABLE

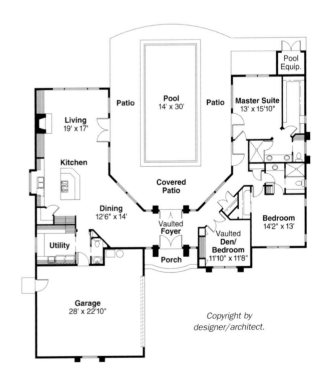

Patio

Pool
14' x 30'

Patio

Pool Equip.

Living
19' x 17'

Master Suite
13' x 15'10"

Kitchen

Covered Patio

Dining
12'6" x 14'

Bedroom
14'2" x 13'

Vaulted Foyer

Utility

Vaulted Den/Bedroom
11'10" x 11'8"

Porch

Garage
28' x 22'10"

Copyright by designer/architect.

Plan #361470

Dimensions: 68' W x 60' D

Levels: 1

Square Footage: 2,313

Bedrooms: 3

Bathrooms: 2

Foundation: Crawl space

Material List Available: No

Price Category: E

Images provided by designer/architect.

Copyright by designer/architect.

Plan #361258

Dimensions: 96'6" W x 67'9" D

Levels: 1

Square Footage: 2,714

Bedrooms: 4

Bathrooms: 2½

Foundation: Crawl space

Material List Available: No

Price Category: F

Images provided by designer/architect.

Copyright by designer/architect.

Images provided by designer/architect.

Plan #111013

Dimensions: 33' W x 59' D

Levels: 1

Square Footage: 1,606

Bedrooms: 3

Bathrooms: 2

Foundation: Slab

Materials List Available: No

Price Category: D

This is the home you have been looking for to fit on that narrow building lot.

Features:

- **Living Room:** Entering this home from the front porch, you arrive in this gathering area. The corner fireplace adds warmth and charm to the area.

- **Kitchen:** This island kitchen features two built-in pantries and is open to the breakfast room. The oversize laundry room is close by and has room for the large items the kitchen needs to store.

- **Master Suite:** Located toward the rear of the home to give some extra privacy, this suite boasts a large sleeping area. The master bath has amenities such as his and her walk-in closets, dual vanities, and a whirlpool tub.

- **Rear Porch:** Just off the breakfast room is this covered rear porch with storage area. On nice days you can sit outside in the shaded area and watch the kids play outside.

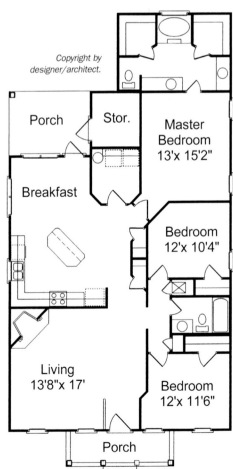

Copyright by designer/architect.

Porch

Stor.

Master Bedroom
13'x 15'2"

Breakfast

Bedroom
12'x 10'4"

Living
13'8"x 17'

Bedroom
12'x 11'6"

Porch

Plan #191012

Dimensions: 60' W x 76' D

Levels: 1

Square Footage: 2,123

Bedrooms: 3

Bathrooms: 2½

Foundation: Crawl space or slab

Materials List Available: No

Price Category: D

Images provided by designer/architect.

The wraparound porch adds to the charm of this home.

Features:

- Porches: The front wraparound porch will be the perfect spot to greet neighbors as they stroll by. The rear porch is a private place to relax and enjoy a beautiful day.

- Great Room: This large gathering area features a 10-ft.-high ceiling and large windows, which offer a view of the backyard. There is even room for a formal dining table.

- Master Suite: Located on the opposite side of the home from the secondary bedrooms, this retreat offers a large sleeping area. The master bath will pamper you with an oversize shower, a tub, and dual vanities.

- Secondary Bedrooms: Two similarly sized bedrooms have ample closet space and share a full bathroom.

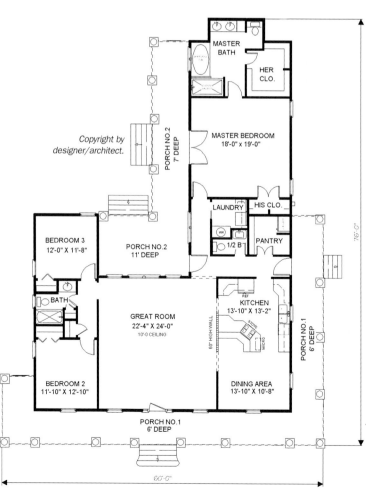

Copyright by designer/architect.

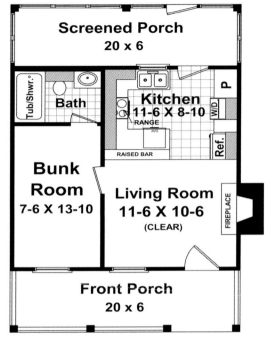

CAD FILE AVAILABLE

Rear View

Plan #351091

Dimensions: 22' W x 32' D

Levels: 1

Square Footage: 400

Bedrooms: 1

Bathrooms: 1

Foundation: Crawl space or slab

Material List Available: Yes

Price Category: B

Screened Porch
20 x 6

Tub/Shwr.

Bath

Kitchen
11-6 X 8-10

RANGE

RAISED BAR

W/D

P

Ref.

Bunk
Room
7-6 X 13-10

Living Room
11-6 X 10-6
(CLEAR)

FIREPLACE

Front Porch
20 x 6

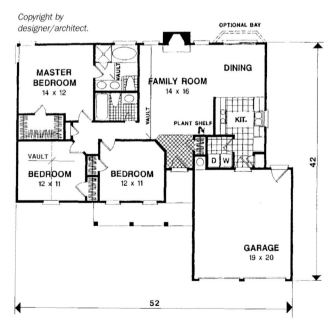

Plan #101023

Dimensions: 52' W x 42' D

Levels: 1

Square Footage: 1,197

Bedrooms: 3

Bathrooms: 2

Foundation: Crawl space, slab

Materials List Available: No

Price Category: B

CAD FILE AVAILABLE

OPTIONAL BAY

MASTER
BEDROOM
14 x 12

VAULT

FAMILY ROOM
14 x 16

DINING

VAULT

PLANT SHELF

KIT.

VAULT

BEDROOM
12 x 11

BEDROOM
12 x 11

D

W

GARAGE
19 x 20

42

52

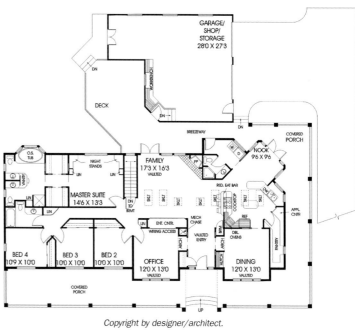

Plan #501497

Dimensions: 76' W x 69" D

Levels: 1

Square Footage: 2,415

Bedrooms: 4

Bathrooms: 3

Foundation: Basement

Material List Available: No

Price Category: E

Images provided by designer/architect.

Copyright by designer/architect.

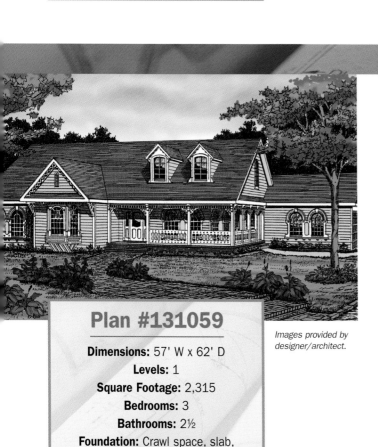

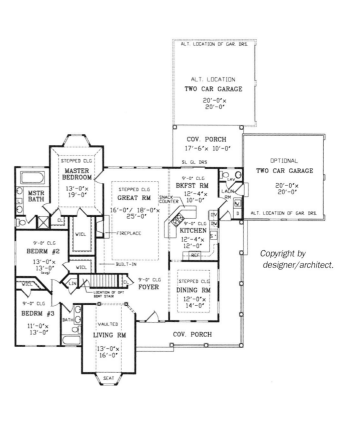

Plan #131059

Dimensions: 57' W x 62' D

Levels: 1

Square Footage: 2,315

Bedrooms: 3

Bathrooms: 2½

Foundation: Crawl space, slab, or basement

Material List Available: Yes

Price Category: F

Images provided by designer/architect.

Copyright by designer/architect.

Plan #151490

Dimensions: 52' W x 69'6" D

Levels: 1

Square Footage: 1,869

Bedrooms: 3

Bathrooms: 2

Foundation: Crawl space or slab

CompleteCost List Available: Yes

Price Category: D

Images provided by designer/architect.

CAD FILE AVAILABLE

Bonus Area Floor Plan

BONUS ROOM 12'-10" X 20'-4"

Copyright by designer/architect.

Plan #151360

Dimensions: 39' W x 72' D

Levels: 1

Square Footage: 1,915

Bedrooms: 3

Bathrooms: 2

Foundation: Crawl space or slab

CompleteCost List Available: Yes

Price Category: D

Images provided by designer/architect.

CAD FILE AVAILABLE

Copyright by designer/architect.

Plan #161116

Dimensions: 52'8" W x 45' D

Levels: 1

Square Footage: 1,442

Bedrooms: 3

Bathrooms: 2

Foundation: Basement

Material List Available: Yes

Price Category: B

Images provided by designer/architect.

Deck

Master Bedroom 12'7" x 13' 8' CTR. CLG. HT

Great Room 18'8" x 14'

CLOSET HIGH FLOOR

Bedroom 11'4" x 10'8"

Bath

Bath

Laun.

WALK IN CLOSET

Dining 18'8" x 10'

LIN.

Bedroom 12'4" x 10'10"

WALK IN CLOSET

Two Car Garage 19'10" x 24'8"

Kitchen 11'7 x 10'4"

Foyer

CLOS

Porch

SEAT

Copyright by designer/architect.

Rear Elevation

Plan #151333

Dimensions: 43' W x 63'6" D

Levels: 1

Square Footage: 1,387

Bedrooms: 2

Bathrooms: 2

Foundation: Crawl space or slab

CompleteCost List Available: Yes

Price Category: B

Images provided by designer/architect.

CAD FILE AVAILABLE

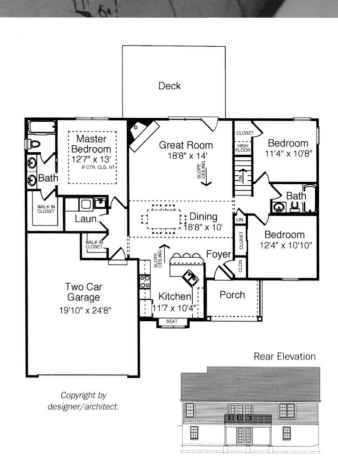

43' 0"

COVERED PORCH 17'-2" X 6'-4"

DINING RM. 12'-0" X 11'-2"

MASTER SUITE 12'-10" X 14'-8"

GREAT ROOM 16'-10" X 15'-5"

KITCHEN 12'-0" X 13'-0"

FOYER 8'-8" X 6'-8"

63'-6"

M. BATH 9'-0" X 13'-4"

LAU. 9'-1" X 6'-3"

PORCH 8'-0" X 6'-2"

GOLF CART

BEDROOM 2 12'-0" X 11'-4"

GARAGE 19'-4" X 26'-10"

Copyright by designer/architect.

Plan #151638

Dimensions: 66' W x 63'8"D
Levels: 1
Square Footage: 2,246
Bedrooms: 4
Bathrooms: 2
Foundation: Crawl space or slab
CompleteCost List Available: Yes
Price Category: E

This charming, traditional home is perfect for the growing family, with plenty of amenities for children and adults alike.

Features:

- **Outdoor Space:** This large front porch allows you to sit out on warm summer nights, talking to passersby. The rear grilling porch, with access from the master suite and the great room, provides a relaxing retreat or an extra entertainment area.

- **Kitchen:** Here, the family chef has all he needs to create anything from macaroni and cheese to filet mignon. There are three dining possibilities – the adjacent snack bar, the formal dining room, and the sunny breakfast room.

- **Master Suite:** This master suite has enough space for something extra, like an entertainment or sitting area. The full bath features his and her vanities, a whirlpool tub, large glass shower, and a sizeable walk-in closet.

- **Secondary Bedrooms:** These two additional bedrooms have ample closet space and access to a semiprivate full bathroom. Need another bedroom? Convert the spacious study into a fourth.

Copyright by designer/architect.

Plan #351093

Dimensions: 30' W x 32' D

Levels: 1

Square Footage: 600

Bedrooms: 1

Bathrooms: 1

Foundation: Crawl space or slab

Material List Available: Yes

Price Category: B

CAD FILE AVAILABLE

This home was designed as a weekend getaway spot. It's perfect for the woods, the lake, or the beach.

Features:

- Porches: Relax and enjoy the day on either the front or rear porch. Invite a neighbor over to enjoy a glass of lemonade.

- Living Room: Enter from the front porch and arrive in this gathering area. A coat closet is located near the front door.

- Kitchen: Compact in size, but large on functionality, this kitchen has everything you need to prepare meals and snacks. A raised bar open to the living room adds extra seating.

- Storage: This expansive 12 x 30-ft. storage space is ideal for stowing all the stuff your family has accumulated.

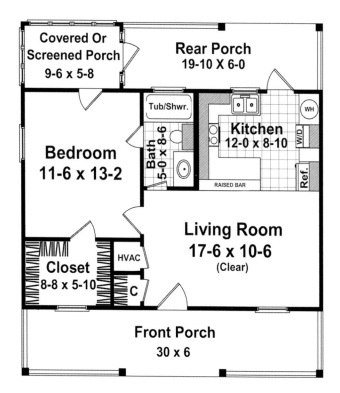

Covered Or Screened Porch
9-6 x 5-8

Rear Porch
19-10 X 6-0

Tub/Shwr.

Kitchen
12-0 x 8-10

WH

Bath
5-0 x 8-6

W/D

Bedroom
11-6 x 13-2

RAISED BAR

Ref.

Closet
8-8 x 5-10

HVAC

C

Living Room
17-6 x 10-6
(Clear)

Front Porch
30 x 6

Plan #121163

Dimensions: 65'10" W x 75'6" D
Levels: 1
Square Footage: 2,679
Bedrooms: 4
Bathrooms: 3
Foundation: Slab; basement for fee
Material List Available: Yes
Price Category: F

Large rooms give this home a spacious feel in a modest footprint.

Features:

- **Family Room:** This area is the central gathering place in the home. The windows to the rear fill the area with natural light. The fireplace take the chill off on cool winter nights.

- **Kitchen:** This peninsula kitchen with raised bar is open into the family room and the breakfast area. The built-in pantry is a welcomed storage area for today's family.

- **Master Suite:** This secluded area features large windows with a view of the backyard. The master bath boasts a large walk-in closet, his and her vanities and a compartmentalized lavatory area.

- **Secondary Bedrooms:** Bedroom 2 has its own access to the main bathroom, while bedrooms 3 and 4 share a Jack-and-Jill bathroom. All bedrooms feature walk-in closets.

Images provided by designer/architect.

Copyright by designer/architect.

Plan #181218

Dimensions: 38' W x 28'8" D

Levels: 1

Square Footage: 946

Bedrooms: 2

Bathrooms: 1

Foundation: Basement

Materials List Available: Yes

Price Category: A

With a showcase front porch trimmed by quaint railings and carved brackets, this design uses all of its space beautifully and practically.

Features:

- **Living room:** This company-loving room waits just inside the entrance.

- **Kitchen:** This creative U-shaped kitchen has a bounty of counter and cabinet space as well as a breakfast counter that stretches into the dining area and doubles as a serving board.

- **Utility Areas:** The full bathroom is paired with the laundry area, and a side door near the kitchen leads to a smaller covered porch.

- **Bedrooms:** Two spacious bedrooms sit comfortably beside each other.

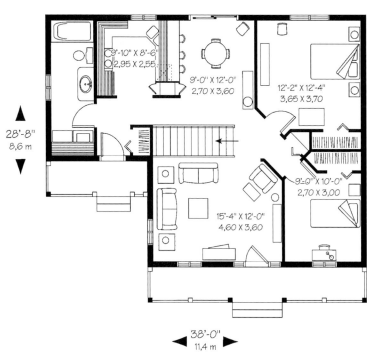

Plan #181308

Dimensions: 50'4" W x 48' D

Levels: 1

Square Footage: 2,161

Bedrooms: 3

Bathrooms: 2

Foundation: Basement

Materials List Available: Yes

Price Category: D

Images provided by designer/architect.

This charming home will draw the warm affection of its occupants, guests, and neighbors alike.

Features:

- **Great Room:** This area will always be warmly lit, either by the glowing fireplace or the bright windows lining the walls. Two doors open into the backyard for easy access to the outdoors on a beautiful day.

- **Dining Room:** This area is adjacent to the kitchen, yet separate from it to retain a sense of formality and leave the messy part of the meal behind the scenes.

- **Kitchen:** Featuring ample workspace and storage, as well as an island and snack bar, this kitchen is also close to the dining room for simple transitions from meal preparation to dining.

- **Master Suite:** With room enough for both an entertainment and a sitting area, this master bedroom will be your own retreat. The full bath features a walk-in closet, his and her vanities, large tub, and a separate stall shower.

- **Secondary Bedrooms:** Both additional bedrooms include ample closet space and room for a sitting area. The second bedroom also has a workspace.

Copyright by designer/architect.

Plan #211155

Dimensions: 96'6" W x 43' D
Levels: 1
Square Footage: 2,719
Bedrooms: 4
Bathrooms: 2½
Foundation: Slab; crawl space for fee
Material List Available: Yes
Price Category: F

Clean lines and a well-designed layout create the relaxed, easy-living atmosphere of this ranch-style home.

Images provided by designer/architect.

Features:

- Entry: An inviting front porch with attractive columns and planter boxes opens to this airy entry.

- Family Room: This huge central family room features a 14-ft.-high vaulted exposed-beam ceiling and a handsome fireplace with a built-in wood box. A nice desk and plenty of bookshelves give the room a distinguished feel.

- Kitchen: A distinguished arched brick opening connects this kitchen to the family room. Double doors open to the intimate formal dining room, which includes a built-in china hutch.

- Bedrooms: The isolated sleeping wing includes four bedrooms. The enormous master suite has a giant walk-in closet and a private bath. A compartmentalized bath with two vanities serves the remaining bedrooms.

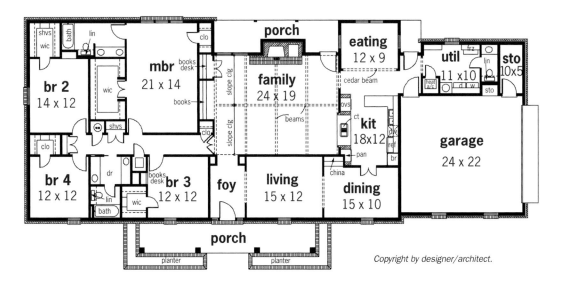

Copyright by designer/architect.

Plan #241033

Dimensions: 56'1" W x 52'1" D

Levels: 1

Square Footage: 1,684

Bedrooms: 3

Bathrooms: 2

Foundation: Slab

Materials List Available: No

Price Category: C

This charming country home features beautiful stonework and roof dormers that add character to the exterior of the home.

Features:

• Great Room: This room is large and efficiently located near the kitchen for a pleasant effect. A fireplace and large windows create romance and ambience.

• Dining Room: Experience formal dining and entertaining in this centrally located room.

• Kitchen: Featuring an eating bar, an island, and a sunny breakfast nook, this room is sure to be a place where family congregates over a light meal or cooks for enjoyment. A full pantry and utility room make the room functional, and the unique design adds flair.

• Master Suite: Enjoy the luxury of dual vanities, a separate shower, a tub, and a walk-in closet in this spacious area.

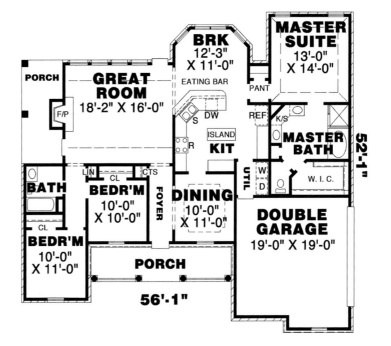

Plan #181310

Dimensions: 32'8" W x 42' D

Levels: 1

Square Footage: 1,094

Bedrooms: 2

Bathrooms: 1

Foundation: Basement

Materials List Available: Yes

Price Category: B

Images provided by designer/architect.

This home is uncomplicated and charismatic, both inside and out.

Features:

- **Great Room:** Welcome guests into your home to gather by the warm light of the fireplace, or enjoy watching your favorite program with the family.

- **Kitchen:** The open design of this kitchen and adjacent dining area provide the family chef with plenty of elbow room for preparing meals.

- **Master Bedroom:** With plenty of room to spare, this space will be your personal retreat. It features a sitting area and a walk-in closet. Adjacent is a full bathroom with a large tub and separate standing shower.

- **Second Bedroom:** Ample closet space and the adjacent full bathroom provide this bedroom's inhabitant with everything he or she needs to feel at home.

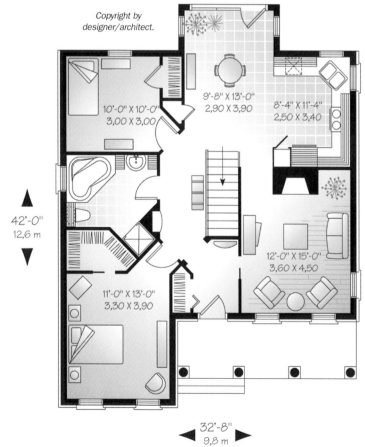

Copyright by designer/architect.

10'-0" X 10'-0"
3,00 X 3,00

9'-8" X 13'-0"
2,90 X 3,90

8'-4" X 11'-4"
2,50 X 3,40

12'-0" X 15'-0"
3,60 X 4,50

11'-0" X 13'-0"
3,30 X 3,90

42'-0"
12,6 m

32'-8"
9,8 m

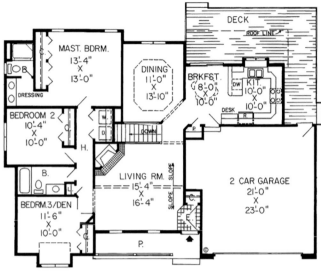

Plan #391211

Dimensions: 58' W x 40' D

Levels: 1

Square Footage: 1,461

Bedrooms: 3

Bathrooms: 2

Foundation: Basement

Material List Available: Yes

Price Category: B

Images provided by designer/architect.

Copyright by designer/architect.

Plan #621006

Dimensions: 89'4" W x 54' D

Levels: 1

Square Footage: 2,619

Bedrooms: 3

Bathrooms: 3

Foundation: Slab

Material List Available: No

Price Category: F

Images provided by designer/architect.

CAD FILE AVAILABLE

Copyright by designer/architect.

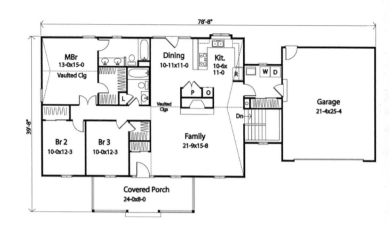

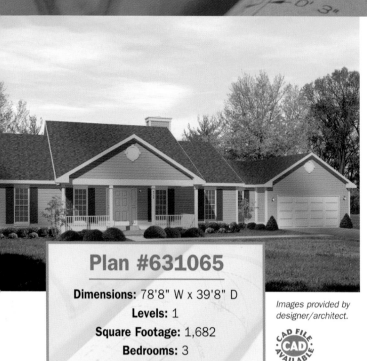

Plan #631065

Dimensions: 78'8" W x 39'8" D

Levels: 1

Square Footage: 1,682

Bedrooms: 3

Bathrooms: 2

Foundation: Basement

Material List Available: Yes

Price Category: C

Images provided by designer/architect.

CAD FILE AVAILABLE

Copyright by designer/architect.

Rear Elevation

Plan #351203

Dimensions: 73'6" W x 62' D

Levels: 1

Square Footage: 2,447

Bedrooms: 4

Bathrooms: 2½

Foundation: Basement

Material List Available: Yes

Price Category: E

Images provided by designer/architect.

CAD FILE AVAILABLE

Copyright by designer/architect.

Rear Elevation

Bonus Level Plan

Plan #521040

Dimensions: 42'2" W x 57' D
Levels: 1
Square Footage: 1,555
Bedrooms: 3
Bathrooms: 2½
Foundation: Slab
Material List Available: No
Price Category: C

Beautifully and intelligently designed, this house has everything you want and everything you need.

CAD FILE AVAILABLE

Features:

- **Porches:** The front porch provides a covered entry while still being open to the sights and sounds of the outdoors, ideal for sitting outside on a lovely evening. On the opposite end of the house is a screened-in porch that opens into the master suite, the living room, and the deck. It is perfect for keeping out unwanted pests and bringing in the breeze. Next to that is the deck, great for soaking up the sun and barbecuing.

- **Living Room:** With light from the dining-area windows and the deck and warmth from the fireplace, this room can become anything you want it to be: warm and cozy or light and airy.

- **Kitchen:** This working area has a walk-in pantry and plenty of workspace and storage, and it opens freely into the dining room. As the busiest part of any home, the kitchen is perfect for gatherings or simple family dinners, making the transition between preparing and serving simple.

- **Master Suite:** A spacious full bath, a large walk-in closet, and a direct entrance to the screened porch make this the ideal place to rest and relax. It is truly a master's bedroom.

- **Bedrooms:** The secondary bedrooms each have their highlights. Bedroom No. 2 has a wide closet and lots of light from its three extended windows while being a short distance from the second full bathroom. Bedroom No. 3 has a direct connection with the bathroom and a small walk-in closet. Both are also a short distance from the large laundry room.

Copyright by designer/architect.

Front View

This home, as shown in the photographs, may differ from the actual blueprints. For more detailed information, please check the floor plans carefully.

Rear View

Plan #341096

Dimensions: 50'6" W x 31'2"D

Levels: 1

Square Footage: 1,447

Bedrooms: 3

Bathrooms: 2

Foundation: Crawl space, slab, basement, or walkout

Material List Available: No

Price Category: B

The perfect-size plan and a pretty facade add up to a great home for your family.

Features:

- Family Room: This casual gathering area boasts a corner fireplace and a vaulted ceiling. The open layout allows friends and family to flow among the family room, kitchen, and breakfast nook.

- Dining Room: Located off of the entry, this formal dining area features a serving counter with cabinets above.

- Office: This large home office will make working at home feel easy. Its private entrance will allow clients to come and go without disturbing the family.

- Master Suite: You'll be close to your family, but in a world of your own, in this master suite. The design simplifies your life with a walk-in closet, his and her sinks, and a stall shower.

Images provided by designer/architect.

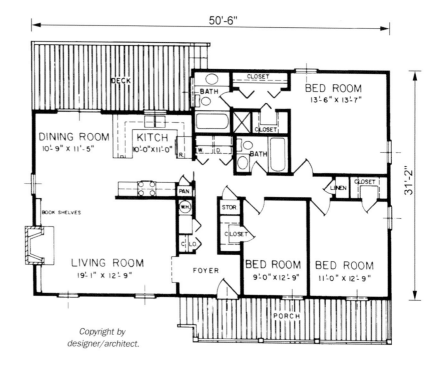

Copyright by designer/architect.

Plan #351116

Dimensions: 50' W x 86' D
Levels: 1
Square Footage: 2,050
Bedrooms: 3
Bathrooms: 2
Foundation: Crawl space or slab
Material List Available: Yes
Price Category: F

Images provided by designer/architect.

This Southern-style design will welcome you with old-fashioned down-home hospitality.

Features:

- **Great Room:** The spacious foyer leads directly into this room, which visually opens to the rear yard, providing natural light and outdoor charm.

- **Kitchen:** This kitchen maximizes space and efficiency with simple transitions and plenty of workspace. The laundry room is adjacent for easy cleanup.

- **Master Suite:** Look for luxurious amenities, such as double sinks, a walk-in closet, and a separate tub and shower, in the master bath. The master bedroom has a stepped ceiling and a walk-in closet.

- **Bedroom:** Two secondary bedrooms complete this design. They share a full bathroom. Bedroom 3 boasts a walk-in closet.

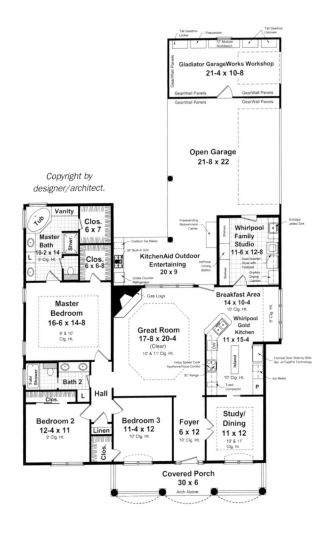

Copyright by designer/architect.

Plan #211062

Dimensions: 96'6" W x 43' D

Levels: 1

Square Footage: 2,719

Bedrooms: 4

Bathrooms: 2½

Foundation: Slab

Materials List Available: Yes

Price Category: F

Images provided by designer/architect.

If you're looking for a beautiful home that combines luxurious amenities with a separate, professional office space, this could be the one.

Features:

- **Living Room:** Enjoy an 11-ft. ceiling, brick fireplace, and built-in shelving in this room.

- **Dining Room:** A 2-story ceiling gives presence to this room.

- **Kitchen:** A breakfast bar here is open to the breakfast room beyond for ease of serving.

- **Breakfast Room:** A built-in corner china closet adds to the practicality you'll find here.

- **Office:** A separate entrance makes it possible to run a professional business from this home.

- **Master Suite:** Separated for privacy, this suite includes two vanities and a walk-in closet.

- **Porch:** The rear screened porch opens to a courtyard where you'll love to entertain.

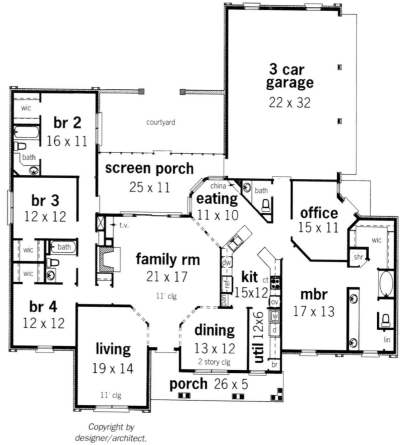

Copyright by designer/architect.

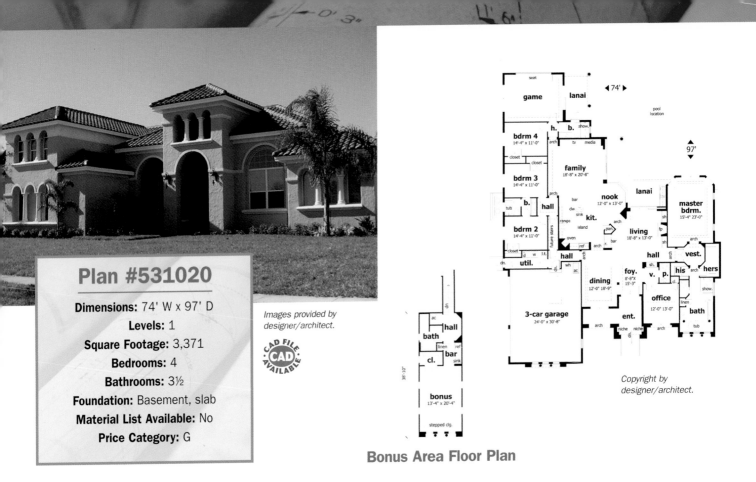

Plan #531020

Dimensions: 74' W x 97' D

Levels: 1

Square Footage: 3,371

Bedrooms: 4

Bathrooms: 3½

Foundation: Basement, slab

Material List Available: No

Price Category: G

Images provided by designer/architect.

CAD FILE AVAILABLE

Copyright by designer/architect.

Bonus Area Floor Plan

Plan #191004

Dimensions: 58' W x 68' D

Levels: 1

Square Footage: 1,856

Bedrooms: 3

Bathrooms: 3

Foundation: Crawl space

Material List Available: No

Price Category: D

Images provided by designer/architect.

Copyright by designer/architect.

Dining Room

Kitchen

Plan #241015

Dimensions: 67'2" W x 46'10" D

Levels: 1

Square Footage: 1,609

Bedrooms: 3

Bathrooms: 2

Foundation: Slab

Materials List Available: No

Price Category: C

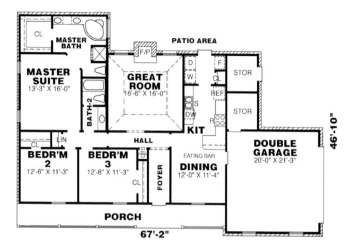

Images provided by designer/architect.

Copyright by designer/architect.

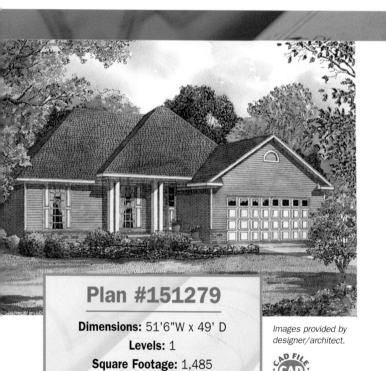

Plan #151279

Dimensions: 51'6"W x 49' D

Levels: 1

Square Footage: 1,485

Bedrooms: 3

Bathrooms: 2

Foundation: Basement, crawl space, slab, or walkout

CompleteCost List Available: Yes

Price Category: B

Images provided by designer/architect.

Copyright by designer/architect.

Rear Porch
16-0 x 8-0

Bedroom 3
12-6 x 11-0
(Clear)
9-0 CLG. HT.

Eating Area
10-0 x 11-10
9-0 CLG. HT.

Kitchen
9-8 x 11-10

Master
Bedroom
11-8 x 14-6
(Clear)
9-0 CLG. HT.

Closet

Mstr. Bath
9-6 x 9-10

Jet Tub

Shwr.

Clos.

Bath 2

Hall

Laun.
6-8 x 5-6

Closet

Clos.

Great Room
17-2 x 18-6
10-0 CLG. HT.

Fireplace

Hall

Bedroom 2
12-6 x 11-0
9-0 CLG. HT.

Built-in

Bath 3

Bedroom 4
12-0 x 11-8
9-0 CLG. HT.

Tub/Shower

Covered Porch
20-0 x 6-0

Two Car
Garage
21-6 x 23-0

Images provided by designer/architect.

Copyright by designer/architect.

Plan #351099

Dimensions: 55' W x 64'4" D

Levels: 1

Square Footage: 1,750

Bedrooms: 4

Bathrooms: 3

Foundation: Crawl space or slab

Material List Available: Yes

Price Category: D

Dining
or Sunroom
12 x 18-6
9' Ceiling

Rear
Porch
7 x 14-2

Patio
14-8 x 14-2

Bedroom 2
11-6 x 13
9' Ceiling

Laun.
5 x 6-6

Raised Bar

9' Ceiling

10' Ceiling

Master
Bedroom
15-10 x 12-6

Jet Tub

Bath

Clos.

Kitchen
12 x 12

Bath

Clos.

Clos.

Shwr.

Coat

Raised Bar

Entry

Storage
8-8 x 4-2

Hall

Great
Room
17-6 x 15
(Clear)

VAULT

Gas Logs

Bedroom 3
11-6 x 13
9' Ceiling

VAULT

Two Car Garage
21-4 x 21-4
(Clear)

Front Porch
17-6 x 5-0

Images provided by designer/architect.

Copyright by designer/architect.

Plan #351097

Dimensions: 51'8" W x 59' D

Levels: 1

Square Footage: 1,610

Bedrooms: 3

Bathrooms: 2

Foundation: Crawl space or slab

Material List Available: Yes

Price Category: D

Plan #371007

Dimensions: 72'10" W x 48'4½" D

Levels: 1

Square Footage: 1,944

Bedrooms: 4

Bathrooms: 2

Foundation: Slab;
crawl space option available for fee

Materials List Available: No

Price Category: D

*Images provided by
designer/architect.*

Copyright by designer/architect.

Plan #391060

Dimensions: 58' W x 34'4" D

Levels: 1

Square Footage: 1,359

Bedrooms: 3

Bathrooms: 2

Foundation: Crawl space, slab
or basement

Materials List Available: Yes

Price Category: B

*Images provided by
designer/architect.*

Rear View

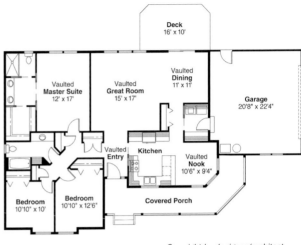

Plan #361448

Dimensions: 68' W x 40' D

Levels: 1

Square Footage: 1,634

Bedrooms: 3

Bathrooms: 2

Foundation: Crawl space or basement

Material List Available: No

Price Category: C

Images provided by designer/architect.

Copyright by designer/architect.

Plan #321121

Dimensions: 30' W x 44' D

Levels: 1

Square Footage: 1,320

Bedrooms: 3

Bathrooms: 2

Foundation: Crawl space

Material List Available: Yes

Price Category: B

Images provided by designer/architect.

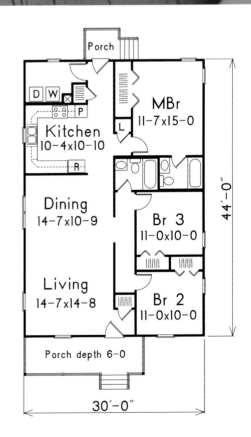

Copyright by designer/architect.

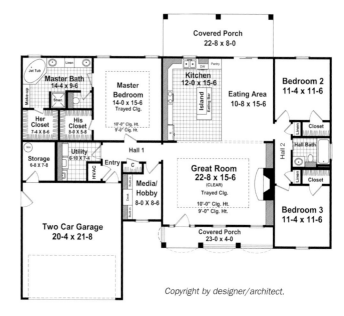

Covered Porch
22-8 x 8-0

Jet Tub

Master Bath
14-4 x 9-6

Make-up

Shwr.

Her
Closet
7-4 X 8-6

His
Closet
8-0 X 5-8

Master
Bedroom
14-0 x 15-6
Trayed Clg.

10'-0" Clg. Ht.
9'-0" Clg. Ht.

Kitchen
12-0 x 15-6

Island

Eating Bar

Pantry

DW

Eating Area
10-8 x 15-6

Bedroom 2
11-4 x 11-6

Linen
Closet

Hall Bath

Hall 2

Linen
Closet

Storage
6-8 X 7-8

Utility
6-10 X 7-4

HVAC

Entry

C

Hall 1

Media/
Hobby
8-0 X 8-6

Great Room
22-8 x 15-6
(CLEAR)
Trayed Clg.

10'-0" Clg. Ht.
9'-0" Clg. Ht.

Bedroom 3
11-4 x 11-6

Two Car Garage
20-4 x 21-8

Covered Porch
23-0 x 4-0

*Images provided by
designer/architect.*

Copyright by designer/architect.

Plan #351101

Dimensions: 64' W x 53'10" D

Levels: 1

Square Footage: 1,865

Bedrooms: 3

Bathrooms: 2

Foundation: Crawl space or slab

Material List Available: Yes

Price Category: E

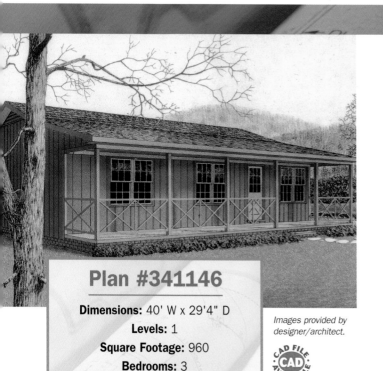

Plan #341146

Dimensions: 40' W x 29'4" D

Levels: 1

Square Footage: 960

Bedrooms: 3

Bathrooms: 2

Foundation: Crawl space, slab, basement, or walkout

Material List Available: No

Price Category: A

*Images provided by
designer/architect.*

STOOP

DINING

D

W

BATH

LIN

W.H.

KITCHEN
15'-0" X 11'-4"

R

BATH

BEDROOM
9'-4" X 9'-0"

COATS

CLOSET

CLOSET

BEDROOM
12'-0" X 11'-4"

CLOS.

LIVING ROOM
14'-6" X 11'-4"

BEDROOM
9'-4" X 9'-0"

PORCH

29'-4"

40'-0"

Copyright by designer/architect.

Plan #151529

Dimensions: 43' W x 66'6" D

Levels: 1

Square Footage: 1,474

Bedrooms: 2

Bathrooms: 2

Foundation: Crawl space or slab

CompleteCost List Available: Yes

Price Category: B

Images provided by designer/architect.

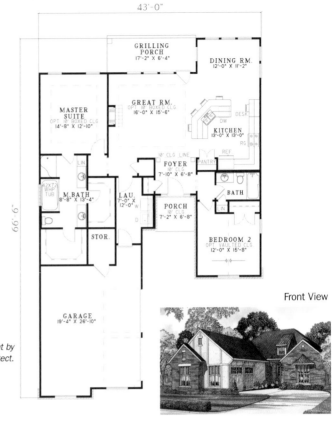

Copyright by designer/architect.

Front View

Plan #371009

Dimensions: 51'5½" W x 52' D

Levels: 1

Square Footage: 1,223

Bedrooms: 3

Bathrooms: 2

Foundation: Slab

Materials List Available: No

Price Category: B

Images provided by designer/architect.

Copyright by designer/architect.

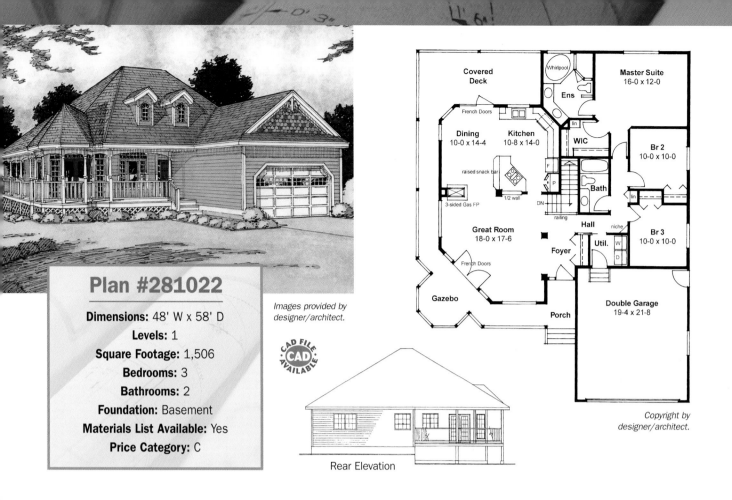

Covered Deck

Whirlpool

Master Suite
16-0 x 12-0

Ens

French Doors

Dining
10-0 x 14-4

Kitchen
10-8 x 14-0

WIC

Br 2
10-0 x 10-0

lin

raised snack bar

1/2 wall

F

Bath

lin

3-sided Gas FP

P

DN

railing

niche

Br 3
10-0 x 10-0

Great Room
18-0 x 17-6

Hall

Util.

W
D

French Doors

Foyer

Gazebo

Porch

Double Garage
19-4 x 21-8

Images provided by designer/architect.

CAD FILE AVAILABLE

Rear Elevation

Copyright by designer/architect.

Plan #281022

Dimensions: 48' W x 58' D

Levels: 1

Square Footage: 1,506

Bedrooms: 3

Bathrooms: 2

Foundation: Basement

Materials List Available: Yes

Price Category: C

PORCH

DINING
11/2 X 12/8
9' CLG.

VAULTED
MASTER
12/8 X 15/2

VAULTED
GREAT RM.
16/8 X 17/0

SHELVES

BUILT-INS

11/4 X 12/10

REF

MEDIA

GARAGE
20/6 X 21/0

48'

FOYER
10' CLG.

BR. 3/
DEN
10/6 X 11/4
9' CLG.

BR. 2
11/0 X 10/0
9' CLG.

PORCH

50'

Images provided by designer/architect.

CAD FILE AVAILABLE

Rear Elevation

Copyright by designer/architect.

Plan #441003

Dimensions: 50' W x 48' D

Levels: 1

Square Footage: 1,580

Bedrooms: 3

Bathrooms: 2½

Foundation: Crawl space; slab or basement available for fee

Materials List Available: No

Price Category: C

Plan #441015

Dimensions: 130'3" W x 79'3" D
Levels: 1
Square Footage: 4,732
Main Level Sq. Ft.: 2,902
Lower Level Sq. Ft.: 1,830
Bedrooms: 4
Bathrooms: 3 full, 2 half
Foundation: Walkout basement
Materials List Available: No
Price Category: I

An artful use of stone was employed on the exterior of this rustic hillside home to complement other architectural elements, such as the angled, oversize four-car garage and the substantial roofline.

CAD FILE AVAILABLE · CAD

Features:

- **Great Room:** This massive vaulted room features a large stone fireplace at one end and a formal dining area at the other. A built-in media center and double doors separate the great room from a home office with its own hearth and built-ins.

- **Kitchen:** This kitchen features a walk-in pantry and snack counter and opens to a skylighted outdoor kitchen. Its appointments include a cooktop and a corner fireplace.

- **Home Theatre:** This space has a built-in viewing screen, a fireplace, and double terrace access.

- **Master Suite:** This private space is found at the other side of the home. Look closely for

expansive his and her walk-in closets, a spa tub, a skylighted double vanity area, and a corner fireplace in the salon.

- **Bedrooms:** Three family bedrooms are on the lower level; bedroom 4 has a private bathroom and walk-in closet.

- **Garage:** This large garage has room for four cars; don't miss the dog shower and grooming station just off the garage.

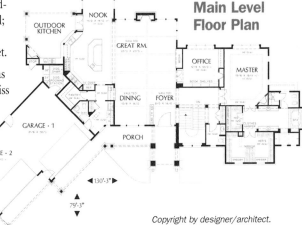

Main Level Floor Plan

Entry

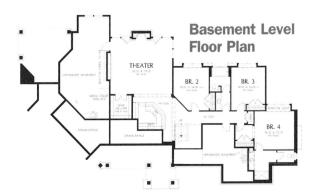

Basement Level Floor Plan

Plan #321005

Dimensions: 69' W x 53'8" D
Levels: 1
Square Footage: 2,483
Bedrooms: 3
Bathrooms: 2
Foundation: Basement
Materials List Available: Yes
Price Category: E

You'll love the grand feeling of this home, which combines with the very practical features that make living in it a pleasure.

Features:

- Porch: The open brick arches and Palladian door set the tone for this magnificent home.

- Great Room: An alcove for the entertainment center and vaulted ceiling show the care that went into designing this room.

- Dining Room: A tray ceiling sets off the formality of this large room.

- Kitchen: The layout in this room is designed to make your work patterns more efficient and to save you steps and time.

- Study: This quiet room can be a wonderful refuge, or you can use it for a fourth bedroom if you wish.

- Master Suite: Made for relaxing at the end of the day, this suite will pamper you with luxuries.

Images provided by designer/architect.

CAD FILE AVAILABLE

Copyright by designer/architect.

Patio

MBr
16-7x16-0
vaulted clg

Great Rm
19-6x23-10
vaulted clg

Brkfst
14-9x13-0
vaulted clg

Kitchen
14-4x12-11
vaulted clg

Br 2
12-0x11-0

Dn

Menu Desk

Laundry

Br 3
12-0x11-5

Entry

Dining
12-0x15-0
tray clg

Study
14-4x11-0
vaulted clg

Porch

Garage
22-4x20-4

53'-8"

69'-0"

SMARTtip

Art in Pools

The tiled walls and floor of a pool make great canvases for art, so incorporate a serious or whimsical design. Also, make the stairs wide and shallow to form a wading area for kids.

Plan #441012

Dimensions: 65' W x 55' D
Levels: 1
Square Footage: 3,682
Main Level Sq. Ft.: 2,192
Basement Level Sq. Ft.: 1,490
Bedrooms: 4
Bathrooms: 4
Foundation: Walk out
Materials List Available: No
Price Category: H

Images provided by designer/architect.

Accommodating a site that slopes to the rear, this home is not only good-looking but practical.

Features:

- Den: Just off the foyer is this cozy space, complete with built-ins.

- Great Room: This vaulted gathering area features a lovely fireplace, a built-in media center, and a view of the back yard.

- Kitchen: This island kitchen is ready to handle the daily needs of your family or aid in entertaining your guests.

- Lower Level: Adding even more livability to the home, this floor contains the games room with media center and corner fireplace, two more bedrooms (each with a full bathroom), and the wide covered patio.

Rear Elevation

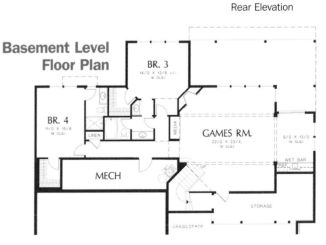

Copyright by designer/architect.

Plan #371033

Dimensions: 73' W x 33' 4" D

Levels: 1

Square Footage: 1,724

Bedrooms: 3

Bathrooms: 2

Foundation: Slab

Materials List Available: No

Price Category: C

This beautiful brick-and-stone country home will be the envy of the neighborhood.

Features:

- Front Porch: This charming yet functional porch welcomes you home.

- Family Room: This large room, with its cathedral ceiling and cozy fireplace, is ideal for entertaining.

- Kitchen: This gourmet kitchen has all the necessities you will ever need, including a raised bar area.

- Master Suite: This cozy area features a stepped ceiling. The luxurious bath boasts a marble tub and two walk-in closets.

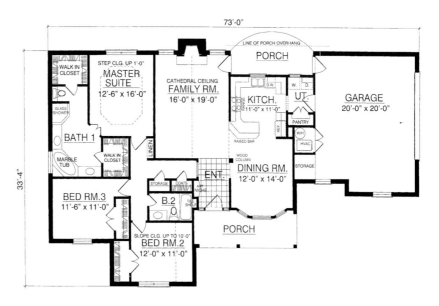

Copyright by designer/architect.

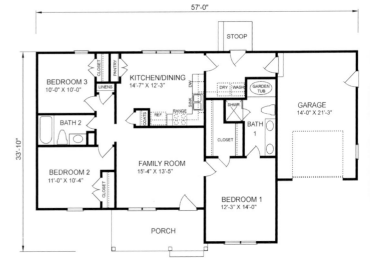

57'-0"

STOOP

BEDROOM 3
10'-0" X 10'-0"

KITCHEN/DINING
14'-7" X 12'-3"

DRY WASH

GARDEN TUB

GARAGE
14'-0" X 21'-3"

BATH 2

FAMILY ROOM
15'-4" X 13'-5"

BATH 1

BEDROOM 2
11'-0" X 10'-4"

BEDROOM 1
12'-3" X 14'-0"

33'-10"

PORCH

Copyright by designer/architect.

Plan #341173

Images provided by designer/architect.

CAD FILE AVAILABLE CAD

Dimensions: 57' W x 33'10" D

Levels: 1

Square Footage: 1,220

Bedrooms: 3

Bathrooms: 1½

Foundation: Crawl space; slab or basement for fee

Material List Available: No

Price Category: B

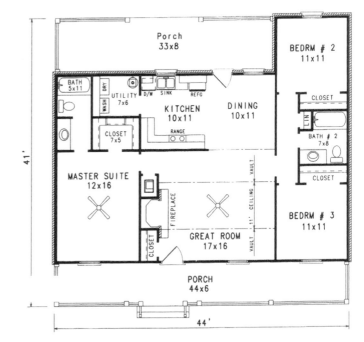

Porch
33x8

BEDRM # 2
11x11

BATH
5x11

UTILITY
7x6

KITCHEN
10x11

DINING
10x11

CLOSET

LIN

BATH # 2
7x8

CLOSET
7x5

RANGE

CLOSET

MASTER SUITE
12x16

11' VAULT CEILING

BEDRM # 3
11x11

41'

FIREPLACE

GREAT ROOM
17x16

VAULT

PORCH
44x6

44'

Plan #171001

Images provided by designer/architect.

Dimensions: 44' W x 41' D

Levels: 1

Square Footage: 1,277

Bedrooms: 3

Bathrooms: 2

Foundation: Crawl space or slab

Material List Available: Yes

Price Category: B

Copyright by designer/architect.

Plan #651026

Dimensions: 40' W x 36' D

Levels: 1

Square Footage: 1,145

Bedrooms: 3

Bathrooms: 2

Foundation: Slab

Material List Available: No

Price Category: B

Images provided by designer/architect.

CAD FILE AVAILABLE

CLOSET 8 x 5

STORAGE 5 x 5

MASTER BATH

"COFFERED" MASTER BEDROOM 11 x 14

LIN.

F.

BATH #2

DINING 8 x 11

KITCHEN 9 x 11

P.

36'

HALL

UTILITY

LIN.

"COFFERED" FAMILY AREA 15 x 13

BEDROOM #3 10 x 10

CLO.

CLO.

BEDROOM #2 10 x 11

E.

PORCH

40'

Copyright by designer/architect.

Plan #351102

Dimensions: 67' W x 56' D

Levels: 1

Square Footage: 2,000

Bedrooms: 3

Bathrooms: 2½

Foundation: Basement, crawl space, or slab

Material List Available: Yes

Price Category: F

Images provided by designer/architect.

CAD FILE AVAILABLE

Ref.

Outdoor Kitchen

Covered Porch 23-0 x 8-0

Patio

Garden Tub

M. Bath 15-4 x 9-6

L

9-0 Ceiling 10-0 Ceiling

Master Bedroom 14-0 x 15-6

S

Clos. 7-6 x 5-8

Clos. 7-6 x 5-8

Kitchen 11-6 x 15-6

DW Pan.

Island

Ref.

Pantry

Eating 11-2 x 15-6 9-0 Ceiling

Bedroom 2 13-4 x 11-6 9-0 Ceiling

Brm.

C

Stor. 6-4 x 7-4

Utility 10-6 x 7-2

D

C

Entry

Half Bath

9-0 Ceiling 10-0 Ceiling

Great Room 22-8 x 15-6

Cabs

Hall

Bath

Tub/ Shwr.

Lin.

Media/ Hobby 8-0 x 7-10

Cabs

2 Car Garage 21-4 x 23-10

Covered Porch 23-0 x 5-0

Bedroom 3 13-4 x 11-6 9-0 Ceiling

Copyright by designer/architect.

Plan #141005

Dimensions: 38' W x 66' D
Levels: 1
Square Footage: 1,532
Bedrooms: 3
Bathrooms: 2
Foundation: Slab, basement
Materials List Available: Yes
Price Category: C

Images provided by designer/architect.

Board and batten combine with shake siding to give this cottage an appealing Tudor style.

Features:

- Ceiling Height: 8 ft. unless otherwise noted.

- Entry: This front entry is highlighted by a dormer that opens to the cathedral ceiling of the spacious open great room.

- Open Floor Plan: The living room, dining areas, and kitchen all flow together to create the feeling of a much larger home.

- Kitchen: This kitchen is defined by a curved bar, which can house a bench seat to service a small cafe-style table.

- Master Suite: This private suite is separated from the rest of the bedrooms. It features a volume ceiling and separate sitting area.

- Basement Option: The house is designed primarily for a slab on a narrow lot but can also be built over a basement.

Rear View

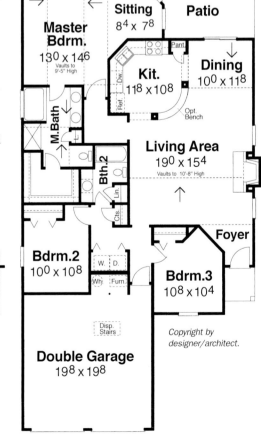

Optional Study

Copyright by designer/architect.

Plan #401041

Dimensions: 38' W x 31' D
Levels: 1
Square Footage: 1,108
Bedrooms: 3
Bathrooms: 2
Foundation: Basement
Materials List Available: Yes
Price Category: B

Craftsman styling and a welcoming porch create marvelous curb appeal for this design. A compact footprint allows economy in construction.

Features:

• **High Ceiling:** This volume ceiling in the living and dining rooms and the kitchen make the home live larger than its modest square footage suggests.

• **Kitchen:** This area features generous cabinet space and flows directly into the dining room to create a casual country feeling. (Note the optional buffet.)

• **Master Bedroom:** This room offers a walk-in closet, a full bath, and a bumped-out window overlooking the rear yard.

• **Expansion:** The lower level provides room for an additional bedroom, den, family room, and full bath.

CAD FILE AVAILABLE

Images provided by designer/architect.

Copyright by designer/architect.

DECK

mbr 13'8x11'4

din 9'x11'4 VAULTED

VAULTED **K** 8'6x11'4

OPTIONAL BUFFET

DN

VAULTED **liv** 15'2x13'4

SKYLIGHT

br2 9'4x11'

br3 9'4x12'8

DN

PORCH

front Elevation

Rear Elevation

Left Side Elevation

Right Side Elevation

FUTURE FAMILY

D
W

UNFINISHED BASEMENT 468 SQ.FT.

UP

FUTURE BEDROOM

FUTURE DEN

DN

Optional Basement Level Floor Plan

Plan #121121

Dimensions: 47'4" W x 45'8"D
Levels: 1
Square Footage: 1,341
Bedrooms: 3
Bathrooms: 2
Foundation: Basement;
crawl space for fee
Material List Available: Yes
Price Category: C

Images provided by designer/architect.

This traditional home is charming and bound to make your life simpler with all its amenities.

Features:

• Great Room: Already equipped with an entertainment center, bookcase and a fireplace by which you can enjoy those books, this room has endless possibilities. This is a room that will bring the whole family together.

• Kitchen: This design includes everything you need and everything you want: a pantry waiting to be filled with your favorite foods, plenty of workspace, and a snack bar that acts as a useful transition between kitchen and breakfast room.

• Breakfast Room: An extension of the kitchen, this room will fill with the aroma of coffee and a simmering breakfast, so you'll be immersed in your relaxing morning. With peaceful daylight streaming in through a window-lined wall, this will easily become the best part of your day.

• Master Suite: Plenty of breathing room for both of you, there will be no fighting for sink or closet space in this bedroom. The full master bath includes dual sinks, and the walk-in closet will hold everything you both need. Another perk of this bathroom is the whirlpool bathtub.

• Garage: This two-car garage opens directly into the home, so there is no reason to get out of your warm, dry car and into unpleasant weather.

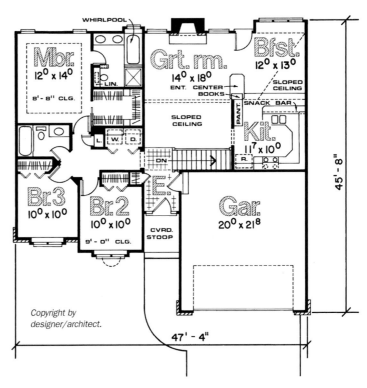

Plan #121125

Dimensions: 54' W x 58'8" D
Levels: 1
Square Footage: 1,978
Bedrooms: 3
Bathrooms: 2½
Foundation: Basement;
crawl space for fee
Material List Available: Yes
Price Category: D

Images provided by designer/architect.

You'll love this plan if you are looking for a home with fantastic curb appeal outside and comfortable amenities inside.

Features:

- **Living Room:** Family and friends will love to gather in this large area, which features a 10-ft.-high ceiling.

- **Dining Room:** This formal dining area is open to the entry foyer and features a stepped ceiling. The triple-window unit, with the transom above, floods the space with natural light.

- **Kitchen:** Convenience marks this well-laid-out kitchen, where you'll love to cook for family and friends. Open to both the family room and the breakfast room, the space has an airy feeling.

- **Master Suite:** The 10-ft.-high boxed ceiling in the sleeping area makes this space feel airy. The master bath features dual vanities and a whirlpool tub.

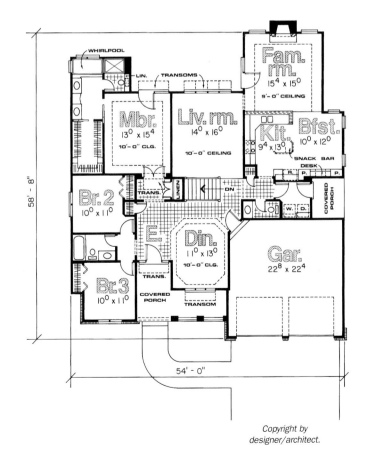

Copyright by designer/architect.

Selecting Colors for Kids' Rooms

Ask kids about color. Kids *love* color, and they usually have a favorite one before they are old enough to start school. You may be choosing a color scheme for the nursery, but by the time your child reaches the toddler stage, she will already show a preference for a particular color. Usually by mid-elementary school age, she will want to help decide on the scheme for her room. And you can count on your preteen or teenage child to insist on a color palette that expresses her individuality.

Experts say that babies distinguish shapes and contrast most clearly, as opposed to different colors. Perhaps black-and-white contrasts are more interesting to a newborn, who may miss the nuances of subtle contrasts until his eyes develop more fully, but it won't be long until he can distinguish sharply defined, bright colors.

If you've planned a soft pastel palette for your baby's room, don't worry: you can add bright colors and contrasts to a nursery through toys, linens, or accessories. In fact, some older babies may need the calming effect of soft colors rather than the sight stimulation of bold, primary hues. The bottom line: use the colors you like best in the nursery. For the most part, the only things that matter to your baby are sleep and the next feeding.

the new Smart Approach to
CREATIVE HOMEOWNER®

kids' rooms

The following article was reprinted from *The New Smart Approach to Kids' Rooms* (Creative Homeowner 2005).

Don't be afraid to experiment, especially on furniture, opposite. Pieces like this can become a focal point.

With white providing the balance, left, primary colors red and blue are dynamic in this boys' room.

Neutral walls are versatile, bottom left. Change accessories easily for new looks and to introduce color accents.

Bold or contrasting patterns, such as stripes, may be stimulating to newborns, bottom right.

If your child is older but not quite old enough to choose a favorite color, there are clues you might observe. For example, look over her drawings. Is there a dominant color that you see repeatedly? What does she like to wear most? Most kids choose clothes based on color preference. Make a game of it. Sit down with your child, and ask her to pick out her favorite colored blocks and organize them by preference. You can do this with crayons, markers, paints, toys, or any other multicolored resource around the house. Sometimes a special object, such as

a much-loved blanket or quilt, a poster or framed print, a cartoon character, or a favorite stuffed animal, can inspire an idea for a color accent or even an entire room's color scheme.

By the time most children are three or four years old, they have developed definite color preferences. Typically, they'll gravitate toward bright hues. (Not every little girl favors pink and purple.) Their tastes start to become more sophisticated, sometimes even offbeat, as they enter their adolescent and teen years.

Should you insist that the colors chosen by your kids for their rooms coordinate with the scheme you've selected for the rest of the house? That's entirely up to you. But even the most outlandish color preferences can be expressed, if not on every surface in the room, at least in linens, in accessories, or on walls that can easily be repainted later. Plain white walls may seem unimaginative and boring, perhaps. But neutral surfaces allow you to introduce an unlimited number of colors and patterns in other ways. Plus, there's the advantage of being able to change the entire look of a room by simply hanging new curtains or changing to another color bedspread or quilt. All-white walls also let your trend-conscious youngster introduce a few faddish colors or prints to the room that can be discarded inexpensively when something new comes along.

One of the smartest things you can do before committing to a color scheme is to learn how to use color effectively, and with professional flair.

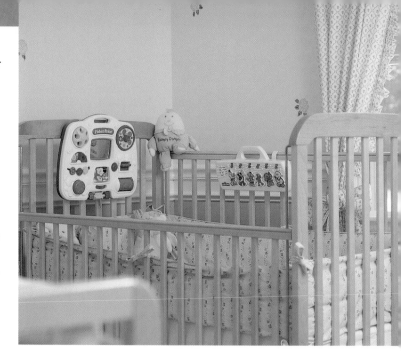

Yellow is a warm hue, above, that energizes a room, sometimes too much. In a bedroom, use the softest, most toned-down version. That way, the room will be cozy and calm.

Linens and accessories, left, provide plenty of opportunities for your child to express her color preferences. Plus, they're easy to change when a new look is desired.

How Color Works

Light reflected through a prism creates a rainbow, known as the "color spectrum." Each band of color blends into the next, from red to ultraviolet. The longest band is red, then orange, yellow, green, blue, violet. Color theory takes those bands and forms them into a circle called the color wheel in order to show the relationship of one color to another.

The color wheel includes primary colors (red, blue, yellow), secondary colors (green, orange, violet), and tertiary colors (red-blue, blue-red, for example). Secondary colors are made by mixing two primaries, such as blue and yellow to make green. A primary color and a secondary color are mixed to make tertiary colors, such as blue and green to make turquoise.

Colors vary in their intensity—that is, the level of the color's purity or saturation. The primaries, secondaries, and tertiaries represent colors at their full intensity. There are several ways to lessen a color's intensity. You can lighten it with white to form a *tint*, darken it with black to create a *shade*, or add gray to arrive

SMARTtip

Color Basics

Use color effectively to enhance the perception of the space itself. Make a large room feel cozy with warm colors, which tend to advance. Conversely, open up a small room with cool colors or neutrals, which tend to recede. The less-intense version of a color will generally reduce its tendency to advance or recede, as well. Other tricks: sharp contrasts often have the same impact as a dark color, reducing perceived space. Monochromatic schemes enlarge space. Neutrals of similar value make walls appear to retreat.

at a *tone*. In addition to changing the intensity of a color, these methods affect what is known as the color's value. *Value* is the lightness or darkness of a color. Tinting gives a color a lighter value; shading gives it a darker value. A hue is simply another term for color or a family of colors.

Color Wheel Combinations

The color wheel is a useful tool for pairing colors. Basically, it presents the spectrum of hues as a circle. The primary colors (yellow, blue, and red) are combined in the remaining colors (orange, green, and violet). The following are the most often used configurations for creating color schemes.

Basic Color Wheel   Analogous   Complementary

Split Complementary   Triad   Tetrad

Putting the Color Wheel to Work for You

Color schemes are developed by combining colors, using their relationship to one another on the color wheel as a guide. Once you've decided on a basic or main color, you can develop an outstanding scheme around it. Use the color wheel to help you envision certain color combinations for your child's room.

Monochromatic schemes are the easiest to develop because they use just one color; examples include totally pink rooms or totally blue rooms. You can use the color in various intensities and with different textures and patterns to create interest. To freshen the look of a monochromatic scheme over the years, all you have to do is change the accent colors. Introduce new colors with accessories or new curtains, for example.

Analogous schemes are invariably pleasing, as well as easy to develop, because they use colors that are next to one another on the color wheel. An example of an analogous color scheme is pink (technically, red tinted with white) and purple (actually, violet-red) a popular combination with young girls. Another combination, one that is often favored for boys, is blue and green-blue. You can play with variations in value, intensity, and texture to add interest to these color schemes.

Complementary schemes are achieved by using two colors that are directly opposite each another on the color wheel. Two such hues are also called contrasting colors. A bright-blue-and-orange bedroom? Well, yes, in full intensity that combination of these two contrasting colors might be hard to stomach, but consider a powdery blue room with pale peach-tone accents. The same complements in varying intensities can make an attractive, soothing combination, while equal amounts of both colors create conflicting tension. The dominance of one color, however, helps to settle things down. Complementary schemes tend to be livelier than others. They consist of a pleasing balance of warm and cool. Strong contrasts may need some tempering, which you can apply by adding a lot of neutral surfaces or by starting with a neutral background (walls) and then using complementary accent colors.

Triadic schemes consist of three or more colors equidistant on the color wheel. Imagine a nursery decorated in palest pink, blue, and yellow. True primaries of red, blue, and yellow often dominate preschoolers' rooms, where everything from toys to storage accessories comes in these colors.

Split-complementary schemes come together when you combine one color with the colors on both sides of the first color's complementary colors. An example is the combination of violet with orange-yellow and yellow-green.

Tetrad schemes are composed by combining any two pairs of complementary colors—for example, orange and blue with red and green.

So far, you've been thinking about color in terms of personal preference, but there are other things to keep in mind when making a choice. First, color has a psychology about it. For example, warm hues (red, yellow, orange, peach, and cream) tend to energize the atmosphere. They're good choices in places where there's a lot of activity. Cool hues (blue, violet, and green) are more restful. They work well in a room intended for relaxing and unwinding. Your child will play and sleep in his room, so try to find a pleasing balance of both types in your scheme, taking your child's personality into account as well. If he's on the busy side and finds it hard to settle down at nap time, predominantly warm hues may be too stimulating. A restful blue or a calming green may be a better choice in this case.

Light and Color

Lighting can alter color dramatically. The quality of natural light changes through the course of the day, too. Consider this when you choose color for your child's room. Paint some test samples on the wall, and watch how the colors shift throughout the day. Do they need adjustment? Rooms with northern exposures will be filled with bluer, cooler light, which weakens warm colors but intensifies cool hues. Rooms with windows that face

A coordinated line of wallcovering and fabrics, left, takes the guesswork out of mixing and matching patterns.

Natural and artificial light affect the way colors appear, above. Test paint samples under both conditions before committing.

Carry out your color scheme, mixing florals, stripes, and solids, if you like. Subdue the look with neutral walls.

want to overpower the space—or your child. That doesn't mean rule it out completely, but perhaps use it sparingly. Small-scale patterns appear to recede, making small spaces seem larger. They can also be used effectively to camouflage odd angles or corners, such as eaves. Try a subtle, nondirectional pattern for this kind of application. In a large room, a small pattern can get lost, unless it contrasts sharply with the background color.

For interest, try to vary the scale of patterns. In general, use large-print fabrics on similar-scale furnishings, medium prints on medium-size pieces, and small prints on accent items. Rules, however, can always be broken. Case in point: you want to include a large upholstered chair in your teenage daughter's relatively small room. Choose a small print to de-emphasize the scale of the piece. Conversely, you found a terrific but small, old ottoman at a garage sale that would make a unique accent piece in the room. Cover it in a large-scale print fabric to call attention to it. When you think about it, applying the ideas of scale and proportion to pattern selection is really a matter of using your own common sense.

How to Mix Patterns

It's not as difficult to mix patterns as it looks, especially if you shop for coordinated lines of fabric and wallpaper, which take the guesswork—and the intimidation—out of using more than one pattern in a room. If you prefer to mix your own patterns, provide links with scale, color, and motif. The regularity of checks, stripes, textural looks, and geometrics (if they are small and low-contrast) tends to make them easy-to-mix "neutrals." A small checked pattern can play off a thin ticking stripe, while a strong plaid may require a bold stripe as a same-scale foil. The most-effective link between disparate patterns is shared colors that are of a similar level of intensity—all pastel tones, for example. A solid-color fabric that pulls out a hue that is shared by more than one pattern in the room provides another way of making a visual connection.

Texture

Texture doesn't have the obvious impact on a room that color and pattern wield. But how a material feels, as well as how it looks, is important. The easiest way to incorporate texture into a design is with fabric. Obviously, you won't be using brocades and damasks in your child's room; you'll want something that's sturdy and washable but soft to the touch. Cottons and chenilles are good choices for curtains and bedding. Fabrics, however, are

south will have a warmer, yellowish light. Rooms with windows that face east are sunny in the morning, while those with a western exposure bring in the late afternoon light. Other factors, such as window treatments and artificial light sources, can alter these conditions, however.

Although these generalizations are not absolute, they're good starting points for making initial judgments.

Pattern

Pattern is another way to add personality to a room, establish a theme, visually alter the size or shape of a room, or camouflage minor surface imperfections. You can introduce pattern in a variety of ways—wallpaper and fabric being the two most popular. Because pattern is largely a vehicle for color, the same rules that guide the selection of color effectively narrow the field when it comes to choosing a pattern or a complement of patterns. Scale, is an-other important consideration.

Large-scale patterns are like warm colors in that they appear to come toward you. They can create a lively and stimulating atmosphere and generally make a large space seem cozier. In a small room, handle a large-scale pattern with care if you don't just the beginning. Tactile interest or texture can emanate from any material that is coarse or smooth, hard or soft, matte or shiny, but you should avoid anything that is very rough and can injure a child. Coarse and matte surfaces, such as some carpeting and cork, absorb light and sound. Glossy and smooth surfaces, which range from metal and glass to silk and enamel, reflect light.

Texture can alter a room spatially. Coarse or matte surfaces will make a room seem smaller and cozier. The glossy surfaces of some contemporary bedroom furniture can seem cold and uninviting without a cozy quilt on the bed to add warmth and contrast. Smooth and shiny surfaces do the reverse—they make space appear larger and brighter. A room that looks confined, for instance, may open up with the addition of a large mirror or a light-color floor. Light reflected off either one will brighten the room.

Keep in mind that texture also affects pattern and color. With fabrics, texture can either soften or intensify a pattern. With paint, a coarse texture subdues the intensity of the color, but adds subtle variations and shadings. On the other hand, a highly polished or glossy finish heightens a color.

Relatively featureless rooms can be improved by adding contrasting textures with wallpaper, paint finishes, or architectural embellishments such as cornices, crown moldings, and wainscoting.

Window treatments are another natural outlet for texture. Fabric choices for draperies and curtains as well as the fabrics and other materials available for blinds and shades are enormous and varied. Texture can be enhanced by the way fabric is hung. Pleating, for example, creates a play of light and shadow. You can combine layers of fabric, or fabric with blinds or shades, to show off different textures.

On the floor, carpets can be smooth, knobby, sculpted, or flecked for visual texture. Rugs, wood, or cork are warming texture options. Varying the materials can make the overall effect more interesting.

A delightful play of textures and patterns, above, creates interest in this scheme of mostly neutrals and earth tones.

Images provided by designer/architect.

Plan #111051

Dimensions: 63' W x 76' D

Levels: 1

Square Footage: 2,471

Bedrooms: 4

Bathrooms: 2½

Foundation: Slab

Materials List Available: No

Price Category: F

You'll find everything you want in this traditional cottage-style home, and it's all on one floor!

Features:

- **Living Room:** Both this room and the dining room are just off the foyer for convenience. A corner fireplace and windows overlooking the backyard give character to the room.

- **Kitchen:** The kitchen island contains a sink and dishwasher as well as a bar. A nearby hall way leads to a half-bath, the utility room, and the two-car garage.

- **Breakfast Area:** Adjacent to the kitchen, the large breakfast area leads to the back porch.

- **Master Suite:** Featuring a walk-in closet and bath with a garden tub, standing shower, and private toilet area, this room opens to the back porch.

- **Additional Bedrooms:** Walk-in closets in two bedrooms and a wide closet with a double door in the third provide good storage space.

Kitchen/Breakfast Area

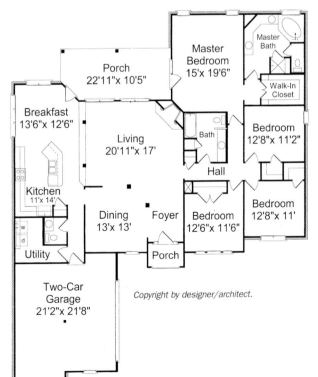

Copyright by designer/architect.

Plan #161001

Dimensions: 67'2" W x 47' D

Levels: 1

Square Footage: 1,782

Bedrooms: 3

Bathrooms: 2

Foundation: Basement

Materials List Available: Yes

Price Category: C

An all-brick exterior displays the solid strength that characterizes this gracious home.

Features:

- Great Room: A feeling of spaciousness permeates the gathering area created by the foyer, great room, and dining room. Multiple windows provide natural light that dances along a sloped ceiling, spilling onto decorative columns and a fireplace.

- Breakfast Area: A continuation of the sloped ceiling leads to the breakfast area where French doors open to a screened porch.

- Kitchen: An abundance of cabinets and counter space are the hallmarks of this large kitchen with its easy access to a spacious laundry room and storage area.

- Master Suite: A tray ceiling and spacious walk-in closet in the master bedroom, along with a whirlpool tub and double-bowl vanity in the bathroom, enable you to pamper yourself.

Images provided by designer/architect.

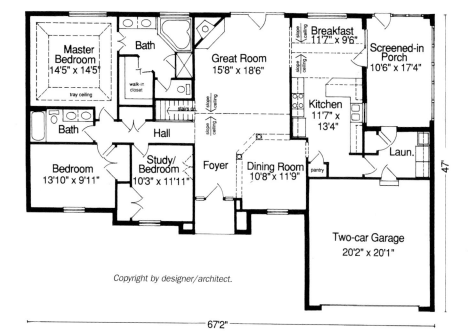

Copyright by designer/architect.

Great Room/Foyer

Rear Elevation

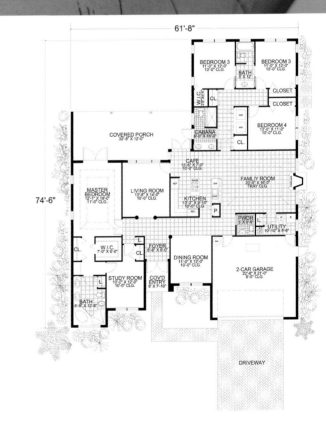

Plan #201062

Dimensions: 70'10" W x 59'5" D

Levels: 1

Square Footage: 2,551

Bedrooms: 4

Bathrooms: 2½

Foundation: Crawl space, slab

Materials List Available: Yes

Price Category: E

Images provided by designer/architect.

Copyright by designer/architect.

Plan #611110

Dimensions: 61'8" W x 74'6" D

Levels: 1

Square Footage: 2,762

Bedrooms: 5

Bathrooms: 3½

Foundation: Slab

Materials List Available: No

Price Category: F

Images provided by designer/architect.

CAD FILE AVAILABLE

Copyright by designer/architect.

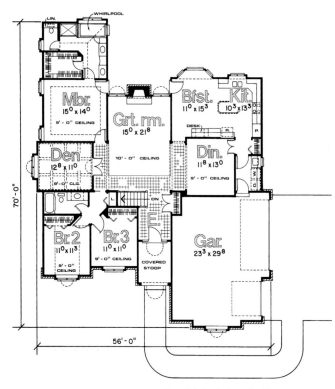

Plan #121052

Dimensions: 56' W x 70' D

Levels: 1

Square Footage: 2,093

Bedrooms: 4

Bathrooms: 2

Foundation: Basement

Materials List Available: Yes

Price Category: D

Images provided by designer/architect.

Copyright by designer/architect.

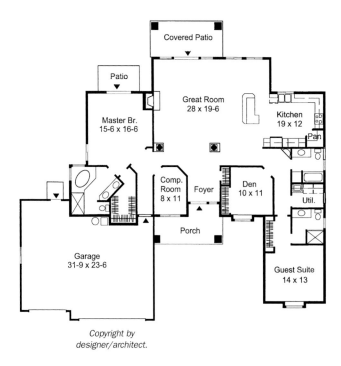

Plan #231003

Dimensions: 74' W x 69' D

Levels: 1

Square Footage: 2,254

Bedrooms: 2

Bathrooms: 3

Foundation: Crawl space

Materials List Available: No

Price Category: E

Illustration provided by designer/architect.

Copyright by designer/architect.

Plan #121004

Dimensions: 55'4" W x 48' D
Levels: 1
Square Footage: 1,666
Bedrooms: 3
Bathrooms: 2
Foundation: Basement
Materials List Available: Yes
Price Category: C

Images provided by designer/architect.

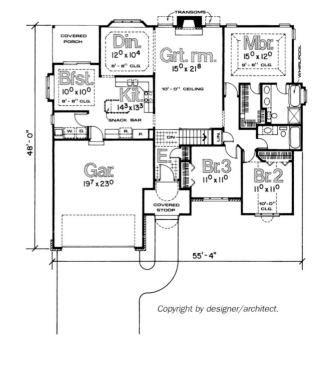

Copyright by designer/architect.

Plan #151054

Dimensions: 67' W x 54'10" D
Levels: 1
Square Footage: 1,746
Bedrooms: 3
Bathrooms: 2
Foundation: Crawl space or slab; basement option for fee
CompleteCost List Available: Yes
Price Category: C

Images provided by designer/architect.

Copyright by designer/architect.

SMARTtip

Mixing and Matching Windows

Windows, both fixed and operable, are made in various styles and shapes. While mixing styles should be carefully avoided, a variety of interesting window sizes and shapes may nevertheless be combined to achieve symmetry, harmony, and rhythm on the exterior of a home.

Plan #321019

Dimensions: 70'8" W x 70' D

Levels: 1

Square Footage: 2,452

Bedrooms: 4

Bathrooms: 2½

Foundation: Basement

Materials List Available: Yes

Price Category: E

Images provided by designer/architect.

CAD FILE AVAILABLE

Copyright by designer/architect.

Plan #311039

Dimensions: 74' W x 50' D

Levels: 1

Square Footage: 1,609

Bedrooms: 3

Bathrooms: 3

Foundation: Crawl space, slab or basement

Material List Available: No

Price Category: D

Images provided by designer/architect.

Bonus Level Floor Plan

Copyright by designer/architect.

Plan #661289

Dimensions: 113'8" W x 97'4" D

Levels: 1

Square Footage: 5,342

Bedrooms: 4

Bathrooms: 2 half

Foundation: Slab

Material List Available: No

Price Category: J

Images provided by designer/architect.

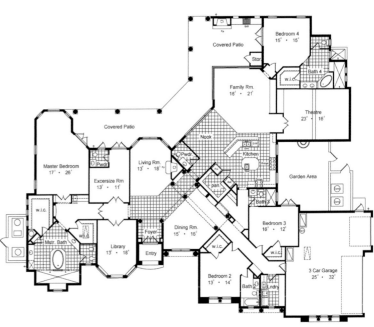

Copyright by designer/architect.

Plan #151057

Dimensions: 73'6" W x 80'6" D

Levels: 1

Square Footage: 2,951

Bedrooms: 4

Bathrooms: 3

Foundation: Crawl space, slab, or basement

CompleteCost List Available: Yes

Price Category: G

Images provided by designer/architect.

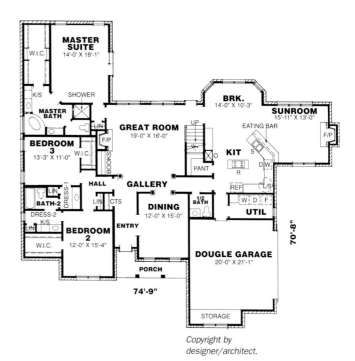

Plan #241004

Dimensions: 74'9" W x 70'8" D

Levels: 1

Square Footage: 2,771

Bedrooms: 3

Bathrooms: 2½

Foundation: Slab

Materials List Available: No

Price Category: F

Images provided by designer/architect.

Copyright by designer/architect.

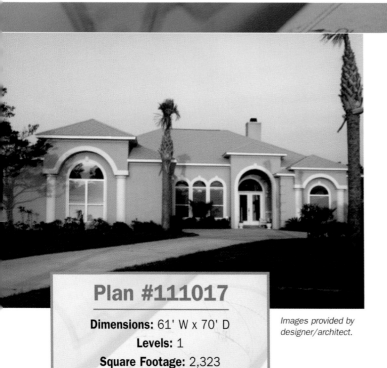

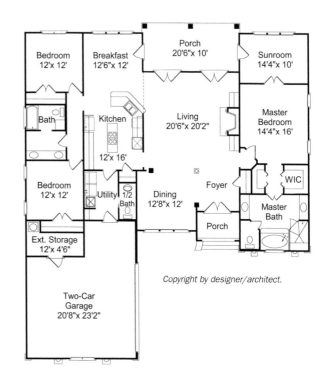

Plan #111017

Dimensions: 61' W x 70' D

Levels: 1

Square Footage: 2,323

Bedrooms: 3

Bathrooms: 2½

Foundation: Monolithic slab

Materials List Available: No

Price Category: F

Images provided by designer/architect.

Copyright by designer/architect.

Plan #121003

Dimensions: 76' W x 55'4" D

Levels: 1

Square Footage: 2,498

Bedrooms: 4

Bathrooms: 2½

Foundation: Basement

Materials List Available: Yes

Price Category: E

Images provided by designer/architect.

Repeated arches bring style and distinction to the interior and exterior of this spacious home.

Features:

- Ceiling Height: 8 ft. except as noted.

- Den: A decorative volume ceiling helps make this spacious retreat the perfect place to relax after a long day.

- Formal Living Room: The decorative volume ceiling carries through to the living room that invites large formal gatherings.

- Formal Dining Room: There's plenty of room for all the guests to move into this gracious formal space that also features a decorative volume ceiling.

- Master Suite: Retire to this suite with its glamorous bayed whirlpool, his and her vanities, and a walk-in closet.

- Optional Sitting Room: With the addition of French doors, one of the bedrooms can be converted into a sitting room for the master suite.

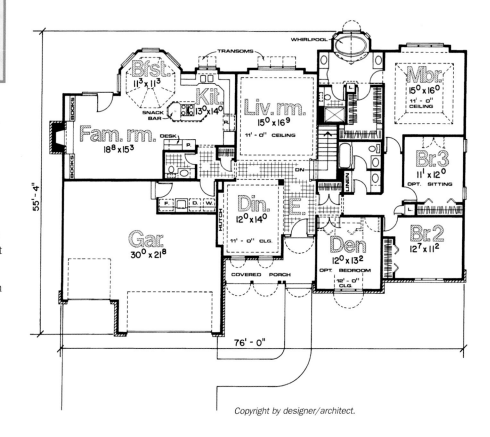

Copyright by designer/architect.

Plan #481028

Dimensions: 86'8" W x 53' D
Levels: 1
Square Footage: 3,980
Main Level Sq. Ft.: 2,290
Lower Level Sq. Ft.: 1,690
Bedrooms: 3
Bathrooms: 2½
Foundation: Walkout basement
Material List Available: No
Price Category: H

- Lower Level: For fun times, this lower level is finished to provide a wet bar and a recreation room. Two bedrooms, which share a full bathroom, are also on this level. Future expansion can include an additional bedroom.

Rear View

This home, with its Southwestern flair, invites friends and family in for some down-home hospitality.

Features:

- Foyer: A 12-ft-high ceiling extends an open welcome to all. With a view through the great room, the open floor plan makes the home feel large and open.

- Kitchen: This spacious gourmet kitchen opens generously to the hearth room, which features an angled fireplace. A two-level island, which contains a two-bowl sink, provides casual seating and additional storage.

- Master Suite: This romantic space features a 10-ft.-high stepped ceiling and a compartmentalized full bath that includes his and her sinks and a whirlpool tub.

Copyright by designer/architect.

Basement Level Floor Plan

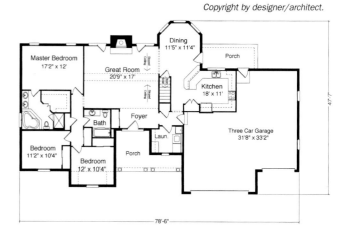

Plan #161006

Dimensions: 78'6" W x 47'7" D

Levels: 1

Square Footage: 1,755

Bedrooms: 3

Bathrooms: 2

Foundation: Basement

Materials List Available: No

Price Category: C

Images provided by designer/architect.

Rear Elevation

Plan #151169

Dimensions: 51'6" W x 49'10" D

Levels: 1

Square Footage: 1,525

Bedrooms: 3

Bathrooms: 2

Foundation: crawl space, slab, basement, or daylight basement

CompleteCost List Available: Yes

Price Category: C

Images provided by designer/architect.

Rear Elevation

Plan #121008

Dimensions: 62' W x 56' D
Levels: 1
Square Footage: 1,651
Bedrooms: 2
Bathrooms: 2
Foundation: Basement
Materials List Available: Yes
Price Category: C

Images provided by designer/architect.

CAD FILE AVAILABLE

Optional Bedroom

Copyright by designer/architect.

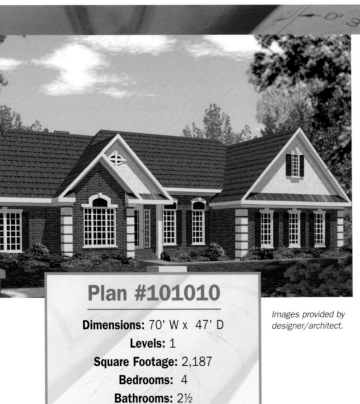

Plan #101010

Dimensions: 70' W x 47' D
Levels: 1
Square Footage: 2,187
Bedrooms: 4
Bathrooms: 2½
Foundation: Crawl space, slab, or basement
Materials List Available: Yes
Price Category: E

Images provided by designer/architect.

Copyright by designer/architect.

SMARTtip

Using Slipcovers in Your Dining Area

Change the look of your dining room by slipcovering chairs. Short-skirted slipcovers give a more informal appearance; fabrics in graphic patterns, such as checks or floral prints, complement this style of slipcover best. Long-skirted covers are elegant additions to a formal dining room, particularly in solid color or tone-on-tone fabrics. Ties, buttons, or trim can add personality.

Plan #151006

Dimensions: 54'2" W x 52'10" D

Levels: 1

Square Footage: 1,758

Bedrooms: 3

Bathrooms: 2

Foundation: Crawl space, slab, basement, or walkout

CompleteCost List Available: Yes

Price Category: C

Images provided by designer/architect.

This home, as shown in the photograph, may differ from the actual blueprints. For more detailed information, please check the floor plans carefully.

You'll love the expansive feeling of the open, spacious rooms in this home and wonder how you ever did without the amenities it offers.

Features:

- **Foyer:** A foyer with a 10-ft. ceiling provides the perfect transition between the columned front porch and the interior of this home.

- **Great Room:** A fireplace, 9-ft. boxed ceiling, and access to the rear grilling porch and back yard make this room the heart of the home.

- **Dining Room:** The 10-ft. ceiling and boxed columns provide a touch of formality.

- **Kitchen:** Convenience marks this well-designed kitchen that opens to the breakfast room.

- **Master Suite:** With a 9-ft. boxed ceiling, this elegant room will be your favorite retreat. The bath has a whirlpool tub with glass blocks, a shower, and double vanities.

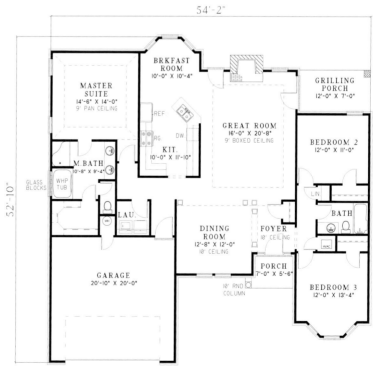

Copyright by designer/architect.

Plan #271063

Dimensions: 61'4" W x 70' D
Levels: 1
Square Footage: 2,572
Bedrooms: 3
Bathrooms: 2
Foundation: Daylight basement
Materials List Available: No
Price Category: E

European detailing gives this home a unique flair and elegant curb appeal.

Features:

• Entry Rotunda: This welcoming area opens to a quiet den with a cozy fireplace.

• Living Room: This open space leads back to a wall of windows overlooking a backyard deck.

• Country Kitchen: A central island and dramatic overhead glass make for a great spot for meal preparation and eating. A four-season porch is nearby.

• Master Suite: Double doors and a coffered ceiling enhance this secluded suite. The private bath has everything you can imagine, including a whirlpool tub.

**Basement Level
Floor Plan**

Plan #151008

Dimensions: 42' W x 66'10" D

Levels: 1

Square Footage: 1,892

Bedrooms: 3

Bathrooms: 2

Foundation: Crawl space, slab, basement, or daylight basement

CompleteCost List Available: Yes

Price Category: D

Images provided by designer/architect.

This home, as shown in the photograph, may differ from the actual blueprints. For more detailed information, please check the floor plans carefully.

Copyright by designer/architect.

Plan #211058

Dimensions: 74'6" W x 68' D

Levels: 1

Square Footage: 2,564

Bedrooms: 4

Bathrooms: 4

Foundation: Slab

Materials List Available: No

Price Category: E

Images provided by designer/architect.

Copyright by designer/architect.

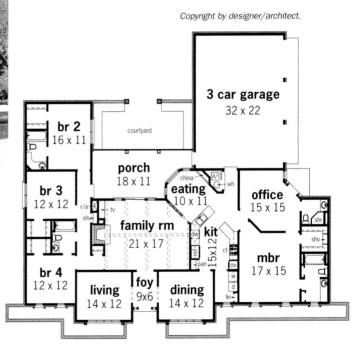

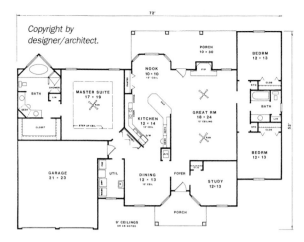

Images provided by designer/architect.

Plan #171004

Dimensions: 72' W x 52' D
Levels: 1
Square Footage: 2,256
Bedrooms: 3
Bathrooms: 2
Foundation: Crawl space, slab
Materials List Available: Yes
Price Category: E

SMARTtip

Windows – Privacy

You can easily stencil a work of art onto a windowpane, perhaps only as a border around the edge. Choose or create a design that gives you as little or as much privacy and light control as you need. Use a ready-made stencil or a piece of openwork fabric such as lace, or mask a design onto the glass using tape and a razor knife. Then apply glass paint or frosted glass spray, referring to the instructions and guidelines that come with the product.

Plan #151117

Dimensions: 66' W x 55' D
Levels: 1
Square Footage: 1,957
Bedrooms: 3
Bathrooms: 3
Foundation: Crawl space, slab, or basement
CompleteCost List Available: Yes
Price Category: D

Images provided by designer/architect.

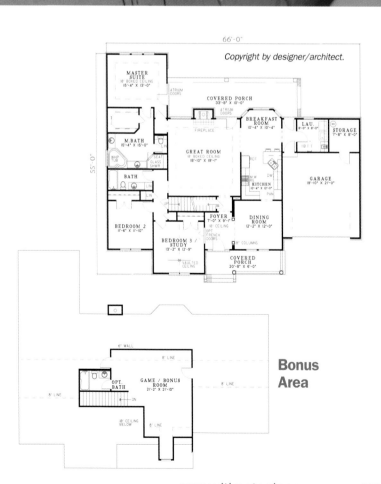

Bonus Area

Plan #121092

Dimensions: 65'4" W x 52'8" D
Levels: 1
Square Footage: 3,225
Main Level Sq. Ft.: 1,887
Basement Level Sq. Ft.: 1,338
Bedrooms: 3
Bathrooms: 2½
Foundation: Basement
Materials List Available: Yes
Price Category: D

Images provided by designer/architect.

This is the design if you want a home that will be easy to expand as your family grows.

Features:

- Entry: Both the dining room and great room are immediately accessible from this lovely entry.

- Great Room: The transom-topped bowed windows highlight the spacious feeling here.

- Gathering Room: Also with an angled ceiling, this room has a fireplace as well as a built-in entertainment center and bookcases.

- Dining Room: This elegant room features a 13-ft. boxed ceiling and majestic window around which you'll love to decorate.

- Kitchen: Designed for convenience, this kitchen includes a lovely angled ceiling and gazebo-shaped breakfast area.

- Basement: Use the plans for finishing a family room and two bedrooms when the time is right.

Main Level Floor Plan

Basement Level Floor Plan

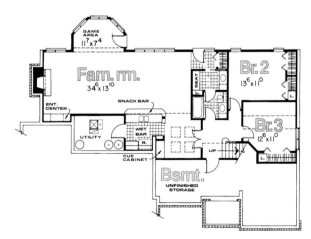

Copyright by designer/architect.

Plan #131011

Dimensions: 75'2" W x 60'9" D
Levels: 1
Square Footage: 1,897
Bedrooms: 4
Bathrooms: 2
Foundation: Crawl space, slab, or basement
Materials List Available: Yes
Price Category: E

Images provided by designer/architect.

You'll love this home if you're looking for a plan for a sloping lot or flat one or if you want to orient the rear porch to face into or away from the sun.

Features:

• Ceiling Height: 8 ft.

• Living Area: The whole family will find it easy to congregate in this lovely room.

• Kitchen: The angle of this home makes the kitchen especially convenient while also giving it an unusual amount of character.

• Study: Located near the front door, this room can serve as a home office or fourth bedroom as easily as it does a private study.

• Master Suite: Located at the opposite end of the home from the other two bedrooms, this master suite offers privacy and quiet.

• Additional Bedrooms: These two bedrooms share a distinctive hall bathroom.

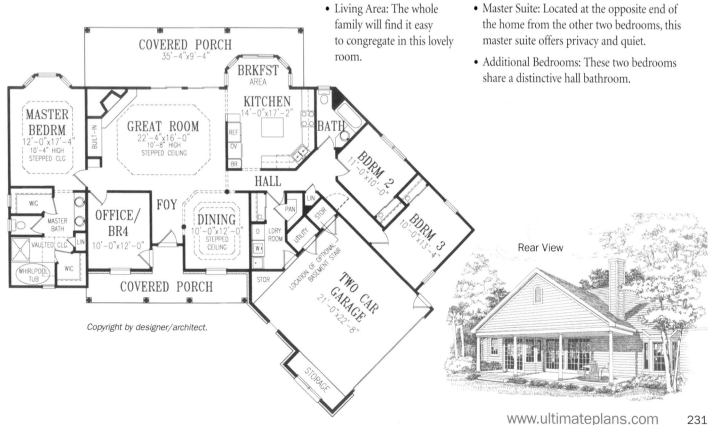

Copyright by designer/architect.

Rear View

Plan #351001

Dimensions: 72'8" W x 51' D

Levels: 1

Square Footage: 1,855

Bedrooms: 3

Bathrooms: 2½

Foundation: Crawl space, slab, or basement

Materials List Available: Yes

Price Category: D

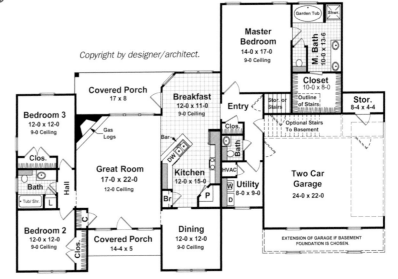

Copyright by designer/architect.

Images provided by designer/architect.

From the lovely arched windows on the front to the front and back covered porches, this home is as comfortable as it is beautiful.

Features:

- Great Room: Come into this room with 12-ft. ceilings, and you're sure to admire the corner gas fireplace and three windows overlooking the porch.

- Dining Room: Set off from the open design, this room is designed to be used formally or not.

- Kitchen: You'll love the practical walk-in pantry, broom closet, and angled snack bar here.

- Breakfast Room: Brightly lit and leading to the covered porch, this room will be a favorite spot.

- Bonus Room: Develop a playroom or study in this area.

- Master Suite: The large bedroom is complemented by the private bath with garden tub, separate shower, double vanity, and spacious walk-in closet.

Kitchen

Bonus Area Floor Plan

Plan #161005

Dimensions: 60' W x 48'10" D
Levels: 1
Square Footage: 1,593
Bedrooms: 3
Bathrooms: 2
Foundation: Basement
Materials List Available: Yes
Price Category: C

Rear Elevation

This delightful ranch home includes many thoughtful conveniences and a full basement to expand your living enjoyment.

Features:

- Great Room: Take pleasure in welcoming guests through a spacious foyer into the warm and friendly confines of this great room with corner fireplace, sloped ceiling, and view to the rear yard.

- Kitchen: Experience the convenience of enjoying meals while seated at the large island that separates the dining area from this well-designed kitchen. Also included is an over-sized pantry with an abundance of storage.

- Master Suite: This master suite features a compartmented bath, large walk-in closet, and master bedroom that has a tray ceiling with 9-ft. center height.

- Porch: Retreat to this delightful rear porch to enjoy a relaxing evening.

Copyright by designer/architect.

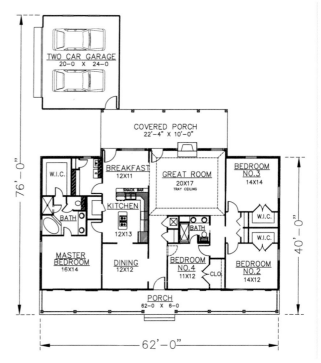

Plan #191009

Dimensions: 62' W x 76' D

Levels: 1

Square Footage: 2,172

Bedrooms: 4

Bathrooms: 2

Foundation: Crawl space, slab

Materials List Available: No

Price Category: D

Images provided by designer/architect.

Copyright by designer/architect.

Plan #271076

Dimensions: 69' W x 57' D

Levels: 1

Square Footage: 2,188

Bedrooms: 2-4

Bathrooms: 1½-2½

Foundation: Daylight basement

Materials List Available: No

Price Category: D

Images provided by designer/architect.

CAD FILE AVAILABLE

Optional Basement Level Floor Plan

Copyright by designer/architect.

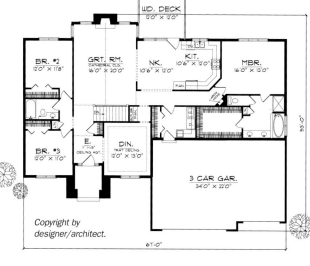

Images provided by designer/architect.

Plan #221018

Dimensions: 67' W x 53' D

Levels: 1

Square Footage: 2,007

Bedrooms: 3

Bathrooms: 2

Foundation: Basement

Materials List Available: No

Price Category: D

CAD FILE AVAILABLE

Rear Elevation

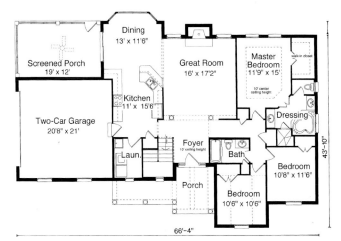

Copyright by designer/architect.

Images provided by designer/architect.

Plan #161007

Dimensions: 66'4" W x 43'10" D

Levels: 1

Square Footage: 1,611

Bedrooms: 3

Bathrooms: 2

Foundation: Basement; crawl space option for fee

Materials List Available: Yes

Price Category: C

CAD FILE AVAILABLE

Rear Elevation

Plan #151002

Dimensions: 67' W x 66' D

Levels: 1

Square Footage: 2,444

Bedrooms: 3

Bathrooms: 2½

Foundation: Crawl space, slab, or basement

CompleteCost List Available: Yes

Price Category: E

• Kitchen: An eat-in bar is a great place to snack, and the handy computer nook allows the kids to do their homework while you cook.

• Breakfast Room: Opening from the kitchen, this area gives added space for the family to gather any time.

• Master Suite: Featuring a 10-ft. boxed ceiling, the master bedroom also has a door-way that opens onto the covered rear porch. The master bathroom has a step-up whirlpool tub, separate shower, and twin vanities with a makeup area.

This gracious, traditional home is designed for practicality and convenience.

Features:

• Ceiling Height: 9 ft. except as noted below.

• Great Room: This room is ideal for entertaining, thanks to its lovely fireplace and French doors that open to the covered rear porch. Built-in cabinets give convenient storage space.

• Family Room: With access to the kitchen as well as the rear porch, this room will become your family's "headquarters."

• Study: Enjoy the quiet in this room with its 12-ft. ceiling and doorway to a private patio on the side of the house.

• Dining Room: Take advantage of the 8-in. wood columns and 12-ft. ceilings to create a formal dining area.

Plan #131019

Dimensions: 83'6" W x 53'4" D
Levels: 1
Square Footage: 2,243
Bedrooms: 3
Bathrooms: 2½
Foundation: Crawl space, slab, or basement
Materials List Available: Yes
Price Category: F

Drama marks this contemporary, angled ranch-style home which can be placed to suit any site, even the most difficult.

Features:

- Great Room: Imagine having an octagonal great room! The shape alone makes it spectacular, but the view to the backyard from its four exterior sides adds to the impression it creates, and you'll love its 16-ft. tray ceiling, fireplace, and wall designed to fit a large entertainment center.

- Kitchen: This room is adjacent to and visually connected to the great room but has

excellent features of its own that make it an easy place to cook or clean.

- Master Suite: Separated from the other bedrooms, this suite is planned for privacy. You'll love the bath here and look forward to the quiet you can find at the end of the day.

- Additional Bedrooms: In a wing of their own, the other two bedrooms share a bath.

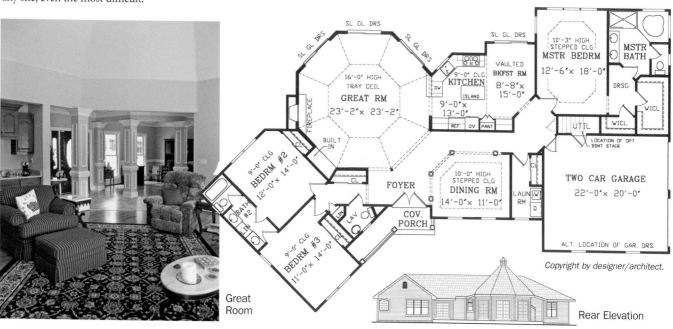

Great Room

Rear Elevation

Copyright by designer/architect.

Plan #241008

Dimensions: 65' W x 56'8" D
Levels: 1
Square Footage: 2,526
Bedrooms: 4
Bathrooms: 3
Foundation: Crawl space, slab, or basement
Materials List Available: No
Price Category: E

A covered back porch—with access from the master suite and the breakfast area—makes this traditional home ideal for sitting near a golf course or with a backyard pool.

Features:

• Great Room: From the foyer, guests enter this spacious and comfortable great room, which features a handsome fireplace.

• Kitchen: This kitchen—the hub of this family-oriented home—is a joy in which to work, thanks to abundant counter space, a pantry, a convenient eating bar, and an adjoining breakfast area and sunroom.

• Master Suite: Enjoy the quiet comfort of this coffered-ceiling master suite, which features dual vanities and separate walk-in closets.

• Additional Bedrooms: Two secondary bedrooms, which share a full bath, are located at the opposite end of the house from the master suite. Bedroom 4—in front of the house—can be converted into a study.

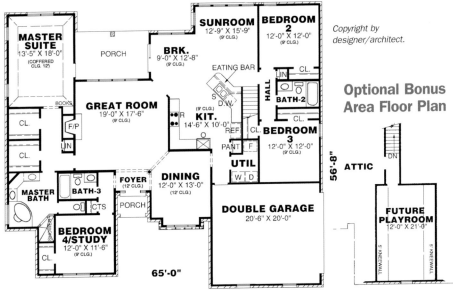

Optional Bonus Area Floor Plan

SMARTtip

Traditional-Style Kitchen Cabinetry

You can modify stock kitchen cabinetry to enjoy fine furniture-quality details. Prefabricated trims may be purchased at local lumber mills and home centers. For example, crown molding, applied to the top of stock cabinetry and stained or painted to match the door style, may be all you need. Likewise, you can replace hardware with reproduction polished-brass door and drawer knobs or pulls for a finishing touch.

Plan #211010

Dimensions: 81' W x 84' D
Levels: 1
Square Footage: 2,503
Bedrooms: 3
Bathrooms: 2½
Foundation: Slab
Materials List Available: Yes
Price Category: E

A well-designed floor plan makes maximum use of space and creates convenience and comfort.

Features:

• Ceiling Height: 10 ft. unless otherwise noted.

• Living Room: A stepped ceiling gives this living room special architectural interest. There's a full-service wet bar designed to handle parties of any size. When the weather gets warm, step out of the living room into a lovely screened rear porch.

• Master Bedroom: You'll love unwinding at the end of a busy day in this master suite. It's located away from the other bedrooms for more privacy.

• Study: This charming study adjoins the master bedroom. It's the perfect quiet spot to get some work done, surf the internet, or pay the bills.

Images provided by designer/architect.

SMARTtip

Deck Railings

Install caps and post finials to your railings. A rail cap protects the cut ends of the posts from the weather. Finials add another decorative layer to your design, and the styles are endless—ball, chamfered, grooved, and top hat are a few.

Copyright by designer/architect.

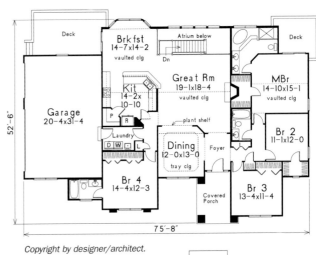

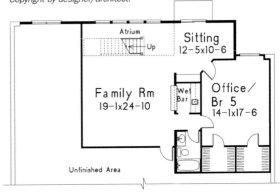

Plan #321034

Dimensions: 75'8" W x 52'6" D

Levels: 1

Square Footage: 3,508

Bedrooms: 4

Bathrooms: 3

Foundation: Basement, walkout

Material List Available: Yes

Price Category: H

Images provided by designer/architect.

**Optional
Basement Level
Floor Plan**

Copyright by designer/architect.

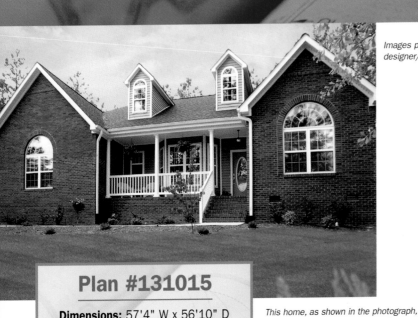

Images provided by designer/architect.

Copyright by designer/architect.

Plan #131015

Dimensions: 57'4" W x 56'10" D

Levels: 1

Square Footage: 1,860

Bedrooms: 3

Bathrooms: 2

Foundation: Crawl space, slab, or basement

Materials List Available: Yes

Price Category: E

This home, as shown in the photograph, may differ from the actual blueprints. For more detailed information, please check the floor plans carefully.

Rear Elevation

Great Room

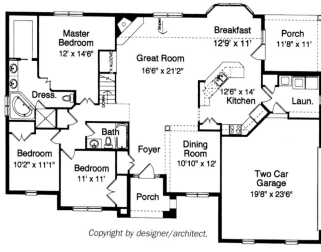

Copyright by designer/architect.

Plan #161008

Dimensions: 64'2" W x 46'6" D

Levels: 1

Square Footage: 1,860

Bedrooms: 3

Bathrooms: 2

Foundation: Slab

Materials List Available: No

Price Category: D

Images provided by designer/architect.

SMARTtip

Espaliered Fruit Trees

Try a technique used by the royal gardeners at Versailles—espalier. They trained the fruit trees to grow flat against the walls, creating patterns. It's not difficult, especially if you go to a reputable nursery and purchase an apple or pear tree that has already been espaliered. Plant it against a flat surface that's in a sunny spot.

Plan #151170

Dimensions: 57' W x 64'4" D

Levels: 1

Square Footage: 1,965

Bedrooms: 4

Bathrooms: 2

Foundation: Crawl space, slab; basement or daylight basement for fee

CompleteCost List Available: Yes

Price Category: D

Images provided by designer/architect.

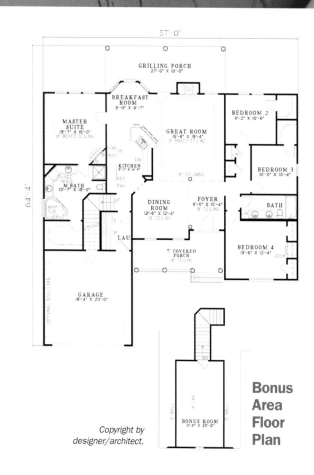

Copyright by designer/architect.

Bonus Area Floor Plan

Plan #151003

Dimensions: 51'6" W x 52'4" D
Levels: 1
Square Footage: 1,680
Bedrooms: 3
Bathrooms: 2
Foundation: Crawl space, slab, or basement
CompleteCost List Available: Yes
Price Category: C

Images provided by designer/architect.
This home, as shown in the photograph, may differ from the actual blueprints. For more detailed information, please check the floor plans carefully.

A lovely front porch, bay windows, and dormers add sparkle to this country-style home.

Features:

- **Great Room:** Perfect for entertaining, this room features a tray ceiling, wet bar, and a quiet screened porch nearby.

- **Dining Room:** This bayed dining room facing the front porch is cozy yet roomy enough for family parties during the holidays.

- **Kitchen:** This eat-in kitchen also faces the front and is ideal for preparing meals for any occasion.

- **Master Suite:** The tray ceiling here gives an added feeling of space, while the distance from the other bedrooms allows for all the privacy you'll need.

Copyright by designer/architect.

Plan #211006

Dimensions: 61' W x 77' D
Levels: 1
Square Footage: 2,177
Bedrooms: 3
Bathrooms: 2
Foundation: Crawl space or slab
Materials List Available: Yes
Price Category: D

SMARTtip

Deck Furniture Style

Mix-and-match tabletops, frames, and legs are stylish. Combine materials such as glass, metal, wood, and mosaic tiles.

This traditional home with a stucco exterior is distinguished by its 9-ft. ceilings throughout and its sleek, contemporary interior.

Features:

- **Living Room:** A series of arched openings that surround this room adds strong visual interest. Settle down by the fireplace on cold winter nights.

- **Dining Room:** Step up to enter this room with a raised floor that sets it apart from other areas.

- **Kitchen:** Ideal for cooking as well as casual socializing, this kitchen has a stovetop island and a breakfast bar.

- **Master Suite:** The sitting area in this suite is so big that you might want to watch TV here or make it a study. In the bath, you'll find a skylight above the angled tub with a mirror surround and well-placed plant ledge.

- **Rear Porch:** This 200-sq.-ft. covered porch gives you plenty of space for entertaining.

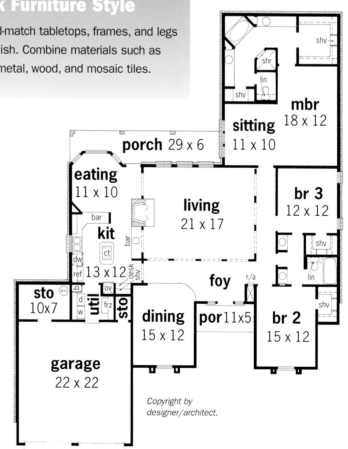

Copyright by designer/architect.

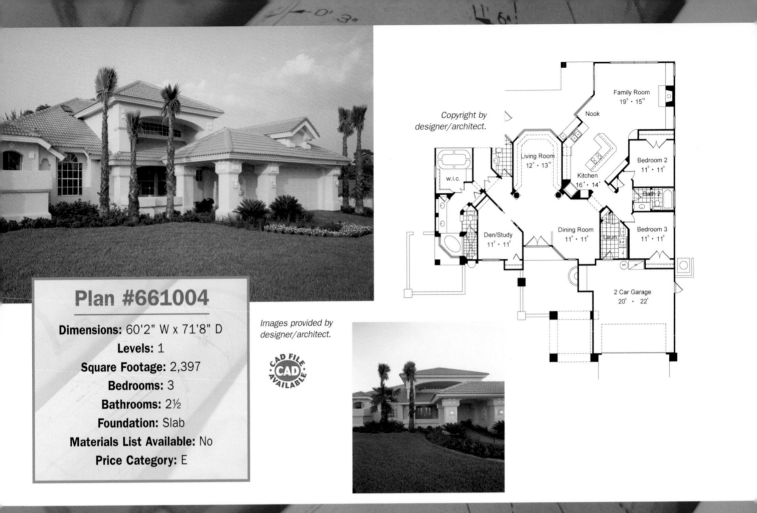

Plan #661004

Dimensions: 60'2" W x 71'8" D

Levels: 1

Square Footage: 2,397

Bedrooms: 3

Bathrooms: 2½

Foundation: Slab

Materials List Available: No

Price Category: E

Images provided by designer/architect.

Copyright by designer/architect.

Plan #391004

Dimensions: 66' W x 52' D

Levels: 1

Square Footage: 1,750

Bedrooms: 2

Bathrooms: 2

Foundation: Crawl space, slab, or basement

Materials List Available: Yes

Price Category: C

Images provided by designer/architect.

Copyright by designer/architect.

This home, as shown in the photograph, may differ from the actual blueprints. For more detailed information, please check the floor plans carefully.

Rear View

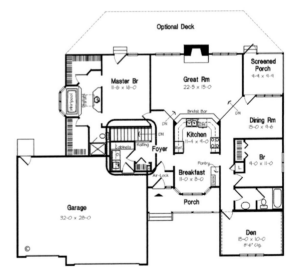

Crawl Space/Slab Optio

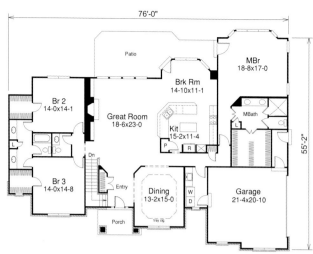

Plan #321007

Dimensions: 76' W x 55'2" D

Levels: 1

Square Footage: 2,695

Bedrooms: 3

Bathrooms: 2½

Foundation: Basement

Materials List Available: Yes

Price Category: F

Images provided by designer/architect.

CAD FILE AVAILABLE · CAD

SMARTtip

Decorative Poles

Drapery poles are supported by the brackets fastened to the window frame or wall. The brackets that are provided with the poles generally coordinate and blend in with the pole finish. Brackets can be simple but also decorative. If you opt for a spectacular, attention-grabbing bracket, consider choosing less showy finials for the ends of the pole.

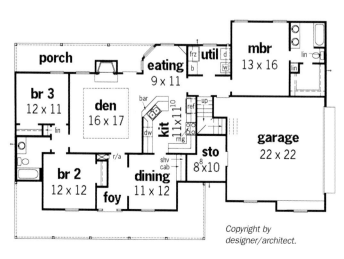

Plan #201086

Dimensions: 68'6" W x 46' D

Levels: 1

Square Footage: 1,573

Bedrooms: 3

Bathrooms: 2

Foundation: Crawl space, slab

Materials List Available: Yes

Price Category: F

Images provided by designer/architect.

Plan #151004

Dimensions: 64'8" W x 62'1" D

Levels: 1

Square Footage: 2,107

Bedrooms: 4

Bathrooms: 2½

Foundation: Crawl space, slab, or basement

CompleteCost List Available: Yes

Price Category: D

Images provided by designer/architect.

You'll love the spacious feeling in this comfortable home designed for a family.

Features:

- Foyer: A 10-ft. ceiling greets you in this home.

- Great Room: A 10-ft. ceiling complements this large room, with its fireplace, built-in cabinets, and easy access to the rear covered porch.

- Dining Room: The 9-ft. boxed ceiling in this large room helps to create a beautiful formal feeling.

- Kitchen: The island in this kitchen is open to the breakfast room for true convenience.

- Breakfast Room: Morning light will stream through the bay window here.

- Master Suite: A 9-ft. pan ceiling adds a distinctive note to this room with access to the rear porch. In the bath, you'll find a whirlpool tub, separate shower, double vanities, and two walk-in closets.

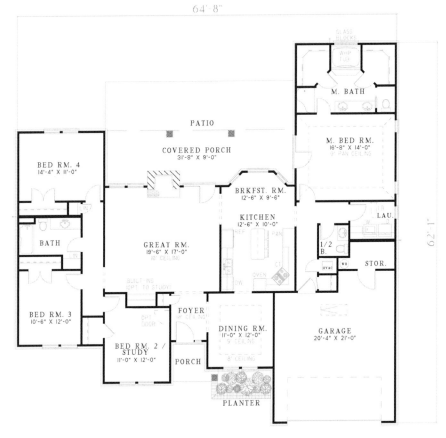

Copyright by designer/architect.

Plan #221057

Dimensions: 89'4" W x 67' D

Levels: 1

Square Footage: 2,551

Bedrooms: 4

Bathrooms: 2½

Foundation: Walkout

Material List Available: No

Price Category: E

Perfect for a growing family, this ranch-style home is spacious and beautiful.

Features:

• Porches: Whether cozying up on the front porch or relaxing in the evening on one of the private porches off of the master bedroom

and kitchen, you're sure to enjoy the outdoors from the comfort of your own home.

• Great Room: Boasting cathedral ceilings and a formal entrance, this enticing room is sure to be a favorite. Wood beams accent the ceilings and are an impressive addition to the room.

• Dining Room: Entertaining family and friends in this gorgeous room with cathedral ceilings is literally a breeze. Enjoy fresh air by keeping the door to the porch open. Chat with guests in the dining room while you cook.

• Master Suite: Take pleasure in privacy without sacrificing space in this resort-like area. Dual

vanities, a shower, and a tub add elegance and practicality to the suite.

• Garages: This three-car garage is wonderful for families with more than one driver. The area also adds valuable storage space or a place to keep equipment for outdoor hobbies.

Images provided by designer/architect.

Rear Elevation

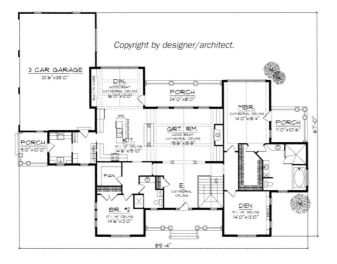

Copyright by designer/architect.

Basement Level Floor Plan

Images provided by designer/architect.

Plan #321004

Dimensions: 91'8" W x 62'4" D
Levels: 1
Square Footage: 2,808
Bedrooms: 3
Bathrooms: 2½
Foundation: Basement
Materials List Available: Yes
Price Category: F

You'll love the sophistication of this design, with its three porches and elegance at every turn.

Features:

• Entry: This impressive space welcomes guests into the living room on one side and the dining room on the other.

• Living Room: This spacious room will be a family favorite, especially in warm weather when you can use the adjoining porch as an outdoor extension of this area.

• Dining Room: Decorate this room to highlight its slightly formal feeling or to create a more casual ambiance for large family dinners.

• Kitchen: The family cooks will appreciate the thought that went into designing the convenient counter space and generous storage areas here.

• Master Suite: A vaulted ceiling, bath with a corner tub, double vanities, walk-in closet, and secluded screened porch make this area a joy.

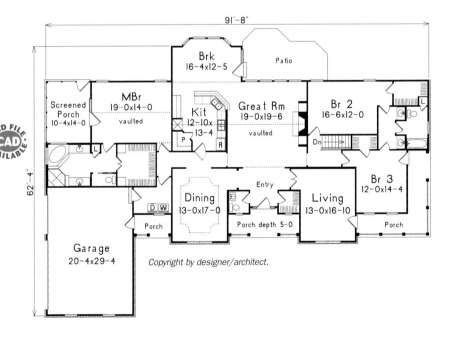

Copyright by designer/architect.

SMARTtip

Ornaments in a Garden

Placement is everything with ornaments in a garden. Some elements are best sitting by themselves. Others are better when they are part of a cohesive whole, perhaps placed in the greenery at a corner or flanking a structure.

Plan #211004

Dimensions: 64' W x 62' D
Levels: 1
Square Footage: 1,828
Bedrooms: 4
Bathrooms: 2
Foundation: Crawl space, slab, or basement
Materials List Available: Yes
Price Category: D

This super-energy-efficient home has the curb appeal of a much larger house.

Features:

- Ceiling Height: 9 ft.

- Kitchen: You will love cooking in this bright, airy, and efficient kitchen. It features an angled layout that allows a great view to the outside through a window wall in the breakfast area.

- Breakfast Area: With morning sunlight streaming through the wall of windows in this area, you won't be able to resist lingering over a cup of coffee.

- Rear Porch: This breezy rear porch is designed to accommodate the pleasure of old-fashioned rockers or swings.

- Master Bedroom: Retreat at the end of a long day to this bedroom, which is isolated for privacy yet conveniently located a few steps from the kitchen and utility area.

- Attic Storage: No need to fuss with creaky pull-down stairs. This attic has a permanent stairwell to provide easy access to its abundant storage.

SMARTtip

Resin Furniture

Resin furniture is made of molded plastic. Most resin pieces are quite affordable, but lacquered resin with brass fittings is a high-end item. Resin doesn't corrode and cleans easily, but a scratched finish cannot be repaired. However, lacquered resin can be touched up.

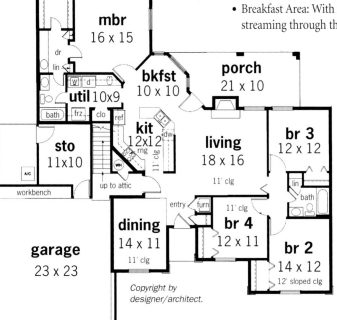

mbr 16 x 15

dr

lin

util 10x9

bath

frz

bkfst 10 x 10

porch 21 x 10

sto 11x10

A/C

workbench

kit 12x12

rng

11' clg

up to attic

WH

living 18 x 16

11' clg

br 3 12 x 12

lin

bath

entry

furn

11' clg

dining 14 x 11

11' clg

br 4 12 x 11

br 2 14 x 12

12' sloped clg

garage 23 x 23

Copyright by designer/architect.

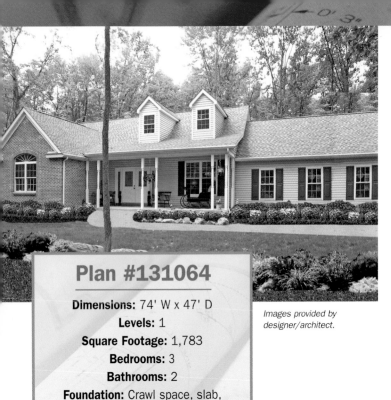

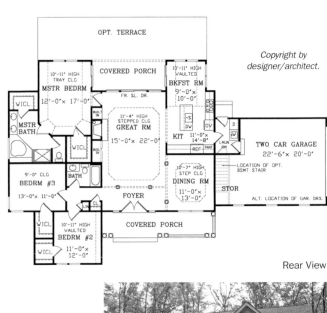

OPT. TERRACE

COVERED PORCH

10'-11" HIGH
TRAY CLG
MSTR BEDRM
12'-0"x 17'-0"

WICL

MSTR
BATH

BKFST RM
10'-11" HIGH
VAULTED
9'-0"x
10'-0"

FR. SL. DR.

BUILT IN

WICL

11'-4" HIGH
STEPPED CLG
GREAT RM
15'-0"x 22'-0"

BUILT IN

KIT
11'-0"x
14'-8"

DW

DV

LAUN
RM

REF PANT

D
W

TWO CAR GARAGE
22'-6"x 20'-0"

LOCATION OF OPT.
BSMT STAIR

9'-0" CLG
BEDRM #3
13'-0"x 11'-0"

BATH

DINING RM
10'-7" HIGH
STEP CLG
11'-0"x
13'-0"

STOR

ALT. LOCATION OF GAR. DRS.

FOYER

WICL

10'-11" HIGH
VAULTED
BEDRM #2
11'-0"x
12'-0"

WICL

COVERED PORCH

*Images provided by
designer/architect.*

Plan #131064

Dimensions: 74' W x 47' D

Levels: 1

Square Footage: 1,783

Bedrooms: 3

Bathrooms: 2

Foundation: Crawl space, slab, or basement

Material List Available: Yes

Price Category: D

Rear View

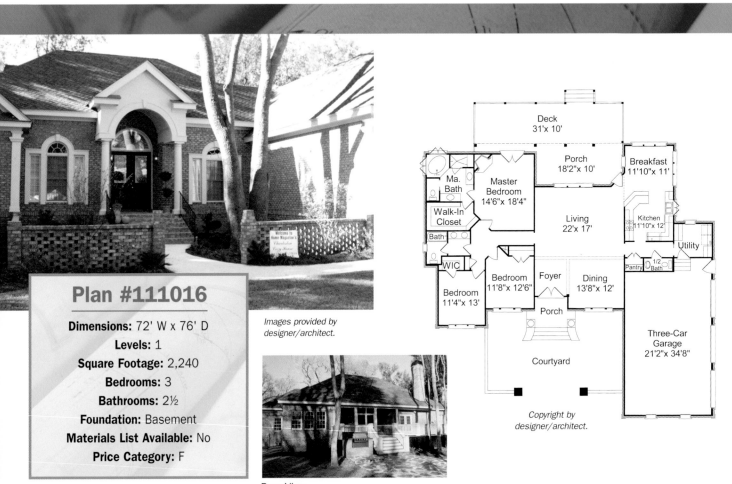

Deck
31'x 10'

Porch
18'2"x 10'

Breakfast
11'10"x 11'

Ma.
Bath

Master
Bedroom
14'6"x 18'4"

Kitchen
11'10"x 12'

Walk-In
Closet

Living
22'x 17'

Utility

Bath

WIC

Bedroom
11'8"x 12'6"

Foyer

Dining
13'8"x 12'

Pantry

1/2
Bath

Bedroom
11'4"x 13'

Porch

Three-Car
Garage
21'2"x 34'8"

Courtyard

Plan #111016

Dimensions: 72' W x 76' D

Levels: 1

Square Footage: 2,240

Bedrooms: 3

Bathrooms: 2½

Foundation: Basement

Materials List Available: No

Price Category: F

*Images provided by
designer/architect.*

Rear View

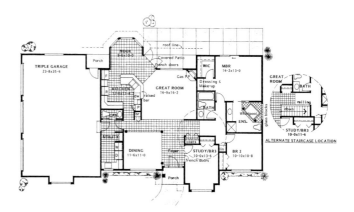

Plan #281008

Dimensions: 74' W x 45' D

Levels: 1

Square Footage: 1,731

Bedrooms: 3

Bathrooms: 2½

Foundation: Basement, crawl space

Materials List Available: Yes

Price Category: C

Images provided by designer/architect.

CAD FILE AVAILABLE

Copyright by designer/architect.

Rear Elevation

Copyright by designer/architect.

Plan #321018

Dimensions: 88'4" W x 48'4" D

Levels: 1

Square Footage: 2,523

Bedrooms: 3

Bathrooms: 2

Foundation: Basement

Materials List Available: Yes

Price Category: E

Images provided by designer/architect.

CAD FILE AVAILABLE

SMARTtip

Tiebacks

You don't have to limit yourself to tiebacks made from matching or contrasting fabric. Achieve creative custom looks by making tiebacks from unexpected items. Some materials to consider are old cotton bandannas or silk scarves, strings of beads, lengths of leather, or old belts and chains.

Plan #151007

Dimensions: 54'2" W x 56'2" D

Levels: 1

Square Footage: 1,787

Bedrooms: 3

Bathrooms: 2

Foundation: Crawl space, slab, basement, or walkout

CompleteCost List Available: Yes

Price Category: C

This home, as shown in the photograph, may differ from the actual blueprints. For more detailed information, plase check the floor plans carefully.

Images provided by designer/archi

This compact, well-designed home is graced with amenities usually reserved for larger houses.

Features:

- Foyer: A 10-ft. ceiling creates unity between the foyer and the dining room just beyond it.

- Dining Room: 8-in. boxed columns welcome you to this dining room, with its 10-ft. ceilings.

- Great Room: The 9-ft. boxed ceiling suits the spacious design. Enjoy the fireplace in the winter and the rear-grilling porch in the summer.

- Breakfast Room: This bright room is a lovely spot for any time of day.

- Master Suite: Double vanities and a large walk-in closet add practicality to this quiet room with a 9-ft. pan ceiling. The master bath includes whirlpool tub with glass block and a separate shower.

- Bedrooms: Bedroom 2 features a bay window, and both rooms are convenient to the bathroom.

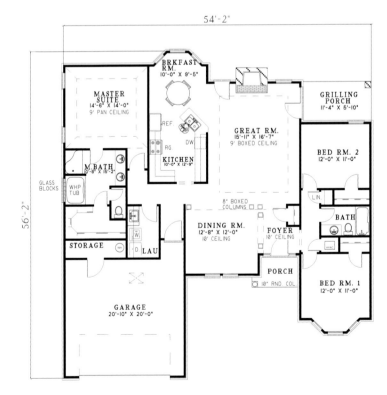

Copyright by designer/architect.

Plan #221039

Dimensions: 89'8" W x 64' D
Levels: 1
Square Footage: 2,839
Bedrooms: 3
Bathrooms: 2½
Foundation: Basement
Materials List Available: No
Price Category: F

This Southwestern design, with its exterior stone masonry and detail-oriented flair, make this home charming and beautiful.

Features:

• Great Room: This enchanting room, with its high ceilings and other comforts, will become the perfect gathering place for you and your loved ones. An added bonus: the view from the great room is of the nature surrounding your home.

• Dining Room: This space opens into a bar and kitchen area, making trips to and from the kitchen short, but the separation of the rooms allows for an elegant dining atmosphere.

• Kitchen: This functional workspace will make meal prep a snap. A breakfast nook is a charming addition to the room, a place where your family can enjoy morning coffee and conversation.

Images provided by designer/architect.

• Master Suite: Containing a large bath with a spa tub, and with luxuries such as his and her walk-in closets and high ceilings, this retreat has sumptuous appeal.

• Additional Bedrooms: Two large bedrooms with walk-in closets are attached to a full bathroom and are perfect for making guests feel right at home, or for children getting ready in the morning.

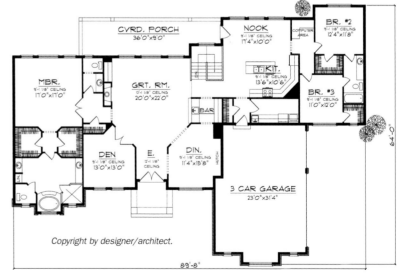

Copyright by designer/architect.

Rear Elevation

Plan #121053

Dimensions: 66' W x 68' D

Levels: 1

Square Footage: 2,456

Bedrooms: 3

Bathrooms: 2½

Foundation: Basement

Materials List Available: Yes

Price Category: E

Images provided by designer/architect.

This home, as shown in the photograph, may differ from the actual blueprints. For more detailed information, please check the floor plans carefully.

If you're looking for a home that gives comfort at every turn, this could be the one.

Features:

- Entry: Airy and open, this entry imparts a welcoming feeling.

- Great Room: You'll love the style built into this centrally located room. A row of transom-topped windows adds natural light, and a fireplace gives it character.

- Dining Room: Just off the entry for convenience, this formal room has a boxed ceiling that accentuates its interesting angled shape.

- Gathering Room: This lovely room features an angled ceiling, snack bar, built-in entertainment center, built-in desk, and abundance of windows. A door leads to the large, covered rear porch with skylights.

- Master Suite: Relax in comfort after a long day, or sit on the adjoining, covered rear porch to enjoy the evening breezes.

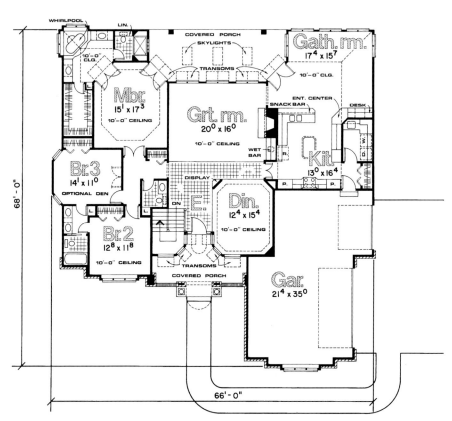

Copyright by designer/architect.

Plan #211059

Dimensions: 68' W x 84' D

Levels: 1

Square Footage: 2,299

Bedrooms: 3

Bathrooms: 2

Foundation: Slab or basement

Materials List Available: No

Price Category: E

Images provided by designer/architect.

This well designed home features plenty of space and all the amenities you seek.

Features:

- Ceiling Height: 9 ft.

- Living Room: This living room is the center of the home's activity. It boasts an attractive, unique angled fireplace and a built-in entertainment room.

- Sunroom: This glass room fills the living room with light. In fact, if you open its interior door on a sunny winter day, it can bring solar heat into the home. The sunroom also has direct access to the porch.

- Master Suite: This suite is located opposite the other bedrooms for maximum privacy. This is truly a master retreat. The private bath features two convenient entries, his and her walk-in closets, dual-sink vanity, luxurious tub, and separate shower.

- Bonus Room: Located over the garage, this room offers 352 ft. of additional space.

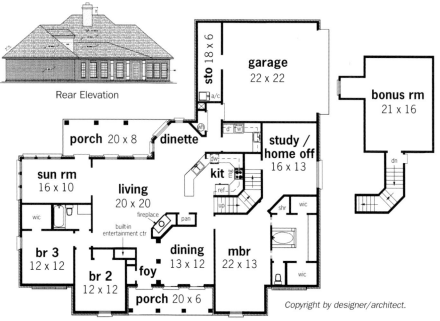

Rear Elevation

Copyright by designer/architect.

SMARTtip

Outdoor Decorating

Arrange outdoor spaces as you would an interior room. Choose a dominant element around which everything else flows. It can be a pool, a fire pit, or the garden. One major furniture piece, such as a dining table, can anchor an area.

Plan #161028

Dimensions: 84'6" W x 69'4" D

Levels: 1

Square Footage: 3,570

Optional Finished Basement
Sq. Ft.: 2,367

Bedrooms: 3

Bathrooms: 3½

Foundation: Basement

Materials List Available: Yes

Price Category: H

Images provided by designer/architect.

From the gabled stone-and-brick exterior to the wide-open view from the foyer, this home will meet your greatest expectations.

Features:

- Great Room/Dining Room: Columns and 13-ft. ceilings add exquisite detailing to the dining room and great room.

- Kitchen: The gourmet-equipped kitchen with an island and a snack bar merges with the cozy breakfast and hearth rooms.

- Master Suite: The luxurious master bed room pampers with a separate sitting room with a fireplace and a dressing room boasting a tub and two vanities.

- Additional: Two bedrooms include a private bath and walk-in closet. The optional finished basement solves all your recreational needs: bar, media room, billiards room, exercise room, game room, as well as an office and fourth bedroom.

Rear Elevation

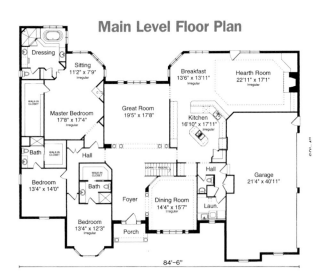

Main Level Floor Plan

Basement Level Floor Plan

Copyright by designer/architect.

Plan #121051

Dimensions: 64' W x 44' D
Levels: 1
Square Footage: 1,808
Bedrooms: 3
Bathrooms: 2½
Foundation: Basement
Materials List Available: Yes
Price Category: D

Images provided by designer/architect.

You'll love the way that natural light pours into this home from the gorgeous windows you'll find in room after room.

Features:

- **Great Room:** You'll notice the bayed, transom-topped window in this lovely great room as soon as you step into the home. A wet-bar makes the room a natural place for entertaining, and the see-through fireplace makes it cozy on chilly days and winter evenings.

- **Kitchen:** This well-designed kitchen will be a delight for everyone who cooks here, not only because of the ample counter and cabinet space but also because of its location in the home.

- **Master Suite:** Angled ceilings in both the bedroom and the bathroom of this suite make it feel luxurious, and the picturesque window in the bedroom gives it character. The bath includes a corner whirlpool tub where you'll love to relax at the end of the day.

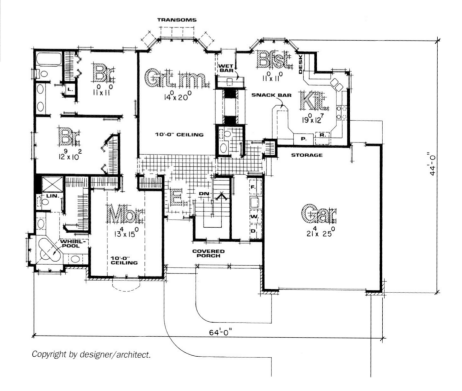

Copyright by designer/architect.

Plan #211001

Dimensions: 52' W x 66' D
Levels: 1
Square Footage: 1,655
Bedrooms: 3
Bathrooms: 2
Foundation: Slab
Materials List Available: Yes
Price Category: C

Images provided by designer/architect.

You'll love this elegant one-story home, both practical and gorgeous, with its many amenities.

Features:

- **Entry:** A covered porch and three glass doors with transoms announce this home.

- **Living Room:** At the center of the house, this living room has a 15-ft. ceiling and a fireplace. A glass door flanked by windows opens to a skylighted porch at the rear of the home.

- **Dining Room:** This elegant octagonal room, which is shaped by columns and cased openings, overlooks both backyard porches.

- **Kitchen:** A 14-ft. sloped ceiling with a skylight adds drama.

- **Master Suite:** Enjoy the seclusion of this area at the rear of the home, as well as its private access to a rear porch. The bath features an oval spa tub, separate shower, dual vanities, and huge walk-in closet.

Copyright by designer/architect.

SMARTtip

Plotting a Potting Space

Whether you opt for a simple corner potting bench or a multipurpose shed or greenhouse, organization is key. You'll need a work surface —a counter or table that's a convenient height for standing while at work—plus storage accommodations for hand tools, long-handled tools, watering cans, extra lengths of hose, hose nozzles, flowerpots, bags of fertilizer and potting soil, gardening books, and notebooks. Plastic garbage cans (with lids) are good for soil and seeds. Most of these spaces are small, so use hooks and stacking bins, which keep items neat and at hand's reach. High shelves free up floor space while holding least-used things.

Plan #321036

Dimensions: 78'4" W x 68'6" D
Levels: 1
Square Footage: 2,900
Bedrooms: 4
Bathrooms: 2½
Foundation: Basement
Materials List Available: No
Price Category: F

This classic contemporary is wrapped in brick.

Features:

- **Great Room:** This grand-scale room offers a vaulted ceiling and Palladian windows flanking an 8-ft.-wide brick fireplace.

- **Kitchen:** This built-in-a-bay room features a picture window above the sink, a huge pantry, and a cooktop island. It opens to the large morning room.

- **Breakfast Area:** Open to the kitchen, this area features 12 ft. of cabinetry.

- **Master Bedroom:** This room features a coffered ceiling, and a walk-in closet gives you good storage space in this luxurious bedroom.

- **Garage:** This area can fit three cars with plenty of room to spare.

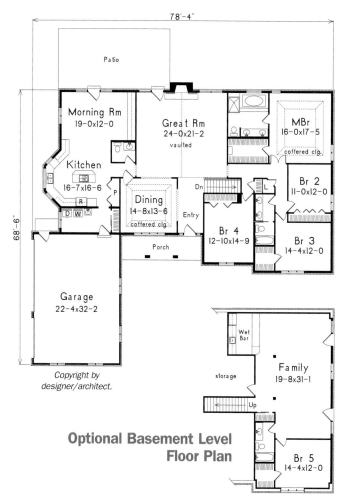

CAD FILE AVAILABLE

Copyright by designer/architect.

Optional Basement Level Floor Plan

Plan #151010

Dimensions: 38'4" W x 68'6" D

Levels: 1

Square Footage: 1,379

Bedrooms: 3

Bathrooms: 2

Foundation: Crawl space, slab

CompleteCost List Available: Yes

Price Category: B

Images provided by designer/architect.

Copyright by designer/architect.

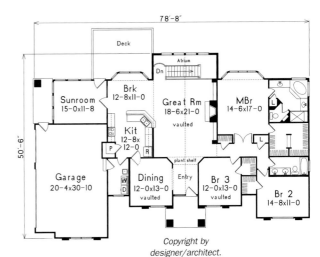

Plan #321037

Dimensions: 78'8" W x 50'6" D

Levels: 1

Square Footage: 2,397

Bedrooms: 3

Bathrooms: 2

Foundation: Basement or walkout

Materials List Available: Yes

Price Category: E

Images provided by designer/architect.

Copyright by designer/architect.

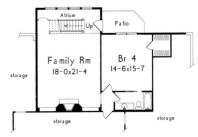

Optional Basement Level Floor Plan

Images provided by designer/architect.

Plan #391008

Dimensions: 50' W x 40' D

Levels: 1

Square Footage: 1,312

Bedrooms: 3

Bathrooms: 2

Foundation: Crawl space, slab, or basement

Materials List Available: Yes

Price Category: B

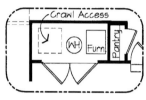

Crawl Space Option

Images provided by designer/architect.

Plan #301003

Dimensions: 84' W x 55'8" D

Levels: 1

Square Footage: 2,485

Bedrooms: 3

Bathrooms: 2½

Foundation: Crawl space, basement

Materials List Available: Yes

Price Category: E

SMARTtip

Making Mitered Returns

Cut the small return piece from a substantial board that you can hold safely and securely against the saw fence.

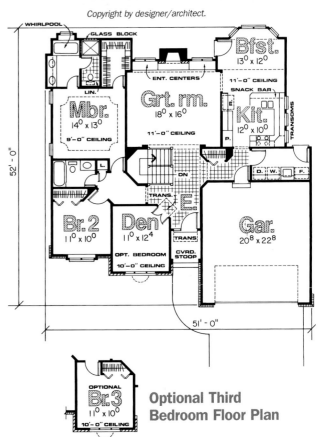

Images provided by
designer/architect.

Plan #121055

Dimensions: 51' W x 52' D

Levels: 1

Square Footage: 1,622

Bedrooms: 3

Bathrooms: 2

Foundation: Basement

Materials List Available: Yes

Price Category: C

Optional Third Bedroom Floor Plan

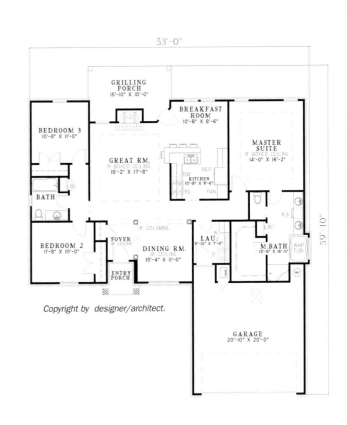

Plan #151043

Dimensions: 53' W x 59'10" D

Levels: 1

Square Footage: 1,636

Bedrooms: 3

Bathrooms: 2

Foundation: Crawl space, slab;
basement option for fee

CompleteCost List Available: Yes

Price Category: E

Images provided by
designer/architect.

Plan #351008

Dimensions: 64'6" W x 61'4" D

Levels: 1

Square Footage: 2,002

Bedrooms: 3

Bathrooms: 2

Foundation: Crawl space or basement

Materials List Available: Yes

Price Category: E

Images provided by designer/architect.

CAD FILE AVAILABLE CAD

Copyright by designer/architect.

Plan #211039

Dimensions: 62' W x 64' D

Levels: 1

Square Footage: 1,868

Bedrooms: 3

Bathrooms: 2

Foundation: Slab

Materials List Available: Yes

Price Category: D

Images provided by designer/architect.

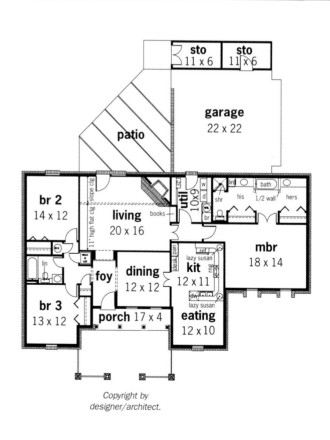

Copyright by designer/architect.

Plan #121057

Dimensions: 64' W x 57'2" D

Levels: 1

Square Footage: 2,311

Bedrooms: 3

Bathrooms: 2½

Foundation: Basement

Materials List Available: Yes

Price Category: E

You'll love to entertain in this home because of its tall ceilings, spacious feeling, open design, and conveniences for both hosts and guests.

Features:

- Entry: The 10-ft. ceiling here sets the stage for the open feeling in this home.

- Great Room: For beauty, this room has a 10-ft. ceiling, arched windows, and a handsome fireplace. The pass-through wet bar and buffet make it a pleasure to entertain here.

- Kitchen: You'll wonder how you ever cooked without the amenities you'll find here—a pantry for extra storage and an island with a wrapped snack bar.

- Master Suite: A corridor gives privacy to this suite, where you'll find two walk-in closets, a sunlit whirlpool tub, a separate shower, and two lavatories.

- Bedroom Wing: An arched opening makes a graceful transition to this wing.

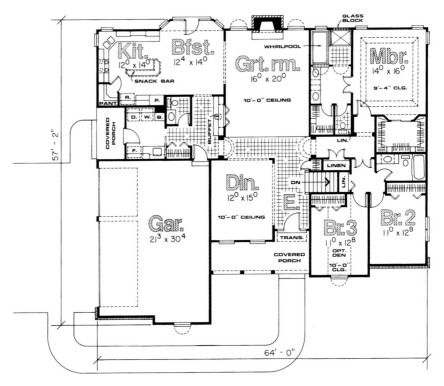

Plan #211050

Dimensions: 68' W x 64' D
Levels: 1
Square Footage: 2,000
Bedrooms: 3
Bathrooms: 2
Foundation: Slab
Materials List Available: Yes
Price Category: D

SMARTtip

Lighting

For lighting in hard-to-reach areas, use a lamp (bulb) with a long life so that you don't have to replace it often.

Stucco siding creates a distinctive counterpoint to the columned front porch.

Features:

- Ceiling Height: 9 ft. unless otherwise noted.

- Living Room: This truly massive living room will accommodate parties of any size, from large formal affairs to more intimate family gatherings.

- Kitchen: This U-shaped kitchen offers generous counter space to make food preparation a pleasure.

- Dinette: Open to the living room, this dinette is the perfect spot for informal family dining.

Images provided by designer/architect.

- Sunroom: There's nothing more pleasant than basking indoors in the warmth of the sun on a cold winter day. When the winter sun is bright, just throw open the double doors between the living room and this delightful sunroom.

- Master Bedroom: This lush retreat boasts a large bedroom and an adjoining study or home office. The master bath has a spa tub, separate shower, dual sinks, and two walk-in closets.

Floor plan labels:
garage 22 x 22
covered porch 20 x 8
eating
util
sto 9 x 9
sun rm 16 x 10
living 20 x 17 — 12' clg
kit 13x11
study 11 x 9
porch
entertainment ctr
pan
br 3 12 x 12
dining 13 x 12 — 12' clg
mbr 22 x 13
br 2 12 x 12
foy
porch 20 x 6

Copyright by designer/architect.

Images provided by
designer/architect.

Plan #151059

Dimensions: 41'10" W x 53' D

Levels: 1

Square Footage: 1,382

Bedrooms: 3

Bathrooms: 2

Foundation: Crawl space, slab;
basement for fee

CompleteCost List Available: Yes

Price Category: B

*Copyright by
designer/architect.*

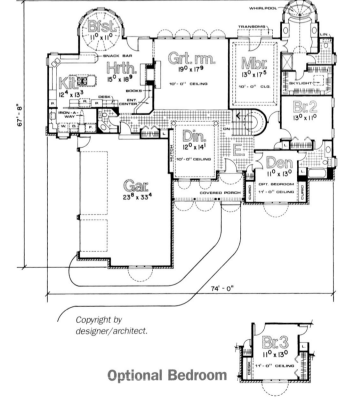

Images provided by
designer/architect.

Plan #121007

Dimensions: 74' W x 67'8" D

Levels: 1

Square Footage: 2,512

Bedrooms: 3

Bathrooms: 2½

Foundation: Basement

Materials List Available: Yes

Price Category: E

*Copyright by
designer/architect.*

Optional Bedroom

Images provided by designer/architect.

Copyright by designer/architect.

Plan #151173

Dimensions: 58' W x 53'6" D
Levels: 1
Square Footage: 1,739
Bedrooms: 3
Bathrooms: 2
Foundation: Crawl space, slab, basement, or walkout
CompleteCost List Available: Yes
Price Category: C

CAD FILE AVAILABLE · CAD

Images provided by designer/architect.

Copyright by designer/architect.

Optional Upper Level Floor Plan

Plan #131036

Dimensions: 72' W x 69'10" D
Levels: 1
Square Footage: 2,585
Bedrooms: 4
Bathrooms: 3
Foundation: Crawl space, slab, or basement
Materials List Available: Yes
Price Category: F

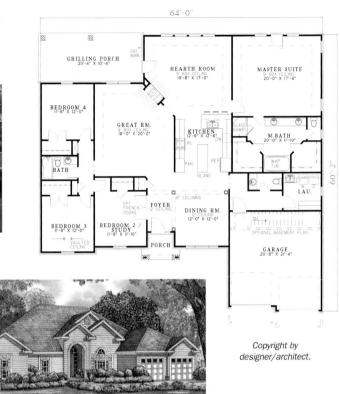

Plan #151063

Dimensions: 64' W x 60'2" D

Levels: 1

Square Footage: 2,554

Bedrooms: 4

Bathrooms: 2½

Foundation: Crawl space or slab; basement or walkout for a fee

CompleteCost List Available: Yes

Price Category: E

Images provided by designer/architect.

This home, as shown in the photograph, may differ from the actual blueprints. For more detailed information, please check the floor plans carefully.

Rear View

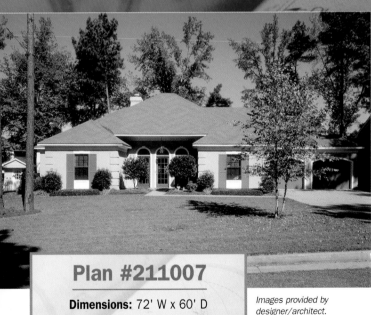

Plan #211007

Dimensions: 72' W x 60' D

Levels: 1

Square Footage: 2,252

Bedrooms: 4

Bathrooms: 2

Foundation: Slab

Materials List Available: Yes

Price Category: E

Images provided by designer/architect.

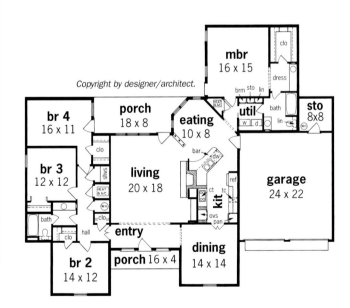

Front View

Optional Basement Level Floor Plan

Copyright by designer/architect.

Plan #391064

Dimensions: 54' W x 28' D

Levels: 1

Square Footage: 988

Bedrooms: 3

Bathrooms: 2

Foundation: Crawl space, basement

Materials List Available: Yes

Price Category: A

Images provided by designer/architect.

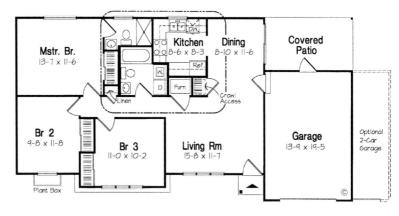

Plan #151711

Dimensions: 64' W x 60'2" D

Levels: 1

Square Footage: 2,554

Bedrooms: 4

Bathrooms: 2½

Foundation: Crawl space or slab

CompleteCost List Available: Yes

Price Category: E

CAD FILE AVAILABLE

Images provided by designer/architect.

This home, as shown in the photograph, may differ from the actual blueprints. For more detailed information, please check the floor plans carefully.

Copyright by designer/architect.

Front View

65'-2"

63'-0"

KNEE SPACE

M.BATH
14'-10" X 14'-4"

WHIRL TUB

9" COLUMNS

MASTER SUITE
14'-10" X 15'-6"

COVERED PORCH
16'-2" X 9'-0"

GRILLING PORCH
12'-4" X 6'-0"

12" + 12" BRICK COLUMNS

BREAKFAST ROOM
11'-8" X 10'-6"

ATRIUM DOOR

LAU.
9'-0" X 6'-6"

STORAGE
11'-8" X 5'-8"

OFFICE
14'-4" X 10'-6"

GREAT ROOM
16'-2" X 20'-0"

FIREPLACE

KITCHEN
11'-8" X 12'-0"

D.W.

REF

GARAGE
20'-10" X 20'-0"

BUILT-INS

BATH

LIN.

FOYER
7'-0" X 9'-6"

DINING ROOM
11'-8" X 11'-6"

BEDROOM 2
11'-10" X 11'-6"

PAN.

BEDROOM 3
11'-10" X 11'-2"

PORCH
7'-0" X 4'-4"

VAULT

VAULT

Plan #151684

Dimensions: 65'2" W x 63' D

Levels: 1

Square Footage: 1,994

Bedrooms: 3

Bathrooms: 2

Foundation: Crawl space, slab, basement, or walkout

CompleteCost List Available: Yes

Price Category: D

Images provided by designer/architect.

Copyright by designer/architect.

Rear Elevation

Patio

Porch

Bedroom
15'9"x 13'1"

Breakfast
13'5"x 11'7"

Master Bedroom
14'5"x 18'7"

Bath

Kitchen
13'9"x14'

Living
20'x 19'3"

WIC

Dress

Bedroom
12'1"x 13'1"

WIC

Master Bath

Utility

Dining
12'7"x 16'1"

Foyer

Bedroom
14'7"x 13'1"

Storage
12'1"x 6'3"

Porch

Two-Car Garage
21'3"x 22'3"

Copyright by designer/architect.

Plan #111018

Dimensions: 67' W x 79' D

Levels: 1

Square Footage: 2,745

Bedrooms: 4

Bathrooms: 3½

Foundation: Basement

Materials List Available: No

Price Category: G

Images provided by designer/architect.

Plan #151336

Dimensions: 39'4" W x 63'2" D

Levels: 1

Square Footage: 1,480

Bedrooms: 3

Bathrooms: 2

Foundation: Crawl space or slab

CompleteCost List Available: Yes

Price Category: B

Images provided by designer/architect.

Copyright by designer/architect.

Front View

Plan #111001

Dimensions: 66'8" W x 76'11" D

Levels: 1

Square Footage: 2,832

Bedrooms: 4

Bathrooms: 2½

Foundation: Crawl space or slab

Materials List Available: No

Price Category: G

Images provided by designer/architect.

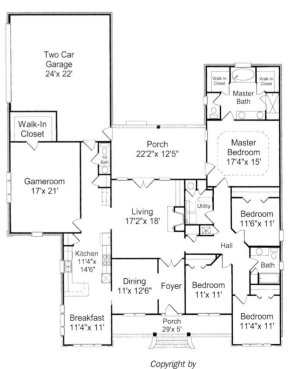

Copyright by designer/architect.

Kitchens and Baths

Of all the rooms in a house, kitchens present unique decorating challenges because so much tends to happen in these spaces. In addition to preparing meals, most families use kitchens as gathering and entertaining areas. Kitchens need to be functional, comfortable, and inviting.

Who can't relate to this scenario: you turn on the oven to preheat it, but wait, did you take out the large roasting pan first?

How about the lasagna dish, muffin tins, pizza stone, and cookie sheets that are in there, too? Now where can you put everything that was in the oven while the casserole is baking and the countertop is laden with the rest of tonight's dinner ingredients? Good cabinetry outfitted with an assortment of organizing options can help you there. It can make your kitchen more efficient and a whole lot neater while establishing a style, or "look," for the room.

Cabinet Construction

Basically, cabinets are constructed in one of two ways: framed or frameless. Framed cabinets have a traditional look, with a full frame across the face of the cabinet box that may show between closed doors. This secures adjacent cabinets and strengthens wider cabinet boxes with a center rail. Hinges on framed cabinets may or may not be visible around doors when they are closed. The door's face may be ornamented with raised or recessed panels, trimmed or framed panels, or a framed-glass panel with or without muntins (the narrow vertical and horizontal strips of wood that divide panes of glass).

Frameless Cabinets. Also known as European-style cabinets, although American manufacturers also make them, frameless cabinets are built without a face frame and sport a clean, contemporary look, often not befitting a Southern or Country style. There's no trim or molding with this simple design. Close-fitting doors cover the entire front of the box, no ornamentation appears on the face of the doors, and hinges are typically hidden inside the cabinet box.

Selecting Cabinets

Choosing one type over another is generally a matter of taste, although framed units offer slightly less interior space. But the quality of construction is a factor that should always be taken into consideration. How do you judge it? Solid wood is too expensive for most of today's budgets, but it might be used on just the doors and frames. More typical is plywood box construction, which offers good structural support and solid wood on the doors and frames. To save money, cabinetmakers sometimes use strong plywood for support elements, such as the box and frame, and medium-density fiberboard for other parts,

such as doors and drawer fronts. In yet another alternative, good-quality laminate cabinets can be made with high-quality, thick particleboard underneath the laminate finish.

Quality Points. There are other things to look for in cabinet construction. They include dovetail or mortise-and-tenon joinery and solidly mortised hinges. Also, make sure that the interior of every cabinet is well finished, with adjustable shelves that are a minimum ⅝ inch thick to prevent bowing.

Bead-board paneled doors, opposite, are at home in Southern-style kitchens.

Framed cabinets, above, offer a traditional look to an otherwise modern kitchen.

Country-style designs have many attributes of Cottage decor, right.

Unless you have the time and skill to build the cabinets yourself or can hire someone else to do it, you'll have to purchase them in one of four ways. **Knockdown cabinetry** (also known as RTA, ready to assemble) is shipped flat and, sometimes, unfinished because you put the pieces together. **Stock cabinetry** comes in standard sizes but limited styles and colors; it is often available on the spot or can be delivered quickly. Like stock, **semicustom cabinetry** comes in standard styles, but it is manufactured to fit a homeowner's specific size and finish needs. **Custom cabinetry** is not limited in terms of style or size because it is built to the designer's specifications.

The Decorative Role of Cabinets

The look you create in your kitchen will be largely influenced by the cabinetry you select. Finding a style that suits you and how you will use your new kitchen is similar to shopping for furniture. In fact, don't be surprised to see many furniture details dressing up the cabinets on view in showrooms and home centers today.

Details That Stand Out. Besides architectural elements such as fluted pilasters, corbels, moldings, and bull's-eye panels, look for details such as fretwork, rope motifs, gingerbread trim, balusters, composition ornamentation (it looks like carving), even footed cabinets that mimic separate furniture pieces. If your taste runs toward less fussy design, you'll also find handsome door and drawer styles that feature minimal decoration, if any. Woods and finishes are just as varied, and range from informal looks in birch, oak, ash, and maple to rich mahogany and cherry. Laminate finishes, though less popular than they were a decade ago, haven't completely disappeared from the marketplace, but an array of colors has replaced the once-ubiquitous almond and white finishes.

Color

Color is coming on strong on wood cabinetry, too. Accents in one, two, or more hues are pairing with natural wood tones. White-painted cabinets take on a warmer glow with tinted shades of this always pop-ular neutral. Special "vintage" finishes, such as translucent color glazes, continue to grow in popularity, as do distressed finishing techniques such as wire brushing and rubbed-through color that add both another dimension and the appeal of handcraftmanship, even on mass-produced items.

If you're shy about using color on such a high-ticket item as cabinetry, try it as an accent on molding, door trim, or island cabinetry. Just as matched furniture suites have become passé in other rooms of the house, the same is true for the kitchen, where mixing several looks can add sophistication and visual interest.

Cabinet Hardware

Another way to emphasize your kitchen's style is with hardware. From exquisite reproductions in brass, pewter, wrought iron, or ceramic to handsome bronze, chrome, nickel, glass, steel, plastic, rubber, wood, or stone creations, a smorgasbord of shapes and designs is available. Some pieces are highly polished; others are matte-finished, smooth, or hammered. Some are abstract or geometrical; others are simple,

elegant shapes. Whimsical designs take on the forms of animals or teapots, vegetables or flowers. Even just one or two great-looking door or drawer pulls can be showstoppers in a kitchen that may otherwise be devoid of much personality. Like mixing cabinet finishes, a combination of two hardware styles—perhaps picked up from other materials in the room—makes a big design statement. As the famed architect Mies Van der Rohe once stated, "God is in the details," and the most perfect detail in your new kitchen may be the artistic hardware that you select.

Cabinet style will set the tone for the design of the entire kitchen. The simple door styles keeps the room at left airy and casual.

The rustic look of the cabinets above is tailor-made for any Country style kitchen.

Color accents, such as the splash of color on the kitchen island shown right, can customize any simple cabinet design.

Cabinet hardware should complement the cabinet door and drawer designs, but it should also be easy for everyone in the household to grasp, above.

Kitchen storage comes in a variety of forms, including cabinets, drawers, pullout extensions, and the glass-front bins shown to the right.

Besides looks, consider the function of a pull or knob. You have to be able to grip it easily and comfortably. If your fingers or hands get stiff easily, or if you have arthritis, select C- or U-shaped pulls. If you like a knob, try it out in the showroom to make sure it isn't slippery or awkward when you grab it. Knobs and pulls can be inexpensive if you can stick to unfinished ones that you can paint in an accent color picked up from the tile or wallpaper. If you don't plan to buy new cabinets, changing the hardware on old ones can redefine their style. The right knob or pull can suggest any one of a number of vintage looks or decorative styles, from Colonial to Victorian, and reinforce your decor.

Types of Storage

Storage facilities can make or break a kitchen, so choose the places you'll put things with care. Here's a look at a few alternatives:

Pantries. How often you shop and how many groceries you typically bring home determine the amount of food storage space your family needs. If you like to stock up or take advantage of sales, add a pantry

to your kitchen. To maximize a pantry's convenience, plan shallow, 6-inch-deep shelves so that cans and packages will never be stored more than two deep. This way, you'll easily be able to see what you've got on hand. Pantries range in size from floor-to-ceiling models to narrow units designed to fit between two standard-size cabinets.

Appliance Garages. Appliance garages make use of dead space in a corner, but they can be installed anywhere in the vertical space between wall-mounted cabinets and the countertop. A tambour (rolltop) door hides small appliances like a food processor or anything else you want within reach but hidden from view.

Lazy Susans and Carousel Shelves. Rotating shelves like lazy Susans and carousels maximize dead corner storage and put items like dishes or pots and pans within easy reach. A lazy Susan rotates 360 degrees, so just spin it to find what you're looking for. Carousel shelves, which attach to two right-angled doors, rotate 270 degrees; open the doors, and the shelves swing out allowing you to reach items easily.

Pivoting Shelves. Door-mounted shelves and in-cabinet swiveling shelf units offer easy access to kitchen supplies. Taller units serve as pantries that hold a great deal in minimal space.

Pullout Tables and Trays. In tight kitchens, pullout tables and trays are excellent ways to gain eating space or an extra work surface. Pullout cutting boards come in handy near cooktops, microwaves, and food prep areas. Pullout tea carts are also available.

Customized Organizers. If you decide to use value-priced cabinets or choose to forego the storage accessories offered by manufacturers, consider refitting their interiors with cabinet organizers you purchase yourself. These plastic, plastic-coated wire, or enameled-steel racks and hangers are widely available at department stores, hardware stores, and home centers.

Some of these units slide in and out of base cabinets, similar to the racks in a dishwasher. Others let you mount shallow drawers to the undersides of wall cabinets.

Still others consist of stackable plastic bins with plenty of room to hold kitchen sundries.

Beware of the temptation to overspecialize your kitchen storage facilities. Sizes and needs for certain items change, so be sure to allot at least 50 percent of your kitchen's storage to standard cabinets with one or more movable shelves. And don't forget to allow for storing recyclable items.

Today's cabinets can be customized with storage accessories, right.

Full-height pantries, above, provide a number of different types of storage near where you need the items. This pantry is next to the food-prep area.

Base cabinets can be outfitted with accessories for kitchen storage or for wet bar storage as shown in the cabinet below.

Storage Checklist

Here's a guide to help you get your storage needs in order.

■ **Do you like kitchen gadgets?**
Plan drawer space, countertop sorters, wall magnets, or hooks to keep these items handy near where you often use them.

■ **Do you own a food processor, blender, mixer, toaster oven, electric can opener, knife sharpener, juicer, coffee maker, or coffee mill?**
If you're particularly tidy, you may want small appliances like these tucked away in an appliance garage or cupboard to be taken out only when needed. If you pre-

fer to have frequently used machines sitting on the counter, ready to go, plan enough space, along with conveniently located electrical outlets.

■ **Do you plan to store large quantities of food?**
Be sure to allow plenty of freezer, bin, and shelf space for the kind of food shopping you do.

■ **Do you intend to do a lot of freezing or canning?**
Allow a work space and place to stow equipment. Also plan adequate storage for the fruits of your labor—an extra stand-alone freezer, a good-sized food safe in the kitchen, or a separate pantry or cellar.

■ **Do you bake often?**
Consider a baking center that can house your equipment and serve as a separate baking-ingredients pantry.

■ **Do you collect pottery, tinware, or anything else that might be displayed in the kitchen?**
Soffits provide an obvious place to hang small objects like collectible plates. Eliminating soffits provides a shelf on top of the wall cabinets for larger light-weight objects like baskets. Open shelving, glass-front cupboards, and display cabinets are other options.

■ **Do you collect cookbooks?**
If so, you'll need expandable shelf space and perhaps a bookstand.

Personal Profile of You and Your Family

■ **How tall are you and everyone else who will use your kitchen?**
Adjust your counter and wall-cabinet heights to suit. Multilevel work surfaces for special tasks are a necessity for good kitchen design.

■ **Do you or any of your family members use a walker, leg braces, or a wheelchair?**
Plan a good work height, knee space, grab bars, secure seating, slide-out work

Fold-down ironing boards, above left, are a true luxury. If you have the space, install one near the kitchen or laundry room.

Corner cabinets often contain storage space you can't reach. Make it accessible by installing swing-out shelves, above right, or a lazy Susan.

Glass doors put your kitchen items on display. The owners of the kitchen below chose distinctive pottery and glassware for their glass-door cabinets.

boards, and other convenience features to make your kitchen comfortable for all who will use it.

■ **Are you left- or right-handed?**
Think about your natural motion when you choose whether to open cupboards or refrigerator doors from the left or right side, whether to locate your dishwasher to the left or right of the sink, and so on.

■ **How high can you comfortably reach?**
If you're tall, hang your wall cabinets high. If you're petite, you may want to hang the cabinets lower and plan a spot to keep a step stool handy.

■ **Can you comfortably bend and reach for something in a base cabinet? Can you lift heavy objects easily and without strain or pain?**
If your range is limited in these areas, be sure to plan roll-out shelving on both upper and lower tiers of your base cabinets. Also, look into spring-up shelves designed to lift mixer bases or other heavy appliances to counter height.

■ **Do you frequently share cooking tasks with another family member?**
If so, you may each prefer to have your own work area.

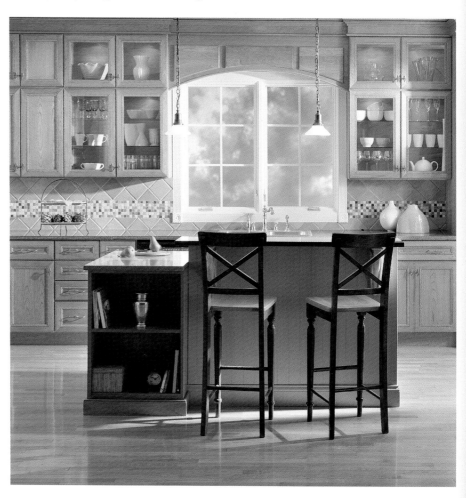

ous plan demands this kind of attention. Even if you are designing a modest bath, you can greatly increase its performance and your ultimate comfort by thoughtfully planning out every square inch of floor and wall space. In fact, small spaces require more attention to details than larger spaces.

Types of bathrooms

The most-common-size American bathroom measures 60 x 84 inches or 60 x 96 inches. The most common complaint about it is the lack of space. The arrangement may have suited families 50 years ago, but times and habits have changed. If it's the only bathroom in the house, making it work better becomes even more important.

When planning the layout, try angling a sink or shower unit in a corner to free up some floor space. Unlike a traditional door, which swings into the room and takes up wall space when it is open, a pocket door slides into the wall. Another smart way to add function to a small bathroom is to remove the drywall and install shelves between the studs.

The Importance of Lighting. You can also make a small bathroom feel roomier by bringing in natural light with a skylight or roof window or by replacing one small standard window with several small casement units that can be installed high on the wall to maintain privacy while admitting light.

Bath Design

Many professionals believe that bathrooms may be the most difficult rooms in the house to design properly. The space is often small, yet it must be able to accommodate a variety of large fixtures. In addition, many homeowners tend to focus, at least initially, on the way the bathroom looks. They fall in love with the whirlpool tub that is really too large for the space or the exquisite hand-painted sink that, while beautiful, demands too much effort to keep it

looking that way. Design your bath to be functional as well as beautiful.

Architect Louis Sullivan said, "Form follows function." That does not mean that style has to be subservient to function, but there must be a balance between the two. So even if you have a clear picture about how you want the new bathroom to look, put that thought on hold—temporarily— and think about how it will work.

Thorough Planning. Don't mislead yourself into believing that only a luxuri-

The Master Bath

The concept of the master bath has come of age in the past decade. It is one of the most popular rooms for splurging on high-end items and gives one of the highest returns on investment upon resale. It's where you can create that sought-after getaway—the home version of a European spa.

Latest Trends. Some popular amenities to include in your plan are a sauna, greenhouse, exercise studio, fireplace, audio and video systems, faucets and sprayers with full massaging options, steam room,

Windows placed high on the wall let in light while maintaining privacy, opposite.

Master baths, above, often contain an attached dressing area.

Traditional designs do not prevent you from using the latest shower products, right.

Cottage baths tend to be bright and airy, such as the one shown to the left.

A simple floral design decorates the border of the medicine cabinet above.

Traditional bathroom cabinetry should be simple in design, below.

whirlpool tub, and dressing table. You are only limited by size and imagination.

Planning for Extras. Extras can be tempting but may require special planning. For example, you may need additional support in the floor, as well as supplemental heating and ventilation. You would not want to slip into a tub and have it fall two floors to the middle of the living room.

Some of the best floor plans for the modern adult bath also include a separate room for the toilet and bidet, a detached tub and shower, and dual sinks on opposite sides of the room with adjacent dressing rooms and walk-in closets. Modern couples

want to share a master bed and bath, but they also want to have privacy and the ease of getting ready in the morning without tripping over their mates. The only way to do this harmoniously is to mingle the parts of the room that invite sharing and separate those elements that are always private. Such items as a sauna, exercise area, and a whirlpool tub would be part of shared space. Dressing tables and clothes closets would be private spaces.

The Powder Room

The guest bath. The half bath. It has a lot of names, and it may be the most efficient room in the house, providing just what you

need often in tight quarters. A powder room normally includes nothing more than a lavatory and a toilet. You can find small-scale fixtures specifically designed for the powder room, from the tiniest lavs to unusually narrow toilets.

Keep a small powder room as light and open as possible. Plan to install good lighting because the powder room is often used for touching up makeup.

Focal Points. In the powder room, the vanity is often the focal point. The room offers the best opportunity to showcase a decorative piece, such as a hand-painted pedestal sink or a custom-made vanity.

Because the powder room is often for guests and is normally located on the ground floor near the living area, take extra care to ensure privacy. If possible, the best location is in a hallway, away from the living room, kitchen, and dining area. This room can also handle stronger wall colors—either dark or bright ones—as well as larger, bolder wallpaper patterns because it is a short-stay room.

The Family Bath

Compartmentalizing is the best way to start planning the family bath. But remember, when you separate the bathroom into smaller, distinct areas, you run the risk of making the room feel cramped. Try to alleviate this with extra natural light, good artificial lighting, and translucent partitions made of glass blocks or etched glass. Anything that divides with privacy while also allowing light to enter will help ease the closed-in feeling.

Separate Areas. If separating the fixtures is not possible because of the size of the room, include a sink in the dressing area within the master bedroom to provide a second place for applying makeup or shaving. It will help relieve bottlenecks when everyone is dressing in the morning.

Investigate building a back-to-back bath in lieu of one large shared room. Another popular option is to locate the bathing fixtures, both the tub and separate shower, in the center of the room; install the bidet, a toilet, and sink on either side in their own separate areas. To make the arrangement work, keep each side of the room accessible to the door.

There are other options you can use. It is important to remember that you don't need to do them all at once; you can do some remodeling once you've moved into your house.

Ceramic-tile counters for bathroom vanities are easy to clean and can stand up to abuse.

Plan #111006

Dimensions: 56' W x 67' D
Levels: 1
Square Footage: 2,241
Bedrooms: 4
Bathrooms: 2½
Foundation: Slab
Materials List Available: No
Price Category: F

You'll love this plan if you're looking for a home with fantastic curb appeal on the outside and comfortable amenities on the inside.

Features:

- Foyer: This lovely foyer opens to both the living and dining rooms.

- Dining Room: Three columns in this room accentuate both its large dimensions and its slightly formal air.

- Living Room: This room gives an airy feeling, and the fireplace here makes it especially inviting when the weather's cool.

- Kitchen: This G-shaped kitchen is designed to save steps while you're working, and the ample counter area adds even more to its convenience. The breakfast bar is a great gathering area.

- Master Suite: Two walk-in closets provide storage space, and the bath includes separate vanities, a standing shower, and a deluxe corner bathtub.

Images provided by designer/architect.

Copyright by designer/architect.

Plan #161100

Dimensions: 89' W x 59'2" D
Levels: 1
Square Footage: 5,377
Main Level Sq. Ft.: 2,961
Basement Level Sq. Ft.: 2,416
Bedrooms: 3
Bathrooms: 2 full, 2 half
Foundation: Walkout;
basement for fee
Material List Available: No
Price Category: J

This luxury home is perfect for you and
your family.

Images provided by designer/architect.

Features:

- Foyer: This beautiful foyer showcases the two-sided fireplace, which warms its space, as well as that of the great room.

- Gathering Areas: The kitchen, breakfast area, and hearth room will quickly become a favorite gathering area, what with the warmth of the fireplace and easy access to a covered porch. Expansive windows with transoms create a light and airy atmosphere.

- Master Suite: This suite makes the most of its circular sitting area and deluxe dressing room with platform whirlpool tub, dual vanities, commode room with closet, and two-person shower.

- Lower Level: This lower level is finished with additional bedrooms and areas dedicated to entertaining, such as the wet bar, billiards area, media room, and exercise room

Rear View

*Copyright by
designer/architect.*

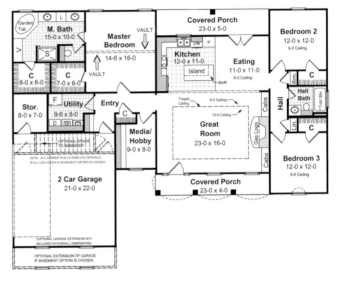

Plan #351002

Dimensions: 64' W x 45'10" D

Levels: 1

Square Footage: 1,751

Bedrooms: 3

Bathrooms: 2

Foundation: Crawl space, slab, or basement

Materials List Available: Yes

Price Category: D

Images provided by designer/architect.

CAD FILE AVAILABLE

Copyright by designer/architect.

Plan #351141

Dimensions: 69' W x 75'10" D

Levels: 1

Square Footage: 2,021

Bedrooms: 3

Bathrooms: 2½

Foundation: Basement

Material List Available: Yes

Price Category: F

Images provided by designer/architect.

CAD FILE AVAILABLE

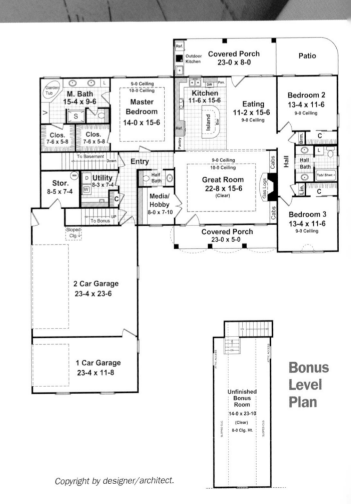

Copyright by designer/architect.

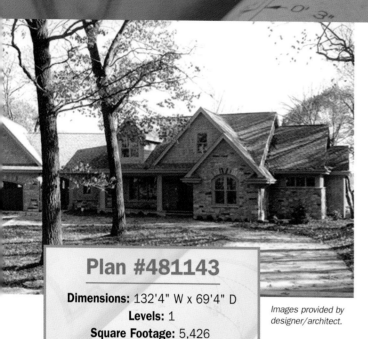

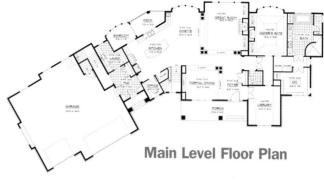

Main Level Floor Plan

Basement Level Floor Plan

Copyright by designer/architect.

Plan #481143

Dimensions: 132'4" W x 69'4" D
Levels: 1
Square Footage: 5,426
Main Level Sq. Ft.: 3,046
Lower Level Sq. Ft.: 2,380
Bedrooms: 4
Bathrooms: 3½
Foundation: Walkout
Material List Available: No
Price Category: J

Images provided by designer/architect.

Copyright by designer/architect.

Plan #151850

Dimensions: 66' W x 52' D
Levels: 1
Square Footage: 2,075
Bedrooms: 4
Bathrooms: 3
Foundation: Crawl space or slab; basement or walkout for fee
CompleteCost List Available: Yes
Price Category: D

Images provided by designer/architect.

CAD FILE AVAILABLE

Images provided by designer/architect.

CAD FILE AVAILABLE

Plan #351126

Dimensions: 69' W x 63'10" D

Levels: 1

Square Footage: 2,021

Bedrooms: 3

Bathrooms: 2½

Foundation: Crawl space, slab or basement

Material List Available: Yes

Price Category: F

Bonus Area Floor Plan

Copyright by designer/architect.

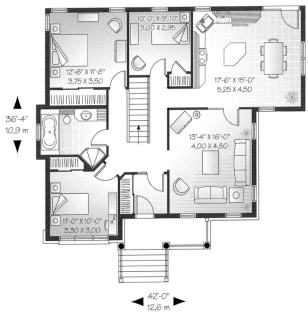

Images provided by designer/architect.

CAD FILE AVAILABLE

Plan #181715

Dimensions: 42' W x 36'4" D

Levels: 1

Square Footage: 1,309

Bedrooms: 3

Bathrooms: 1

Foundation: Basement

Material List Available: Yes

Price Category: B

Copyright by designer/architect.

Plan #151841

Dimensions: 53'8" W x 64'8" D

Levels: 1

Square Footage: 1,747

Bedrooms: 3

Bathrooms: 2

Foundation: Crawl space or slab; basement or walkout for fee

CompleteCost List Available: Yes

Price Category: C

Images provided by designer/architect.

Copyright by designer/architect.

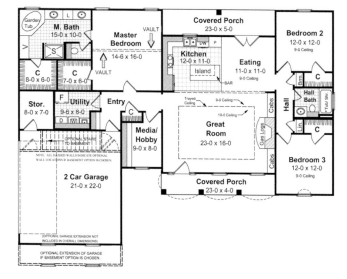

Plan #351003

Dimensions: 64' W x 45'10" D

Levels: 1

Square Footage: 1,751

Bedrooms: 3

Bathrooms: 2

Foundation: Crawl space, slab, or basement

Materials List Available: Yes

Price Category: D

Images provided by designer/architect.

Copyright by designer/architect.

Plan #561005

Dimensions: 58'4" W x 71' D
Levels: 1
Square Footage: 2,358
Bedrooms: 3
Bathrooms: 2
Foundation: Basement
Material List Available: No
Price Category: E

This magnificent farmhouse design, with its traditional front porch and rear screened-in porch, is more than just a home.

Features:

- Great Room: Gather by the glowing fire on cold nights, or expand your entertaining space any other time. This great room is at the center of everything and has plenty of space for friends, family, and anyone else you can think to invite.

- Kitchen: A built-in pantry and ample counter space make a great work area for the family cook and the aspiring chef alike. An open transition to the breakfast area simplifies morning chaos, while a defined separation formalizes the dining room.

- Master Suite: This area is a welcome retreat where you can shut out the frenzied world and simply relax. The attached master bath includes dual walk-in closets, his and her sinks, a standing shower, and a separate tub – perfect for busy mornings and romantic evenings.

- Secondary Bedrooms: These bedrooms boast ample closet space and equal distance to a full bathroom. They're also off the beaten path, creating a calmer space for study and sleep.

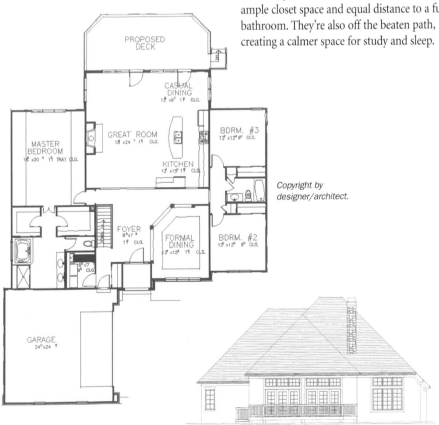

Rear Elevation

Plan #181728

Dimensions: 60' W x 30' D
Levels: 1
Square Footage: 1,322
Bedrooms: 3
Bathrooms: 1
Foundation: Basement
Material List Available: Yes
Price Category: B

CAD FILE AVAILABLE

Images provided by designer/architect.

This home radiates country charm.

Features:

- **Entry:** The excitement builds as you step inside this welcoming entry. A pocket door can close off the living room, creating an air lock for energy conservation.

- **Living Room:** A bay window and a fireplace set the mood in this gathering area. Friends and family will enjoy the serenity of the room.

- **Kitchen:** With an abundance of cabinet and counter space, this kitchen will please the family chef. The attached dinette area features a sliding glass door leading to the future deck.

- **Bedrooms:** Three bedrooms are provided in the home. The master bedroom features a walk-in closet. All bedrooms share a full bathroom, which includes a stall shower and a deluxe tub.

Copyright by designer/architect.

Images provided by designer/architect.

Plan #441014

Dimensions: 119'6" W x 87'6" D
Levels: 1
Square Footage: 3,940
Bedrooms: 3
Bathrooms: 3 full, 2 half
Foundation: Crawl space; slab or basement available for fee
Materials List Available: No
Price Category: H

Though this is but a single-story home, it satisfies and delights on many levels. The exterior has visual appeal, with varied rooflines, a mixture of materials, and graceful traditional lines.

Features:

- **Great Room:** This huge room boasts a sloped, vaulted ceiling, a fireplace, and built-ins. There is also a media room with double-door access.

- **Kitchen:** This kitchen has an island, two sink prep areas, a butler's pantry connecting it to the formal dining room, and a walk-in pantry.

- **Bedrooms:** Family bedrooms sit at the front of the plan and are joined by a Jack-and-Jill bathroom.

- **Master Suite:** This master suite is on the far right side. Its grand salon has an 11-ft.-high ceiling, a fireplace, built-ins, a walk-in closet, and a superb bathroom.

- **Garage:** If you need extra space, there's a bonus room on an upper level above the three-car garage.

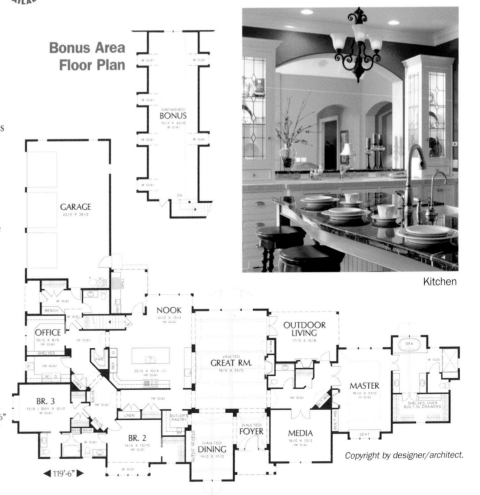

Kitchen

Copyright by designer/architect.

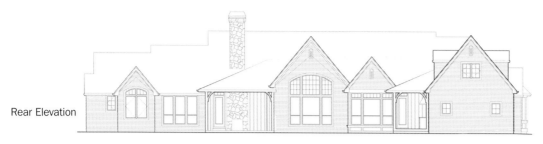

Rear Elevation

Dining Room

Master Bath

Great Room

Kitchen

Plan #101033

Dimensions: 62' W x 69'2" D

Levels: 1

Square Footage: 2,260

Bedrooms: 3

Bathrooms: 3

Foundation: Basement

Material List Available: No

Price Category: E

The standing-seam roof over the entry porch makes this home stand out.

Features:

• Family Room: This gathering area features an over-13-ft.-tall ceiling, a built-in entertainment center, and a fireplace.

• Kitchen: This large kitchen has a built-in pantry and is open to the breakfast nook.

• Master Suite: This suite provides a dramatic extended bow-window wall with a clear view to the pool. It also offers his and her walk-in closets, a sitting area, and direct access to the covered rear porch.

• Bedrooms: The two additional bedrooms share a Jack-and-Jill bathroom Bedroom 2 has a walk-in closet.

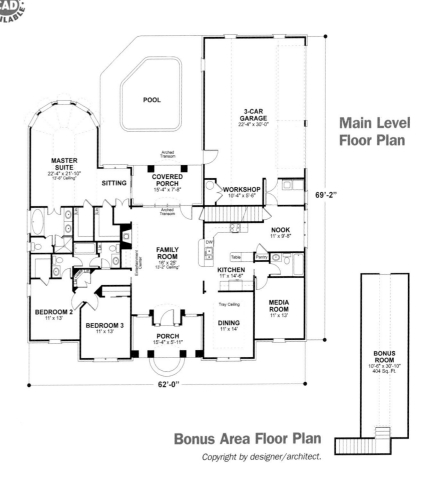

Main Level Floor Plan

Bonus Area Floor Plan

Plan #181652

Dimensions: 29' W x 44' D
Levels: 2
Square Footage: 1,579
Main Level Sq. Ft.: 709
Upper Level Sq. Ft.: 870
Bedrooms: 3
Bathrooms: 1½
Foundation: Basement
Material List Available: Yes
Price Category: C

This is an attractive home with an appealing Mediterranean look.

Images provided by designer/architect.

Features:

- Entry: This covered entry welcomes you home. The sidelights on the front door flood the interior with light. A coat closet and a half bath add convenience.
- Family Room: Open to the kitchen for an airy feel, this gathering area will be the place to unwind after a long day.
- Kitchen: The family chef will love this kitchen. The room contains extra seating at the island and a convenient breakfast nook. A three-panel sliding-glass door brings plenty of natural light to the area.
- Upper Level: Three bedrooms, a full bathroom, and the laundry area are located on this level.

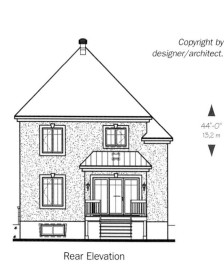

Rear Elevation

Main Level Floor Plan

Copyright by designer/architect.

14'-8" X 19'-0"
4,40 X 5,70

12'-8" X 14'-0"
3,80 X 4,20

12'-0" X 20'-8"
3,60 X 6,20

44'-0"
13,2 m

29'-0"
8,7 m

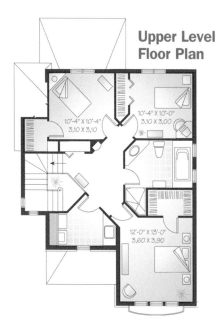

Upper Level Floor Plan

10'-4" X 10'-4"
3,10 X 3,10

10'-4" X 10'-0"
3,10 X 3,00

12'-0" X 13'-0"
3,60 X 3,90

Plan #191058

Dimensions: 80' W x 56' D

Levels: 1

Square Footage: 2,550

Bedrooms: 5

Bathrooms: 3

Foundation: Slab

Material List Available: No

Price Category: E

Images provided by designer/architect.

Designed for today's family, this house has everything you want and everything you need.

Features:

- **Great Room:** This large gathering area boasts a beautiful gas fireplace. There are built-in cabinets on either side of the fireplace, which would be a perfect entertainment center.

- **Dining Room:** Accented by an arched opening and columns, this dining room is able to handle all formal gatherings. Its location adjacent to the kitchen and the great room allows friends and family to have easy access to these two areas.

- **Kitchen:** This peninsula kitchen has an abundance of cabinets and counter space. The open counter, which reaches into the great room, allows these two areas to work as one space.

- **Master Suite:** A vaulted-ceiling retreat is provided to remove the stress from your day. The luxurious master bath pampers you with a whirlpool bath, dual vanities, and separate toilet area.

Copyright by designer/architect.

Kitchen

Rear View

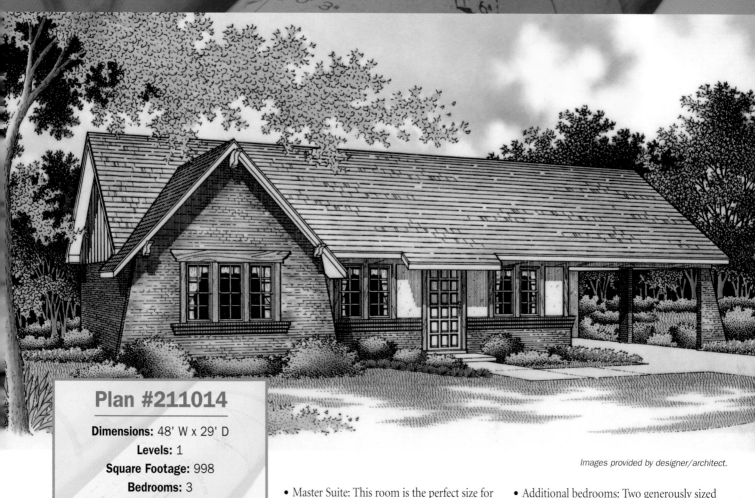

Plan #211014

Dimensions: 48' W x 29' D
Levels: 1
Square Footage: 998
Bedrooms: 3
Bathrooms: 1
Foundation: Slab; crawl space for fee
Material List Available: Yes
Price Category: A

This traditional-style home has cozy, rustic charm.

Features:

- Living Room: Spacious and placed centrally, this family area opens up into the dining room as well as the front hallway. The adjoining rooms make the area ideal for entertaining or for cozying up with loved ones after dinner.

- Dining Room: Featuring the perfect amount of space for a large table, this room offers a beautiful retreat from the hustle and bustle of kitchen activity. A bar area, where high-backed chairs can be added, is perfect for less formal dining.

- Kitchen: This convenient setup offers every thing a cook needs. An area for the refrigerator is placed near the entrance so that reaching for a quick item from the fridge won't interfere with the busy chef.

- Master Suite: This room is the perfect size for two. Its features include a large walk-in closet, as well as its own separate entrance to the bathroom.

- Additional bedrooms: Two generously sized bedrooms offer ample closet space and are spacious enough to accommodate each member of your family.

Images provided by designer/architect.

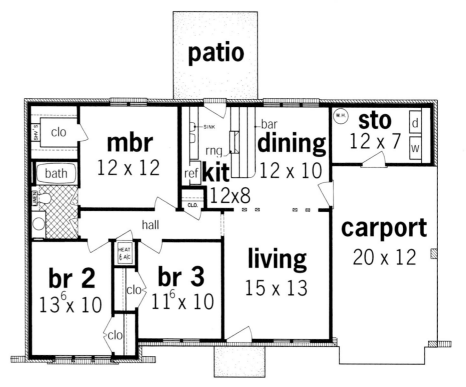

Copyright by designer/architect.

Images provided by designer/architect.

Plan #481036

Dimensions: 84'8" W x 82'4" D
Levels: 1
Square Footage: 4,258
Main Level Sq. Ft.: 2,440
Basement Level Sq. Ft.: 1,818
Bedrooms: 4
Bathrooms: 3½
Foundation: Walkout
Material List Available: No
Price Category: I

Old-world style with a modern floor plan makes this home perfect for you.

Features:

• Great Room: With a 12-ft.-high ceiling and a glowing fireplace, this room welcomes you home. Relax with your family, or entertain your friends.

• Study: Located off the foyer, this room would make a perfect home office; clients can come and go without disturbing the family.

• Master Suite: Unwind in this private space,

and enjoy its many conveniences. The full master bath includes a standing shower, his and her sinks, a large tub, and a spacious walk-in closet.

• Garage: This large storage space has room for three full-size cars and includes a convenient sink. The stairs to the storage area in the basement will help keep things organized.

Main Level Floor Plan

Basement Level Floor Plan

Copyright by designer/architect.

Plan #101030

Dimensions: 63' W x 63' D

Levels: 1

Square Footage: 2,071

Bedrooms: 3

Bathrooms: 2½

Foundation: Crawl space or basement

Materials List Available: No

Price Category: D

This lovely three-bedroom brick home with an optional bonus room above the three-car garage is just what you've been looking for.

Features:

- **Family Room:** This large room, with its high ceiling and cozy fireplace, is great for entertaining.

- **Kitchen:** This kitchen boasts a built-in pantry and a peninsula opening into the breakfast nook.

- **Master Suite:** This suite, with its 14-ft.-high ceiling and private sitting area, is a perfect place to relax after a long day. The bath has a double vanity, large walk-in closet, and soaking tub.

- **Bedrooms:** Two additional bedrooms feature walk-in closets and share a private bathroom.

Images provided by designer/architect.

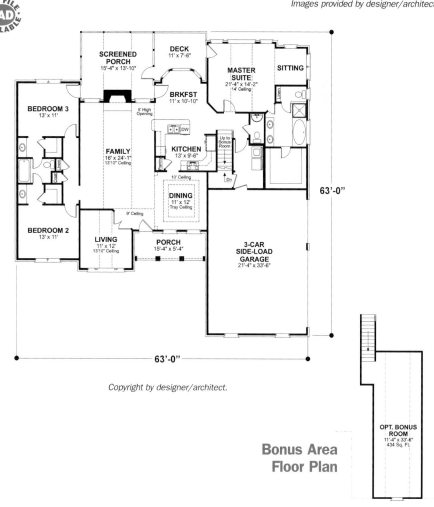

Copyright by designer/architect.

Bonus Area Floor Plan

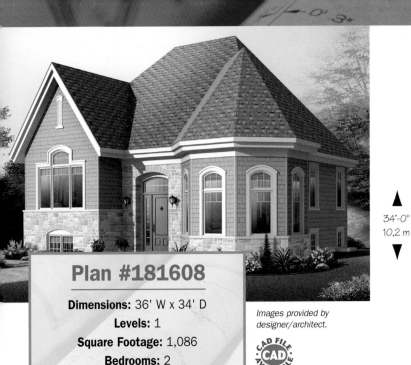

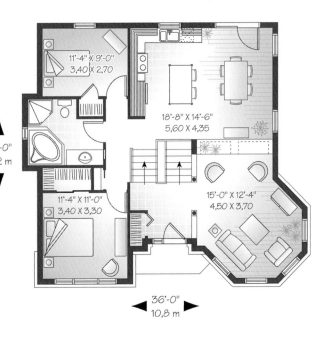

Plan #181608

Dimensions: 36' W x 34' D

Levels: 1

Square Footage: 1,086

Bedrooms: 2

Bathrooms: 1

Foundation: Basement

Material List Available: Yes

Price Category: B

Images provided by designer/architect.

CAD FILE AVAILABLE

34'-0"
10,2 m

11'-4" X 9'-0"
3,40 X 2,70

18'-8" X 14'-6"
5,60 X 4,35

11'-4" X 11'-0"
3,40 X 3,30

15'-0" X 12'-4"
4,50 X 3,70

36'-0"
10,8 m

Copyright by designer/architect.

Plan #211012

Dimensions: 33'9" W x 43' D

Levels: 1

Square Footage: 984

Bedrooms: 2

Bathrooms: 1½

Foundation: Slab; crawl space for fee

Materials List Available: Yes

Price Category: A

Images provided by designer/architect.

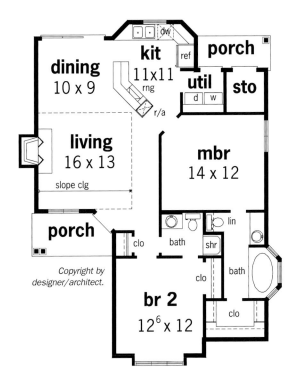

kit
11x11
rng

ref

porch

dining
10 x 9

util
d w

sto

living
16 x 13

mbr
14 x 12

slope clg

porch

clo

bath

shr

lin

clo

bath

br 2
12⁶ x 12

clo

Copyright by designer/architect.

Copyright by designer/architect.

Plan #351138

Dimensions: 69' W x 71'10" D
Levels: 1
Square Footage: 2,000
Bedrooms: 3
Bathrooms: 2½
Foundation: Crawl space, slab
Material List Available: Yes
Price Category: F

Images provided by designer/architect.

CAD FILE AVAILABLE
CAD

Upper Level Floor Plan

Plan #131003

Dimensions: 60' W x 39'10" D
Levels: 1
Square Footage: 1,466
Bedrooms: 3
Bathrooms: 2
Foundation: Crawl space, slab, or basement
Materials List Available: Yes
Price Category: C

Images provided by designer/architect.

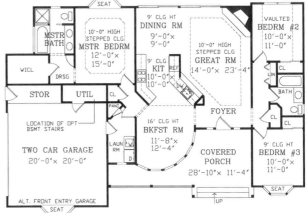

This home, as shown in the photograph, may differ from the actual blueprints. For more detailed information, plsea check the floor plans carefully.

Kitchen/Great Room

Kitchen

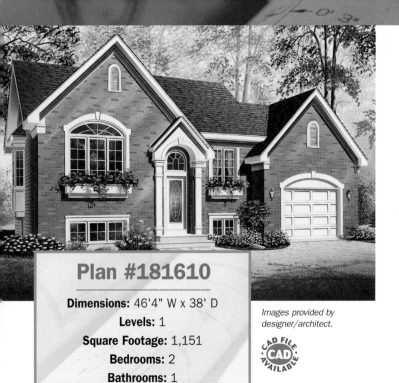

Plan #181610

Dimensions: 46'4" W x 38' D

Levels: 1

Square Footage: 1,151

Bedrooms: 2

Bathrooms: 1

Foundation: Basement

Material List Available: Yes

Price Category: B

Images provided by designer/architect.

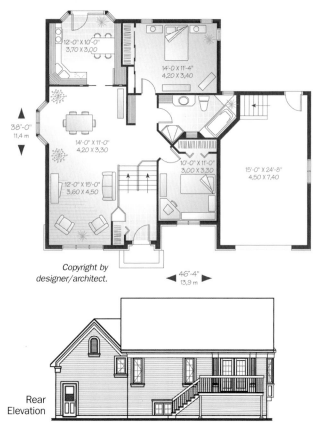

Copyright by designer/architect.

Rear Elevation

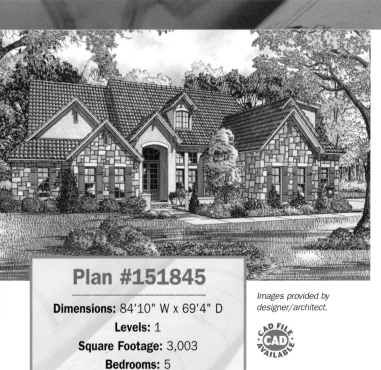

Plan #151845

Dimensions: 84'10" W x 69'4" D

Levels: 1

Square Footage: 3,003

Bedrooms: 5

Bathrooms: 4

Foundation: Crawl space, slab

CompleteCost List Available: Yes

Price Category: G

Images provided by designer/architect.

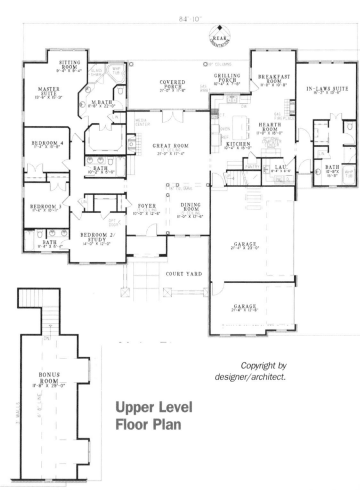

Copyright by designer/architect.

Upper Level Floor Plan

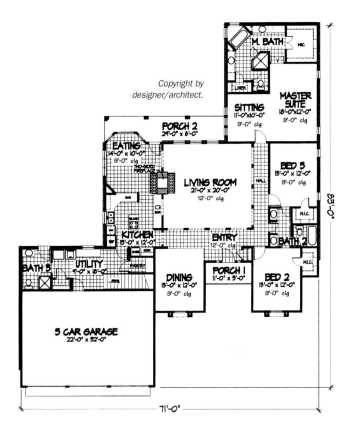

Plan #271080

Dimensions: 71' W x 83' D

Levels: 1

Square Footage: 2,581

Bedrooms: 3

Bathrooms: 3

Foundation: Basement

Materials List Available: Yes

Price Category: E

Images provided by designer/architect.

CAD FILE AVAILABLE

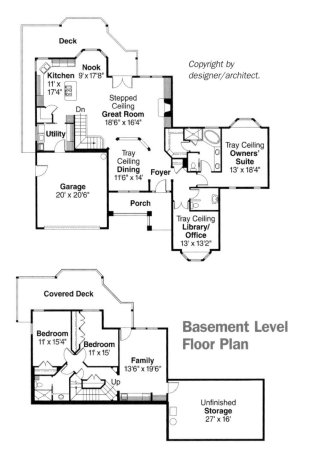

Basement Level Floor Plan

Plan #151820

Dimensions: 67' W x 64'10" D

Levels: 1

Square Footage: 2,744

Main Level Sq. Ft.: 1,902

Lower Level Sq. Ft.: 842

Bedrooms: 3

Bathrooms: 2½

Foundation: Basement

CompleteCost List Available: Yes

Price Category: F

Images provided by designer/architect.

CAD FILE AVAILABLE

Images provided by designer/architect.

Plan #151536

Dimensions: 37' W x 74'4" D
Levels: 1
Square Footage: 1,933
Bedrooms: 3
Bathrooms: 2
Foundation: Crawl space or slab
CompleteCost List Available: Yes
Price Category: D

The design of this home reflects the attention to detail of the Craftsman style.

Features:

• Foyer: The covered porch leads to this foyer, which separates the secondary bedrooms from the rest of the home.

• Great Room: This gathering room has eight-inch-diameter columns that add to the drama of the design. Additional amenities include a media center, a cozy fireplace, and a hidden computer center for study time or to serve as a small office.

• Kitchen: This spacious kitchen, with snack bar seating, has a wall of windows for plenty of natural light. Conveniently located just off the kitchen is a kids' play nook that helps keep the work area clutter free.

• Master Suite: A 10-ft.-high boxed ceiling, a large walk-in closet, whirlpool tub, and a separate shower, with built-in seat, make this master suite the ultimate in privacy and relaxation.

Copyright by designer/architect.

Plan #181622

Dimensions: 44'8" W x 38' D

Levels: 1

Square Footage: 1,007

Bedrooms: 2

Bathrooms: 1

Foundation: Basement

Material List Available: Yes

Price Category: B

CAD FILE CAD AVAILABLE

Images provided by designer/architect.

With its fine detailing, this is a home created for the ages.

Features:

- **Foyer:** The covered porch protects the entry, which has a transom and sidelights to brighten this interior space.

- **Living Room:** Equipped with a bay window to increase floor space, this gathering area will welcome friends and family.

- **Kitchen:** This efficient peninsula kitchen opens directly into the living room and the eating area. It also opens out onto the future patio, ideal for barbecues with family and friends.

- **Garage:** This attached one-car garage offers a storage area in addition to space to park your car.

Rear Elevation

38'-0"
11,4 m

12'-0"x 22'-4"
3,60 x 6,70

9'-0"x 12'-0"
2,70 x 3,60

10'-4"x 14'-0"
3,10 x 4,20

11'-0"x 9'-0"
3,30 x 2,70

11'-0"x 11'-0"
3,30 x 3,30

12'-0"x 17'-4"
3,60 x 5,20

Copyright by designer/architect.

44'-8"
13,4 m

Plan #211049

Dimensions: 73' W x 66' D
Levels: 1
Square Footage: 2,023
Bedrooms: 3
Bathrooms: 2
Foundation: Slab
Materials List Available: Yes
Price Category: D

Images provided by designer/architect.

This European-style home features an open floor plan that maximizes use and flexibility of space.

Features:

- Ceiling Height: 8 ft. unless otherwise noted.
- Living/Dining Area: This combined living-and-dining area features high ceilings, which make the large area seem even more spacious. Corner windows will fill the room with light. The wet bar and cozy fireplace make this the perfect place for entertaining.
- Backyard Porch: This huge covered backyard

porch is accessible from the living/dining area, so the entire party can step outdoors on a warm summer night.

- Kitchen: More than just efficient, this modern kitchen is actually an exciting place to cook. It features a dramatic high ceiling and plenty of work space.
- Utility Area: Located off the kitchen, this area has extra freezer space, a walk-in pantry, and access to the garage.
- Eating Nook: Informal family meals will be a true delight in this nook that adjoins the kitchen and faces a lovely private courtyard.

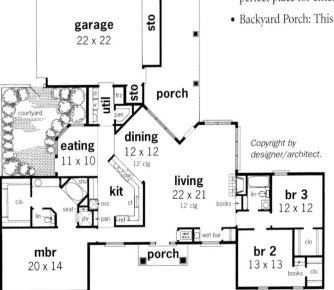

Copyright by designer/architect.

SMARTtip
Outdoor Lighting Safety

Lighting is necessary for walkways, paths, stairways, and transition areas (from the deck to the yard, hot tub, or pool) to prevent accidents. Choose from low-voltage rail, path, and post lighting for these areas. The corners of planters or built-in seating should also be delineated with lighting. Consider installing floodlights near doorways or large open spaces for security reasons.

Plan #211151

Dimensions: 68' W x 72' D
Levels: 1
Square Footage: 2,328
Bedrooms: 3
Bathrooms: 2
Foundation: Slab
Material List Available: No
Price Category: E

This beautiful Tudor-style home offers a unique exterior design that's both luxurious and inviting.

Features:

- Living Room: This sleek L-shaped room opens to a sunroom and breakfast nook. The wide-open space and high ceilings, along with the separation into individual areas, are an enticing combination.

- Dining Room: Enjoy meals in style in this generously sized area. Connected to the foyer and main entrance to the home, the room greets guests with its impressive high ceilings and luxurious fireplace.

Copyright by designer/architect.

- The Office/Nursery: Perfect for those who work from home, this area functions as a place where family members can use a computer and work quietly without everyday distractions. Or use the area, which is attached to the master bedroom, as a nursery. New moms and dads will love the added comfort of knowing their little one is close by.

- Kitchen: This U-shaped design is perfect for the busy cook, offering generous counter space, as well as easy access to all kitchen accessories. A large utility space connected to the kitchen is an added bonus of this home.

- Master Suite: Featuring a sitting area that doubles as a comfortable retreat, or as a great place for a vanity, this master bedroom opens into a generously sized bathroom, which includes a separate shower and tub. Dual sinks and a large walk-in closet make the area the perfect haven for carefree mornings.

- Additional bedrooms: Two additional bedrooms located near another full bathroom is the perfect setup for families with busy teenagers.

Plan #351114

Dimensions: 37' W x 84' D

Levels: 1

Square Footage: 1,733

Bedrooms: 3

Bathrooms: 2

Foundation: Crawl space or slab

Material List Available: Yes

Price Category: C

This home includes many of the most-popular features normally found in much larger homes.

Features:

- Front Porch: Enjoy the views during a relaxing evening on your front porch.

- Great Room: This expansive great room features a tray ceiling, a built-in entertainment center, and easy access to the dining room and kitchen.

- Kitchen: This large kitchen contains a popular feature: a raised bar for meals and conversations with family and friends.

- Master Suite: Enjoy this isolated master suite, with its oversize spa tub, separate shower, large walk-in closet, and dual sinks.

Plan #181621

Dimensions: 49' W x 37'4" D

Levels: 1

Square Footage: 1,129

Bedrooms: 2

Bathrooms: 1

Foundation: Basement

Material List Available: Yes

Price Category: B

CAD FILE AVAILABLE

Images provided by designer/architect.

Rear Elevation

This quaint cottage-style home would make a great first home.

Features:

- **Living Room:** This cozy gathering area, accented by a bay window, will be the favorite spot to sit and read a book. The two-sided fireplace will add warmth to the room.

- **Kitchen:** An L-shape layout, with an island, makes this kitchen very functional. The attached dinette area makes serving meals a snap.

- **Bedrooms:** Two bedrooms that have ample closet space share a luxurious bathroom, which features a spa-style tub.

- **Garage:** Plenty of storage is provided in this front-loading one-car garage, which has access to the entry foyer.

12'-0" X 9'-8"
3,60 X 2,90

20'-4" X 13'-4"
6,10 X 4,00

13'-4" X 21'-8"
4,00 X 6,50

37'-4"
11,2 m

13'-0" X 16'-8"
3,90 X 5,00

12'-0" X 12'-4"
3,60 X 3,70

49'-0"
14,7 m

Copyright by designer/architect.

Plan #171019

Dimensions: 68' W x 60' D

Levels: 1

Square Footage: 1,878

Bedrooms: 3

Bathrooms: 2

Foundation: Slab

Materials List Available: Yes

Price Category: D

Large columns on the front porch and brick accents give this home great curb appeal.

Features:

- **Living Room:** This gathering area is perfect for friends and family to relax. The corner fireplace adds charm and warmth to the area. The wall of windows allows a view of the rear porch and backyard.

- **Kitchen:** This kitchen boasts an efficient cabinet layout and room for the family chef to prepare the meals. The large windows in the adjacent eating area will bring the natural light into the space. A convenient utility space located just off the kitchen features the washer and dryer.

- **Master Suite:** Located in a private wing of the home, this retreat boasts ample space for furnishings in the sleeping area. The master bath includes a walk-in closet, dual vanities, a whirlpool tub, and a compartmentalized lavatory.

- **Garage:** This side-loading two-car garage can hold two full-size cars and has an added storage room.

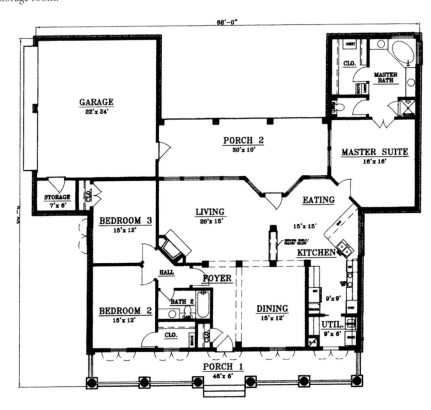

Plan #161093

Dimensions: 70'8" W x 64' D
Levels: 1
Square Footage: 4,328
Main Level Sq. Ft.: 2,582
Basement Sq. Ft.: 1,746
Bedrooms: 3
Bathrooms: 3½
Foundation: Walkout
Materials List Available: No
Price Category: I

Detailed stucco and stone accents impart warmth and character to the exterior of this one level home.

Images provided by designer/architect.

Features:

- Great Room: This gathering room, which features a fireplace and a decorative ceiling, offers an extensive view of the rear yard.

- Kitchen: Spacious and up-to-date, this extra-large combination gourmet kitchen and breakfast room is an ideal area for doing chores and hosting family gatherings.

- Main Level: The extravagant master suite, with its private bathroom and dressing area, the library with built-in shelves, and the formal dining room round out the main floor. Accented by a wood rail, the extra-wide main stairway leads to the lavish lower level.

- Lower Level: The two additional bedrooms, adjoining bathroom, media room, billiard room, and exercise room comprise this fantastic finished lower level.

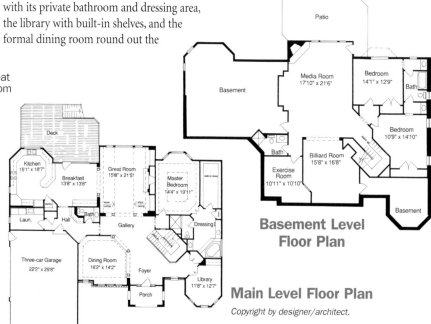

Great Room

Basement Level Floor Plan

Main Level Floor Plan

Copyright by designer/architect.

Images provided by
designer/architect.

Plan #131052

Dimensions: 67' W x 63'10" D

Levels: 1

Square Footage: 2,367

Bedrooms: 2

Bathrooms: 2

Foundation: Crawl space, slab,
or basement; walkout for fee

Materials List Available: Yes

Price Category: E

Rear
Elevation

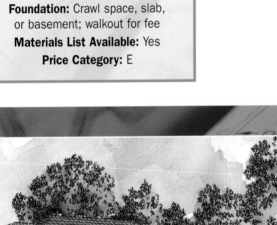

Plan #361261

Dimensions: 70' W x 60' D

Levels: 1

Square Footage: 2,396

Bedrooms: 3

Bathrooms: 2½

Foundation: Slab

Material List Available: No

Price Category: E

Images provided by
designer/architect.

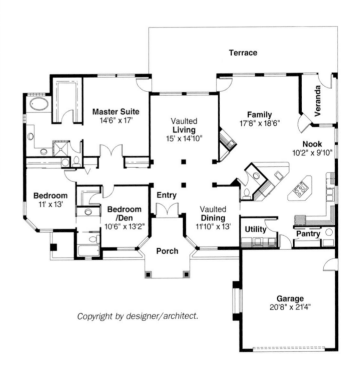

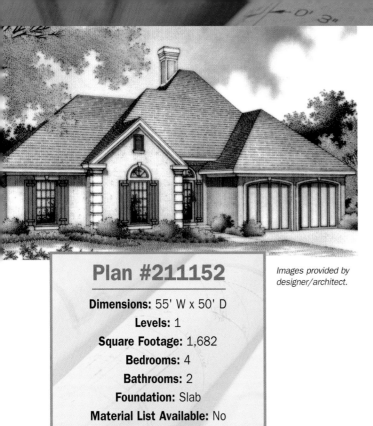

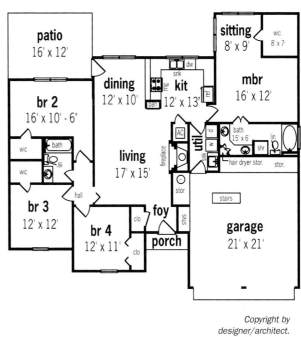

Images provided by designer/architect.

Plan #211152

Dimensions: 55' W x 50' D

Levels: 1

Square Footage: 1,682

Bedrooms: 4

Bathrooms: 2

Foundation: Slab

Material List Available: No

Price Category: C

Copyright by designer/architect.

patio 16' x 12'

dining 12' x 10'

kit 12' x 13'

sitting 8' x 9'

wic 8' x 7'

mbr 16' x 12'

br 2 16' x 10' - 6"

living 17' x 15'

bath 15' x 6'

br 3 12' x 12'

br 4 12' x 11'

foy

porch

garage 21' x 21'

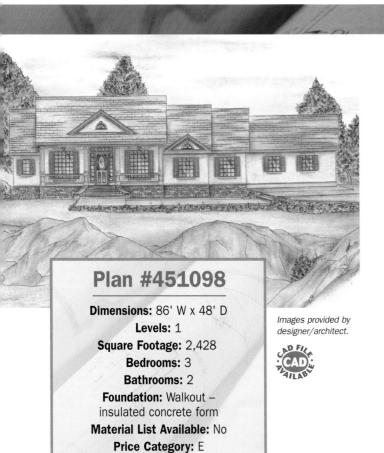

Plan #451098

Dimensions: 86' W x 48' D

Levels: 1

Square Footage: 2,428

Bedrooms: 3

Bathrooms: 2

Foundation: Walkout – insulated concrete form

Material List Available: No

Price Category: E

Images provided by designer/architect.

CAD FILE AVAILABLE

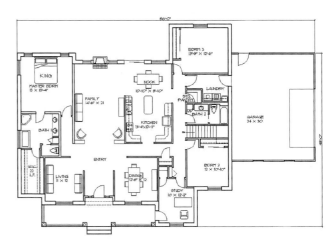

Copyright by designer/architect.

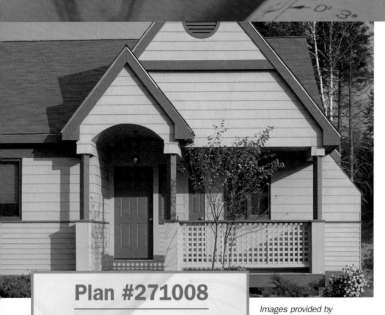

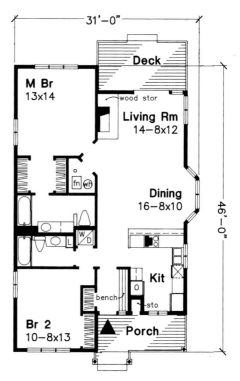

Images provided by
designer/architect.

CAD FILE AVAILABLE

Copyright by
designer/architect.

Plan #271008

Dimensions: 31' W x 46' D

Levels: 1

Square Footage: 1,199

Bedrooms: 2

Bathrooms: 2

Foundation: Slab

Materials List Available: No

Price Category: B

Images provided by
designer/architect.

Copyright by
designer/architect.

CAD FILE AVAILABLE

Rear
Elevation

Plan #181600

Dimensions: 34' W x 33'8" D

Levels: 1

Square Footage: 1,065

Bedrooms: 2

Bathrooms: 1

Foundation: Basement

Material List Available: Yes

Price Category: B

Plan #361057

Dimensions: 54' W x 46'8" D

Levels: 1

Square Footage: 1,564

Bedrooms: 3

Bathrooms: 2

Foundation: Crawl space

Material List Available: No

Price Category: C

Images provided by designer/architect.

CAD FILE AVAILABLE

Patio

Bedroom
10' x 11'

Vaulted
Nook
8'8" x 9'8"

Kitchen

Vaulted
Family
15'6" x 15'8"

Master Suite
17'2" x 12'

Utility

Entry

Living
15' x 13'

Vaulted
Bedroom/
Study
10' x 11'

Porch

Garage
19' x 21'

Plan #271303

Dimensions: 55'4" W x 70' D

Levels: 1

Square Footage: 2,345

Bedrooms: 3

Bathrooms: 2

Foundation: Slab

Material List Available: No

Price Category: E

Images provided by designer/architect.

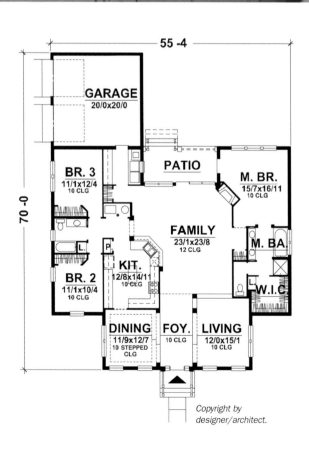

55 -4

GARAGE
20/0x20/0

70 -0

BR. 3
11/1x12/4
10 CLG

PATIO

M. BR.
15/7x16/11
10 CLG

FAMILY
23/1x23/8
12 CLG

M. BA.

KIT.
12/8x14/11
10 CLG

BR. 2
11/1x10/4
10 CLG

W.I.C.

DINING
11/9x12/7
10 STEPPED
CLG

FOY.
10 CLG

LIVING
12/0x15/1
10 CLG

Plan #121059

Dimensions: 52' W x 59'4" D

Levels: 1

Square Footage: 1,782

Bedrooms: 3

Bathrooms: 2

Foundation: Basement

Materials List Available: Yes

Price Category: C

Images provided by designer/architect.

CAD FILE AVAILABLE

Copyright by designer/architect.

Copyright by designer/architect.

Plan #181348

Dimensions: 32' W x 36' D

Levels: 1

Square Footage: 1,068

Bedrooms: 2

Bathrooms: 1

Foundation: Basement

Material List Available: Yes

Price Category: B

Images provided by designer/architect.

CAD FILE AVAILABLE

Rear Elevation

Plan #361483

Dimensions: 71' W x 76'6" D

Levels: 1

Square Footage: 2,507

Bedrooms: 5

Bathrooms: 3

Foundation: Crawl space

Material List Available: No

Price Category: E

Images provided by designer/architect.

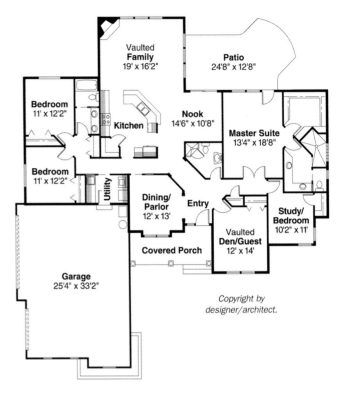

Vaulted Family 19' x 16'2"

Patio 24'8" x 12'8"

Bedroom 11' x 12'2"

Kitchen

Nook 14'6" x 10'8"

Master Suite 13'4" x 18'8"

Bedroom 11' x 12'2"

Utility

Dining/Parlor 12' x 13'

Entry

Study/Bedroom 10'2" x 11'

Garage 25'4" x 33'2"

Covered Porch

Vaulted Den/Guest 12' x 14'

Copyright by designer/architect.

Plan #181717

Dimensions: 43'8" W x 40'8" D

Levels: 1

Square Footage: 1,578

Bedrooms: 3

Bathrooms: 1

Foundation: Basement

Material List Available: Yes

Price Category: C

Images provided by designer/architect.

16'-4" X 14'-8"
4,90 X 4,40

12'-8" X 11'-0"
3,80 X 3,30

13'-4" X 13'-0"
4,00 X 3,90

40'-8"
12,2 m

11'-0" X 9'-0"
3,30 X 2,70

11'-0" X 10'-0"
3,30 X 3,00

12'-0" X 13'-4"
3,60 X 4,00

43'-8"
13,1 m

Copyright by designer/architect.

Plan #161095

Dimensions: 59' W x 49'8" D

Levels: 1

Square Footage: 3,620

Main Level Sq. Ft.: 2,068

Basement Level Sq. Ft.: 1,552

Bedrooms: 3

Bathrooms: 3

Foundation: Walkout basement

Material List Available: No

Price Category: H

This elegant ranch design has everything your family could want in a home.

Features:

- **Dining Room:** This column-accented formal area has a sloped ceiling and is open to the great room.

- **Great Room:** Featuring a cozy fireplace, this large gathering area offers a view of the backyard.

- **Kitchen:** This fully equipped island kitchen has everything the chef in the family could want.

- **Master Suite:** Located on the main level for privacy, this suite has a sloped ceiling in the sleeping area. The master bath boasts a whirlpool tub, a walk-in closet, and dual vanities.

Main Level Floor Plan

Rear View

Lower Level Floor Plan

Copyright by designer/architect.

Plan #441005

Dimensions: 50' W x 59' D
Levels: 1
Square Footage: 1,800
Bedrooms: 3
Bathrooms: 2
Foundation: Crawl space; slab or basement for fee
Materials List Available: No
Price Category: D

Images provided by designer/architect.

This home looks as if it's a quaint little abode—with its board-and-batten siding, cedar shingle detailing, and column-covered porch—but even a quick peek inside will prove that there is much more to this plan than meets the eye.

CAD FILE AVAILABLE

Features:

- Foyer: This entry area rises to a 9-ft.-high ceiling. On one side is a washer-dryer alcove with a closet across the way; on the other is another large storage area. Just down the hallway is a third closet.

- Kitchen: This kitchen features a center island, built-in desk/work center, and pantry. This area and the dining area also boast 9-ft.-high ceilings and are open to a vaulted great room with corner fireplace.

- Dining Room: Sliding doors in this area lead to a covered side porch, so you can enjoy outside dining.

- Master Suite: This suite has a vaulted ceiling. The master bath is wonderfully appointed with a separate shower, spa tub, and dual sinks.

- Bedrooms: Three bedrooms (or two plus an office) are found on the right side of the plan.

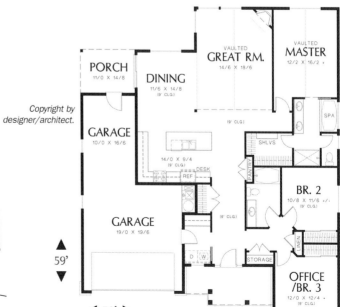

Copyright by designer/architect.

Rear Elevation

Plan #181387

Dimensions: 54' W x 52' D

Levels: 1

Square Footage: 1,572

Bedrooms: 2

Bathrooms: 1½

Foundation: Basement

Material List Available: Yes

Price Category: B

CAD FILE AVAILABLE · CAD

This home has a classically designed exterior and an innovatively designed interior.

Features:

- Sitting Areas: Two sitting areas flank the formal dining room, creating a cozy and relaxing atmosphere for entertaining guests.

- Kitchen: The curvature of this kitchen creates a more efficient use of space. It features ample workspace and storage, as well as a sizeable snack bar for meals on the go.

- Office: In this well-appointed office, illuminated by a wall of windows, you can enjoy the peace and quiet while working from home or simply keeping home matters in order.

- Master Suite: This spacious bedroom features a walk-in closet and private access to the full bath. The bath includes his and her sinks, a large tub, and a separate stall shower.

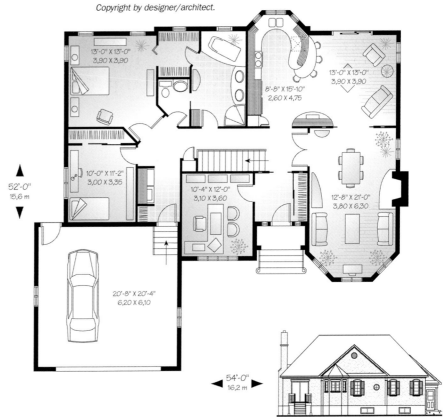

Rear Elevation

Plan #441001

Dimensions: 44' W x 68' D
Levels: 1
Square Footage: 1,850
Bedrooms: 3
Bathrooms: 2
Foundation: Crawl space; slab or basement for fee
Materials List Available: No
Price Category: D

Images provided by designer/architect.

With all the tantalizing elements of a cottage and the comfortable space of a family-sized home, this Arts and Crafts-style one-story design is the best of both worlds. Exterior accents such as stone wainscot, cedar shingles under the gable ends, and mission-style windows just add to the effect.

CAD FILE AVAILABLE

Features:

• Great Room: A warm hearth lights this room—right next to a built-in media center.

• Dining Room: This area features a sliding glass door to the rear patio for a breath of fresh air.

• Den: This quiet area has a window seat and a vaulted ceiling, giving the feeling of openness and letting your mind wander.

• Kitchen: This open corner kitchen features a 42-in. snack bar and a giant walk-in pantry.

• Master Suite: This suite boasts a tray ceiling and a large walk-in closet.

Rear Elevation

Copyright by designer/architect.

Plan #161102

Dimensions: 99'6" W x 84'2" D
Levels: 1
Square Footage: 6,659
Main Level Sq. Ft.: 3,990
Lower Level Sq. Ft: 2,669
Bedrooms: 4
Bathrooms: 4 full, 2 half
Foundation: Walkout; basement for fee
Material List Available: Yes
Price Category: K

A brick-and-stone exterior with limestone trim and arches decorates the exterior, while the interior explodes with design elements and large spaces to dazzle all who enter.

Features:

- Great Room: The 14-ft. ceiling height in this room is defined with columns and a fireplace wall. Triple French doors with an arched transom create the rear wall, and built-in shelving adds the perfect spot to house your big-screen TV.

- Kitchen: This spacious gourmet kitchen opens generously to the great room and allows everyone to enjoy the daily activities. A two-level island with cooktop provides casual seating and additional storage.

- Breakfast Room: This room is surrounded by windows, creating a bright and cheery place to start your day. Sliding glass doors to the covered porch in the rear add a rich look for outdoor entertaining, and the built-in fireplace provides a cozy, warm atmosphere.

- Master Suite: This master bedroom suite is fit for royalty, with its stepped ceiling treatment, spacious dressing room, and private exercise room.

- Lower Level: This lower level is dedicated to fun and entertaining. A large media area, billiards room, and wet bar are central to sharing this spectacular home with your friends.

Foyer/Dining Room

Rear Elevation

Images provided by designer/architect.

Copyright by designer/architect.

Basement Level Floor Plan

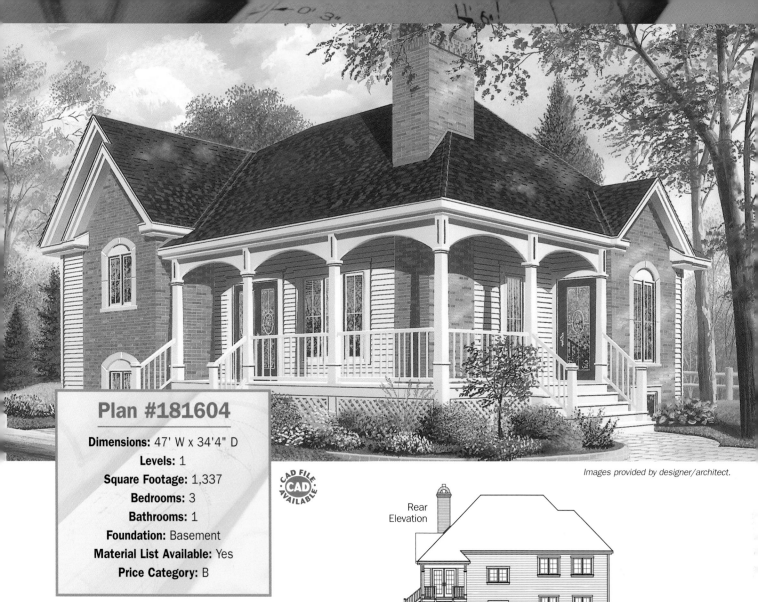

Plan #181604

Dimensions: 47' W x 34'4" D

Levels: 1

Square Footage: 1,337

Bedrooms: 3

Bathrooms: 1

Foundation: Basement

Material List Available: Yes

Price Category: B

Images provided by designer/architect.

There will be many good times in this home, which is perfect for weekend getaways or as a full-time residence.

Features:

- **Porch:** This wraparound front porch welcomes friends and family to your wonderful home. The kitchen has direct access to the porch to aid in unloading the groceries.

- **Living Room:** Imagine coming home after a long day to this warm, inviting space and being greeted by the glow of soft light from the fireplace.

- **Kitchen:** This island kitchen, complete with a small pantry, will make meal preparation easy. The adjacent dinette has access to the future rear deck.

- **Bedrooms:** Three bedrooms are located a few steps up from the living room. The full bathroom features a tub and a separate shower.

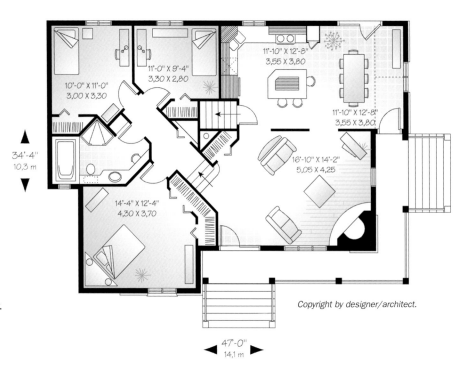

Rear Elevation

10'-0" X 11'-0"
3,00 X 3,30

11'-0" X 9'-4"
3,30 X 2,80

11'-10" X 12'-8"
3,55 X 3,80

11'-10" X 12'-8"
3,55 X 3,80

16'-10" X 14'-2"
5,05 X 4,25

14'-4" X 12'-4"
4,30 X 3,70

34'-4"
10,3 m

47'-0"
14,1 m

Copyright by designer/architect.

Plan #441006

Dimensions: 48' W x 64' D
Levels: 1
Square Footage: 1,891
Bedrooms: 3
Bathrooms: 2
Foundation: Crawl space; slab or basement for fee
Materials List Available: No
Price Category: D

If you prefer the look of Craftsman homes, you'll love the details this plan includes. Wide-based columns across the front porch, Mission-style windows, and a balanced mixture of exterior materials add up to true good looks.

Features:

- Great Room: A built-in media center and a fireplace in this room make it distinctive.

- Kitchen: A huge skylight over an island eating counter brightens this kitchen. A private office space opens through double doors nearby.

- Dining Room: This room has sliding glass doors opening to the rear patio.

- Bedrooms: Two bedrooms with two bathrooms are located on the right side of the plan. One of the bedrooms is a master suite with a vaulted salon and a bath with a spa tub.

- Garage: You'll be able to reach this two-car garage via a service hallway that contains a laundry room, a walk-in pantry, and a closet.

Images provided by designer/architect.

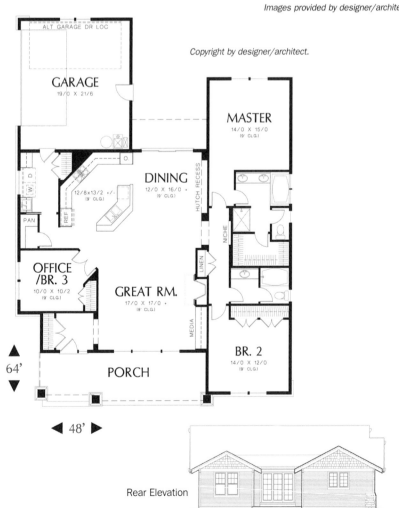

Copyright by designer/architect.

Rear Elevation

Plan #271075

Dimensions: 80' W x 52' D
Levels: 1
Square Footage: 2,233
Bedrooms: 2
Bathrooms: 1½
Foundation: Basement
Materials List Available: No
Price Category: E

CAD FILE AVAILABLE

With open space for recreation and relaxation, this traditional-style home is perfect for busy families who enjoy downtime at home.

Features:

- Great Room: This spacious welcoming area greets you with a tray ceiling and a romantic peninsula fireplace.

- Kitchen: Island style, with a full range and generous counter space, this room is perfect for preparing delicious meals to be served in an elegant dining room.

- Laundry Room/Mudroom: Your little athletes will have a place to put muddy cleats, rain-soaked gear, and the like, and you'll have a spacious area to do laundry and ironing.

- Master Suite: Perhaps the most enticing area in the home with its dual vanities, private toilet, and separate sitting area, you're sure to enjoy this chic and luxurious combination.

- The three-car garage accesses a huge hobby room, perfect for music-lovers to display CD's and guitars, or use the space as a guest room.

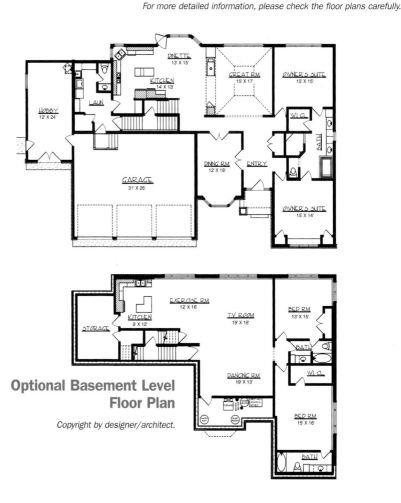

Optional Basement Level Floor Plan

Copyright by designer/architect.

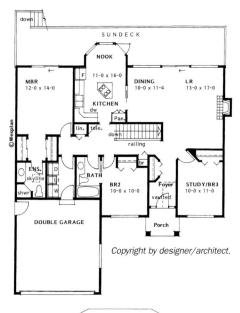

Copyright by designer/architect.

Images provided by designer/architect.

Rear Elevation

Plan #281009

Dimensions: 46' W x 52' D

Levels: 1

Square Footage: 1,423

Bedrooms: 3

Bathrooms: 2

Foundation: Walk-out basement

Materials List Available: Yes

Price Category: B

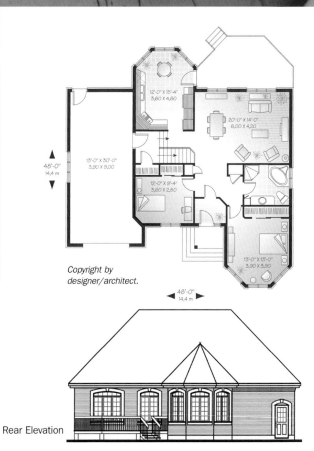

Copyright by designer/architect.

Images provided by designer/architect.

CAD FILE AVAILABLE

Rear Elevation

Plan #181585

Dimensions: 48' W x 48' D

Levels: 1

Square Footage: 1,207

Bedrooms: 2

Bathrooms: 1

Foundation: Basement

Material List Available: Yes

Price Category: B

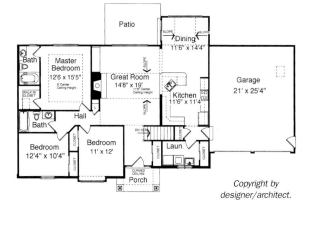

Copyright by designer/architect.

Images provided by designer/architect.

Plan #161090

Dimensions: 69'4" W x 42'4" D

Levels: 1

Square Footage: 1,563

Bedrooms: 3

Bathrooms: 2

Foundation: Basement

Materials List Available: Yes

Price Category: C

Rear Elevation

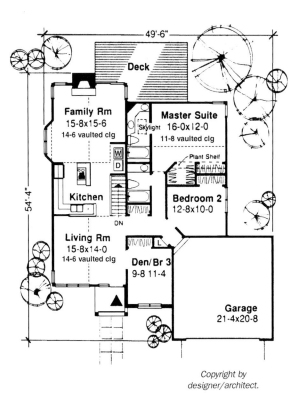

Plan #271006

Dimensions: 50' W x 55' D

Levels: 1

Square Footage: 1,444

Bedrooms: 2

Bathrooms: 2

Foundation: Basement

Materials List Available: Yes

Price Category: B

Images provided by designer/architect.

This home, as shown in the photograph, may differ from the actual blueprints. For more detailed information, please check the floor plans carefully.

Copyright by designer/architect.

Plan #181424

Dimensions: 36' W x 42' D

Levels: 1

Square Footage: 1,196

Bedrooms: 3

Bathrooms: 1

Foundation: Basement

Material List Available: Yes

Price Category: B

Images provided by designer/architect.

Rear Elevation

Alternate Floor Plan

Copyright by designer/architect.

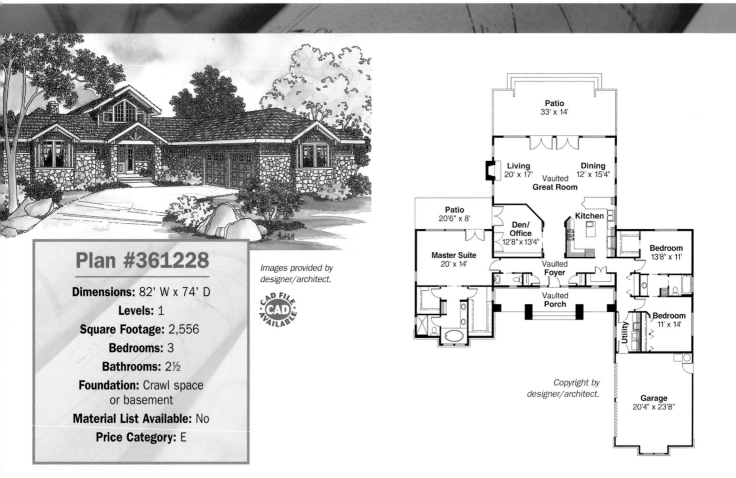

Plan #361228

Dimensions: 82' W x 74' D

Levels: 1

Square Footage: 2,556

Bedrooms: 3

Bathrooms: 2½

Foundation: Crawl space or basement

Material List Available: No

Price Category: E

Images provided by designer/architect.

Copyright by designer/architect.

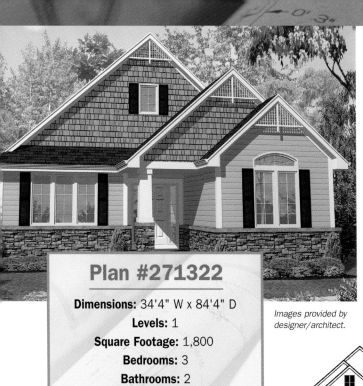

Plan #271322

Dimensions: 34'4" W x 84'4" D

Levels: 1

Square Footage: 1,800

Bedrooms: 3

Bathrooms: 2

Foundation: Basement

Material List Available: No

Price Category: D

Images provided by designer/architect.

Rear Elevation

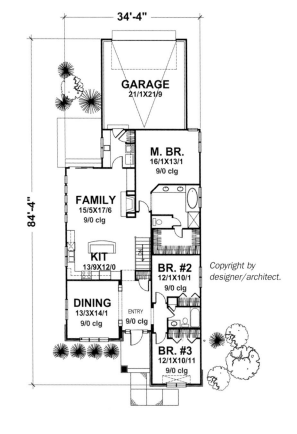

Copyright by designer/architect.

GARAGE 21/1X21/9

M. BR. 16/1X13/1 9/0 clg

FAMILY 15/5X17/6 9/0 clg

KIT 13/9X12/0

DINING 13/3X14/1 9/0 clg

ENTRY 9/0 clg

BR. #2 12/1X10/1 9/0 clg

BR. #3 12/1X10/11 9/0 clg

34'-4"

84'-4"

Plan #181603

Dimensions: 38'4" W x 38'9" D

Levels: 1

Square Footage: 1,220

Bedrooms: 2

Bathrooms: 1

Foundation: Basement

Material List Available: Yes

Price Category: B

Images provided by designer/architect.

CAD FILE AVAILABLE

Rear Elevation

Copyright by designer/architect.

Optional Basement Level Floor Plan

Plan #441007

Dimensions: 70' W x 64' D

Levels: 1

Square Footage: 2,197

Bedrooms: 4

Bathrooms: 2½

Foundation: Crawl space

Materials List Available: No

Price Category: D

Images provided by designer/architect.

Welcome to this roomy ranch, embellished with a brick facade, intriguing roof peaks, and decorative quoins on all the front corners.

CAD FILE AVAILABLE

Features:

- **Great Room:** There's a direct sightline from the front door through the trio of windows in this room. The rooms are defined by columns and changes in ceiling height rather than by walls, so light bounces from dining room to breakfast nook to kitchen.

- **Kitchen:** The primary workstation in this kitchen is a peninsula, which faces the fireplace. The peninsula is equipped with a sink, dishwasher, downdraft cooktop, and snack counter.

- **Den/Home Office:** Conveniently located off the foyer, this room would work well as a home office.

- **Master Suite:** The double doors provide an air of seclusion for this suite. The vaulted bedroom features sliding patio doors to the backyard and an arch-top window. The adjoining bath is equipped with a whirlpool tub, shower, double vanity, and walk-in closet.

- **Secondary Bedrooms:** The two additional bedrooms, each with direct access to the shared bathroom, occupy the left wing of the ranch.

Rear Elevation

Copyright by designer/architect.

Plan #351085

Dimensions: 70'6" W x 65' D

Levels: 1

Square Footage: 2,200

Bedrooms: 3

Bathrooms: 2½

Foundation: Crawl space or slab

Material List Available: Yes

Price Category: E

Images provided by designer/architect.

This attractive European-style country home was designed to meet the needs of your family.

Features:

- **Great Room:** This oversized gathering area boasts a raised ceiling and built-in cabinets, which makes it perfect for entertaining. Brick arches frame the spacious kitchen and dining area.

- **Office:** This office is conveniently located near the master bedroom and could serve as a guest bedroom or nursery.

- **Master Suite:** This master suite has a vaulted ceiling along with his and her walk-in closets and dual lavatories. There is also an additional vanity for her.

- **Garage:** A two-car side-load garage is provided to store either cars or any other items you need to keep out of the weather.

Copyright by designer/architect.

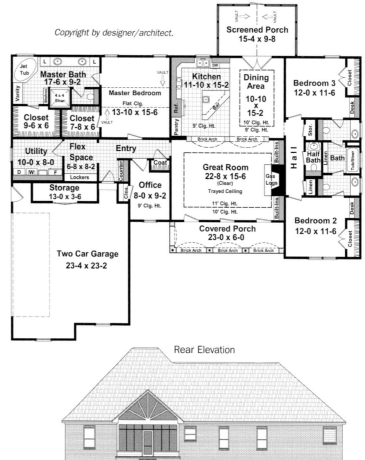

Plan #351098

Dimensions: 51'8" W x 60' D
Levels: 1
Square Footage: 1,655
Bedrooms: 3
Bathrooms: 2
Foundation: Crawl space or slab
Material List Available: Yes
Price Category: D

CAD FILE AVAILABLE

This is a great home for those who enjoy a casual lifestyle.

Features:

• Great Room: This gathering area features a vaulted ceiling and a gas fireplace. The built-ins that flank the fireplace can function as an entertainment center.

• Kitchen: Centrally located, this kitchen is the heart of this home. The two raised bars, one opening to the dining room and the other transitioning to the great room, makes serving meals or snacks a breeze.

• Master Suite: This suite includes a raised ceiling in the master bedroom and a large walk-in closet. The master bath boasts a jetted tub and a stall shower.

• Garage: This side-load two-car garage has room for cars in addition to added storage area.

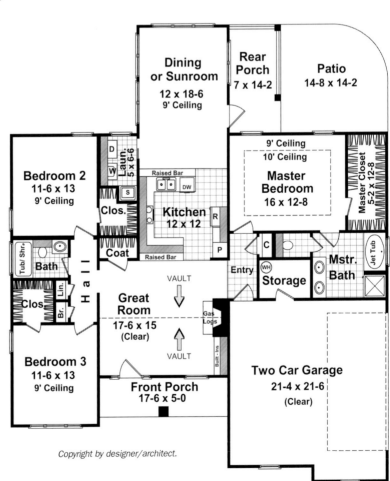

Copyright by designer/architect.

Plan #401023

Dimensions: 76' W x 63'4" D
Levels: 1
Square Footage: 2,806
Bedrooms: 3
Bathrooms: 2½
Foundation: Basement, walkout
Materials List Available: Yes
Price Category: F

The lower level of this magnificent home includes unfinished space that could have a future as a den and a family room with a fireplace. This level could also house extra bedrooms or an in-law suite.

Images provided by designer/architect.

Features:

- **Foyer:** On the main level, this foyer spills into a tray ceiling living room with a fireplace and an arched, floor-to-ceiling window wall.

- **Family Room:** Up from the foyer, a hall introduces this vaulted room with built-in media center and French doors that open to an expansive railed deck.

- **Kitchen:** Featured in this gourmet kitchen are a food-preparation island with a salad sink, double-door pantry, corner-window sink, and breakfast bay.

- **Master Bedroom:** The vaulted master bedroom opens to the deck, and the deluxe bath offers a raised whirlpool spa and a double-bowl vanity under a skylight.

- **Bedroom:** Two family bedrooms share a compartmented bathroom.

Rear Elevation

Copyright by designer/architect.

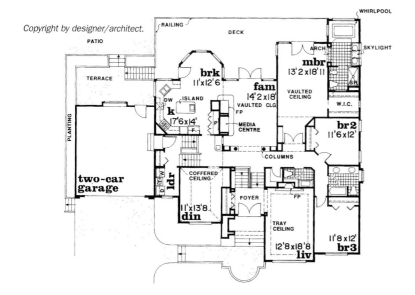

Optional Floor Plan

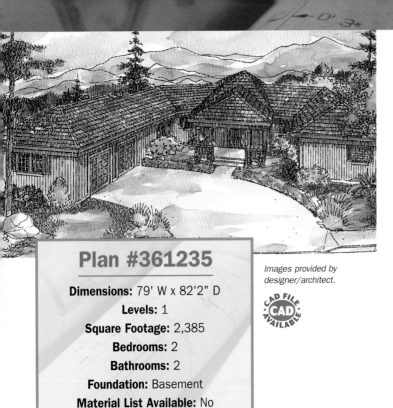

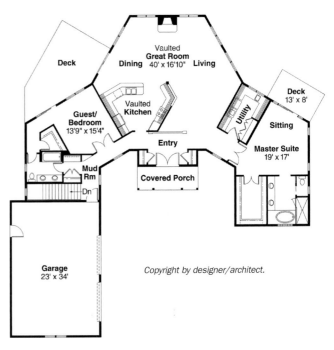

Plan #361235

Dimensions: 79' W x 82'2" D

Levels: 1

Square Footage: 2,385

Bedrooms: 2

Bathrooms: 2

Foundation: Basement

Material List Available: No

Price Category: E

Images provided by designer/architect.

CAD FILE AVAILABLE

Copyright by designer/architect.

Plan #541028

Dimensions: 77' W x 58' D

Levels: 1

Square Footage: 2,737

Bedrooms: 4

Bathrooms: 2½

Foundation: Basement; crawl space, slab, walkout for fee

Material List Available: No

Price Category: F

Images provided by designer/architect.

CAD FILE AVAILABLE

MAIN FLOOR PLAN

Copyright by designer/architect.

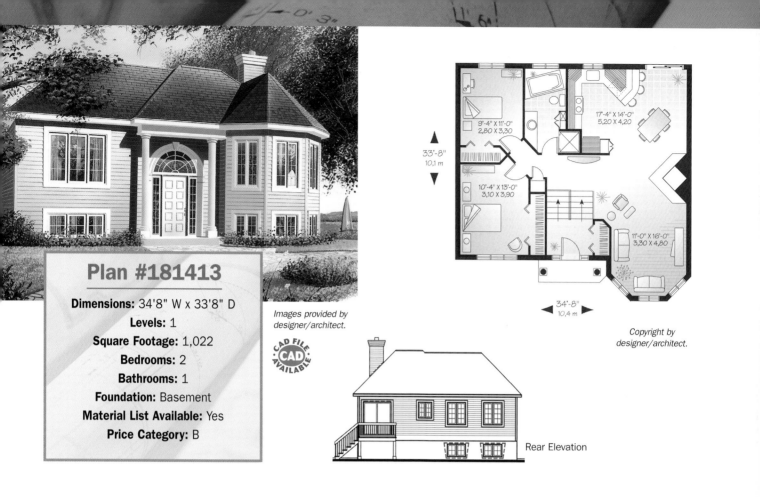

Plan #181413

Dimensions: 34'8" W x 33'8" D

Levels: 1

Square Footage: 1,022

Bedrooms: 2

Bathrooms: 1

Foundation: Basement

Material List Available: Yes

Price Category: B

Images provided by designer/architect.

CAD FILE AVAILABLE

Copyright by designer/architect.

9'-4" X 11'-0"
2,80 X 3,30

17'-4" X 14'-0"
5,20 X 4,20

10'-4" X 13'-0"
3,10 X 3,90

11'-0" X 16'-0"
3,30 X 4,80

33'-8"
10,1 m

34'-8"
10,4 m

Rear Elevation

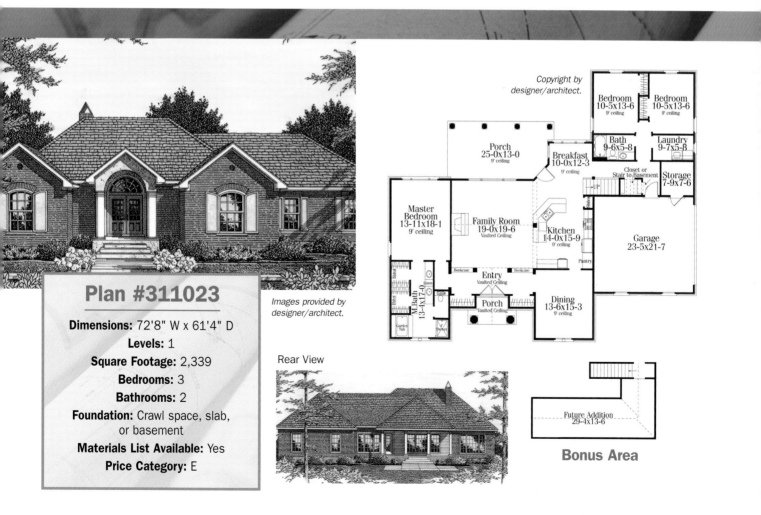

Plan #311023

Dimensions: 72'8" W x 61'4" D

Levels: 1

Square Footage: 2,339

Bedrooms: 3

Bathrooms: 2

Foundation: Crawl space, slab, or basement

Materials List Available: Yes

Price Category: E

Images provided by designer/architect.

Copyright by designer/architect.

Bedroom
10-5x13-6
9' ceiling

Bedroom
10-5x13-6
9' ceiling

Porch
25-0x13-0
9' ceiling

Breakfast
10-0x12-3
9' ceiling

Bath
9-6x5-8

Laundry
9-7x5-8

Closet or Stair to Basement

Storage
7-9x7-6

Master Bedroom
13-11x18-1
9' ceiling

Family Room
19-0x19-6
Vaulted Ceiling

Kitchen
14-0x15-9
9' ceiling

Garage
23-5x21-7

Bookcase

Bookcase

Pantry

M.Bath
13-4x17-4

Linen

Entry
Vaulted Ceiling

Porch
Vaulted Ceiling

Dining
13-6x15-3
9' ceiling

Garden Tub

Rear View

Future Addition
29-4x13-6

Bonus Area

Plan #101028

Dimensions: 57'8" W x 57'6" D

Levels: 1

Square Footage: 1,963

Bedrooms: 3

Bathrooms: 2

Foundation: Basement

Materials List Available: No

Price Category: D

Images provided by designer/architect.

CAD FILE AVAILABLE

Copyright by designer/architect.

SITTING

MASTER SUITE
23'-4" x 15'
Tray Ceiling

DECK
17'-4" x 12'

SCREENED PORCH
17'-4" x 7'-10"
Skylight   Skylight

BEDROOM 3
13' x 12'-10"

KITCHEN
12'-9" x 10'

BREAKFAST
12'-3" x 12'-2"

FAMILY
18' x 16'-2"

BEDROOM 2
13' x 11'

Stairs to Bonus Room
Stairs to Basement

DINING
11' x 15'-4"

PORCH
19'-8" x 7'-4"

2-CAR SIDE-LOAD GARAGE
23'-4" x 20'-2"

57'-6"

57'-8"

BONUS ROOM
14'-2" x 30'-2"
309 Sq. Ft.

Bonus Area Floor Plan

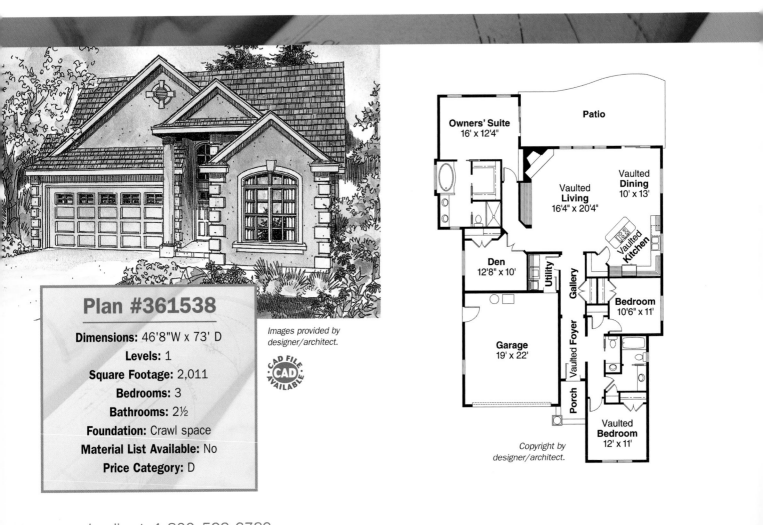

Plan #361538

Dimensions: 46'8"W x 73' D

Levels: 1

Square Footage: 2,011

Bedrooms: 3

Bathrooms: 2½

Foundation: Crawl space

Material List Available: No

Price Category: D

Images provided by designer/architect.

CAD FILE AVAILABLE

Owners' Suite
16' x 12'4"

Patio

Vaulted Living
16'4" x 20'4"

Vaulted Dining
10' x 13'

Den
12'8" x 10'

Utility

Gallery

Vaulted Kitchen

Bedroom
10'6" x 11'

Garage
19' x 22'

Vaulted Foyer

Porch

Vaulted Bedroom
12' x 11'

Copyright by designer/architect.

Plan #271304

Dimensions: 55'4" W x 77'6" D

Levels: 1

Square Footage: 2,360

Bedrooms: 3

Bathrooms: 2

Foundation: Slab

Material List Available: No

Price Category: E

Images provided by designer/architect.

Copyright by designer/architect.

Rear Elevation

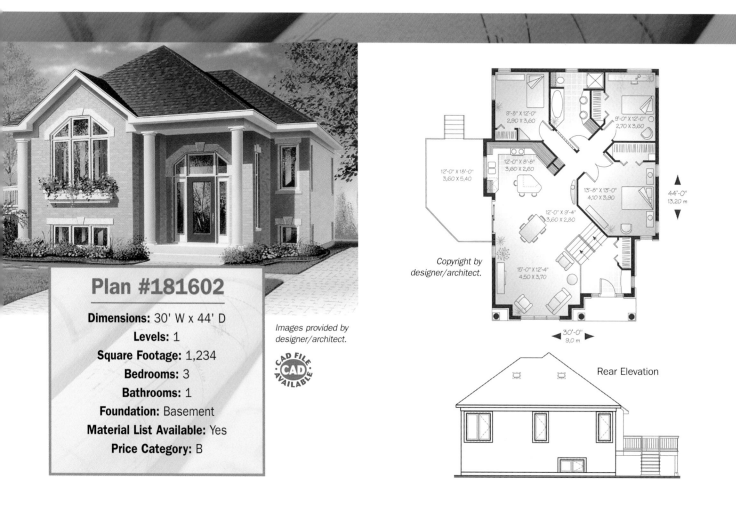

Plan #181602

Dimensions: 30' W x 44' D

Levels: 1

Square Footage: 1,234

Bedrooms: 3

Bathrooms: 1

Foundation: Basement

Material List Available: Yes

Price Category: B

Images provided by designer/architect.

CAD FILE AVAILABLE

Copyright by designer/architect.

Rear Elevation

Images provided by designer/architect.

Plan #271005

Dimensions: 48'4" W x 48'4" D
Levels: 1
Square Footage: 1,368
Bedrooms: 3
Bathrooms: 2
Foundation: Basement
Materials List Available: Yes
Price Category: B

This traditional home boasts an open floor plan that is further expanded by soaring vaulted ceilings.

Features:

- Great Room: Front and center, this large multipurpose room features a gorgeous corner fireplace, an eye-catching boxed out window, and dedicated space for casual dining—all beneath a vaulted ceiling.

- Kitchen: A vaulted ceiling crowns this galley kitchen and its adjoining breakfast nook.

- Master Suite: This spacious master bedroom, brightened by a boxed-out window, features a vaulted ceiling in the sleeping chamber and the private bath.

48'-4"

Mas. Suite
14x12-6
12 vaulted clg

Br 2
12x10

Patio

Den/
Br 3
11x9

DN

Kit/Brkfst
19x10-8
12 vltd
clg

Dining

Garage
21-4x19-4

DN

Great Room
19x18
12 vaulted clg

48'-4"

Copyright by designer/architect.

SMARTtip

Design with Computers

Consider using a computer-aided design (CAD) program to plan your deck. Some programs let you see three-dimensional views of your design complete with railings, stairs, planters, hot tubs, and the surrounding landscaping.

Plan #541034

Dimensions: 79'6" W x 58'3"D

Levels: 1

Square Footage: 3,162

Main Level Sq. Ft.: 2,113

Lower Level Sq. Ft.: 1,049

Bedrooms: 3

Bathrooms: 3

Foundation: Walkout; basement for fee

Material List Available: No

Price Category: G

A combination of stone, shutters, and columns blend to create a magnificent exterior.

Features:

- Great Room: A see-through fireplace connects this vaulted gathering area to the kitchen and breakfast nook.

- Den: This den has built-in bookshelves and could serve as an additional bedroom.

- Master Suite: This fantastic suite features an octagonal sitting area. The private bath includes a separate tub and shower, a walk-in closet, double sinks, and a vanity for applying makeup.

- Secondary Bedrooms: Located on the lower level, these two bedrooms share a Jack-and-Jill bathroom.

- Expansion: There is no lack of room to expand as the basement allows for a future sunken family room, another bedroom, and an additional bathroom.

Images provided by designer/architect.

Basement Level Floor Plan

Copyright by designer/architect.

36'-0"
10,8 m

50'-0"
15,0 m

12'-0" X 10'-0"
3,60 X 3,00

9'-4" X 12'-0"
2,80 X 3,60

12'-0" X 15'-4"
3,60 X 4,60

14'-4" X 22'-8"
4,30 X 6,80

12'-0" X 12'-0"
3,60 X 3,60

12'-0" X 16'-8"
3,60 X 5,00

Copyright by designer/architect.

Plan #181023

Dimensions: 50' W x 36' D

Levels: 1

Square Footage: 1,191

Bedrooms: 2

Bathrooms: 1

Foundation: Full basement

Materials List Available: Yes

Price Category: B

Images provided by designer/architect.

CAD FILE
CAD
AVAILABLE

Plan #151277

Dimensions: 67'8" W x 58' D

Levels: 1

Square Footage: 2,216

Bedrooms: 3

Bathrooms: 2½

Foundation: Crawl space or slab

CompleteCost List Available: Yes

Price Category: E

Images provided by designer/architect.

CAD FILE
CAD
AVAILABLE

67'-8"

58'-0"

DECK OR PATIO

HEARTH
ROOM
10'-8" X 13'-4"

GRILLING
PORCH
9'-0" X 6'-0"

M. BATH
9'-8" X 8'-3"

MASTER
SUITE
15'-0" X 13'-0"
9' BOXED CEILING

GREAT RM.
17'-2" X 22'-3"
9' BOXED CEILING

BREAKFAST
ROOM
12'-8" X 12'-4"

KITCHEN
12'-8" X 11'-4"

GALLERY
9' CEILING

BEDROOM 2
11'-0" X 11'-2"
9' CEILING

FOYER
7'-10" X 9'-10"

LAUNDRY
9'-0" X 5'-8"

STORAGE
8'-0" X 5'-8"

BEDROOM 3
11'-4" X 14'-2"
9' CEILING

DINING RM.
11'-4" X 13'-10"
9' BOXED CEILING

GARAGE
22'-0" X 21'-4"

PORCH
7'-0" X 9'-10"

Copyright by designer/architect.

Plan #361200

Dimensions: 99' W x 76'4" D

Levels: 1

Square Footage: 2,568

Bedrooms: 3

Bathrooms: 3

Foundation: Crawl space

Material List Available: No

Price Category: E

Images provided by designer/architect.

CAD FILE AVAILABLE

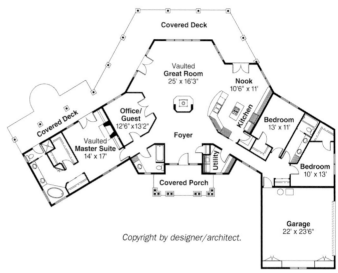

Copyright by designer/architect.

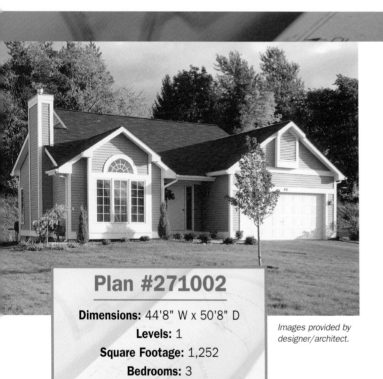

Plan #271002

Dimensions: 44'8" W x 50'8" D

Levels: 1

Square Footage: 1,252

Bedrooms: 3

Bathrooms: 2

Foundation: Basement

Materials List Available: Yes

Price Category: B

Images provided by designer/architect.

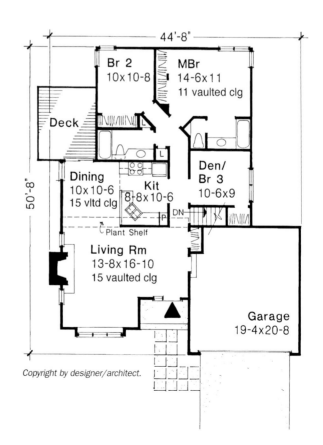

Copyright by designer/architect.

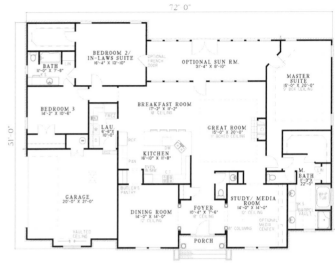

Images provided by
designer/architect.

Plan #151552

Dimensions: 72' W x 51' D

Levels: 1

Square Footage: 2,930

Bedrooms: 3

Bathrooms: 2½

Foundation: Slab

CompleteCost List Available: Yes

Price Category: F

Copyright by
designer/architect.

Plan #181027

Dimensions: 30'8" W x 48' D

Levels: 1

Square Footage: 1,103

Bedrooms: 2

Bathrooms: 1

Foundation: Full basement

Materials List Available: Yes

Price Category: B

Images provided by
designer/architect.

Copyright by designer/architect.

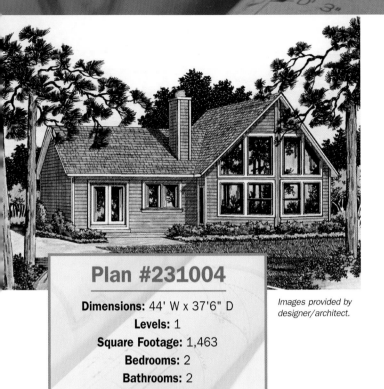

Plan #231004

Dimensions: 44' W x 37'6" D
Levels: 1
Square Footage: 1,463
Bedrooms: 2
Bathrooms: 2
Foundation: Crawl space
Materials List Available: No
Price Category: A

Images provided by designer/architect.

Br #2
12-6 x 9-7

Den
10 x 12

Kit.

PANTRY

Eating

M. Br
18-6 x 11

Living
22 x 21

CATHEDERAL CEILING

Patio

Copyright by designer/architect.

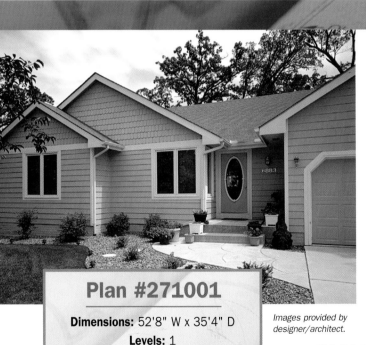

Plan #271001

Dimensions: 52'8" W x 35'4" D
Levels: 1
Square Footage: 1,400
Bedrooms: 3
Bathrooms: 2
Foundation: Basement
Materials List Available: Yes
Price Category: B

Images provided by designer/architect.

Copyright by designer/architect.

Deck

Master Br
15-4x11

Great Room
16-8x19

Dining

Kitchen/ Brkfst
13-8x12-8

Bar

dn

Den/Br 3
11-4x12-4

Garage
19-4x19-4

Br 2
11x10

35'-4"

52'-8'

SMARTtip

Candid Camera for Your Landscaping

To see your home and yard as others see them, take some camera shots. Seeing your house and landscaping on film will create an opportunity for objectivity. Problems will become more obvious, and you will then be better able to prioritize your home improvements, as well as your landscaping plan.

Plan #151306

Dimensions: 58' W x 69'6" D
Levels: 1
Square Footage: 2,189
Bedrooms: 4
Bathrooms: 2
Foundation: Crawl space or slab; basement or walkout for fee
CompleteCost List Available: Yes
Price Category: D

Images provided by designer/architect.

CAD FILE AVAILABLE

Copyright by designer/architect.

Plan #301001

Dimensions: 99'10" W x 46'2" D
Levels: 1
Square Footage: 2,720
Bedrooms: 3
Bathrooms: 2
Foundation: Crawl space, slab
Materials List Available: Yes
Price Category: F

Images provided by designer/architect.

Copyright by designer/architect.

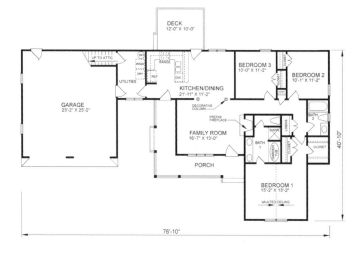

Plan #341128

Dimensions: 76'10" W x 40'10" D

Levels: 1

Square Footage: 1,410

Bedrooms: 3

Bathrooms: 2

Foundation: Crawl space, slab, basement, or walkout

Material List Available: Yes

Price Category: B

Images provided by designer/architect.

CAD FILE AVAILABLE

Copyright by designer/architect.

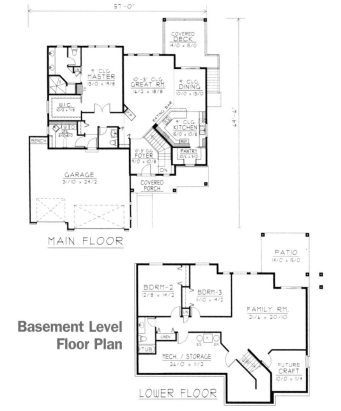

Plan #541031

Dimensions: 57' W x 64'6" D

Levels: 1

Square Footage: 2,803

Main Level Sq. Ft.: 1,670

Lower Level Sq. Ft.: 1,133

Bedrooms: 3

Bathrooms: 2½

Foundation: Walkout; basement for fee

Material List Available: No

Price Category: F

Images provided by designer/architect.

CAD FILE AVAILABLE

MAIN FLOOR

Basement Level Floor Plan

LOWER FLOOR

Copyright by designer/architect.

Plan #211009

Dimensions: 72' W x 60' D

Levels: 1

Square Footage: 2,396

Bedrooms: 4

Bathrooms: 2

Foundation: Slab

Materials List Available: Yes

Price Category: E

Images provided by designer/architect.

Beautiful arched windows lend a luxurious feeling to the exterior of this one-story home.

Features:

- Ceiling Height: 9 ft. unless otherwise noted.

- Entry: Guests will be greeted by a dramatic 12-ft. ceiling in this elegant foyer.

- Living Room: The 12-ft. ceiling continues through the foyer into this inviting living room. Everyone will feel welcomed by the crackling fire in the handsome fireplace.

- Covered Porch: When the weather is warm, invite guests to step out of the living room directly into this covered porch.

- Kitchen: This bright and cheery kitchen is designed for the way we live today. It includes a pantry and an angled eating bar that will see plenty of impromptu family meals.

- Energy-Efficient Walls: All the outside walls are framed with 2x6 lumber instead of 2x4. The extra thickness makes room for more insulation to lower your heating and cooling bills.

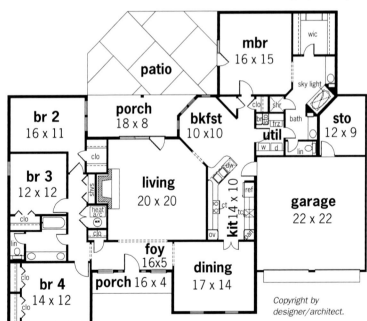

Copyright by designer/architect.

SMARTtip

Ornaments in a Garden

Placement is everything with ornaments in a garden. Some elements are best sitting by themselves. Others are better when they are part of a cohesive whole, perhaps placed in the greenery at a corner or flanking a structure.

Plan #181557

Dimensions: 32' W x 32' D
Levels: 1
Square Footage: 1,806
Main Level Sq. Ft.: 843
Lower Level Sq. Ft.: 963
Bedrooms: 3
Bathrooms: 1½
Foundation: Walkout
Material List Available: Yes
Price Category: D

This home's distinctive architectural design continues from the outside in to provide a unique and comfortable living environment.

Images provided by designer/architect.

CAD FILE AVAILABLE

Features:

- **Great Room:** Whether it's sunlight or starlight filtering in through the wall of windows, it creates a relaxing ambiance in this great room.

- **Kitchen:** A wide open design and a working island with snack bar give the house cook enough elbow room for any creation. A formal dining area located just footsteps away provides an easy transition for entertaining.

- **Bonus Area:** Create a playroom, as pictured here, or use the extra space for any hobby or storage need you might have.

- **Lower Level:** The lower level features another sitting room, three sizable bedrooms, and a full bathroom, as well as plenty of extra closet space.

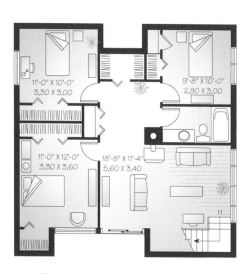

Basement Level Floor Plan

Copyright by designer/architect.

Plan #271318

Dimensions: 55' W x 71' D
Levels: 1
Square Footage: 2,086
Bedrooms: 2
Bathrooms: 2½
Foundation: Basement
Material List Available: No
Price Category: E

With its unique exterior and modern interior, this Craftsman-style design will make you feel at home as soon as you step through the door.

Features:

- Entry: The side-lighted foyer opens to the living room and the adjoining den, as well as the formal dining room that is framed by decorative columns.

- Kitchen: With a quaint, sunlit breakfast nook and efficiently sized island, this kitchen is a place that offers more than just somewhere to cook food—it's a sweet place to relax with family and to get to know guests.

- Master Suite: This master suite enjoys lavish comforts such as a deluxe bath and ample walk-in closet space.

- Additional Bedrooms: Although one additional bedroom is designed into the plan, the den can be used as a third bedroom, making this a perfect home for your family, or a homeowner who loves entertaining guests.

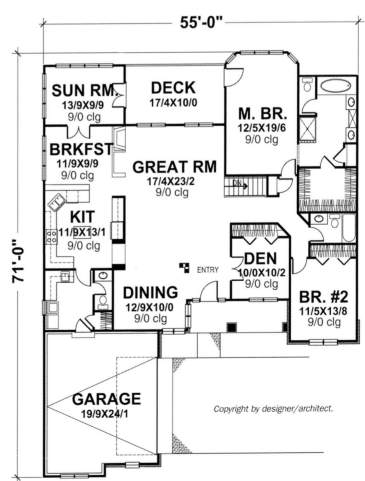

55'-0"

71'-0"

SUN RM
13/9X9/9
9/0 clg

DECK
17/4X10/0

M. BR.
12/5X19/6
9/0 clg

BRKFST
11/9X9/9
9/0 clg

GREAT RM
17/4X23/2
9/0 clg

KIT
11/9X13/1
9/0 clg

ENTRY

DEN
10/0X10/2
9/0 clg

DINING
12/9X10/0
9/0 clg

BR. #2
11/5X13/8
9/0 clg

GARAGE
19/9X24/1

Copyright by designer/architect.

Plan #151383

Dimensions: 70'4" W x 57'2" D
Levels: 1
Square Footage: 2,534
Bedrooms: 3
Bathrooms: 2
Foundation: Crawl space or slab
CompleteCost List Available: Yes
Price Category: E

The arched entry of the covered porch welcomes you to this magnificent home.

Features:

- **Foyer:** Welcome your guests in this warm foyer before leading them into the impressive dining room with magnificent columns framing the entry.

- **Great Room:** After dinner, your guests will enjoy conversation in this spacious room, complete with fireplace and built-ins.

- **Study:** Beautiful French doors open into this quiet space, where you'll be able to concentrate on that work away from the office.

- **Rear Porch:** This relaxing spot may be reached from the breakfast room or your secluded master suite.

Images provided by designer/architect.

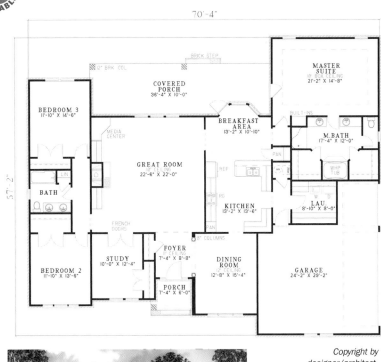

Copyright by designer/architect.

Front View

Plan #341144

Dimensions: 52' W x 30' D

Levels: 1

Square Footage: 1,104

Bedrooms: 3

Bathrooms: 1½

Foundation: Crawl space, slab, basement, or walkout

Material List Available: No

Price Category: B

Images provided by designer/architect.

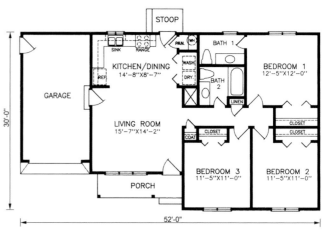

Copyright by designer/architect.

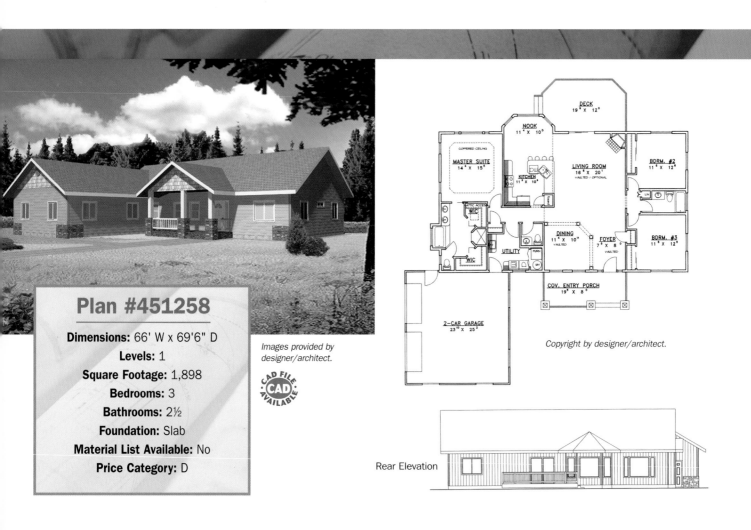

Plan #451258

Dimensions: 66' W x 69'6" D

Levels: 1

Square Footage: 1,898

Bedrooms: 3

Bathrooms: 2½

Foundation: Slab

Material List Available: No

Price Category: D

Images provided by designer/architect.

Copyright by designer/architect.

Rear Elevation

Plan #271448

Dimensions: 34' W x 36' D

Levels: 1

Square Footage: 775

Bedrooms: 1

Bathrooms: 1

Foundation: Crawl space

Material List Available: No

Price Category: A

*Images provided by
designer/architect.*

*Copyright by
designer/architect.*

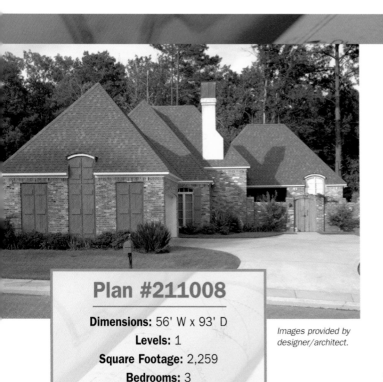

Plan #211008

Dimensions: 56' W x 93' D

Levels: 1

Square Footage: 2,259

Bedrooms: 3

Bathrooms: 2½

Foundation: Slab

Material List Available: Yes

Price Category: E

*Images provided by
designer/architect.*

*Copyright by
designer/architect.*

Front View

Plan #451332

Dimensions: 108' W x 70' D
Levels: 1
Square Footage: 3,202
Bedrooms: 3
Bathrooms: 2½
Foundation: Crawl space – insulated concrete form
Material List Available: No
Price Category: G

Images provided by designer/architect.

Perfectly at home on a tree-lined street in a quiet neighborhood, this great design is a contemporary version of an old-fashioned standard.

Features:

- Entry: Welcome family and friends into this grand foyer. The 12-ft.-high ceiling creates an elegant impression.

- Kitchen: The heart of the home, this kitchen will be the center of all your entertaining. Plenty of workspace, a nearby pantry, and an island complete with cooktop will delight chefs of all skill levels.

- Master Suite: Everyone knows that the master bath makes the master suite, and this home is no different. His and her sinks, a large tub with a view, and a separate standing shower combine to create both a retreat and a remedy for hectic mornings.

- Secondary Bedrooms: Both secondary bedrooms have ample closet space and are similarly sized to quell any sibling rivalry on the subject.

Copyright by designer/architect.

Rear Elevation

Plan #361166

Dimensions: 73'7" W x 79'3"D

Levels: 1

Square Footage: 2,417

Bedrooms: 3

Bathrooms: 2½

Foundation: Crawl space, slab, or basement

Material List Available: No

Price Category: E

Images provided by designer/architect.

A unique floor plan makes this a one-of-a-kind home.

Features:

- **Entry:** Stepping off of the porch you are greeted by this magnificent entry, which includes a large coat closet and a half bath.

- **Family Room:** This large open gathering room, with its massive fireplace, will impress friends and family. French doors allow access to the rear deck.

- **Dining Room:** Formal meals are grand in this dining room located in the center of the home. The ceiling rises up to the clerestory windows, which create a halo of light.

- **Master Suite:** You'll be close to your family but in a world of your own in this master suite. The design simplifies your life with its walk-in closet, his and her sinks, and stall shower.

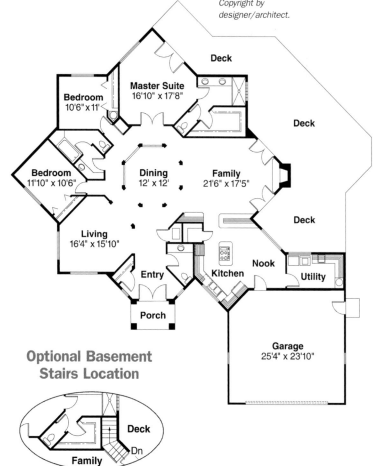

Copyright by designer/architect.

Optional Basement Stairs Location

Plan #271320

Dimensions: 39' W x 75' D

Levels: 1

Square Footage: 1,548

Bedrooms: 2

Bathrooms: 2

Foundation: Basement

Material List Available: No

Price Category: C

Images provided by designer/architect.

Timeless style makes this house stand out in the neighborhood.

Features:

- Living Room: Welcome guests to this space to gather by the warm light of the fireplace, or use the room to spend quality time with your family.

- Kitchen: Featuring ample workspace and storage, this kitchen is located close to the dining room, simplifying the transition from meal preparation to dining.

- Master Suite: This master suite has enough space for something extra, such as an entertainment or sitting area. The full bath features his and her vanities, a whirlpool tub, a large glass shower, and a sizeable walk-in closet.

- Garage: This two-car garage connects to the laundry room and kitchen, allowing for easy unloading of groceries.

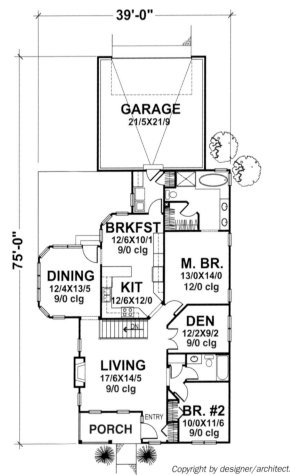

Copyright by designer/architect.

Plan #151055

Dimensions: 82'4" W x 81'6" D

Levels: 1

Square Footage: 3,183

Bedrooms: 4

Bathrooms: 2½

Foundation: Crawl space or slab; basement or walkout available for fee

CompleteCost List Available: Yes

Price Category: E

This stunning large ranch home has a well-designed floor plan that is perfect for today's family.

CAD FILE AVAILABLE

Features:

- Living Room: This large gathering area features a beautiful fireplace and a vaulted ceiling. On nice days, exit through the atrium doors and relax on the grilling porch.

- Kitchen: The raised bar in this island kitchen provides additional seating for informal

Images provided by designer/architect.

meals. The family will enjoy lazy weekend mornings in the adjoining breakfast room and intimate hearth room.

- Master Suite: This retreat, with its built-in media center and romantic fireplace in the sleeping area, features a boxed ceiling. The

master bath boasts a whirlpool tub, his and her vanities and lavatories, and a glass shower.

- Bedrooms: These three family bedrooms are located on the opposite side of the home from the master suite for privacy and share a common bathroom.

Copyright by designer/architect.

Front View

Plan #451245

Dimensions: 43' W x 70'6" D

Levels: 1

Square Footage: 1,584

Bedrooms: 2

Bathrooms: 2

Foundation: Slab

Material List Available: No

Price Category: C

Images provided by designer/architect.

CAD FILE AVAILABLE

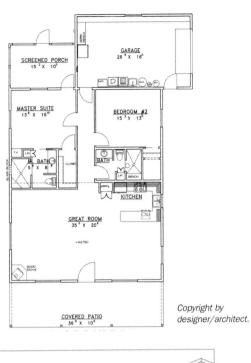

Copyright by designer/architect.

Right Side Elevation

Plan #181024

Dimensions: 58' W x 36' D

Levels: 1

Square Footage: 1,370

Bedrooms: 3

Bathrooms: 1

Foundation: Basement; crawl space or slab for fee

Material List Available: Yes

Price Category: B

Images provided by designer/architect.

CAD FILE AVAILABLE

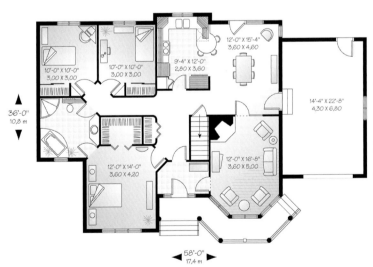

Copyright by designer/architect.

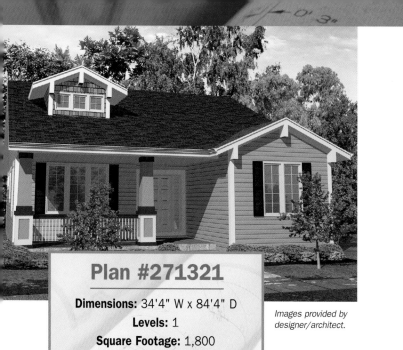

Copyright by designer/architect.

Images provided by designer/architect.

Plan #271321

Dimensions: 34'4" W x 84'4" D

Levels: 1

Square Footage: 1,800

Bedrooms: 3

Bathrooms: 2

Foundation: Basement

Material List Available: No

Price Category: D

Rear Elevation

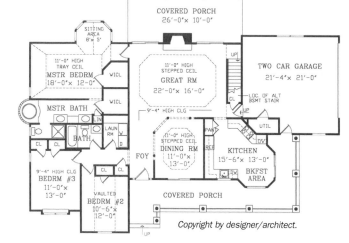

Copyright by designer/architect.

Images provided by designer/architect.

Bonus Area

Plan #131047

Dimensions: 69'10" W x 51'8" D

Levels: 1

Square Footage: 1,793

Bedrooms: 3

Bathrooms: 2

Foundation: Crawl space, slab, or basement

Materials List Available: Yes

Price Category: D

Rear Elevation

Copyright by designer/architect.

Images provided by designer/architect.

Plan #571084

Dimensions: 42' W x 50' D

Levels: 1

Square Footage: 1,524

Bedrooms: 2

Bathrooms: 2

Foundation: Basement

Material List Available: Yes

Price Category: C

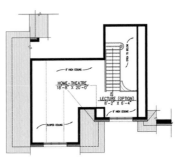

(OPTION) HOME-THEATRE: 430 p.c. / sq. ft.

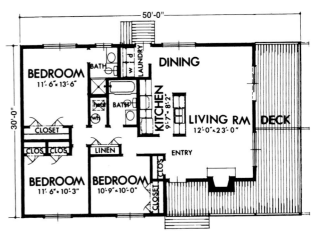

Images provided by designer/architect.

Plan #271450

Dimensions: 42' W x 30' D

Levels: 1

Square Footage: 1,164

Bedrooms: 3

Bathrooms: 2

Foundation: Crawl space

Material List Available: No

Price Category: B

Copyright by designer/architect.

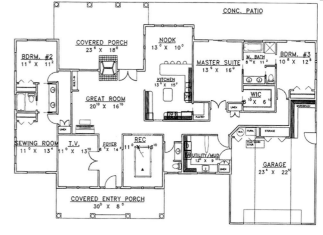

Plan #451210

Dimensions: 83'6" W x 53'3" D

Levels: 1

Square Footage: 2,646

Bedrooms: 3

Bathrooms: 2½

Foundation: Crawl space

Material List Available: No

Price Category: F

Images provided by designer/architect.

Rear Elevation

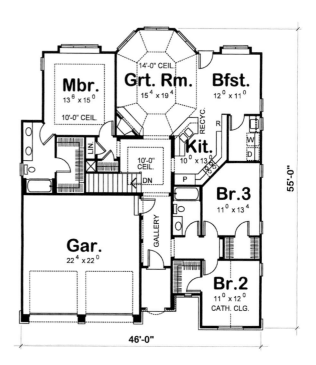

Plan #121165

Dimensions: 46' W x 55' D

Levels: 1

Square Footage: 1,678

Bedrooms: 3

Bathrooms: 2

Foundation: Basement; crawl space for fee

Material List Available: Yes

Price Category: C

Images provided by designer/architect.

This home, as shown in the photograph, may differ from the actual blueprints. For more detailed information, please check the floor plans carefully.

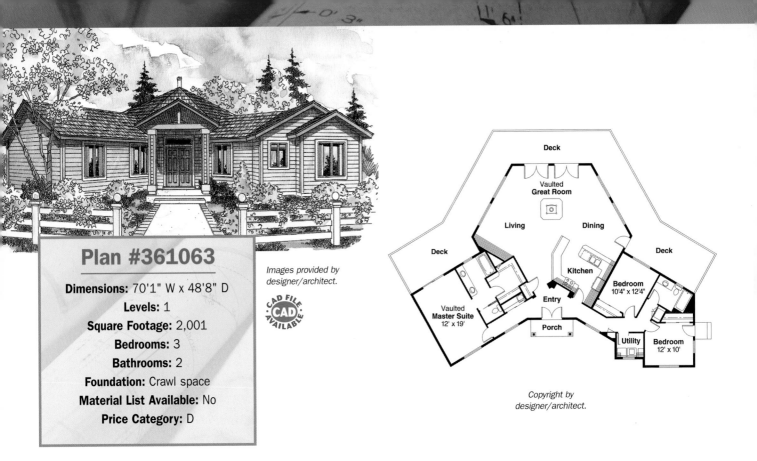

Plan #361063

Dimensions: 70'1" W x 48'8" D

Levels: 1

Square Footage: 2,001

Bedrooms: 3

Bathrooms: 2

Foundation: Crawl space

Material List Available: No

Price Category: D

Images provided by designer/architect.

Copyright by designer/architect.

Plan #161126

Dimensions: 86'2" W x 57'5" D

Levels: 1

Square Footage: 4,896

Main Level Sq. Ft.: 2,850

Lower Level Sq. Ft.: 2,046

Bedrooms: 4

Bathrooms: 4½

Foundation: Basement

Material List Available: Yes

Price Category: I

Images provided by designer/architect.

Basement Level Floor Plan

Copyright by designer/architect.

Plan #161130

Dimensions: 61'10" W x 49'1" D

Levels: 1

Square Footage: 1,619

Bedrooms: 3

Bathrooms: 2

Foundation: Basement

Material List Available: Yes

Price Category: C

Images provided by designer/architect.

Copyright by designer/architect.

Rear Elevation

Plan #661146

Dimensions: 65' W x 65'6" D

Levels: 1

Square Footage: 2,560

Bedrooms: 4

Bathrooms: 2

Foundation: Slab

Materials List Available: No

Price Category: E

Images provided by designer/architect.

Copyright by designer/architect.

Plan #121124

Dimensions: 55'4" W x 56' D
Levels: 1
Square Footage: 1,806
Bedrooms: 3
Bathrooms: 2
Foundation: Basement; crawl space for fee
Material List Available: Yes
Price Category: D

This brick ranch will be the best-looking home in the neighborhood.

Features:

• Great Room: This area is a great place to gather with family and friends. The 10-ft.-high ceiling and arched windows make this room bright and airy. On cold nights, gather by the warmth of the fireplace.

• Dining Room: A column off the entry defines this formal dining area. Arched windows and a 10-ft.-high ceiling add to the elegance of the space.

• Kitchen: This island kitchen will inspire the chef in the family to create a symphony at every meal. The triple window in the adjoining breakfast area floods this area with natural light.

Images provided by designer/architect.

• Master Suite: Located on the opposite side of the home from the secondary bedrooms, this private area features a 10-ft.-high ceiling in the sleeping area. The master bath boasts a compartmentalized lavatory and shower area in addition to dual vanities and a walk-in closet.

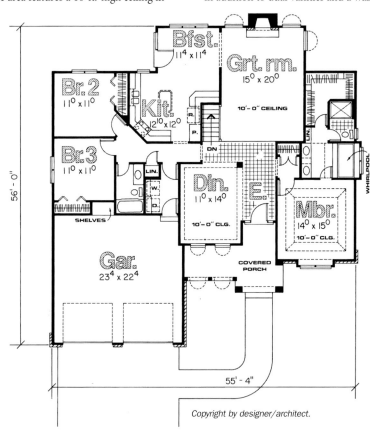

Copyright by designer/architect.

Plan #151387

Dimensions: 64'2" W x 49' D
Levels: 1
Square Footage: 1,989
Bedrooms: 4
Bathrooms: 3
Foundation: Crawl space, slab, basement or walkout
CompleteCost List Available: Yes
Price Category: D

Images provided by designer/architect.

This home is elegantly designed both inside and out. The luxurious amenities will delight you and your guests alike.

Features:

- Entry: Welcome guests in from the cold to enjoy hors d'oeuvres by the fireplace in the spacious great room before enjoying the main course in the formal dining room.

- Kitchen: Expansive counter space and plenty of storage give the house chef ample room to work. A raised bar, which seats four, transitions into the sunlit breakfast room.

- Master Suite: Private entry to the porch and a vast walk-in closet are two special features of this master suite. The full bath includes his and her vanities, a whirlpool tub, and a large corner shower stall.

- Guest Suite: Guests will not only feel at home, they will feel like their at a four-star hotel in this spacious guest suite. Features include a walk-in closet and full bathroom.

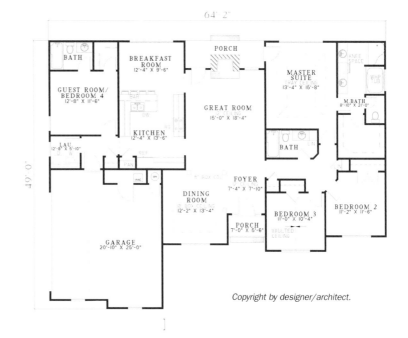

Copyright by designer/architect.

Plan #361101

Dimensions: 87'2" W x 72'6"D

Levels: 1

Square Footage: 1,986

Bedrooms: 3

Bathrooms: 2½

Foundation: Crawl space

Material List Available: No

Price Category: D

This is home with a great layout that does a good job of dividing public areas from private spaces.

Features:

- **Living Room:** Gather by the glowing fire on cold nights, or expand your entertaining space at other times. This living room is at the center of everything, with plenty of space for friends and family.

- **Dining Room:** This vaulted dining room is perfect for both formal and everyday meals. Its location close to the kitchen and living room adds to the versatility of the area.

- **Kitchen:** Plenty of workspace, ample storage, a convenient snack bar, and proximity to both the dining and living rooms make this kitchen ideal for chefs and entertainers of all kinds. The kitchen layout simplifies hectic mornings, family dinners, and formal parties.

- **Secondary Bedrooms:** Both secondary bedrooms have ample closet space and are similarly sized to quell any sibling rivalry on the subject.

Plan #241040

Dimensions: 34' W x 65' D

Levels: 1

Square Footage: 1,468

Bedrooms: 3

Bathrooms: 2

Foundation: Slab

Material List Available: No

Price Category: B

This craftsman-style house is perfect for first time buyers, or for enjoying an active retirement.

Features:

- **Great Room:** A unique design, this area has 12-ft.-high ceilings and a plant ledge that divides the room. A separate niche provides a hideaway for relaxing.

- **Master Suite:** Featuring an 11-ft.-high ceiling, walk-in closet, and ample bathroom space, this suite has everything you need for comfort and relaxation.

- **Additional rooms:** Two bedrooms make this home ideal or family life. The home also features a utility room for the washer and dryer.

- **Garage:** This two-car garage helps make the home functional as well as sweet and appealing.

Images provided by designer/architect.

Copyright by designer/architect.

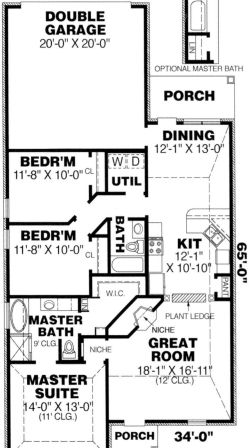

Plan #441010

Dimensions: 108' W x 59' D

Levels: 1

Square Footage: 2,973

Bedrooms: 4

Bathrooms: 4½

Foundation: Crawl space; slab or basement available for fee

Materials List Available: No

Price Category: F

Bordering on estate-sized, this plan borrows elements from Norman, Mediterranean, and English architecture.

CAD FILE AVAILABLE

Images provided by designer/architect.

Features:

- Great Room: This gathering area features a large bay window and a fireplace flanked with built-ins. The vaulted ceiling adds to the large feel of the area.

- Kitchen: This large island kitchen features a walk-in pantry and a built-in desk. The breakfast nook has access to the patio.

- Master Suite: This retreat features a vaulted ceiling in the sleeping area and access to the patio. The master bath boasts dual vanities, a stand-up shower, a spa tub, and a very large walk-in closet.

- Bedrooms: Two family bedrooms, each with its own private bathroom, have large closets.

Copyright by designer/architect.

Rear Elevation

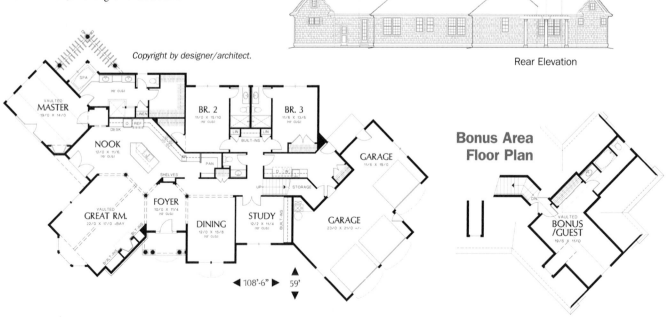

Bonus Area Floor Plan

Plan #121119

Dimensions: 62' W x 48' D
Levels: 1
Square Footage: 1,850
Bedrooms: 3
Bathrooms: 2
Foundation: Basement;
crawl space for fee
Material List Available: Yes
Price Category: C

Images provided by designer/architect.

With beautiful architectural details and abundant amenities, this home will steal your heart.

Features:

• Kitchen: Keeping this kitchen cheerful are walls surrounded by transom windows, bringing the morning sun into your home. The kitchen has everything you want, including an island, a pantry, counter space to spare, and a desk area, and it opens directly into the breakfast room.

• Dining Room: Separated from the kitchen and breakfast room by a hallway, this dining room can adopt an air of elegance and decorum. It has a built-in hutch and, with the right furniture, can be used for family dinners and small dinner parties alike.

• Master Suite: This bedroom, sectioned in two, is simply a dream. Through double doors is a walk-in closet to the left, dual vanities to the front, a skylight above, and a full master bath to the right, equipped with a whirlpool tub, shower stall, and window seat. Here, "staying in" sounds romantic.

• Secondary Bedrooms: If three bedrooms are more than you need, Bedroom 2 will work wonderfully as a den. With transom windows bringing in the sunlight and double doors opening to the entryway, this room would be a welcoming place to entertain guests who have just arrived.

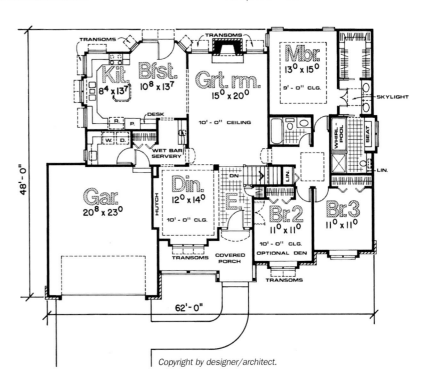

Copyright by designer/architect.

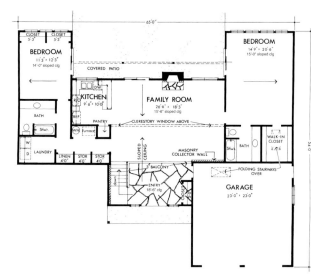

Plan #271458

Dimensions: 65' W x 54' D

Levels: 1

Square Footage: 1,789

Bedrooms: 2

Bathrooms: 2

Foundation: Crawl space

Material List Available: No

Price Category: C

Images provided by designer/architect.

Rear View

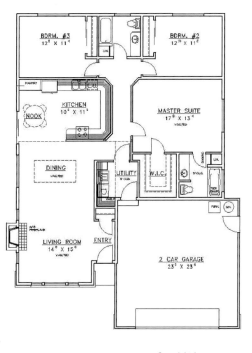

Plan #451172

Dimensions: 43' W x 58' D

Levels: 1

Square Footage: 1,659

Bedrooms: 3

Bathrooms: 2

Foundation: Slab

Material List Available: No

Price Category: C

Images provided by designer/architect.

CAD FILE AVAILABLE

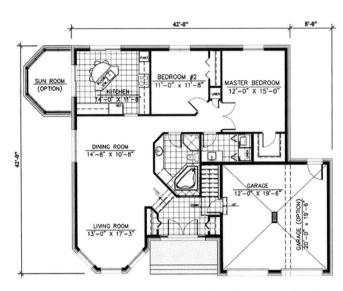

Plan #571045

Dimensions: 42' W x 42' D

Levels: 1

Square Footage: 1,399

Bedrooms: 2

Bathrooms: 1

Foundation: Basement

Material List Available: Yes

Price Category: B

Images provided by designer/architect.

Rear Elevation

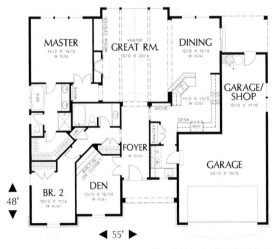

Plan #441004

Dimensions: 55' W x 48' D

Levels: 1

Square Footage: 1,728

Bedrooms: 2

Bathrooms: 2

Foundation: Crawl space; slab or basement available for fee

Materials List Available: No

Price Category: C

Images provided by designer/architect.

CAD FILE AVAILABLE

Rear Elevation

Plan #121137

Dimensions: 42' W x 54' D

Levels: 1

Square Footage: 1,392

Bedrooms: 3

Bathrooms: 2

Foundation: Basement; crawl space for fee

Material List Available: Yes

Price Category: B

Images provided by designer/architect.

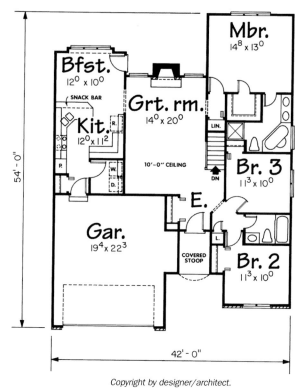

Copyright by designer/architect.

Plan #451161

Dimensions: 87'8" W x 66'10" D

Levels: 1

Square Footage: 5,042

Main Level Sq. Ft.: 2,521

Lower Level Sq. Ft.: 2,521

Bedrooms: 6

Bathrooms: 4½

Foundation: Walkout

Material List Available: No

Price Category: I

Images provided by designer/architect.

Basement Level Floor Plan

Copyright by designer/architect.

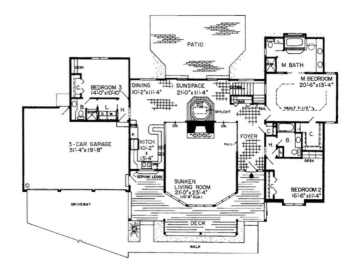

Copyright by designer/architect.

Plan #391168

Dimensions: 93'6" W x 48' D

Levels: 1

Square Footage: 2,352

Bedrooms: 3

Bathrooms: 2½

Foundation: Basement

Material List Available: Yes

Price Category: E

Images provided by designer/architect.

Plan #151688

Dimensions: 68'6" W x 64'8" D

Levels: 1

Square Footage: 2,388

Bedrooms: 4

Bathrooms: 2½

Foundation: Slab

CompleteCost List Available: Yes

Price Category: E

Images provided by designer/architect.

CAD FILE AVAILABLE

Copyright by designer/architect.

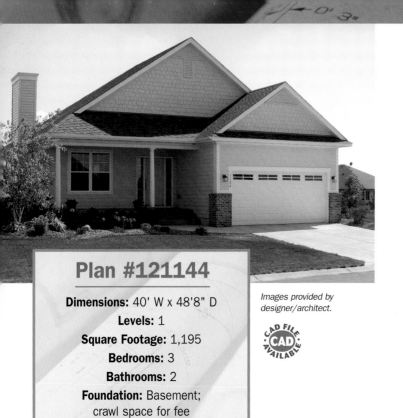

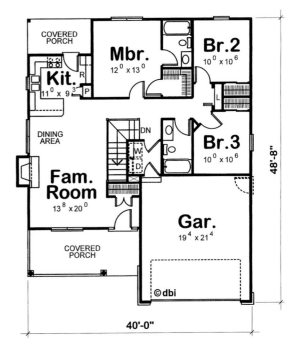

Images provided by designer/architect.

CAD FILE AVAILABLE

Copyright by designer/architect.

Plan #121144

Dimensions: 40' W x 48'8" D

Levels: 1

Square Footage: 1,195

Bedrooms: 3

Bathrooms: 2

Foundation: Basement; crawl space for fee

Material List Available: Yes

Price Category: B

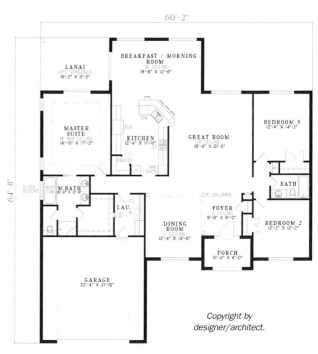

Images provided by designer/architect.

CAD FILE AVAILABLE

Copyright by designer/architect.

Plan #151500

Dimensions: 60'2" W x 64'8" D

Levels: 1

Square Footage: 2,237

Bedrooms: 3

Bathrooms: 2

Foundation: Slab

CompleteCost List Available: Yes

Price Category: E

Plan #451153

Dimensions: 52' W x 50' D
Levels: 1
Square Footage: 1,605
Bedrooms: 3
Bathrooms: 2½
Foundation: Crawl space
Material List Available: No
Price Category: C

Images provided by designer/architect.

CAD FILE CAD AVAILABLE

Copyright by designer/architect.

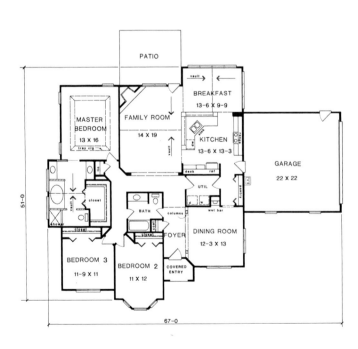

Plan #461090

Dimensions: 67' W x 51' D
Levels: 1
Square Footage: 1,922
Bedrooms: 3
Bathrooms: 2
Foundation: Crawl space or slab; basement for fee
Material List Available: No
Price Category: D

Images provided by designer/architect.

Copyright by designer/architect.

Plan #121117

Dimensions: 76' W x 46' D

Levels: 1

Square Footage: 2,172

Bedrooms: 4

Bathrooms: 3

Foundation: Basement; crawl space for fee

Material List Available: Yes

Price Category: D

Tall ceilings and an efficient design complement this home's stately exterior.

Features:

- Great Room: Whether welcoming guests in for an elegant evening or just spending time with the family, this great room provides plenty of space and is warmed by a built-in fireplace.

- Kitchen: This unique design includes a walk-in pantry, desk, and large square island. The kitchen drinks in the sunlight from the adjacent breakfast room, which provides a simple transition from meal preparation to dining.

- Master Suite: With windows flanking one wall of the bedroom and a skylight in the bathroom, natural light romanticizes this space. Other features include a large walk-in closet, a whirlpool tub with a view, and a separate stall shower.

- Secondary Bedrooms: Two equally sized bedrooms each have access to their own semiprivate full bathrooms. A living area by the entry can serve as a third bedroom for a growing family or a guest bedroom for the occasional visitor.

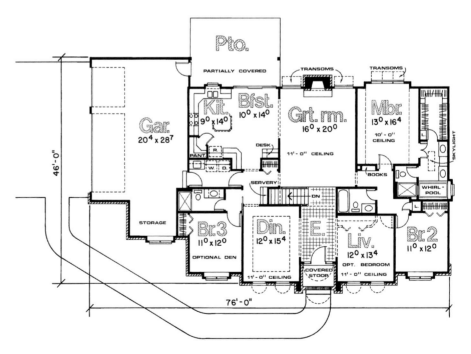

Plan #481033

Dimensions: 78' W x 73' D
Levels: 1
Square Footage: 5,667
Main Level Sq. Ft.: 3,042
Lower Level Sq. Ft.: 2,625
Bedrooms: 4
Bathrooms: 4 full, 2 half
Foundation: Walkout basement
Material List Available: No
Price Category: J

This outstanding home has all the charm of the Tudor style. The siding consists of brick and cedar shingles and complements the brick-and-stone chimney.

Images provided by designer/architect.

Features:

- Reception Area: This fabulous reception area opens to the formal dining room, which features a beamed ceiling.

- Kitchen: This combined kitchen and dinette area share a see-through fireplace with the family room. Sliding doors lead to a unique curved deck. The island and butler's pantry make meal preparation a breeze.

- Master Suite: Discover this retreat located on the other side of the home. The suite features a tray ceiling, a bay window, and a secluded bath with dual walk-in closets and an angled garden tub.

- Lower Level: A recreation room, a game room with a kitchenette, and a wine room make up one-half of this level. An exercise room, two bedrooms with walk-in closets, and a bathroom complete the area.

Basement Level Floor Plan

Copyright by designer/architect.

Plan #541039

Dimensions: 99'4" W x 66'6"D
Levels: 1
Square Footage: 4,466
Main Level Sq. Ft.: 2,846
Lower Level Sq. Ft.: 1,620
Bedrooms: 4
Bathrooms: 3½
Foundation: Walkout; basement for fee
Material List Available: No
Price Category: I

Images provided by designer/architect.

Unsurpassed street appeal is only the beginning of this outstanding design.

Features:

- **Great Room:** This vaulted gathering area offers exposed beams, a fireplace, and a view out to the covered deck.

- **Kitchen:** This spacious kitchen includes a large island with a raised eating bar, double ovens, a china cabinet, and a huge walk-in pantry.

- **Office:** An additional desk is located outside of this cozy office. The room's convenient location just off of the breakfast nook allows for a productive work environment.

- **Master Suite:** A coffer ceiling enhances this fabulous master suite, which includes his and her walk-in closets. Separate vanities, a vaulted ceiling, a soaking tub, a large shower, and private access to the covered deck complete the master bath.

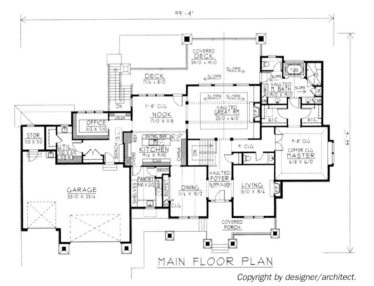

MAIN FLOOR PLAN

Copyright by designer/architect.

Basement Level Floor Plan

BASEMENT PLAN

Plan #121116

Dimensions: 72' W x 56' D
Levels: 1
Square Footage: 2,276
Bedrooms: 3
Bathrooms: 2½
Foundation: Basement; crawl space for fee
Material List Available: Yes
Price Category: E

Images provided by designer/architect.

This charming country home is filled with ingenious design and sumptuous spaces.

Features:

- Great Room: This spacious entertainment area can be kept formal for guests while the den holds all of the embarrassing family clutter.

- Kitchen: Uniquely laid out, this kitchen includes two pantries, a desk, a snack bar, and an adjacent wet bar. Transitioning right into the breakfast area means more natural light for the kitchen and simple shifting from meal preparation to dining.

- Master Suite: This master bedroom was planned with couples in mind. His and her closets and vanities simplify getting ready. A built-in entertainment center, whirlpool tub, and separate shower stall are added bonuses.

- Secondary Bedrooms: In a space all their own, these bedrooms have ample closet space, a nearby full bathroom, and are identically sized to keep siblings from squabbling.

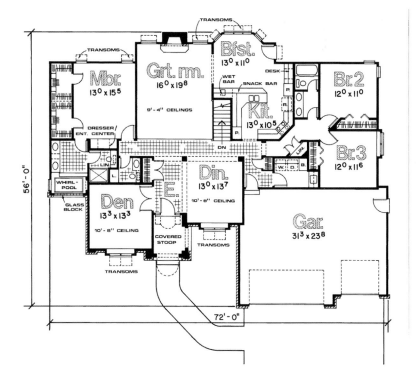

Copyright by designer/architect.

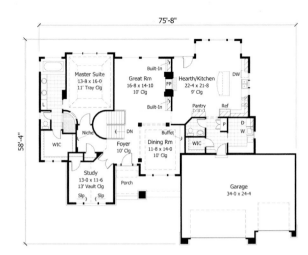

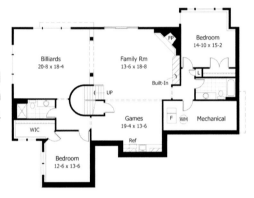

Plan #481029

Dimensions: 75'8" W x 58'4" D

Levels: 1

Square Footage: 4,048

Main Level Sq. Ft.: 2,147

Lower Level Sq. Ft.: 1,901

Bedrooms: 4

Bathrooms: 3½

Foundation: Walkout basement

Material List Available: No

Price Category: I

Images provided by designer/architect.

Basement Level Floor Plan

Copyright by designer/architect.

Plan #451138

Dimensions: 64'4" W x 73' D

Levels: 1

Square Footage: 4,484

Main Level Sq. Ft.: 2,242

Basement Level Sq. Ft.: 2,242

Bedrooms: 4

Bathrooms: 3

Foundation: Basement – insulated concrete form

Material List Available: No

Price Category: I

Images provided by designer/architect.

CAD FILE AVAILABLE

Basement Level Floor Plan

Copyright by designer/architect.

Plan #151502

Dimensions: 81'7" W x 97'2" D

Levels: 1

Square Footage: 3,654

Bedrooms: 3

Bathrooms: 3

Foundation: Slab

CompleteCost List Available: Yes

Price Category: H

Images provided by designer/architect.

Copyright by designer/architect.

Plan #111014

Dimensions: 78' W x 47' D

Levels: 1

Square Footage: 1,865

Bedrooms: 4

Bathrooms: 2

Foundation: Slab

Materials List Available: No

Price Category: E

Images provided by designer/architect.

Copyright by designer/architect.

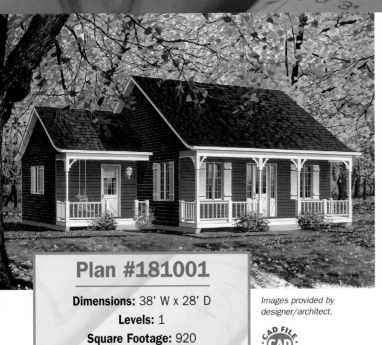

Plan #181001

Dimensions: 38' W x 28' D

Levels: 1

Square Footage: 920

Bedrooms: 2

Bathrooms: 1

Foundation: Basement

Materials List Available: Yes

Price Category: A

Images provided by designer/architect.

CAD FILE AVAILABLE / CAD

28'-0"
8,4 m

19'-0" X 11'-8"
5,70 X 3,50

12'-2" X 11'-8"
3,65 X 3,50

9'-0" X 10'-0"
2,70 X 3,00

15'-4" X 12'-0"
4,60 X 3,60

38'-0"
11,4 m

Plan #481137

Dimensions: 77' W x 66' D

Levels: 1

Square Footage: 4,425

Main Level Sq. Ft.: 2,482

Lower Level Sq. Ft.: 1,943

Bedrooms: 3

Bathrooms: 2½

Foundation: Walkout

Material List Available: No

Price Category: I

Images provided by designer/architect.

Basement Level Floor Plan

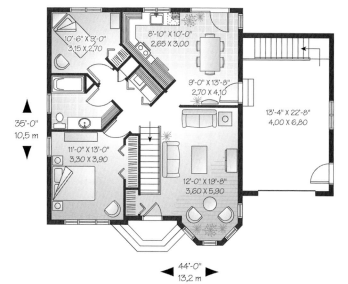

Plan #181595

Dimensions: 44' W x 35' D

Levels: 1

Square Footage: 976

Bedrooms: 2

Bathrooms: 1

Foundation: Basement

Material List Available: Yes

Price Category: A

Images provided by designer/architect.

CAD FILE AVAILABLE

10'-6" X 9'-0"
3,15 X 2,70

8'-10" X 10'-0"
2,65 X 3,00

9'-0" X 13'-8"
2,70 X 4,10

13'-4" X 22'-8"
4,00 X 6,80

11'-0" X 13'-0"
3,30 X 3,90

12'-0" X 19'-8"
3,60 X 5,90

35'-0"
10,5 m

44'-0"
13,2 m

Copyright by designer/architect.

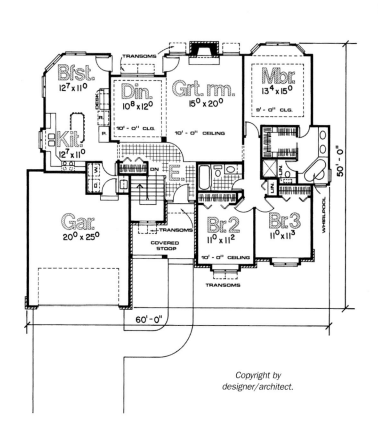

Plan #121109

Dimensions: 60' W x 50' D

Levels: 1

Square Footage: 1,735

Bedrooms: 3

Bathrooms: 2

Foundation: Basement; crawl space for fee

Material List Available: Yes

Price Category: C

Images provided by designer/architect.

This home, as shown in the photograph, may differ from the actual blueprints. For more detailed information, please check the floor plans carefully.

Bfst.
12⁷ x 11⁰

Din.
10⁸ x 12⁰

Grt. rm.
15⁰ x 20⁰

Mbr.
13⁴ x 15⁰
9'-0" CLG.

Kit.
12⁷ x 11⁰

10'-0" CLG.

10'-0" CEILING

TRANSOMS

Gar.
20⁰ x 25⁰

Br. 2
11⁰ x 11²

Br. 3
11⁰ x 11³

10'-0" CEILING

COVERED STOOP

TRANSOMS

WHIRLPOOL

50'-0"

60'-0"

Copyright by designer/architect.

Plan #151616

Dimensions: 84' W x 47'6" D
Levels: 1
Square Footage: 3,246
Main Level Sq. Ft.: 2,024
Lower Level Sq. Ft.: 1,222
Bedrooms: 4
Bathrooms: 2½
Foundation: Crawl space or slab
CompleteCost List Available: Yes
Price Category: G

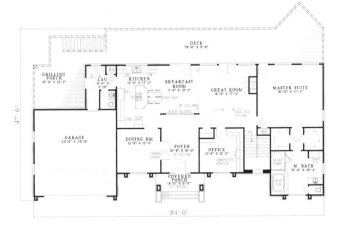

Images provided by designer/architect.

Basement Level Floor Plan

Copyright by designer/architect.

Plan #451092

Dimensions: 100' W x 68'5" D
Levels: 1
Square Footage: 2,752
Bedrooms: 2
Bathrooms: 2½
Foundation: Walkout basement
Material List Available: No
Price Category: E

Images provided by designer/architect.

Main Level Floor Plan

Optional Basement Level Floor Plan

Copyright by designer/architect.

Rear Elevation

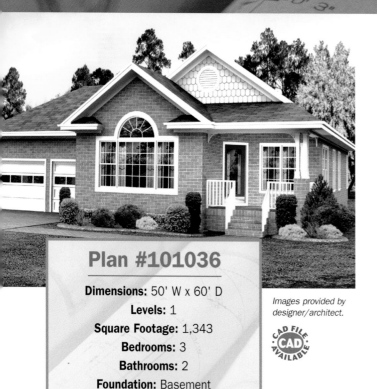

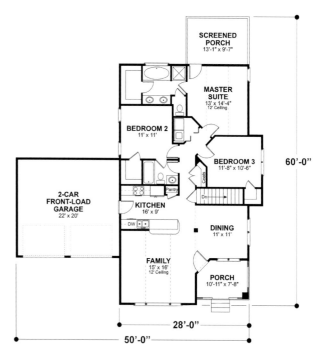

Plan #101036

Dimensions: 50' W x 60' D

Levels: 1

Square Footage: 1,343

Bedrooms: 3

Bathrooms: 2

Foundation: Basement

Materials List Available: No

Price Category: B

Images provided by designer/architect.

CAD FILE AVAILABLE

Copyright by designer/architect.

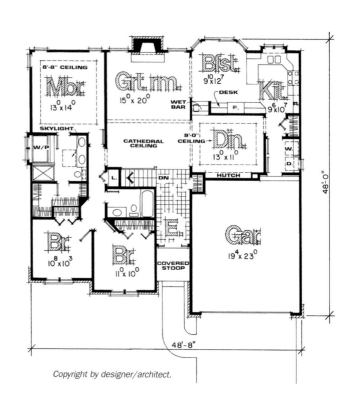

Plan #121107

Dimensions: 48'8" W x 48' D

Levels: 1

Square Footage: 1,604

Bedrooms: 3

Bathrooms: 2

Foundation: Basement; crawl space for fee

Material List Available: Yes

Price Category: C

Images provided by designer/architect.

CAD FILE AVAILABLE

Copyright by designer/architect.

Plan #271077

Dimensions: 69'6" W x 53' D

Levels: 1

Square Footage: 1,786

Bedrooms: 1

Bathrooms: 1½

Foundation: Basement or daylight basement

Materials List Available: No

Price Category: C

Images provided by designer/architect.

This wonderful home has an optional finished basement plan to add three more bedrooms—ideal for a growing family.

Features:

- Great Room: This large gathering room has a fireplace with built-in cabinets on either side.

- Kitchen: This island kitchen, with dinette area, is open to the great room.

- Master Bedroom: This luxurious room provides a view of the backyard.

- Master Bath: This private bathroom has a walk-in closet and double vanities.

Copyright by designer/architect.

Optional Basement Level Floor Plan

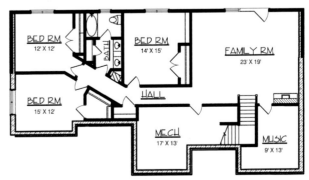

Plan #391049

Dimensions: 78' W x 52'4" D
Levels: 1
Square Footage: 4,064
Bedrooms: 4
Bathrooms: 3
Foundation: Basement
Material List Available: Yes
Price Category: E

Images provided by designer/architect.

This home proves that elegance can be comfortable. No need to sacrifice one for the other. Here, a peaked roofline creates a well-mannered covered front porch and classical columns announce the beauty of the dining room.

Features:

- Living Areas: High windows and a fireplace light up the living room, while an open hearth room shares the glow of a three-sided fireplace with the breakfast area and kitchen.

- Kitchen: To please the cook there's a built-in kitchen desk, cooking island, food-preparation island, double sinks, and pantries.

- Master Suite: To soothe the busy executive, this first-floor master suite includes a lavish bath and a nearby study.

- Recreation: The lower level entertains some big plans for entertaining—a home theater,

wet bar, and large recreation room with a double-sided fireplace.

- Bedrooms: Two additional bedrooms with excellent closet space and a shared full bath keep family or guests in stylish comfort.

Living Room

Copyright by designer/architect.

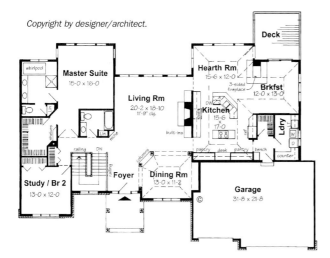

Basement Level Floor Plan

Plan #151001

Dimensions: 70' W x 88'2" D
Levels: 1
Square Footage: 3,124
Bedrooms: 4
Bathrooms: 3½
Foundation: Crawl space, slab
CompleteCost List Available: Yes
Price Category: G

Images provided by designer/architect.

From the double front doors to sleek arches, columns, and a gallery with arched openings to the bedrooms, you'll love this elegant home.

Features:

- Grand Room: With a 13-ft. pan ceiling and column entry, this room opens to the rear covered porch as well as through French doors to the bay-windowed morning room that, in turn, leads to the gathering room.

- Gathering Room: A majestic fireplace, built-in entertainment center, and book shelves give comfort and ease.

- Kitchen: A double oven, built-in desk, and a work island add up to a design for efficiency.

- Master Suite: Enjoy the practicality of walk-in closets, the comfort of a private sitting area, and the convenience of an adjacent study or nursery. The bath features a step-up whirlpool tub and separate shower.

Copyright by designer/architect.

Plan #481132

Dimensions: 109' W x 52' D
Levels: 1
Square Footage: 4,056
Main Level Sq. Ft.: 2,222
Lower Level Sq. Ft.: 1,834
Bedrooms: 4
Bathrooms: 4½
Foundation: Walkout
Material List Available: No
Price Category: I

Designed for a large family that loves to entertain, this home is a dream come true.

Images provided by designer/architect.

Features:

- Great Room: This welcoming space is perfect for relaxing and entertaining. Whether experienced in the bright sun or the warm glow of the fireplace, it will be everyone's favorite place to gather.

- Kitchen: Great for the busy family, this kitchen has all the workspace and storage that the family chef needs, as well as a snack bar that acts as a transition to the large dinette area.

- Master Suite: Located away from the busy areas of the home, this master suite is ideal for shedding your daily cares and relaxing in a romantic atmosphere. It includes a full master bath with his and her sinks, a stall shower, and a whirlpool tub.

- Lower Level: This is the ideal space for entertaining. The huge recreation room contains a wet bar, a billiards nook, and a fireplace flanked by built-in shelves. The space also contains an exercise area, two bathrooms, and two bedrooms.

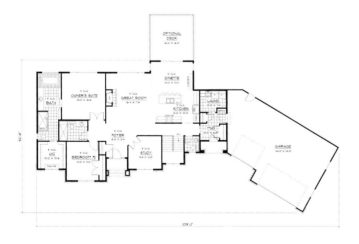

Basement Level Floor Plan

Copyright by designer/architect.

Plan #151626

Dimensions: 72' W x 82' D

Levels: 1

Square Footage: 2,659

Bedrooms: 4

Bathrooms: 2½

Foundation: Crawl space or slab

CompleteCost List Available: Yes

Price Category: F

Images provided by designer/architect.

CAD FILE AVAILABLE

Copyright by designer/architect.

Plan #451083

Dimensions: 82'5" W x 34'6" D

Levels: 1

Square Footage: 1,627

Bedrooms: 3

Bathrooms: 2

Foundation: Slab

Material List Available: No

Price Category: C

Images provided by designer/architect.

CAD FILE AVAILABLE

Copyright by designer/architect.

Plan #481011

Dimensions: 89'2" W x 60'6" D

Levels: 1

Square Footage: 2,758

Main Level Sq. Ft.: 1,670

Lower Level Sq. Ft.: 1,088

Bedrooms: 4

Bathrooms: 3

Foundation: Walkout basement

Material List Available: No

Price Category: F

Images provided by designer/architect.

Basement Level Floor Plan

Copyright by designer/architect.

Rear Elevation

Plan #121106

Dimensions: 74'4" W x 58' D

Levels: 1

Square Footage: 2,133

Bedrooms: 3

Bathrooms: 2½

Foundation: Basement; crawl space for fee

Material List Available: Yes

Price Category: D

Images provided by designer/architect.

CAD FILE AVAILABLE

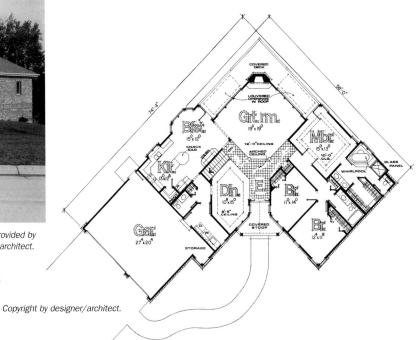

Copyright by designer/architect.

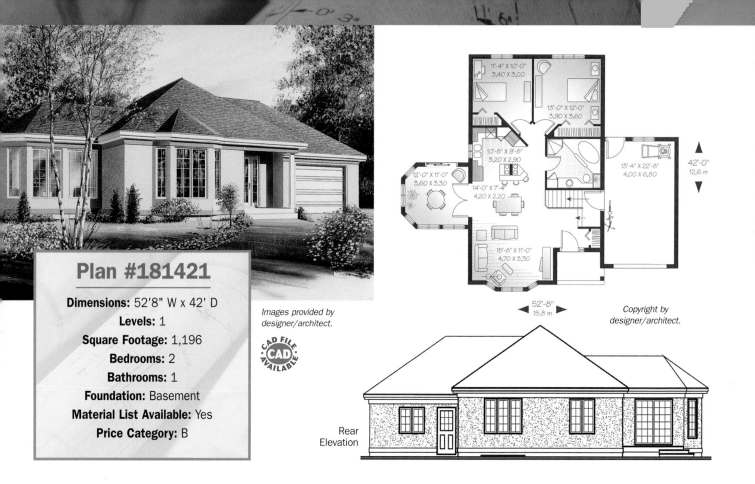

Plan #181421

Dimensions: 52'8" W x 42' D

Levels: 1

Square Footage: 1,196

Bedrooms: 2

Bathrooms: 1

Foundation: Basement

Material List Available: Yes

Price Category: B

Images provided by designer/architect.

CAD FILE AVAILABLE

Copyright by designer/architect.

Rear Elevation

Plan #321006

Dimensions: 76' W x 45' D

Levels: 1, optional lower

Square Footage: 1,977

Optional Basement Level Sq. Ft.: 1,416

Bedrooms: 4

Bathrooms: 2½

Foundation: Basement

Materials List Available: Yes

Price Category: D

Images provided by designer/architect.

CAD FILE AVAILABLE

Optional Basement Level Floor Plan

Copyright by designer/architect.

Plan #461064

Dimensions: 62'6" W x 54'6" D

Levels: 1

Square Footage: 1,677

Bedrooms: 3

Bathrooms: 2

Foundation: Crawl space or slab; basement for fee

Material List Available: No

Price Category: C

Images provided by designer/architect.

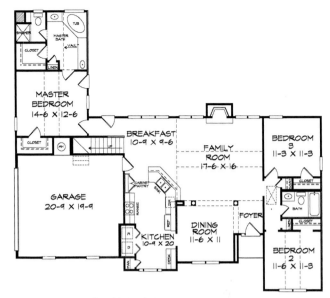

Copyright by designer/architect.

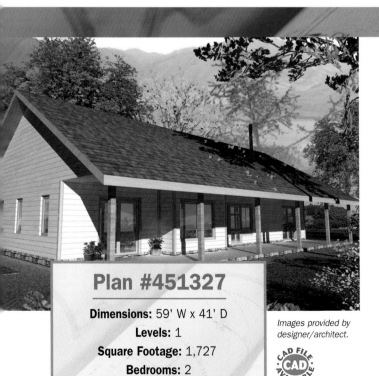

Plan #451327

Dimensions: 59' W x 41' D

Levels: 1

Square Footage: 1,727

Bedrooms: 2

Bathrooms: 2

Foundation: Slab – insulated concrete form

Material List Available: No

Price Category: C

Images provided by designer/architect.

CAD FILE AVAILABLE

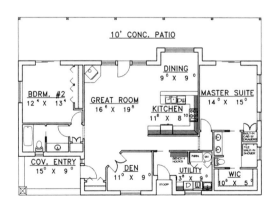

Copyright by designer/architect.

Bedroom 16' x 12'
Bath
Hall
Breakfast/ Family Center 11'7"-16'6" x 20' irreg.
Covered Deck
Master Bedroom 17'10" x 15'
Bedroom 14' x 12'4"
Laun.
Great Room 20' x 16'2"
Dressing
Kitchen 13'9" x 14'4" Irreg.
Dining Room 12'2" x 15'10"
Foyer
Garage 21'8" x 34'2"
Porch
Library 14'10" x 16'2"

FIRST FLOOR PLAN

76'-0"

Copyright by designer/architect.

Plan #161062

Dimensions: 76' W x 68'1" D

Levels: 1

Square Footage: 2,904

Opt. Finished Basement Sq. Ft.: 1,905

Bedrooms: 3

Bathrooms: 2½

Foundation: Basement, walk-out basement

Materials List Available: Yes

Price Category: F

Images provided by designer/architect.

Rear Elevation

Bedroom 15'6" x 15'1"
Game Room
Exercise Area
Bath
Billiards
Media Area
Storage
Bar
Unexcavated
Unfinished Basement
Unexcavated

Optional Basement Level Floor Plan

Plan #181403

Dimensions: 34' W x 32' D

Levels: 1

Square Footage: 1,917

Main Level Sq. Ft.: 1,014

Lower Level Sq. Ft.: 903

Bedrooms: 3

Bathrooms: 2

Foundation: Basement

Material List Available: Yes

Price Category: D

Images provided by designer/architect.

10'-8" X 9'-0" 3,20 X 2,70
12'-0" X 13'-0" 3,60 X 3,90
11'-0" X 10'-0" 3,30 X 3,00
32'-0" 9,6 m
11'-0" X 11'-4" 3,30 X 3,40
34'-0" 10,2 m

11'-0" X 13'-8" 3,30 X 4,10
20'-0" X 14'-0" 6,00 X 4,20

Basement Level Floor Plan

Copyright by designer/architect.

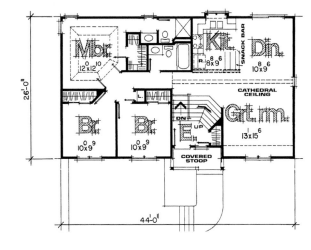

Plan #121105

Dimensions: 44' W x 26' D

Levels: 1

Square Footage: 1,125

Bedrooms: 3

Bathrooms: 2

Foundation: Basement; crawl space for fee

Material List Available: Yes

Price Category: B

Basement Level Floor Plan

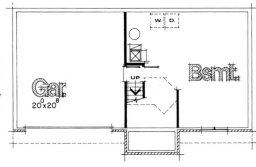

Plan #471002

Dimensions: 38' W x 26' D

Levels: 1

Square Footage: 835

Bedrooms: 2

Bathrooms: 2

Foundation: Crawl space or slab

Material List Available: No

Price Category: A

Plan #461032

Dimensions: 67'6" W x 36' D

Levels: 1

Square Footage: 1,799

Bedrooms: 3

Bathrooms: 2

Foundation: Slab; crawl space or basement for fee

Material List Available: No

Price Category: C

Images provided by designer/architect.

Copyright by designer/architect.

Plan #151498

Dimensions: 70' W x 88'6" D

Levels: 1

Square Footage: 3,167

Bedrooms: 4

Bathrooms: 3½

Foundation: Slab

CompleteCost List Available: Yes

Price Category: G

Images provided by designer/architect.

CAD FILE AVAILABLE

Copyright by designer/architect.

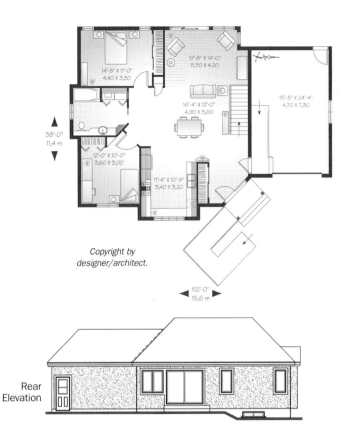

Plan #181385

Dimensions: 52' W x 38' D

Levels: 1

Square Footage: 1,285

Bedrooms: 2

Bathrooms: 1

Foundation: Basement

Material List Available: Yes

Price Category: B

Images provided by designer/architect.

CAD FILE AVAILABLE

Copyright by designer/architect.

Rear Elevation

Plan #471003

Dimensions: 40' W x 36' D

Levels: 1

Square Footage: 920

Bedrooms: 2

Bathrooms: 2

Foundation: Crawl space

Material List Available: Yes

Price Category: A

Images provided by designer/architect.

Copyright by designer/architect.

Plan #441008

Dimensions: 60' W x 50' D

Levels: 1

Square Footage: 2,001

Bedrooms: 3

Bathrooms: 2

Foundation: Crawl space; slab or basement available for fee

Materials List Available: No

Price Category: D

Images provided by designer/architect.

CAD FILE AVAILABLE

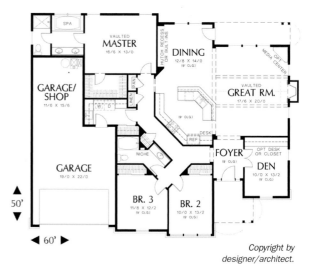

Copyright by designer/architect.

Rear Elevation

Plan #121058

Dimensions: 50' W x 52'8" D

Levels: 1

Square Footage: 1,554

Bedrooms: 2

Bathrooms: 2

Foundation: Basement

Materials List Available: Yes

Price Category: C

Images provided by designer/architect.

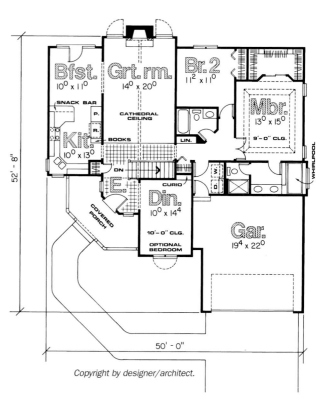

Copyright by designer/architect.

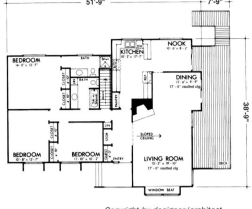

Copyright by designer/architect.

Images provided by designer/architect.

Plan #271084

Dimensions: 51'9" W x 38'9" D

Levels: 1

Square Footage: 1,602

Bedrooms: 3

Bathrooms: 1½

Foundation: Daylight

Materials List Available: Yes

Price Category: C

Optional Basement Level Floor Plan

Copyright by designer/architect.

Images provided by designer/architect.

CAD FILE AVAILABLE

Plan #181342

Dimensions: 39' W x 34' D

Levels: 1

Square Footage: 1,098

Bedrooms: 2

Bathrooms: 1

Foundation: Basement

Material List Available: Yes

Price Category: B

Rear Elevation

Plan #391006

Dimensions: 50' W x 45'4" D

Levels: 1

Square Footage: 1,456

Bedrooms: 3

Bathrooms: 2

Foundation: Crawl space, slab, or basement

Materials List Available: Yes

Price Category: B

Celebrating the union of beauty and function, this single-level layout makes a large appearance, with its peaked rooflines, elongated windowing, and sloping ceilings in the living room and bedroom #3 (or home office).

Features:

- Foyer: Soft angles define the space in the house, beginning with this foyer entry that curves to all the important rooms.

- Master Suite: Private rooms gather on the opposite side of the plan, with this master suite owning special windowing, an enormous walk-in closet, and a highly specialized bathroom with compartments that maintain privacy as two people use the various facilities at once.

- Bedroom: This other secondary bedroom enjoys a full bath and plenty of closet space.

- Utility Areas: Laundry facilities are easy to access, and a two-car garage has convenient front entry.

Images provided by designer/architect.

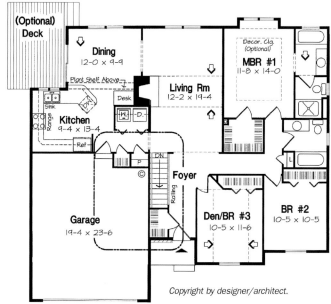

Copyright by designer/architect.

Rear View

Crawl Space/ Slab Option

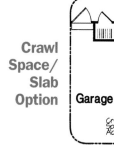

Plan #381092

Dimensions: 92' W x 62' D
Levels: 1
Square Footage: 3,030
Bedrooms: 4
Bathrooms: 2½
Foundation: Basement
Material List Available: Yes
Price Category: G

Images provided by designer/architect.

A stylish arched entry welcomes guests to this expansive residence.

Features:

- Dining Room: Located just off of the foyer is this formal dining room, which has access to the rear brick patio. A pass-through between the dining room and kitchen will aid in serving formal meals.

- Family Room: This large gathering area boasts a fireplace flanked by built-in bookshelves. Large windows flood the room with natural light, and there is access to the brick patio.

- Kitchen: This kitchen is quite sizable and is complete with a walk-in pantry and cooking island.

- Master Suite: At the rear of the house, this generous master suite offers access to the patio. The master bath boasts dual vanities and a whirlpool tub.

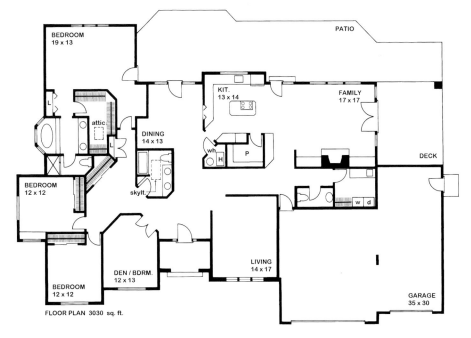

Copyright by designer/architect.

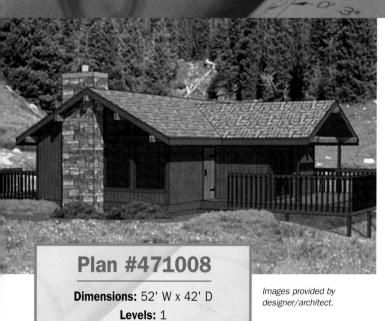

Plan #471008

Dimensions: 52' W x 42' D

Levels: 1

Square Footage: 1,127

Bedrooms: 3

Bathrooms: 2

Foundation: Crawl space or slab

Material List Available: No

Price Category: B

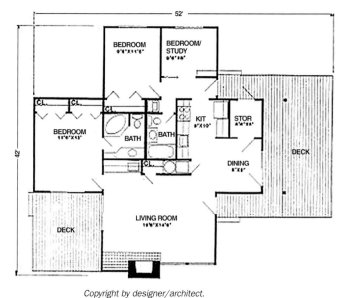

Images provided by designer/architect.

Copyright by designer/architect.

Plan #181598

Dimensions: 37' W x 32'4" D

Levels: 1

Square Footage: 962

Bedrooms: 2

Bathrooms: 1

Foundation: Basement

Material List Available: Yes

Price Category: A

Images provided by designer/architect.

CAD FILE AVAILABLE CAD

Copyright by designer/architect.

Rear Elevation

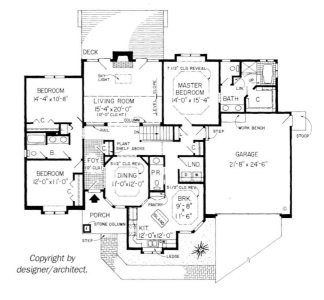

Plan #391059

Dimensions: 68' W x 46' D

Levels: 1

Square Footage: 2,020

Bedrooms: 3

Bathrooms: 2½

Foundation: Basement

Materials List Available: Yes

Price Category: C

Rear View

Plan #471014

Dimensions: 40' W x 26' D

Levels: 1

Square Footage: 950

Bedrooms: 2

Bathrooms: 2

Foundation: Crawl space

Material List Available: No

Price Category: A

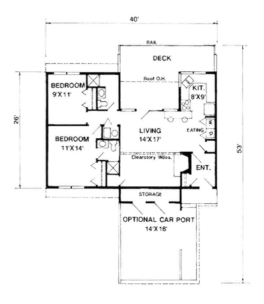

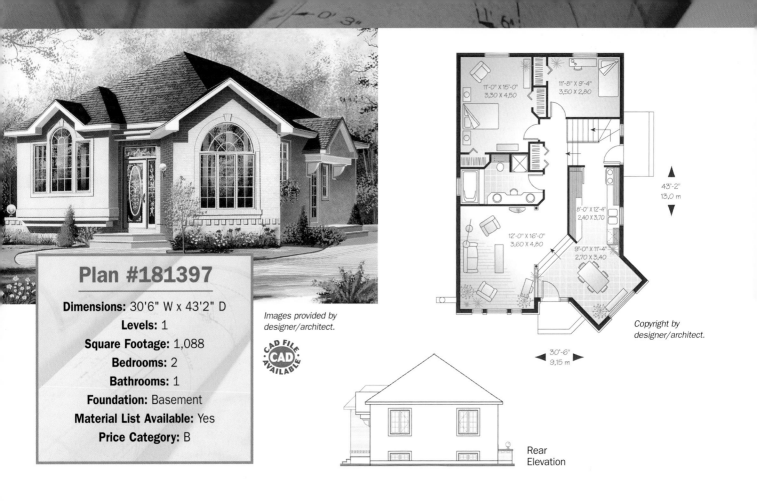

Plan #181397

Dimensions: 30'6" W x 43'2" D

Levels: 1

Square Footage: 1,088

Bedrooms: 2

Bathrooms: 1

Foundation: Basement

Material List Available: Yes

Price Category: B

Images provided by designer/architect.

CAD FILE AVAILABLE

Copyright by designer/architect.

11'-0" X 15'-0"
3,30 X 4,50

11'-8" X 9'-4"
3,50 X 2,80

8'-0" X 12'-4"
2,40 X 3,70

12'-0" X 16'-0"
3,60 X 4,80

9'-0" X 11'-4"
2,70 X 3,40

43'-2"
13,0 m

30'-6"
9,15 m

Rear Elevation

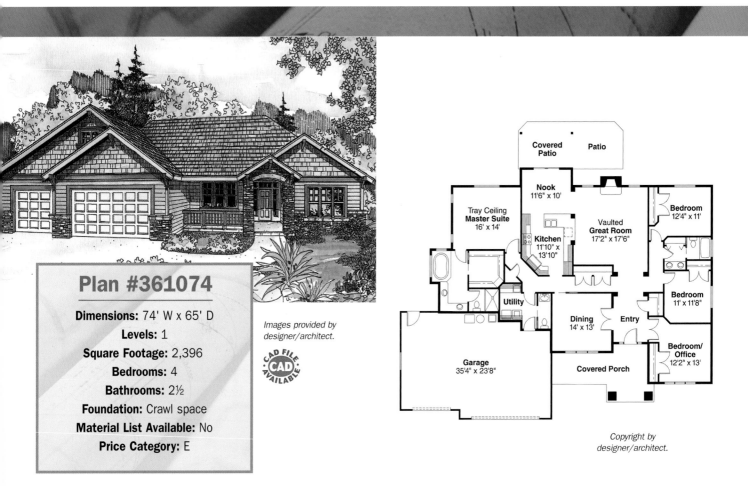

Plan #361074

Dimensions: 74' W x 65' D

Levels: 1

Square Footage: 2,396

Bedrooms: 4

Bathrooms: 2½

Foundation: Crawl space

Material List Available: No

Price Category: E

Images provided by designer/architect.

CAD FILE AVAILABLE

Covered Patio

Patio

Nook
11'6" x 10'

Tray Ceiling
Master Suite
16' x 14'

Kitchen
11'10" x 13'10"

Vaulted
Great Room
17'2" x 17'6"

Bedroom
12'4" x 11'

Utility

Dining
14' x 13'

Entry

Bedroom
11' x 11'8"

Garage
35'4" x 23'8"

Covered Porch

Bedroom/
Office
12'2" x 13'

Copyright by designer/architect.

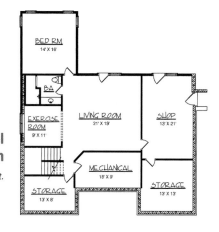

Plan #271078

Dimensions: 83' W x 52' D

Levels: 1

Square Footage: 3,620

Main Level Sq. Ft.: 1,855

Basement Level Sq. Ft.: 1,765

Bedrooms: 2

Bathrooms: 1½

Foundation: Daylight basement

Materials List Available: No

Price Category: H

Images provided by designer/architect.

Basement Level Floor Plan

Copyright by designer/architect.

Plan #181309

Dimensions: 34' W x 39' D

Levels: 1

Square Footage: 1,114

Bedrooms: 2

Bathrooms: 1

Foundation: Basement

Materials List Available: Yes

Price Category: B

Images provided by designer/architect.

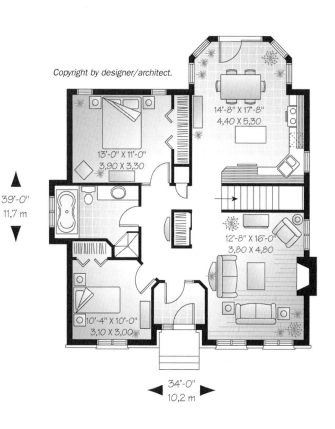

Copyright by designer/architect.

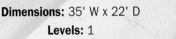

Plan #471024

Dimensions: 35' W x 22' D

Levels: 1

Square Footage: 484

Bedrooms: 1

Bathrooms: 1

Foundation: Crawl space or slab

Material List Available: No

Price Category: A

Images provided by designer/architect.

Copyright by designer/architect.

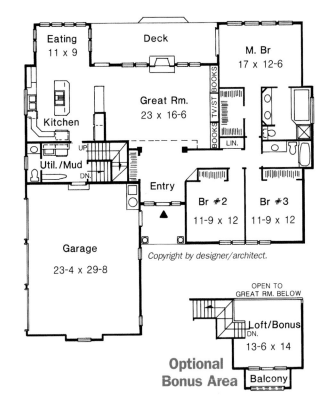

Plan #231008

Dimensions: 60' W x 62' D

Levels: 1

Square Footage: 1,941

Bedrooms: 3

Bathrooms: 2½

Foundation: Basement, crawl space

Materials List Available: No

Price Category: D

Images provided by designer/architect.

Copyright by designer/architect.

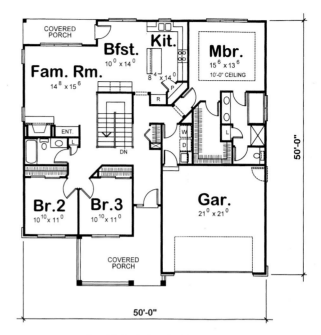

CAD FILE AVAILABLE

Copyright by designer/architect.

Plan #121011

Dimensions: 50' W x 50' D

Levels: 1

Square Footage: 1,724

Bedrooms: 3

Bathrooms: 2

Foundation: Slab, basement

Materials List Available: Yes

Price Category: C

Copyright by designer/architect.

Rear View

Plan #131008

Dimensions: 45'4" W x 36'4" D

Levels: 1

Square Footage: 1,299

Bedrooms: 3

Bathrooms: 2

Foundation: Crawl space, basement

Materials List Available: Yes

Price Category: C

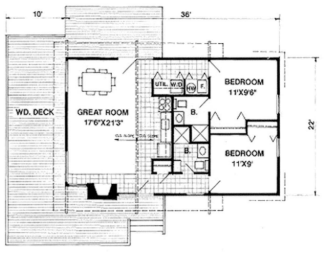

Plan #471017

Dimensions: 30' W x 40' D

Levels: 1

Square Footage: 786

Bedrooms: 2

Bathrooms: 2

Foundation: Crawl space or slab

Material List Available: Yes

Price Category: A

Images provided by designer/architect.

Copyright by designer/architect.

Copyright by designer/architect.

Plan #271059

Dimensions: 67' W x 57' D

Levels: 1

Square Footage: 1,790

Bedrooms: 1-3

Bathrooms: 1½- 2½

Foundation: Daylight basement

Materials List Available: No

Price Category: C

Images provided by designer/architect.

Optional Basement Level Floor Plan

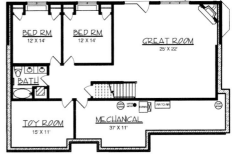

Plan #181148

Dimensions: 36' W x 34' D

Levels: 1

Square Footage: 1,174

Bedrooms: 3

Bathrooms: 1

Foundation: Full basement

Materials List Available: Yes

Price Category: B

Images provided by designer/architect.

CAD FILE AVAILABLE

34'-0"
10,2 m

36'-0"
10,8 m

Copyright by designer/architect.

Plan #391005

Dimensions: 60' W x 40'4" D

Levels: 1

Main Level Sq. Ft.: 1,575

Bedrooms: 3

Bathrooms: 2

Foundation: Crawl space, slab, or basement

Materials List Available: Yes

Price Category: C

Images provided by designer/architect.

Main Level Floor Plan

Copyright by designer/architect.

Front View

Images provided by designer/architect.

Plan #351018

Dimensions: 40'8" W x 38'6" D

Levels: 1

Square Footage: 1,251

Bedrooms: 3

Bathrooms: 2

Foundation: Crawl space or slab

Materials List Available: Yes

Price Category: C

This traditional home has great curb appeal and a great floor plan.

Features:

- Ceilings: All ceilings are a minimum of 9-ft. high.

- Great Room: This entertainment area, with a 12-ft.-high ceiling, features a gas fireplace and has views of the front yard through round-top windows and doors.

- Kitchen: This kitchen fulfills all the needs of the active family, plus it has a raised bar.

- Dining Room: Being adjacent to the kitchen allows this room to be practical as well as beautiful by means of the numerous windows overlooking the porch and backyard.

- Bedrooms: Vaulted ceilings in two of the three bedrooms provide a feeling of spaciousness. One bedroom has its own bathroom.

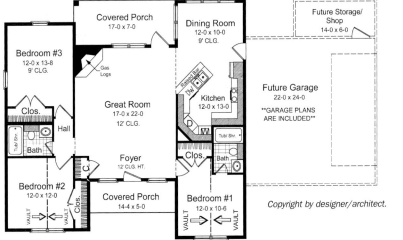

Copyright by designer/architect.

Front View

Plan #271061

Dimensions: 68' W x 52' D
Levels: 1
Square Footage: 1,750
Bedrooms: 1
Bathrooms: 1½
Foundation: Walkout basement
Material List Available: No
Price Category: C

Stucco and a contemporary design give this home a simplistically elegant look.

CAD FILE AVAILABLE · CAD

Features:

- Entry: A small porch area welcomes guests out of the weather and into the warmth. Inside, this entryway provides an inviting introduction to the rest of the home.

- Kitchen: Opening to both the full dining room and a bayed dinette, this kitchen is both beautifully and efficiently designed. The space includes a walk-in pantry and plenty of work-space for the budding gourmet.

- Master Suite: This space is fit for the king (or queen) of the castle. Separated from the rest

of the house by a small entry, the suite includes its own full bath with dual sinks, bathtub, shower stall, and water closet.

- Basement: This area can be finished to include two bedrooms with wide closets, a full bathroom, a family room, and storage space.

- Garage: Whether you actually have three cars you need kept from the climate, you are a collector of things, or you prefer a hobby area, this three-bay garage has plenty of space to fit your needs.

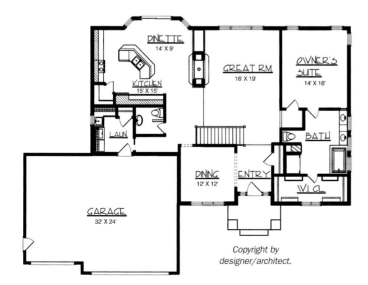

Copyright by designer/architect.

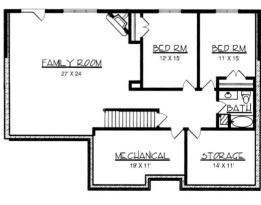

Optional Basement Level Floor Plan

Plan #181022

Dimensions: 46' W x 40'4" D
Levels: 1
Square Footage: 1,098
Bedrooms: 2
Bathrooms: 1
Foundation: Full basement
Materials List Available: Yes
Price Category: B

Images provided by designer/architect.

Copyright by designer/architect.

Plan #131040

Dimensions: 50' W x 37' D
Levels: 1
Square Footage: 1,630
Bedrooms: 3
Bathrooms: 2
Foundation: Crawl space, slab, or basement
Materials List Available: Yes
Price Category: D

Images provided by designer/architect.

Copyright by designer/architect.

Optional Lower Level Floor Plan

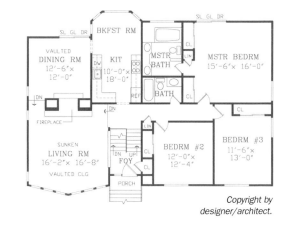

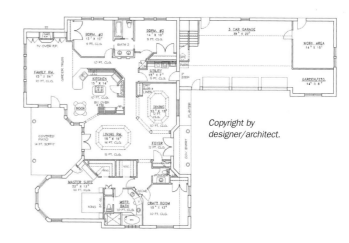

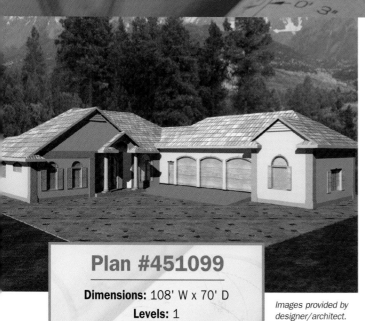

Plan #451099

Dimensions: 108' W x 70' D

Levels: 1

Square Footage: 3,044

Bedrooms: 3

Bathrooms: 2½

Foundation: Crawl space – insulated concrete form

Material List Available: No

Price Category: G

Images provided by designer/architect.

CAD FILE AVAILABLE

Rear Elevation

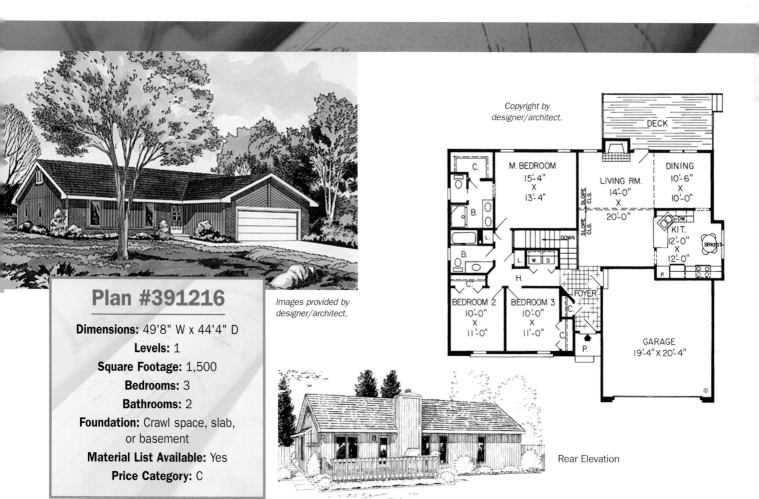

DECK

M. BEDROOM
15'-4" X 13'-4"

LIVING RM.
14'-0" X 20'-0"

DINING
10'-6" X 10'-0"

KIT.
12'-0" X 12'-0"

BRKFST.

DOWN

BEDROOM 2
10'-0" X 11'-0"

BEDROOM 3
10'-0" X 11'-0"

FOYER

GARAGE
19'-4" X 20'-4"

Plan #391216

Dimensions: 49'8" W x 44'4" D

Levels: 1

Square Footage: 1,500

Bedrooms: 3

Bathrooms: 2

Foundation: Crawl space, slab, or basement

Material List Available: Yes

Price Category: C

Images provided by designer/architect.

Rear Elevation

Plan #121009

Dimensions: 50' W x 58' D
Levels: 1
Square Footage: 1,422
Bedrooms: 3
Bathrooms: 2
Foundation: Basement
Materials List Available: Yes
Price Category: B

This amenity-filled home is perfect for the growing family or as a retirement retreat.

Features:

- Ceiling Height: 8 ft. unless otherwise noted.

- Great Room: This inviting space is the perfect place for gatherings of all sizes. It shares 12-ft. ceilings with the dining room and kitchen.

- Dining Room: In addition to the 12-ft. ceiling, arched openings, and built-in book cases make this an elegant place to dine.

- Private Porch: After dinner, step through a door in the dining room to enjoy a summer breeze in this inviting porch.

- Master Suite: The boxed ceiling lends drama to this suite and a walk-in closet adds convenience. Luxury comes from the whirlpool bath.

- Garage: You won't be short of parking and storage space in this two-bay garage. As a bonus there is space for a workbench.

SMARTtip
Window Cornices

You can transform plain rooms by making jogs in cornice molding that will hold shades, blinds, and other window treatments. You can create individual pockets over each window or continue the molding past narrow wall sections between windows to form a more expansive detail. Housings below the cornice can be painted or papered.

Plan #321026

Dimensions: 67' W x 42'4" D
Levels: 1
Square Footage: 1,712
Bedrooms: 3
Bathrooms: 2½
Foundation: Crawl space
Materials List Available: Yes
Price Category: C

Southwestern style is reflected perfectly in this gorgeous home.

Features:

• Great Room: Relax in style in this sunken great room, with its cozy fireplace and large, open area.

• Kitchen: Ample counter space and extra floor space make this kitchen a flexible room, expertly designed with the chef, multitasking owner, and host in mind. The washer and dryer located in a section off to the side makes easy-access cleaning a breeze.

• Master Suite: This private space contains a large walk-in closet. The master bath features dual vanities.

• Bedrooms: Two additional bedrooms, each with its own bathroom, make this home accommodating and luxurious.

• Storage: A garage and crawl space are great for organization and storage of cars or other necessities.

• Patio: This private rear patio adds classy appeal to the home. Great for enjoying the warm sun on your face in the privacy of your home or for having family over for a barbecue, these outdoor extras will have you relaxed in no time.

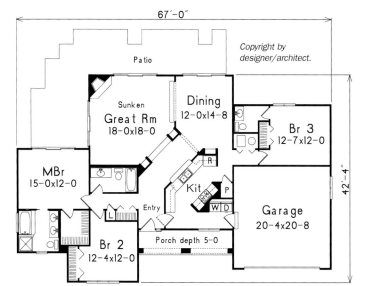

SMARTtip

Deck Design with Computers

Consider using a computer-aided design (CAD) program to plan your deck. Some programs let you see three-dimensional views of your design complete with railings, stairs, planters, hot tubs, and the surrounding landscaping.

Plan #131054

Dimensions: 107'4" W x 75'3" D
Levels: 1
Square Footage: 2,753
Opt. Lower Level Sq. Ft.: 1,127
Bedrooms: 3
Bathrooms: 2½
Foundation: Crawl space, slab, basement, or walkout
Materials List Available: Yes
Price Category: G

The beautifully designed interior area combined with plenty of outdoor living space create a striking and efficient home.

Images provided by designer/architect.

Features:

- Outdoor Living: Sit on the front porch and watch the world go by, enjoy a peaceful moment on the screened-in porch, or entertain on the wooden deck. If you enjoy the outdoors, this home is for you.

- Great Room: A vaulted ceiling, built-in fireplace, and flanking windows create a bright and comfortable space for entertaining or simply hanging out with the family.

- Kitchen: With plenty of workspace and storage, this kitchen suits all cooking styles. An exit onto the back deck and screened-in porch provide outdoor meal options for any kind of weather.

- Master Suite: Down a hallway of its own, this oasis inspires total relaxation. It features two walk-in closets, a desk, his and her vanities, extra large tub, and separate stall shower.

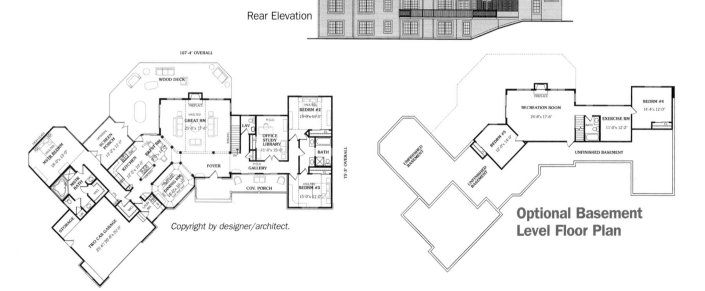

Rear Elevation

Copyright by designer/architect.

Optional Basement Level Floor Plan

Plan #391138

Dimensions: 76' W x 75' D
Levels: 1
Square Footage: 2,194
Bedrooms: 3
Bathrooms: 2
Foundation: Crawl space or basement
Material List Available: Yes
Price Category: D

A truly sensational layout! A beautiful brick courtyard and a swimming pool anchor this unusual design.

Features:

- Living Room: This area is the interior highlight of the home. The large, exciting space features a skylight and large windows that flood the room with light.

- Kitchen: This large U-shaped kitchen has a raised bar, which is open to the living room. A pocket door leads to the dining area.

- Master Suite: This private retreat is located in a wing of its own. The suite has access to the rear patio. The master bath features dual vanities and a glass shower.

- Bedrooms: Two bedrooms are located on the opposite side of the home to give those in the master suite privacy. The family room will act as a playroom for the kids.

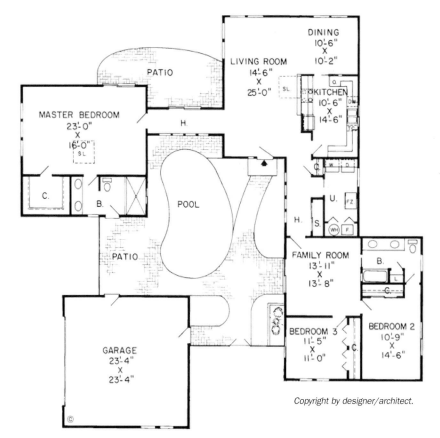

Plan #131045

Dimensions: 81'4" W x 68'3" D
Levels: 1
Square Footage: 2,347
Bedrooms: 4
Bathrooms: 2½
Foundation: Crawl space, slab, or basement
Materials List Available: Yes
Price Category: F

You'll love the character and flexibility in siting that the angled design gives to this contemporary ranch-style home.

Features:

• **Porch:** A wraparound rear porch adds distinction to this lovely home.

• **Great Room:** Facing the rear of the house, this great room has a high, stepped ceiling, fireplace, and ample space for built-ins.

• **Kitchen:** This large room sits at an angle to the great room and is adjacent to both a laundry room and extra powder room.

• **Office:** Use the 4th bedroom as a home office, study, or living room, depending on your needs.

• **Master Suite:** This area is separated from the other bedrooms in the house to give it privacy. The beautiful bay window at the rear, two large walk-in closets, and luxurious bath make it an ideal retreat after a hectic day.

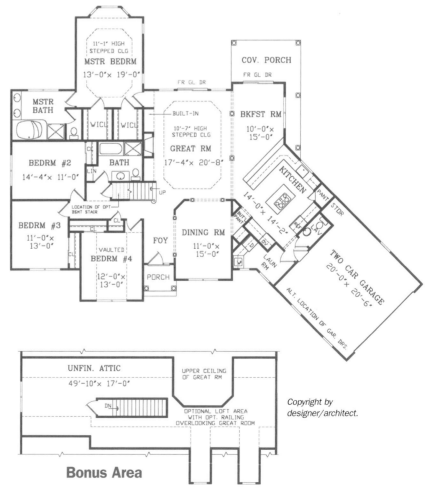

Plan #391156

Dimensions: 96' W x 60'6" D
Levels: 1
Square Footage: 2,450
Bedrooms: 4
Bathrooms: 2
Foundation: Basement or walkout
Material List Available: Yes
Price Category: E

Images provided by designer/architect.

This contemporary home offers many amenities for your family.

Features:

- Entry: This front entry consists of a vestibule, which contains a coat closet, and a separate foyer that leads to the rest of the house.

- Library/Den: This cozy room shares a see-through fireplace with the living room. The room has built-in shelves, a sloped ceiling, and a separate study alcove.

- Kitchen: This modern kitchen, with octagonal island, opens into the dining area. Skylights flood the area with natural light. A large nearby pantry keeps supplies handy and the kitchen neat.

- Master Suite: This private retreat includes a bedroom that is large enough for a comfortable seating area in front of its fireplace. The master bath features a separate room for the toilet, a spa tub, a large shower, and his and her vanities.

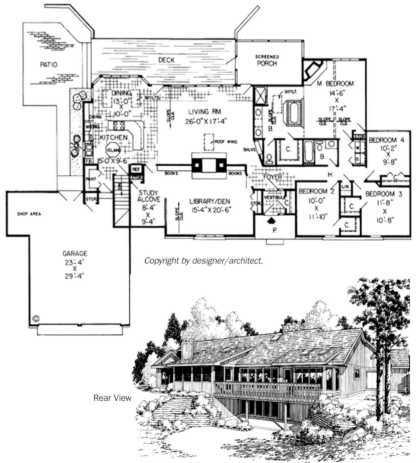

Copyright by designer/architect.

Rear View

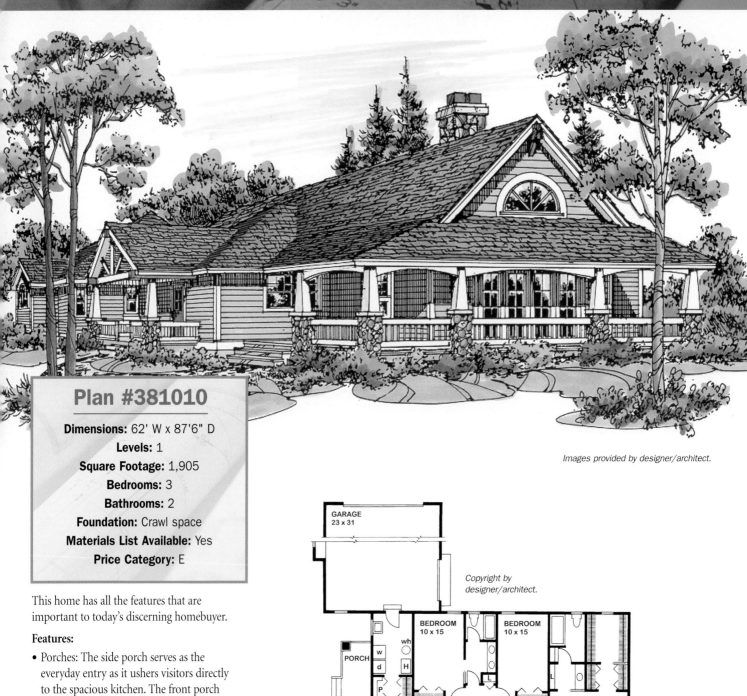

Plan #381010

Dimensions: 62' W x 87'6" D

Levels: 1

Square Footage: 1,905

Bedrooms: 3

Bathrooms: 2

Foundation: Crawl space

Materials List Available: Yes

Price Category: E

Images provided by designer/architect.

This home has all the features that are important to today's discerning homebuyer.

Features:

- Porches: The side porch serves as the everyday entry as it ushers visitors directly to the spacious kitchen. The front porch maintains its distinction as the formal entrance to the home.

- Great Room: The dining and living rooms are combined into this colossal great room. The room features a stone fireplace and a soaring vaulted ceiling with exposed beams. A circular stairway ascends to the loft.

- Kitchen: A vaulted ceiling, abundant cabinets, an island counter, and a dining room pass-through are all part of this very functional kitchen. An adjoining oversized utility room contains a coat closet and a pantry, and it offers access to the three-car garage.

- Master Suite: This master suite boasts a vaulted ceiling, a large walk-in closet, and a private bath.

Copyright by designer/architect.

Plan #131079

Dimensions: 36' W x 38' D

Levels: 1

Square Footage: 792

Bedrooms: 1

Bathrooms: 1

Foundation: Crawl space or slab

Material List Available: Yes

Price Category: B

A great starter home, this cozy space has everything you need. The efficient design makes the house feel larger than it is.

Features:

- Outdoor Space: This long porch in the front is perfect for sitting out on warm summer days, sipping lemonade, and watching the world go by. The second covered porch allows you to enjoy nature with more privacy.

- Great Room: Separate this spacious area into two sitting rooms, or use the fireplace as a focal point for entertaining.

- Kitchen: Everything you need is at hand in this inviting eat-in kitchen. The utility area is close by for quick and easy cleanup.

- Master Suite: With plenty of space for a small sitting area, this bedroom will become your personal retreat. It also features plenty of closet space and windows looking out on both the front and backyards.

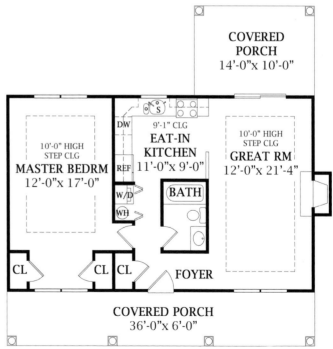

Plan #121005

Dimensions: 48' W x 52' D

Levels: 1

Square Footage: 1,496

Bedrooms: 3

Bathrooms: 2

Foundation: Basement

Materials List Available: Yes

Price Category: B

Images provided by designer/architect.

This home, as shown in the photograph, may differ from the actual blueprints. For more detailed information, please check the floor plans carefully.

A beautiful starter or retirement home with all the amenities you'd expect in a much bigger house.

Features:

- Ceiling Height: 8 ft.

- Great Room: A cathedral ceiling visually expands the great room making it the perfect place for family gatherings or formal entertaining.

- Formal Dining Room: This elegant room is ideal for entertaining dinner guests. It conveniently shares a wet bar and service counter with a bayed breakfast area next door.

- Breakfast Area: In addition to the service area shared with the dining room, this cozy area features a snack bar, pantry, and desk that's perfect for household paperwork.

- Master Suite: The master bedroom features special ceiling details. It's joined by a private bath with a whirlpool, shower, and spacious walk-in closet.

- Garage: The two-bay garage offers plenty of storage space.

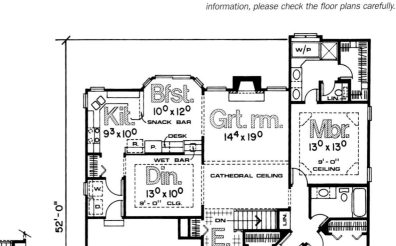

Optional Den

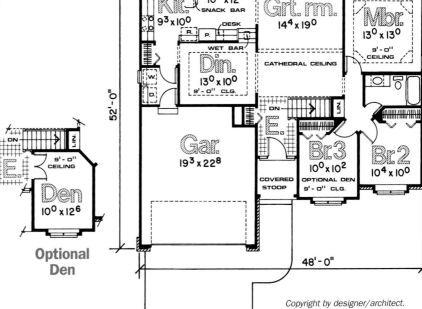

Copyright by designer/architect.

Let Us Help You Plan Your Dream Home

Whether you've always dreamed of building your own home or you can't find the right house from among the dozens you've toured, our collection of 1-story plans can help you achieve the home of your dreams. You could have an architect create a one-of-a-kind home for you, but the design services alone could end up costing up to 15 percent of the cost of construction—a hefty premium for any building project. Isn't it a better idea to select from among the hundreds of unique designs shown in our collection for a fraction of the cost?

What does Creative Homeowner Offer?

In this book, Creative Homeowner provides hundreds of home plans from the country's best architects and designers. Our designs are among the most popular available. Whether your taste runs from traditional to contemporary, Victorian to early American, you are sure to find the best house design for you and your family. Our plans packages include detailed drawings to help you or your builder construct your dream house. **(See page 422.)**

Can I Make Changes to the Plans?

Creative Homeowner offers three ways to help you achieve a truly unique home design. Our customizing service allows for extensive changes to our designs. **(See page 423.)** We also provide reverse images of our plans, or we can give you and your builder the tools for making minor changes on your own. **(See page 426.)**

Can You Help Me Manage My Costs?

To help you stay within your budget, Creative Homeowner has teamed up with the leading estimating company to provide one of the most accurate, complete, and reliable building material take-offs in the industry. **(See page 424.)** If that is too much detail for you, we can provide you with general construction costs based on your zip code. **(See page 426.)** Also, many of our plans come with the option of buying detailed materials lists to help you price out construction costs.

How Can I Begin the Building Process?

To get started building your dream home, fill out the order form on page 427, call our order department at 1-800-523-6789, or visit ulti-mateplans.com. If you plan on doing all or part of the work yourself, or want to keep tabs on your builder, we offer best-selling building and design books available at www.creativehomeowner.com.

Our Plans Packages Offer:

"Square footage" refers to the total "heated square feet" of this plan. This number does not include the garage, porches, or unfinished areas. All of our home plans are the result of many hours of work by leading architects and professional designers. Most of our home plans include each of the following:

Frontal Sheet

This artist's rendering of the front of the house gives you an idea of how the house will look once it is completed and the property landscaped.

Detailed Floor Plans

These plans show the size and layout of the rooms. They also provide the locations of doors, windows, fireplaces, closets, stairs, and electrical outlets and switches.

Foundation Plan

A foundation plan gives the dimensions of basements, walk-out basements, crawl spaces, pier foundations, and slab construction. Each house design lists the type of foundation included. If the plan you choose does not have the foundation type you require, our customer service department can help you customize the plan to meet your needs.

Roof Plan

In addition to providing the pitch of the roof, these plans also show the locations of dormers, skylights, and other elements.

Exterior Elevations

These drawings show the front, rear, and sides of the house as if you were looking at it head on. Elevations also provide information about architectural features and finish materials.

Interior Elevations and Details

Interior elevations show specific details of such elements as fireplaces, kitchen and bathroom cabinets, built-ins, and other unique features of the design.

Cross Sections

These show the structure as if it were sliced to reveal construction requirements, such as insulation, flooring, and roofing details.

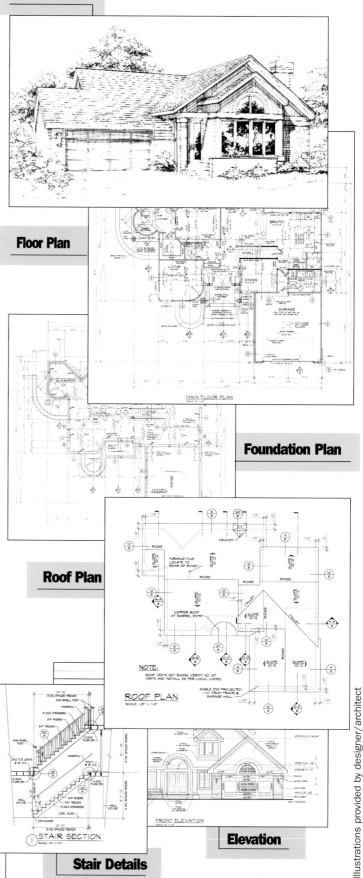

Frontal Sheet

Floor Plan

Foundation Plan

Roof Plan

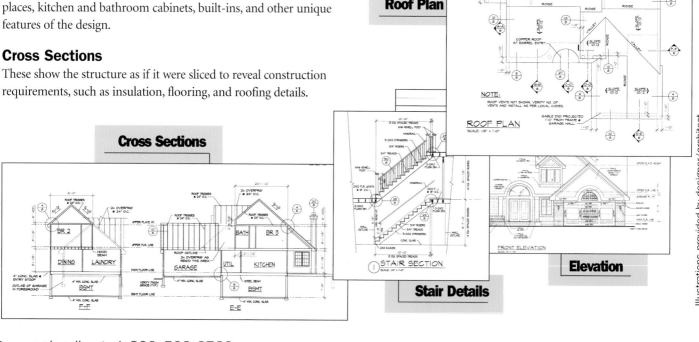

Cross Sections

Stair Details

Elevation

Customize Your Plans in 4 Easy Steps

1 **Select the home plan** that most closely meets your needs. Purchase of a reproducible master is necessary in order to make changes to a plan.

2 **Call 1-800-523-6789 to place your order.** Tell our sales representative you are interested in customizing your plan. To receive your customization cost estimate, we will send you a checklist (via fax or email) for you to complete indicating the changes you would like to make to your plan. There is a $50 nonrefundable consultation fee for this service. If you decide to continue with the custom changes, the $50 fee is credited to the total amount charged.

3 **Fax or email your request** to our modification company. Within three business days of receipt of your request, a detailed cost estimate will be provided to you.

4 **Once you approve the estimate,** a 75% retainer fee is collected and customization work begins. Preliminary drawings typically take 10 to 15 business days. After approval of the design, the balance of your customization fee is due before modified plans can be shipped. You will receive five sets of blueprints, a reproducible master, or CAD files, depending on which package was purchase.

Modification Pricing Guide

Categories	Average Cost For Modification
Add or remove living space	Quote required
Bathroom layout redesign	Starting at $150
Kitchen layout redesign	Starting at $120
Garage: add or remove	Starting at $600
Garage: front entry to side load or vice versa	Starting at $300
Foundation changes	Starting at $220
Exterior building materials change	Starting at $200
Exterior openings: add, move, or remove	$75 per opening
Roof line changes	Starting at $600
Ceiling height adjustments	Starting at $280
Fireplace: add or remove	Starting at $90
Screened porch: add	Starting at $300
Wall framing change from 2x4 to 2x6	Starting at $250
Bearing and/or exterior walls changes	Quote required
Non-bearing wall or room changes	$65 per room
Metric conversion of home plan	Starting at $495
Adjust plan for handicapped accessibility	Quote required
Adapt plans for local building code requirements	Quote required
Engineering stamping only	Quote required
Any other engineering services	Quote required
Interactive illustrations (choices of exterior materials)	Quote required

Note: Any home plan can be customized to accommodate your desired changes. The average prices above are provided only as examples of the most commonly requested changes, and are subject to change without notice. Prices for changes will vary according to the number of modifications requested, plan size, style, and method of design used by the original designer. To obtain a detailed cost estimate, please contact us.

Before Customization

After

Turn your dream home into reality with

Ultimate Estimate

When purchasing a home plan with Creative Homeowner, we recommend you order one of the most complete materials lists in the industry.

1 What comes with an Ultimate Estimate?

Quote

- Basis of the entire estimate.

- Detailed list of all the framing materials needed to build your project, listed from the bottom up, in the order that each one will actually be used.

Comments

- Details pertinent information beyond the cost of materials.

- Includes any notes from our estimator.

Express List

- A version of the Quote with space for SKU numbers listed for purchasing the items at your local lumberyard.

- Your local lumberyard can then price out the materials list.

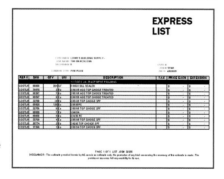

Construction-Ready Framing Diagrams

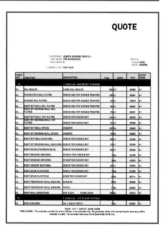

- Your "map" to exact roof and floor framing.

Millwork Report

- A complete count of the windows, doors, molding, and trim.

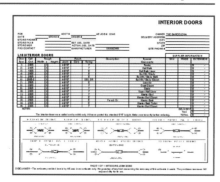

Man-Hour Report

- Calculates labor on a line-by-line basis for all items quoted and presented in man-hours.

Why an Ultimate Estimate?

Accurate. Professional estimators break down each individual item from the blueprints using advanced software, techniques, and equipment.

Timely. You will be able to start your home-building project quickly — knowing the exact framing materials you need to order from your local lumberyard.

Detailed. Work with your local lumberyard associate to complete your quote with the remaining products needed for your new home.

3

So how much does it cost?

Pricing is determined by the total square feet of the home plan — including living area, garages, decks, porches, finished basements, and finished attics.

Square Feet Range	UE Tier*	Price
2,001 to 5,000 total square feet	XB	$345.00
5,001 to 10,000 total square feet	XC	$545.00

*Please see the Plan Index to determine your plan's Ultimate Estimate Tier (UE Tier). Note: All prices subject to change.

Call our toll-free number (800-523-6789), or visit ultimateplans.com to order your Ultimate Estimate.

4

What else do I need to know?

Call our toll-free number (800-523-6789), or visit **ultimateplans.com** to order your Ultimate Estimate.

Turn your dream home into reality.

Decide What Type of Plan Package You Need

How many Plans Should You Order?

Standard 8-Set Package. We've found that our 8-set package is the best value for someone who is ready to start building. The 8-set package provides plans for you, your builder, the subcontractors, mortgage lender, and the building department.

Minimum 5-Set Package. If you are in the bidding process, you may want to order only five sets for the bidding round and reorder additional sets as needed.

1-Set Study Package. The 1-set package allows you to review your home plan in detail. The plan will be marked as a study print, and it is illegal to build a house from a study print alone. It is a violation of copyright law to reproduce a blueprint without permission.

Buying Additional Sets. If you require additional copies of blueprints for your home construction, you can order additional sets within 60 days of the original order date at a reduced price. The cost is $35.00 for each additional set. For more information, contact customer service.

Reproducible Masters

If you plan to make minor changes to one of our home plans, you can purchase reproducible masters. These plans are printed on bond or vellum paper that is easy to alter. They clearly indicate your right to modify, copy, or reproduce the plans. Reproducible masters allow an architect, designer, or builder to alter our plans to give you a customized home design. This package allows you to print as many copies of the modified plans as you need for the construction of one home.

PDF Files

PDF files are a complete set of home plans in electronic file format sent to you via email. These files cannot be altered electronically, once printed changes can be hand drawn. A PDF file gives you the license to modify the plans to fit your needs and build one home. Not available for all plans. Please contact our order department or visit our Web site to check the availability of PDF files for your plan.

CAD (Computer-Aided Design) Files

CAD files are the complete set of home plans in an electronic file format. Choose this option if there are multiple changes you wish made to the home plans and you have a local design professional able to make the changes. Not available for all plans. Please contact our order department or visit our Web site to check the availability of CAD files for your plan.

Mirror-Reverse Sets/Right-Reading Reverse

Plans can be printed in mirror-reverse—we can "flip" plans to create a mirror image of the design. This is useful when the house would fit your site or personal preferences if all the rooms were on the opposite side than shown. As the image is reversed, the lettering and dimensions will also be reversed, meaning they will read backwards. Therefore, when ordering mirror-reverse drawings, you must order at least one set of the original plan unreversed. A $50.00 fee per plan order will be charged for mirror-reverse (regardless of the number of mirror-reverse sets ordered). Some plans are available in right-reading reverse; this feature will show the plan in reverse, but the writing on the plan will be readable. A $150.00 fee per plan order will be charged for right-reading reverse (regardless of the number of right-reading reverse sets ordered). Please contact our order department or visit our website to check the availibility of this feature for your chosen plan.

EZ Quote: Home Cost Estimator

EZ Quote is our response to a frequently asked question we hear from customers: "How much will the house cost me to build?" EZ Quote: Home Cost Estimator will enable you to obtain a calculated building cost to construct your home, based on labor rates and building material costs within your zip code area. This summary is useful for those who want to get an idea of the total construction costs before purchasing sets of home plans. It will also provide a level of comfort when you begin soliciting bids. The cost is $29.95 for the first EZ Quote and $19.95 for each additional one in the same order. Available only in the U.S. and Canada.

Materials List

Available for most of our plans, the Materials List provides you an invaluable resource in planning and estimating the cost of your home. Each Materials List outlines the quantity, dimensions, and type of materials needed to build your home (with the exception of mechanical systems). You will get faster, more-accurate bids from your contractors and building suppliers. A Materials List may only be ordered with the purchase of at least five sets of home plans.

CompleteCost Estimator

CompleteCost Estimator is a valuable tool for use in planning and constructing your new home. It provides more detail than a materials list and will act as a checklist for all items you will need to select or coordinate during your building process. CompleteCost Estimator is only available for certain plans (please see Plan Index) and may only be ordered with the purchase of at least five sets of home plans. The cost is $125.00 for CompleteCost Estimator

Ultimate Estimate (See page 424.)

Before You Order

Our Exchange Policy

Blueprints are nonrefundable. However, should you find that the plan you have purchased does not fit your needs, you may exchange that plan for another plan in our collection within 60 days from the date of your original order. The entire content of your original order must be returned before an exchange will be processed. You will be charged a processing fee of 20% of the amount of the original order, the cost difference between the new plan set and the original plan set (if applicable), and all related shipping costs for the new plans. Contact our order department for more information. Please note: reproducible masters may only be exchanged if the package is unopened. PDF files and CAD files cannot be exchanged and are nonrefundable.

Building Codes and Requirements

All plans offered for sale in this book and on our website (www.ultimateplans.com) are continually updated to meet the latest International Residential Code (IRC). Because building codes vary from area to area, some drawing modifications and/or the assistance of a professional designer or architect may be necessary to comply with your local codes or to accommodate specific building site conditions. We strongly advise you to consult with your local building official for information regarding codes governing your area.

Multiple Plan Discount

Purchase **3** different home plans in the **same order** and receive **5% off** the plan price.

Purchase **5** or more different home plans in the **same order** and receive **10% off** the plan price. (Please Note: Study sets do not apply.)

Blueprint Price Schedule

Price Code	1 Set	5 Sets	8 Sets	Reproducible Masters or PDF Files	CAD	Materials List
A	$410	$470	$545	$660	$1,125	$85
B	$465	$540	$615	$740	$1,310	$85
C	$525	$620	$695	$820	$1,475	$85
D	$575	$670	$745	$870	$1,575	$95
E	$625	$730	$805	$925	$1,675	$95
F	$690	$790	$865	$990	$1,800	$95
G	$720	$820	$895	$1,020	$1,845	$95
H	$730	$830	$905	$1,045	$1,900	$95
I	$995	$1,095	$1,170	$1,290	$2,110	$105
J	$1,190	$1,290	$1,365	$1,490	$2,300	$105
K	$1,195	$1,295	$1,370	$1,495	$2,300	$105
L	$1,240	$1,335	$1,410	$1,535	$2,400	$105

Note: All prices subject to change

Lowe's Material Take-off (MT Tier)

MT Tier*	Price
XB	$345
XC	$545

* Please see the Plan Index to determine your plan's Lowe's Material Take-off (MT Tier).

Shipping & Handling

Shipping & Handling	1–4 Sets	5–7 Sets	8+ Sets or Reproducibles	CAD
US Regular (7–10 business days)	$18	$20	$25	$25
US Priority (3–5 business days)	$25	$30	$35	$35
US Express (1–2 business days)	$40	$45	$50	$50
Canada Express (3–4 business days)	$100	$100	$100	$100
Worldwide Express (3–5 business days)		** Quote Required **		

Note: All delivery times are from date the blueprint package is shipped (typically within 1-2 days of placing order).

Order Form
Please send me the following:

Plan Number: _____ **Price Code:** _____ (See Plan Index.)

Indicate Foundation Type: (Select ONE. See plan page for availability.)
❏ Slab   ❏ Crawl space   ❏ Basement   ❏ Walk-out basement
❏ Optional Foundation for Fee _____ $_____
(Please enter foundation here)
*Please call all our order department or visit our website for optional foundation fee

Basic Blueprint Package	Cost
❏ CAD Files	$_____
❏ PDF Files	$_____
❏ Reproducible Masters	$_____
❏ 8-Set Plan Package	$_____
❏ 5-Set Plan Package	$_____
❏ 1-Set Study Package	$_____
❏ Additional plan sets: __ sets at $35.00 per set	$_____
❏ Print in mirror-reverse: $50.00 per order	$_____

*Please call all our order department or visit our website for availibility

❏ Print in right-reading reverse: $150.00 per order $_____
*Please call all our order department or visit our website for availibility

Important Extras

❏ Lowe's Material Take-off (See Price Tier above.)	$_____
❏ Materials List	$_____
❏ CompleteCost Materials Report at $125.00	$_____

Zip Code of Home/Building Site _____
❏ EZ Quote for Plan #_____ at $29.95 $_____
❏ Additional EZ Quotes for Plan #s_____ $_____
   at $19.95 each

Shipping (see chart above) $_____
SUBTOTAL $_____
Sales Tax (NJ residents only, add 7%) $_____
TOTAL $_____

Order Toll Free: 1-800-523-6789 By Fax: 201-760-2431
Creative Homeowner (Home Plans Order Dept.)
24 Park Way
Upper Saddle River, NJ 07458

Name _____
(Please print or type)

Street _____
(Please do not use a P.O. Box)

City _____ State _____

Country _____ Zip _____

Daytime telephone (___) _____

Fax (___) _____
(Required for reproducible orders)

E-Mail _____

Payment ❏ Bank check/money order. No personal checks.
Make checks payable to Creative Homeowner

❏ VISA   ❏ MasterCard   ❏ American Express Cards   ❏ Discover

Credit card number _____

Expiration date (mm/yy) _____

Signature _____

Please check the appropriate box:
❏ Building home for myself   ❏ Building home for someone else

| SOURCE CODE | CC101 |

Copyright Notice

All home plans sold through this publication are protected by copyright. Reproduction of these home plans, either in whole or in part, including any form and/or preparation of derivative works thereof, for any reason without prior written permission is strictly prohibited. The purchase of a set of home plans in no way transfers any copyright or other ownership interest in it to the buyer except for a limited license to use that set of home plans for the construction of one, and only one, dwelling unit. The purchase of additional sets of the home plans at a reduced price from the original set or as a part of a multiple-set package does not convey to the buyer a license to construct more than one dwelling.

Similarly, the purchase of reproducible home plans (sepias, mylars) carries the same copyright protection as mentioned above. It is gener-

ally allowed to make up to a maximum of 10 copies for the construction of a single dwelling only. To use any plans more than once, and to avoid any copyright license infringement, it is necessary to contact the plan designer to receive a release and license for any extended use. Whereas a purchaser of reproducible plans is granted a license to make copies, it should be noted that because blueprints are copyrighted, making photocopies from them is illegal.

Copyright and licensing of home plans for construction exist to protect all parties. Copyright respects and supports the intellectual property of the original architect or designer. Copyright law has been reinforced over the past few years. Willful infringement could cause settlements for statutory damages to $150,000.00 plus attorney fees, damages, and loss of profits.

Index

For pricing, see page 427.

Index
For pricing, see page 427.

Plan #	Price Code	Page	Total Finished Sq. Ft.	Materials List	CompleteCost	UE Tier
161013	C	14	1509	Y	N	XB
161014	C	14	1698	Y	N	XB
161026	D	48	2041	N	N	XB
161026	D	49	2041	N	N	XB
161028	H	256	3570	N	N	XC
161056	J	76	5068	Y	N	XC
161056	J	77	5068	Y	N	XC
161062	F	392	2904	Y	N	XB
161090	C	327	1563	Y	N	XB
161093	I	311	4328	Y	N	XB
161095	H	318	3620	N	N	XB
161098	E	125	2283	N	N	XB
161100	J	285	5377	N	N	XC
161102	K	322	6659	Y	N	XC
161115	E	98	2253	Y	N	XB
161116	B	173	1442	Y	N	XB
161126	I	360	4896	Y	N	XC
161130	C	361	1619	Y	N	XB
171001	B	200	1804	Y	N	XB
171004	E	229	2256	Y	N	XB
171009	C	83	1771	Y	N	XB
171011	D	111	2069	Y	N	XB
171013	G	35	3084	Y	N	XC
171015	D	118	2089	Y	N	XB
171016	E	244	2482	Y	N	XB
171019	D	310	1878	Y	N	XB
181001	A	380	920	Y	N	XB
181012	D	161	2192	Y	N	XB
181013	B	155	2294	Y	N	XB
181022	B	410	1098	Y	N	XB
181023	B	340	1191	Y	N	XB
181024	B	356	3100	Y	N	XB
181027	B	342	1103	Y	N	XB
181145	A	166	840	Y	N	XB
181148	B	407	1174	Y	N	XB
181218	A	177	946	N	N	XB
181308	D	178	2161	Y	N	XB
181309	B	403	1114	Y	N	XB
181310	B	181	1094	Y	N	XB
181342	B	397	1098	Y	N	XB
181348	B	316	1068	Y	N	XB
181385	B	395	1285	Y	N	XB
181387	B	320	1572	Y	N	XB
181397	B	402	1088	Y	N	XB
181403	D	392	1917	Y	N	XB
181413	B	335	1022	Y	N	XB
181421	B	390	1196	Y	N	XB
181424	B	328	1196	Y	N	XB
181557	D	347	1806	Y	N	XB
181585	B	326	1207	Y	N	XB
181595	A	381	976	Y	N	XB
181598	A	400	962	Y	N	XB
181600	B	314	1065	Y	N	XB
181602	B	337	1234	Y	N	XB
181603	B	329	1220	Y	N	XB
181604	B	323	1337	Y	N	XB
181608	B	300	1086	Y	N	XB
181610	B	302	1151	Y	N	XB
181621	B	309	1129	Y	N	XB
181622	B	305	1007	Y	N	XB
181652	C	295	1579	Y	N	XB
181717	C	317	1578	Y	N	XB
181724	D	189	1808	Y	N	XB
181727	B	288	1350	Y	N	XB
181728	B	291	1322	Y	N	XB
191001	D	99	2156	N	N	XB
191004	D	188	1856	N	N	XB
191009	D	234	2172	N	N	XB
191012	D	169	2123	N	N	XB
191016	E	111	2421	N	N	XB
191021	G	104	3029	N	N	XB
191032	D	42	2091	N	N	XB
191058	E	296	2550	N	N	XB
201062	H	216	2551	Y	N	XB
201084	G	92	2056	Y	N	XB
201086	F	245	1573	Y	N	XB
211001	C	258	1655	Y	N	XB
211002	C	133	1792	Y	N	XB
211003	D	36	1865	Y	N	XB
211004	D	249	1828	Y	N	XB
211005	D	120	2000	Y	N	XB
211006	D	243	2177	Y	N	XB
211007	E	268	2252	Y	N	XB
211008	E	351	2259	Y	N	XB
211009	E	346	2396	Y	N	XB
211010	E	239	2503	Y	N	XB
211011	F	137	2791	Y	N	XB
211012	A	300	984	Y	N	XB
211014	A	297	998	Y	N	XB
211018	B	10	1266	Y	N	XB
211030	C	122	1600	Y	N	XB
211036	D	120	1800	Y	N	XB
211039	D	263	1868	Y	N	XB
211048	D	132	2002	Y	N	XB
211049	D	306	2023	Y	N	XB
211050	D	265	2000	Y	N	XB
211058	E	228	2564	N	N	XB
211059	E	255	2299	N	N	XB
211062	F	187	2682	Y	N	XB
211067	I	131	4038	Y	N	XC
211151	E	307	2328	N	N	XB
211152	C	313	1682	N	N	XB
211155	F	179	2719	Y	N	XB
221001	F	67	2600	N	N	XB
221004	C	62	1763	N	N	XB
221008	C	150	1540	N	N	XB
221015	D	18	1926	N	N	XB
221018	D	235	2007	N	N	XB
221020	D	40	1859	N	N	XB
221039	F	253	2839	N	N	XB
221047	D	302	2067	N	N	XB
221057	E	247	2551	N	N	XB
231003	E	217	2254	N	N	XB
231004	A	343	1463	N	N	XB
231008	D	404	1941	N	N	XB
241004	F	221	2771	N	N	XB
241007	D	85	2036	N	N	XB
241008	E	238	2526	N	N	XB
241015	C	189	1609	N	N	XB
241033	C	180	1684	N	N	XB
241040	B	365	1468	N	N	XB
241041	C	129	1612	N	N	XB
251001	B	86	1253	Y	N	XB
251003	B	116	1393	Y	N	XB
251004	C	107	1550	Y	N	XB
271001	B	343	1400	Y	N	XB
271002	B	341	1252	Y	N	XB
271003	B	123	1452	Y	N	XB
271005	B	338	1368	Y	N	XB
271006	B	327	1444	Y	N	XB
271007	B	136	1283	Y	N	XB
271008	B	314	1199	N	N	XB
271023	D	153	1993	Y	N	XB
271059	C	406	1790	N	N	XB
271060	C	51	1726	N	N	XB
271061	C	409	1750	N	N	XB
271063	E	227	2572	N	N	XB
271073	D	64	1920	N	N	XB
271074	E	115	2400	N	N	XB
271075	E	325	2233	N	N	XB
271076	D	234	2188	N	N	XB
271077	C	384	1786	N	N	XB
271078	H	403	3620	N	N	XB
271079	E	165	2228	N	N	XB
271080	E	303	2581	Y	N	XC
271081	E	24	2539	N	N	XB
271082	D	66	2074	N	N	XB
271084	C	397	1602	Y	N	XB
271285	D	162	1972	N	N	XB
271303	E	315	2345	N	N	XB
271304	E	337	2360	N	N	XB
271318	E	348	2086	N	N	XB
271320	C	354	1548	N	N	XB
271321	D	357	1800	N	N	XB
271322	D	329	1800	N	N	XB
271448	A	351	775	N	N	XB
271450	B	358	1164	N	N	XB
271458	C	368	1789	N	N	XB
281008	C	251	1731	Y	N	XB
281009	B	326	1423	Y	N	XB
281018	C	163	1565	Y	N	XB
281020	C	121	1734	Y	N	XB
281022	C	195	1506	Y	N	XB
281029	D	155	1833	Y	N	XB
291001	C	113	1550	N	N	XB
291002	C	34	1550	N	N	XB
301001	F	344	2720	Y	N	XC
301002	D	19	1845	Y	N	XB
301003	E	261	2485	Y	N	XC
301005	D	80	1930	Y	N	XB
311001	D	50	2085	N	N	XB
311002	E	30	2402	Y	N	XC
311004	D	50	2046	Y	N	XB
311005	E	61	2497	Y	N	XC
311023	E	335	2339	N	N	XB
311032	D	130	4158	N	N	XB
311039	D	219	5938	N	N	XC
311058	C	164	1702	N	N	XB
311060	E	108	2585	N	N	XB
311061	E	103	2570	Y	N	XC

Index

For pricing, see page 427.

Plan #	Price Code	Page	Total Finished Sq. Ft.	Materials List	CompleteCost	UE Tier
321001	C	26	1721	Y	N	XB
321002	B	46	1400	Y	N	XB
321003	C	65	1791	N	N	XB
321004	F	248	2808	N	N	XC
321005	E	197	2483	Y	N	XC
321006	D	390	1977	Y	N	XB
321007	F	245	2695	Y	N	XB
321008	C	37	1761	Y	N	XB
321009	E	158	2295	Y	N	XB
321010	C	15	1787	Y	N	XB
321011	F	57	2874	N	N	XC
321013	B	15	1360	Y	N	XB
321018	E	251	2523	Y	N	XC
321019	E	219	2452	Y	N	XC
321025	A	150	914	Y	N	XB
321026	C	413	1712	Y	N	XB
321030	D	42	2029	Y	N	XB
321033	B	52	1268	Y	N	XB
321034	H	240	3508	Y	N	XC
321035	B	146	1384	Y	N	XB
321036	F	259	2900	Y	N	XC
321037	E	260	2397	Y	N	XB
321038	B	151	1452	Y	N	XB
321040	B	152	1084	Y	N	XB
321121	B	192	1322	Y	N	XB
341035	C	53	1680	Y	N	XB
341039	C	153	3740	Y	N	XB
341096	B	185	1447	N	N	XB
341128	B	345	1410	Y	N	XB
341144	B	350	1104	N	N	XB
341146	A	193	960	N	N	XB
351001	D	232	1855	Y	N	XB
351002	D	286	1751	Y	N	XB
351003	D	289	1751	Y	N	XB
351004	D	81	1852	Y	N	XB
351005	D	52	1501	Y	N	XB
351006	D	43	1638	Y	N	XB
351008	E	263	2002	Y	N	XB
351013	B	109	800	Y	N	XB
351018	C	408	1251	Y	N	XB
351020	C	91	1488	Y	N	XB
351021	D	134	1500	Y	N	XB
351055	F	112	6281	Y	N	XC
351082	E	51	1800	Y	N	XB
351085	E	331	2200	Y	N	XB
351089	F	89	2505	Y	N	XB
351091	B	170	400	Y	N	XB
351093	B	175	600	Y	N	XB
351097	D	190	1610	Y	N	XB
351098	D	332	1655	Y	N	XB
351099	D	190	1750	Y	N	XB
351101	E	193	1865	Y	N	XB
351114	C	308	1733	Y	N	XB
351116	D	186	2050	Y	N	XB
351126	F	288	3461	Y	N	XB
351141	F	286	2850	Y	N	XB
361004	D	58	2191	N	N	XB
361030	F	165	2619	N	N	XB
361057	C	315	1564	N	N	XB
361063	D	360	2001	N	N	XB
361074	E	402	2396	N	N	XB
361101	D	364	1986	N	N	XB
361166	E	353	2417	N	N	XB
361200	E	341	2568	N	N	XB
361213	C	154	1735	N	N	XB
361223	F	127	2966	N	N	XB
361228	E	328	2556	N	N	XB
361235	E	334	2385	N	N	XB
361258	F	167	2714	N	N	XB
361261	E	312	2396	N	N	XB
361444	C	101	1605	N	N	XB
361448	C	192	1634	N	N	XB
361469	E	166	2261	N	N	XB
361470	E	167	2313	N	N	XB
361483	E	317	2507	N	N	XB
361538	D	336	2011	N	N	XB
371007	D	191	1944	N	N	XB
371009	B	194	1223	N	N	XB
371033	C	199	1724	N	N	XB
381010	E	418	1905	Y	N	XB
381092	G	399	3030	Y	N	XB
381164	E	128	2300	Y	N	XB
391004	C	244	1750	Y	N	XB
391005	C	407	1575	Y	N	XB
391006	B	398	1456	Y	N	XB
391008	B	261	1312	Y	N	XB
391019	C	23	1792	Y	N	XB
391034	C	56	1737	Y	N	XB
391038	C	11	1642	Y	N	XB
391042	B	147	1307	Y	N	XB
391049	E	385	4064	Y	N	XC
391059	C	401	2020	Y	N	XB
391060	B	191	1359	Y	N	XB
391064	A	269	988	Y	N	XB
391069	B	151	1492	Y	N	XB
391138	D	415	2194	Y	N	XB
391156	E	417	2450	Y	N	XB
391168	E	371	2352	Y	N	XB
391211	B	182	1461	Y	N	XB
391216	C	411	1500	Y	N	XB
401008	C	201	1541	Y	N	XB
401020	B	156	1230	Y	N	XB
401023	F	333	2806	Y	N	XC
401033	B	148	1405	Y	N	XB
401041	B	203	1108	Y	N	XB
401047	B	119	1064	Y	N	XB
421008	D	119	1954	Y	N	XB
431001	C	100	1792	Y	N	XB
441001	D	321	1850	N	N	XB
441002	D	112	1873	N	N	XB
441003	C	195	1580	N	N	XB
441004	C	369	1728	N	N	XB
441005	D	319	1800	N	N	XB
441006	D	324	1891	N	N	XB
441007	D	330	2197	N	N	XB
441008	D	396	2001	N	N	XB
441009	F	126	2650	N	N	XB
441010	F	366	2973	N	N	XB
441012	H	198	3682	N	N	XB
441014	H	292	3940	N	N	XB
441014	H	293	3940	N	N	XB
441015	I	196	4732	N	N	XC
451083	C	388	1627	N	N	XB
451092	E	382	2752	N	N	XC
451098	E	313	2428	N	N	XB
451099	G	411	3044	N	N	XB
451138	I	378	4484	N	N	XC
451153	C	373	1605	N	N	XB
451161	I	370	5042	N	N	XC
451172	C	368	1659	N	N	XB
451194	F	361	2618	N	N	XB
451210	F	359	2646	N	N	XB
451245	C	356	1584	N	N	XB
451258	D	350	1898	N	N	XB
451316	K	160	6824	N	N	XC
451327	C	391	1727	N	N	XB
451332	G	352	3202	N	N	XB
461032	C	394	1799	N	N	XB
461064	C	391	1677	N	N	XB
461090	D	373	1922	N	N	XB
471002	A	393	835	N	N	XB
471003	A	395	920	Y	N	XB
471008	B	400	1127	N	N	XB
471014	A	401	950	N	N	XB
471017	A	406	786	Y	N	XB
471024	A	404	484	N	N	XB
481011	F	389	2758	N	N	XB
481028	H	223	3980	N	N	XC
481029	I	378	4048	N	N	XC
481031	I	60	4707	N	N	XC
481033	J	375	5667	N	N	XC
481036	I	298	4258	N	N	XC
481132	I	387	4056	N	N	XC
481137	I	380	4425	N	N	XB
481143	J	287	5426	N	N	XC
521017	E	159	2359	N	N	XB
521040	C	184	1555	N	N	XB
531020	G	188	3371	N	N	XB
541031	F	345	2803	N	N	XB
541034	G	339	3162	N	N	XC
541037	I	334	4219	N	N	XC
541039	I	376	4466	N	N	XC
561005	I	290	4142	Y	N	XB
561006	E	88	2408	Y	N	XB
571045	B	369	1399	Y	N	XB
571083	D	371	2036	Y	N	XB
611110	F	216	3286	N	N	XB
621006	F	182	3842	N	N	XB
631065	C	183	2222	Y	N	XB
651026	B	201	1145	N	N	XB
661289	J	220	7247	N	N	XC

UltimateEstimate

The fastest way to get started building your dream home

One of the most complete materials lists in the industry

Work with our order department to get you started today

To learn more go to page 424 or visit

CREATIVE
HOMEOWNER®

online at ultimateplans.com

order direct: 1-800-523-6789